D0857513

NINEVEH
AND ITS REMAINS

TRAVELLERS AND EXPLORERS
General Editor: Robin Hallett

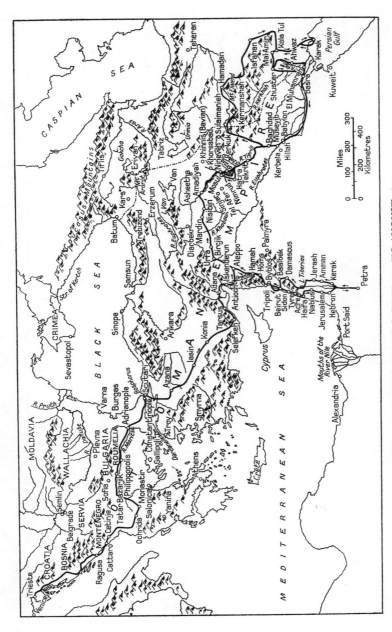

MAP 1. LAYARD'S TRAVELS, JULY 1839 TO AUGUST 1841

Henry Austen Layard in Albanian Dress

NINEVEH
AND ITS REMAINS

HENRY AUSTEN LAYARD

Edited and with an Introduction
and Notes by
H. W. F. SAGGS

FREDERICK A. PRAEGER, *Publishers*
New York · Washington

BOOKS THAT MATTER

Published in the United States of America in 1970
by Frederick A. Praeger, Inc., Publishers
111 Fourth Avenue, New York, N.Y. 10003
© 1969, in London, England. H. W. F. Saggs

Library of Congress Catalog Card Number: 70-77302

Printed in Great Britain

To Sir Max Mallowan, C.B.E., D.Lit., F.B.A.,
Layard's successor at Nimrud,
under whose inspiring direction
I spent happy hours in the palaces
of Assyrian kings

Contents

Plates

Line Illustrations

Maps and Plans

Abbreviations

Autobiography: Sir A. Henry Layard, G.C.B., D.C.L., *Autobiography and Letters from his childhood until his appointment as H.M. Ambassador at Madrid,* edited by the Hon. William N. Bruce. (2 volumes; John Murray, 1903.)

Early Adventures: Sir [A.] Henry Layard, G.C.B., *Early Adventures in Persia, Susiana, and Babylonia including a residence among the Bakhtiyari and other wild tribes before the discovery of Nineveh.* (2 volumes; John Murray, 1887.)

J.R.G.S.:   *Journal of the Royal Geographical Society of London.*

Five-figure numbers denote manuscripts in the Department of Manuscripts of the British Museum.

General Plan of Excavations at Nimroud

The plan overleaf has been redrawn from the original in Layard's Nineveh. For a detailed plan of the same site based on the most recent archaeological research see M. E. L. Mallowan, *Nimrud and its Remains* (Collins, 1966), Vol. 1, p. 32, fig. one.

Henry Austen Layard arranged to change his name to Austen Henry Layard when he left school. His name appears in these two forms in several parts of the book. The publishers regret that this inconsistency extends to the title page, binding and jacket.

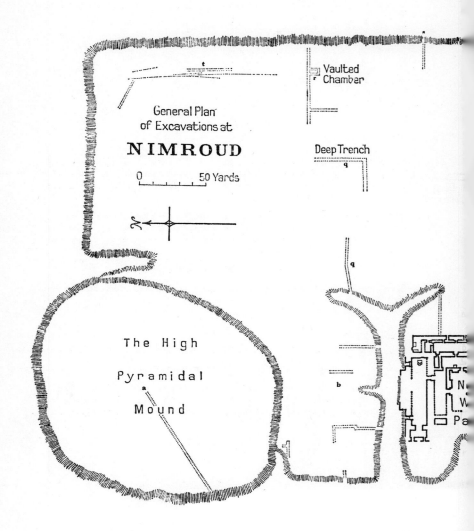

General Plan
of Excavations at

NIMROUD

0 ____ 50 Yards

Vaulted
Chamber

Deep Trench

The High

Pyramidal

Mound

PLAN I. General plan

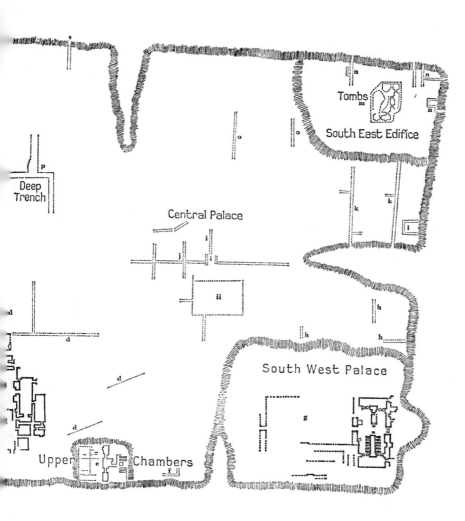

Tombs
m

n

n

j

n

South East Edifice

o

o

Deep
Trench

p

Central Palace

i

j

ii

k

k

l

d

d

d

h

h

h

South West Palace

d

d

g

Upper Chambers

e

f

excavations at Nimroud

Introduction

Italian Childhood[1]

FEW VISITORS TO THE British Museum fail to give their moment of awed admiration to the two pairs of colossal Assyrian lions and bulls which stand some fifty yards to the left of the main entrance. A few yards beyond, in the Nimrud Gallery and other galleries nearby, are to be seen some of the most impressive Assyrian bas-reliefs in the world. These works of art are justly associated with various names, but the names of two men stand supreme; one of them was Henry Austen Layard,[2] the pioneer of British archaeology in Mesopotamia.[3]

It is current cant to describe any great Englishman of the nineteenth century as a typical Victorian. This is not a description which sits well upon Henry Austen Layard. Certainly he possessed many of the qualities which made for Victorian greatness, but there was much in his upbringing and education, in his early career, and in the general cast of his mind, which served to separate him from the stereotype of the typical middle-class Victorian gentleman. He himself records how, when he was eighteen, a Frenchwoman whom he met in the Palais Royal in Paris would not believe that he and his friends were English, because they were so 'gai'.[4] As to upbringing, he was not educated at a Public School in an aura of Anglicanism and Greek, and in the career which his elders had chosen for him his application to his

[1] Quotations up to p. 13, not otherwise identified, are from *Autobiography*.

[2] The surname of the family was pronounced monosyllabically 'laird', not (as commonly amongst Assyriologists) bisyllabically as 'lay-ard'. This is indicated by the writing of the name as 'Laird' by certain correspondents (*e.g.* Colonel Taylor, 38975, 32). One close friend spelt the name 'Laird' inside his letter, though he knew the correct spelling and used it in the address (38976, 149 and 150). Mrs. F. Haley of Smarden Kent kindly informs me that members of the Layard family still prominent in Ceylon up to the end of the British era pronounced their name 'laird'.

[3] The archaeological explorations of Claudius J. Rich (see his *Memoir on the ruins of Babylon* (1813) and *Second memoir on Babylon* (1818)), though important in stimulating interest in the possibilities of Mesopotamian archaeology, were so limited that they can hardly be classed with those of Layard.

[4] 38972, 116.

calling was far from fitting him for the traditional role of the industrious apprentice, although his dereliction of duty was not so grave as his own highly-coloured account in his autobiography might suggest. It was, however, sufficient to mark him in the eyes of his guardian as, if not a notable failure, at least ill-omened for success; and in such circumstances the typical Englishman of gentle birth might well be encouraged to venture to foreign parts, there either to retrieve his fortunes or to die in obscurity. This course, indeed, Layard's uncles proposed for him, but here again Layard failed to conform to the expected behaviour. Leaving England en route for Ceylon, he engaged in a series of what, but for the fact of his survival and subsequent distinction, would have been hailed as foolhardy and pointless adventures, and never came near his intended destination. It was almost incidentally that he came to play a major part in the discovery of ancient Assyria. Layard had great qualities, but it does him less than justice to suggest that they were the qualities of the typical Victorian.

Layard's paternal great-grandfather grandly claimed, like many before and after him, to have traced the descent of his family back into the mists of the eleventh century. The indisputable ancestry of the family went back to a Huguenot officer in the army of King William III. This officer's third son was the great-grandfather already mentioned; though the latter gentleman's aristocratic pretensions were not recognized by the College of Heralds, his social connections as a court physician were not without their value to his sons, two of whom became Generals, whilst the third, Henry Austen Layard's grandfather, achieved some worldly success in the Church. This ecclesiastic, a typical eighteenth century divine well able to surmount the difficulty of combining the service of God and Mammon, ultimately became Dean of Bristol and was supposed, in family tradition, to have been marked out for the episcopacy, when he prematurely killed himself of gout through too much good living. Henry Austen Layard's evident distaste for this ecclesiastical dignitary—whom he described as 'a man of a proud, selfish and overbearing character'—may perhaps be reflected in the distinct coolness which, although no enemy of religion, he always manifested towards the established church.[1]

Henry Austen Layard's father, Henry Peter John Layard, had been

[1] Expressing reluctance to accept an invitation to become godfather to the infant son of the Countess of Aboyne, Layard, writing from Baghdad at the end of 1850, says (38944, 5) 'you know that my opinions on religious subjects differ very materially from those generally proposed in England, altho' as far as all the duties and the spirit of Christianity are concerned I believe we are most completely of one mind.'

sent at the age of nineteen, along with a younger brother Charles Edward, to a writership in the Ceylon Civil Service. Charles Edward remained and prospered, marrying a fecund Dutch lady a year after his arrival and founding a veritable dynasty of twenty-six children. Henry Peter John, on the other hand, found it less easy to settle himself and his affections, and eventually retired with the pension to which twelve years service (1803–14) entitled him.[1] It was enough to enable Henry Peter John, shortly after his return, to marry his child-hood sweetheart, Marianne Austen, the attractive and kindly though (as her son seems to have remembered her) slightly neurotic daughter of a Ramsgate banker. Henry Peter John Layard and his bride event-ually installed themselves in Paris. It was here that their first son was born, on the 5th of March, 1817; the Layards and Austens were good Tory Churchmen and the event demanded a return to England for a family christening, at which the child was given the name Henry Austen.

In the years that followed, Henry Peter John Layard came to suffer increasingly from the twin afflictions of asthma and a limited income. It was in an attempt to alleviate these hardships that the family returned in 1820 to the continent, where they spent the greater part of the next nine years. Most of this period was passed in Florence, where Layard senior found advantage in the climate and delight in the art treasures of the city. There were close bonds of affection between Layard senior and his sons (Henry Austen eventually had four brothers, two of whom died in infancy); and the father would allow Henry Austen to accompany him to the art galleries and museums, pointing out to him the merits and characteristics of the works of the great masters, and teaching the boy to distinguish their various styles. Meanwhile, more conventionally reared contemporaries had their noses to their Greek and Latin primers; but Henry Austen's early training in art criticism was to give him something which excellence in Greek and Latin could not. It stood him in good stead when, as a man, he exposed to view, for the first time in two and a half thousand years, the palaces of two Assyrian capitals, with their wealth of sculpture of a kind hitherto unknown. It was not the classicists but Layard, with his sensitiveness to art styles, who was first able to assign the palaces to their correct chronological sequence.[2]

[1] J. R. Toussaint, *Annals of the Ceylon Civil Service* (1935), 5.
[2] As early as February 1846 Layard was able to date the remains from Nimrud as earlier than those from Khorsabad (40637, 44–45). See also 38941, 23, where Layard writes 'I think I have fully satisfied Botta, Bernouf and others of the greater antiquity of the earlier palace of Nimroud when compared with Khorsabad'.

In Florence, Henry Austen's education was ultimately entrusted to a day school, from which he later somewhat grudgingly admitted receiving at least a useful grounding in Italian. With the sole exception of a boarding school in Geneva, Henry Layard in later life revealed little gratitude to any of the several educational establishments with which the family migrations brought him into brief association. Writing many years later, Layard himself had obviously come to the conclusion that as a schoolboy his tastes, interests and attainments had been so far different from those of the average boy of his age that he tended to be suspect by most of his teachers and a natural target for bullying by his fellow pupils. One suspects that a truer summing-up would be that young Layard, with considerable gifts and often with more opportunities of adult than of childhood companionship, was perilously near to becoming a precocious prig. A little taking-down by his teachers and contemporaries was inevitable, and no ill thing.

More significant than his schools as educational influences were the acquaintances Henry made amongst the English and Italian society of Florence. The older Layard was, as far as his limited income allowed, much given to hospitality; and residents in Florence, or English visitors passing through, were frequent guests at his table, where, according to Henry's later recollection, they all took much notice of him and favoured him with their conversation. Doubtless he some-times took as a tribute to his own boyish intelligence marks of attention directed to him in the ordinary courtesies of social intercourse as the host's eldest son.

Henry fully shared his father's delight in Florentine painting, and his enthusiasm was such that for a while he even wished to make painting his profession. This ambition his father discouraged (quite properly, Layard later conceded), though he did allow him to take drawing lessons. Once again he had no high opinion of his teacher, whom he considered a Catholic bigot; but it was probably under him that he began to acquire techniques destined to be of value in later years in Assyria, when single-handed he sought to make an accurate record with his pencil of the newly discovered sculptures. Henry's fascination with history, early encouraged by his father, was also developing, and he later claimed that before he was twelve 'there [were] few events in [the history] of Florence with which I was not acquainted. . . . There was scarcely a church or a palace of any import-ance of which I did not know something'. Again one has only Layard's

4

own unverifiable claim, but it seems that already he was destined to be either an historian or a prig.

It was understood that Henry Austen Layard, when of a suitable age, was to enter the office of his uncle and godfather, Benjamin Austen Esquire, a successful and childless solicitor, and a man of substance. This uncle, though far from being an enemy to the liberal arts, of which in some measure he was a patron, took the view that researches into Florentine painting and history, and the company of dilettante artists and men of letters, constituted no suitable training for one destined for the Law. The ultimate fruits of Henry Layard's dilettantism no one could foresee, whilst the neglect of his conventional education was evident to everyone, except perhaps his father. Pressure from the Austens was therefore exerted to have Henry (together with one of his brothers) sent to a school in England. He left Florence with great regret in 1829, at the age of twelve, and was entered at a school in Richmond, where he remained for four years. His later memory of the school was a little sour and ungracious.

Apprenticeship to the Law

Henry Layard's maternal uncle, Benjamin Austen, was, as has already been said, well-to-do and childless. He was also Henry's godfather. Since he had taken the responsibilities of the latter relationship so seriously as to bring pressure upon Layard senior in connection with Henry's education, had arranged for his godson to be articled to him as clerk, and had suggested that the young man, christened 'Henry Austen', should use 'Austen' as his first Christian name, the Layards drew certain conclusions as to expectations.

Layard was formally articled to his uncle on the 20th of January, 1834. Benjamin Austen was a conscientious man. He strove to implement the undertaking made in the articles of indenture that he would 'to the best and utmost of his skill and knowledge teach and instruct or cause to be taught and instructed the said Austen Henry Layard in the Business practice and profession of an Attorney and Solicitor',[1] and with this end in view not unreasonably expected young Layard to read the standard works on the subject, which he made available to him. Layard, however, had other views. He could find little interest in the Law. His uncle must have needed to practise considerable forbearance in his relations with Layard, who, by his own confession, consistently failed to fulfil the obligation, entered into by his in-

[1] Lavard's Articles of Indenture, 39055, 1ff.

dentures, that he would 'faithfully soberly and diligently serve him the said Benjamin Austen as his Clerk . . . and in all things acquit and demean himself as an honest and faithful Clerk ought to do'.[1]

One might conclude, from a hasty reading of Layard's *Auto-biography*, that it was a wholly miserable five years which he spent indentured to his uncle. 'My life was then a desolate one', he laments. 'My flute', he adds melodramatically, 'was my only solace'. He may well have been lonely and miserable in London for his first few months —most newcomers are—and in October of the same year he lost his father, to whom he had been much attached; but afterwards he certainly had other consolations. At least once a week he dined at his uncle's house, and devoted to the Law though Benjamin Austen was, his guests included not a few of the kind most likely to interest and stimulate Layard, amongst them many men of letters and the arts. One whom Layard frequently met there was Benjamin Disraeli. When, much later, both men were in the House of Commons, Disraeli, recalling the early acquaintanceship, showed to Layard, as the latter records, 'a marked consideration and forbearance', political opponents though they were.

During the latter half of his period in London Layard was much influenced by Henry Crabb Robinson, a prosperous elderly lawyer of liberal opinions, and a well-known figure in the literary society of his day. Layard, who during his early days in London had been starved of books, was now given access to Robinson's extensive library, and particularly encouraged in his interest in Italian literature and his attempts at serious writing.

During these years of nominal (and apparently minimal) devotion to the Law, Layard began to dabble in political and social issues, speaking at discussions at working men's clubs. His radical sympathies also brought him into contact with Polish revolutionaries in exile in London, for whom on one of his early visits abroad he undertook some congenial melodramatic cloak-and-dagger work, acting as a secret messenger to their countrymen in Paris.

For Layard, unenamoured though he was of the practice of the Law, it had one undeniable advantage—the long vacation, running from the beginning of August into October. Despite his limited allowance, he somehow always found the means, after his first year in London, to embark on a protracted period of foreign travel. In successive years he visited the Italian and Swiss Alps, the south of

[1] *Ibid.*

6

France, northern Italy, and, in the final year of his indenture, Denmark, Finland and Russia. During the first of these tours, in 1835, Layard began to display an interest in ancient oriental antiquities, particularly mentioning in his journal the Egyptian remains in Turin museum. We also find him showing keen interest in Roman inscriptions and remains which he encountered, and discussing the problem of Hannibal's route over the Alps.[1]

The five years of Layard's indenture were duly completed at the beginning of 1839. As the prospect of entering upon a career as attorney and solicitor drew nearer, Layard's distaste for such a course increased. The final blow fell when it became clear that his uncle had no intention for the present of making his rather unsatisfactory nephew a partner in his firm. The volatile Layard was again in the depths of despair, and began to cast around for other means of making a career for himself. Since he himself had acquired some facility at public speaking—one of his diversions had been the membership of various debating societies—he began to consider the possibility of becoming a barrister. There was the objection that, unknown as he was, it might be some time before he was able to support himself by his profession; but he hoped to overcome this difficulty by writing. Layard had displayed, since boyhood, a marked taste for literature and a ready pen. On his various tours abroad he had collected information and statistics and kept journals, which even today are in parts very readable. Several articles of his had been published in the *London Magazine*, to whose publishers, Smith and Elder, he had made himself useful in various ways.[2] He also had a connection with the son of the publisher Murray, for whom he had supplied data concerning Denmark for a handbook.[3] It was thus not an entirely wild hope that he might succeed in supporting himself by his pen.

To the Orient

Whilst Layard was reflecting upon the possibility of such a step, there arrived in England his father's younger brother, Charles Edward Layard. Charles Layard had just retired from the Ceylon Civil Service, in which he had held high office; he was thus not without influence in the island. He now suggested that his nephew Austen Henry should go out to practise as a barrister in Ceylon, where his

[1] 38972 (1835), 194.
[2] 38975, 6–11.
[3] 38975, 1.

admission as an attorney and solicitor would be sufficient qualification, and where family connection might be expected (in the nepotistic society of nineteenth century Ceylon) to be a guarantee of success. Austen Henry decided to put the opportunity to the test. He successfully took the requisite examinations in Law, and on the 10th of June, 1839, found himself a duly admitted, if penniless, Attorney of Her Majesty's court of Queen's Bench at Westminster. He was just twenty-two.

It happened that Charles Layard was acquainted with a certain Edward Ledwich Osbaldeston Mitford. Mitford, five or six[1] years Henry Layard's senior, had already spent some years travelling in Morocco, and was now considering visiting Ceylon, with a view to establishing himself either as a coffee planter or in Government service. He planned to attempt the overland route, much of it on horseback, rather than entrust himself to a long sea voyage. When Charles Layard brought the two younger men together and it was proposed that his nephew should accompany Mitford, Austen Henry jumped at the idea with enthusiasm.

The overland journey to Ceylon could be expected at this time to take anything up to a year, much of it through little known parts where the traveller would be subject to discomforts and hardships and perhaps danger. There was no reason to regard Austen Henry as particularly well equipped for such an arduous enterprise. His apparent qualifications for foreign travel went no further than a good knowledge of French and Italian, the utility of which would rapidly diminish. His enthusiasm was not, however, unaccompanied by intelligent foresight as to the demands and opportunities of the journey, and he took steps to learn something of navigation, of taxidermy (with a view to making a collection of birds), of routes, and of customs and peoples. He also received some elementary instruction in medicine and first-aid, and learnt Arabic script and a little of the Persian language. In addition he avidly read all works available to him on Persia and Babylonia, and even 'such treatises as had then been published ... on the cuneiform and Pehlevi writing, as inscriptions were believed to exist in both these characters in the border mountains of Persia.' In the latter

---

[1] Not ten years, as suggested by G. Waterfield, *Layard of Nineveh* (1963), 25, presumably on the basis of pages 1–2 of E. L. O. Mitford's *Land march from England to Ceylon* (1884), where Mitford loosely refers to the age difference between himself and Henry Layard as 'nearly a decade'. Mitford, writing to Layard in March 1845, speaks of himself as then thirty-three (38976, 147); at that date Layard was just twenty-eight.

connection, one of the works he took with him was a paper by H. C. Rawlinson, which he subsequently repeatedly referred to in the journals of his travels in Mesopotamia and Persia.[1]

Layard's mother was able to allow him £300 for the expenses of his journey. In addition Layard and Mitford jointly obtained from the publishers Smith and Elder a generous advance of £200, repayable with interest after three years unless the two should produce an account of their tour suitable for publication.[2]

Layard left England on the 10th July, 1839, not (so he later said in his autobiography) without some misgivings. He joined Mitford at Brussels, and the two men travelled via Munich, Venice, and Trieste, as far as Fiume. This represented the end of the beaten track for European travellers. 'We were', wrote Layard, 'now about to leave the realms of civilization, and to embark upon our adventurous and perilous journey. We were in high spirits. The novelty of all that we saw around us, and the risks which we were assured we were about to run, added not a little to the charm of our position'.

The next section of their journey brought them into regions where oriental features in costume, habits and even vegetation, began to appear. Wherever they went Layard took the most lively interest in the ruins, in the agriculture and manufactures, and in the appearance of the younger ladies. Layard seems to have been of an amorous nature and obviously had an eye for a pretty girl; both before and after this time he came near to serious trouble for allegedly paying too much attention to other men's wives.

Finally the two men reached the furthest borders of the Austrian Empire, and came to the little independent state of Montenegro. The name (meaning 'black mountain') well described this country, which was everywhere mountainous and mostly covered with dark forests. The Slav inhabitants, who were Christians, had fiercely maintained their independence against Turkish attempts at annexation. Govern-

---

[1] *J.R.G.S.* IX (1839), 26–116, Major Rawlinson, *Notes on a march from Zoháb, at the foot of Zagros, along the mountains to Khúzistán (Susiána), and from thence through the province of Luristan to Kermansháh, in the year 1836.*

[2] 39055, 8–9. A manuscript in suitable form was never forthcoming. Mitford did send a manuscript in 1843, but it was not accepted for publication (38975, 317); he accepted rejection complaisantly and settled down, as he put it, 'to work up my adventures in another form more suitable for the market', and ultimately published them in 1884 under the title *A land march from England to Ceylon forty years ago . . . of which 7000 miles on horseback* (2 volumes). Mitford repaid Smith and Elder his share of the loan at the end of 1843, whilst Layard, after a reminder from Mitford, was able to discharge his debt early in 1845 (39055, 8–9 and 38975, 317).

ment was in the hands of a prince-bishop known as the Vladika, who was supported by a Russian subsidy. Layard and Mitford possessed a letter of introduction to this dignitary and on sending it on to him received a reply in friendly terms, inviting them to visit the Vladika at his capital Cettigne (Cetinje); an escort was sent for this purpose. Layard found the Vladika—a giant of a man of about twenty-seven —something of an enigma. He was an intelligent man with more than a veneer of liberalism, and indignant at reports published abroad attributing backwardness and barbarity to his country. As one of the symbols of civilization he had even provided his modest palace with a billiard table. None the less, head-hunting raids into Turkish territory seem to have remained generally more popular than table games; Layard professes to have been horrified to have had a game of billiards interrupted by a victorious raiding party depositing a bundle of bloody heads at the Vladika's feet. He still displayed a West European sensitivity about such matters, to which his later experiences were to harden him. Layard seems to have remained unaware, even when writing his autobiography many years later, that his host Peter II[1] had been the greatest of Serb poets, and a ruler who opened the first secular elementary schools in his country well before corresponding schools existed in England.

The Montenegrins were the first people Layard had met who had not, to some degree, been under the influence of western industrial civilization. It would be interesting to learn his first impression of them. In his autobiography he says that 'their constant and frequently unprovoked raids upon their neighbours' territories . . . were accompanied by acts of ferocious cruelty. . . . The Mussulman inhabitants of the districts adjacent to the Black Mountain were . . . compelled to submit to the depredations and excesses of their restless and barbarous neighbours. Their villages were burnt, their women and children barbarously mutilated and slain, and a harvest of heads periodically carried off as trophies by their invaders.' Layard, however, wrote this passage at a much later date, when he had had long experience of Eastern life and had acquired an enduring regard for Ottoman Turkey.

Because of the almost perennial hostilities between Montenegrins and Turkish subjects, Layard and Mitford found some difficulty in moving on from Montenegro into Ottoman territory, which began

---

[1] Mitford, *A land march from England to Ceylon*, vol. I, 42, gives the Vladika's name correctly. Layard wrongly refers to him as Danielo (*Autobiography*, vol. I, 129), which was actually the name of his successor.

at Lake Scutari. The move was finally achieved by the use of a leaky boat in which the two travellers were rowed across the lake during the night, arriving in the Albanian town of Scutari, and so for the first time in Turkish territory, next morning.

Layard, who since boyhood had been under the spell of the Arabian Nights and had often pictured oriental life to himself, was fascinated by the scene before him. It was, he said, 'a world of which I had dreamt from my earliest childhood. . . . The booths in the covered alleys of the bazaar, the endless variety of merchandise piled up in them, the embroideries and strange dresses that were suspended around them, the grave Turk seated cross-legged amidst his stores, pipe in hand, the veiled women gliding through the crowd, . . . the savoury messes steaming in the cooks' shops, and the dim and mysterious light of the place, . . . greatly increased the effect that it could not fail to make upon me.'

The usual manner of travelling through Ottoman territories at this time was by post-horse.[1] Government posting stages were maintained at intervals of about twenty miles, and provided, at very small cost, horses available to any traveller armed with the appropriate governmental pass, known as a bouyourouldi. The two travellers presented themselves to the governor of Scutari, a courteous old Turkish gentleman, and duly obtained the requisite passes and letters of introduction to the chiefs through whose territories they would require to proceed.

It was now the end of August [1839], and as Layard and Mitford hoped to get well into Asia Minor before the winter set in, they went on their way without further delay. Travelling through Albania, Roumelia, and Bulgaria, they arrived in Constantinople within a fortnight. Here the travellers required further bouyourouldis, and also a firman from the imperial authorities. These were obtained through the Consul-General, accompanied with a warning that in some areas through which they would be passing the local populations cared little for the authority of the Sultan in Constantinople. There was the additional problem that in the regions through which the two men proposed to travel posting stages would be much less readily available than in the European dominions of Turkey, but this difficulty was overcome by their buying their own mounts and a horse for their

[1] G. Waterfield, *Layard of Nineveh*, 25, states incorrectly that when Layard left England in 1839 he 'had never been astride a horse'. For evidence to the contrary see *Autobiography*, vol. I, 63.

luggage. With a view to provoking as little suspicion as possible in districts where the appearance of European travellers might arouse the hostility or cupidity of the natives, Layard and Mitford replaced their European head-gear by a red Turkish fez. A Greek servant, in native dress, added to the colourfulness of the party.

To those at home in England at this time international political circumstances might well have appeared such as to justify alarm at the prospect of a journey through the centre of Asia Minor. Mohammed Ali, an Albanian commander in the Ottoman army, who had succeeded in getting himself recognized as viceroy in Egypt, had overrun the province of Syria and crossed the Taurus into Turkey itself, thereby throwing parts of south-eastern Turkey into temporary anarchy. But Layard and Mitford had formed the highest opinion of the Turkish authorities and populations they had met in European Turkey, and had no reason to fear that their reception and treatment by officials throughout Asiatic Turkey would be less courteous or helpful.

The two travellers had, before leaving England, been in touch with the Royal Geographical Society and had been invited to attempt to solve certain specific problems. This in part dictated their route, and led them to cross Asia Minor in an approximately straight line from Mudania to Seleucia. Layard kept a route-book for the journey, by means of which he was able to produce a useful map for the Royal Geographical Society.

Throughout, Layard was keeping his eyes open for ruins and antiquities, and used his servant to make enquiries amongst villagers as to the existence of ancient monuments. 'Ancient' being a relative term, especially as used by villagers, this frequently led to disappointment, a tiresome journey often yielding only the remains of a building which had fallen into ruins in quite recent times.

Layard was, on this first visit as always later in his oriental travels, much impressed by the general courtesy of Turks to strangers, and gave several instances of this. He adds however: 'Increased intercourse with Europeans and Christians, and the influence of European contact, has probably changed them for the worse'. Where Layard had occasion to complain of the rapacity or discourtesy of his hosts, it usually proved that they were Christians of some kind. Layard and Mitford crossed Asia Minor without incident, and reached the Mediterranean coast at Seleucia.

Although physical communications were certainly much slower than today, in some respects travel in Layard's time was a deal easier than since the Second World War. No oriental government, and few western governments, would now permit a traveller even to approach an area corresponding to that across which Layard and Mitford were about to ride, abutting on a province which had just fallen to rebel forces. The Turkish army had been defeated by Egyptian rebels in Syria, and the Egyptian forces had penetrated as far as Tarsus, in the south-eastern corner of Turkey. It was to Tarsus that Layard and Mitford now set out. The region impressed Layard more than anything he had yet seen. 'The sun went down in all its glory, lighting up this beautiful coast and the distant mountains of Taurus and Syria, and turning the blue Mediterranean into a sheet of purple and gold. . . . The beauty of the distant mountains, the richness of the vegetation, the utter loneliness and desolation of the country, the wonderful remains of ancient civilisation, the graceful elegance of the monuments, the picturesque aspect of the ruins, the blue motionless sea reflecting every object, with here and there a white sail, all combined to form a scene which it would be difficult to equal and impossible to surpass.'

Having passed into territory under the control of the Egyptian armies, Layard and Mitford stayed for some days at Tarsus, the city of St. Paul. They had now been out of England over four months, and were not more than a third of the way, and that the best known and perhaps the easiest section, to Ceylon. But still they showed no impatience to reach their destination, and when they left Tarsus in mid-November it was to make a detour into Syria. Layard was on the whole favourably impressed with the administration of Ibrahim Pasha, Mohammed Ali's son and his representative in Syria. Taxation was certainly heavy, but at the same time there was peace for the inhabitants and (except for misdemeanours of the troops) security for merchants and travellers. Layard took the view that had Syria remained under Mohammed Ali it would have been spared many calamities. But this was not the view which finally prevailed in the chancelleries of Europe, and finally the western powers (England, Austria and Russia) intervened and compelled Mohammed Ali to withdraw from Syria in 1840.

Palestine and Petra[1]

When, after a visit to Aleppo, the two men set out southwards for Hamah and Homs, they were frankly sight-seeing, since the direct route to Ceylon lay eastwards. Having come so near, they were

[1] Quotations from here to p. 34, not otherwise identified, are from *Early Adventures*.

understandably disinclined to leave the Levant without seeing Jerusalem, and made their way there via Sidon, Tyre and Acre. From Jerusalem, Layard resolved to make a detour still further south to visit Petra, the site of a celebrated ancient city cut in the solid rock. He was strongly advised against this by his European acquaintances in Jerusalem, for the area was not under the control of the Egyptian authorities and the native population was said to be treacherous, fanatical and hostile to Europeans. Mitford, who was no coward but with five years experience of travel in Morocco was able to distinguish between adventure and foolhardiness, refused to take the risk. Layard, however, stubbornly undeterred by warnings, set out, having fixed a date for meeting Mitford in Damascus. He afterwards admitted: 'I had romantic ideas about Bedouin hospitality, and . . . their respect for their guests.' He was to learn otherwise.

Layard, who by this time had a smattering of Arabic, was accompanied only by a Christian Arab lad, Antonio, belonging to a tribe south of the Dead Sea. A sheikh, one Abu Dhaouk of the tribe of Jehalin, was found prepared to undertake to lead Layard to Petra and Kerak, though he added the proviso that he could only guarantee Layard's safety in relation to his own tribe: others might not respect Abu Dhaouk's safe-conduct.

When, after considerable trouble and fatigue, Layard, travelling by camel, reached the sheikh's encampment in the desert, he felt that at last he had found what he was seeking: '[when] it was time for me to retire to my little tent for the night, I remained for some time at the entrance, gazing on the strange and novel scene before me. It was my first acquaintance with an Arab encampment and Arab life. A full moon in all its brilliancy lighted up the Wady, so that every feature in the landscape could be plainly distinguished. The fires in the Arab tents studded the valley with bright stars. The silence of the night was broken by the lowing of the cattle and the hoarse moanings of the camels, and by the long mournful wail of the jackals, which seemed to be almost in the midst of us.'

Eventually, Layard and Antonio were sent off from the encampment by camel with two armed men. The journey to Petra was an anxious one, as they early encountered two robbers, and although their firearms prevented attack, the escorts suspected they were being stalked by a larger party. At Petra Layard met a very unfriendly reception. An ugly scene developed, but Layard pointed out forcibly that if any harm befell him, the Egyptian authorities at Hebron would place the responsibility with sheikh Abu Dhaouk, who would either have to avenge the insult to Egyptian authority by wiping out the tribe at Petra, or lose his own head. The people of Petra were in no doubt as to which alternative he would choose; and with an ill grace permitted Layard to examine the ruins, molesting him no further.

Followed by the curses of the Arabs of Petra, the party returned by the route east of the Dead Sea, through the biblical land of Moab, with a view to seeing Kerak, the site of a great twelfth century crusader fortress. On the way the party was ambushed, but with great presence of mind Layard covered the sheikh of the tribe with his gun, and driving him before him, firmly held him hostage until the party came in sight of an encampment belonging to dependants of the Governor of Kerak.

At the encampment Layard was civilly received. He learned that he was lucky to be alive, since the raiding tribe had the reputation of being the most notorious cut-throats east of the Dead Sea. Only his audacity in taking the sheikh prisoner had saved his party.

In Kerak, arrangements were made for Layard to continue on his way under the protection of a certain sheikh, Suleiman-ibn-Fais, whose encampment was near the ruins of the biblical Rabbath-Ammon (in the district of the present capital of Jordan, Amman, north-east of the Dead Sea). Layard soon discovered that both he and Suleiman-ibn-Fais had been the victims of a trick. His host in Kerak had represented Layard as a wealthy European willing to pay handsomely for an escort, and had received from Suleiman-ibn-Fais a substantial present as a commission on the supposed pickings which had been put in his way. Layard made it clear to his new host that he had neither the means nor the intention of making the generous payment which the sheikh had been led to expect. Suleiman-ibn-Fais alternately cajoled and threatened, but Layard was adamant. The sheikh, in the hope of wearing down Layard's patience, wandered slowly around the desert; but this by no means displeased Layard, to whom it gave the opportunity to see numerous otherwise inaccessible ruins. Finally the sheikh gave up the struggle of wills and led Layard to his main encampment, where he became an honoured guest, and was subsequently given a guide for Amman and Jerash. Except for the annoying importunity for money, Layard formed a very good opinion of Suleiman-ibn-Fais. Suleiman-ibn-Fais did a great deal to disillusion Layard of his romantic ideas about Bedouin generosity; he had learnt that hospitality and cupidity could well go together.

Layard reached Amman without further incident and recorded that the Roman ruins there afforded him 'one of the most striking proofs of the marvellous energy and splendid enterprise of that great people who had subjected the world.'[1] He was even more impressed by the ruins at Jerash, which are mainly Roman from the first and second centuries A.D. 'I was enchanted by the wonderful beauty of the scene. On all sides I saw long avenues of graceful columns leading to temples, theatres, baths, and public edifices, constructed of marble, to which time had given a bright pinkish yellow tint. . . . I passed the day in examining these interesting and wonderful remains. Forcing my way through the tangled brushwood, I succeeded in making in my notebook a hasty and consequently not very accurate plan of them, which is now of no interest or value except as showing how much of the ancient city still existed at the time of my visit, and how much of it has since been destroyed or has disappeared'.

Layard was now over the worst dangers of the desert, but he had new ones to face, in that an epidemic of plague had broken out in the settlements east of the Jordan. He was now well overdue for rejoining Mitford, and in view of this and the danger from plague he began to feel some anxiety to reach Damascus. There were, however, unforeseen difficulties. The Egyptian authorities had put a sanitary cordon around the province of Damascus, which no one was allowed, on pain of death, to enter from the desert. The only practicable possibility open to Layard seemed to be to enter via Palestine. Managing to hire two camels and a guide, Layard, still accompanied by Antonio, struck westwards for the Jordan, crossing it south of the Sea of Galilee to reach Tiberias. Here Antonio left him to return to Jerusalem.

In Tiberias, on the western bank of the Sea of Galilee, Layard was given hospitality by a Polish Jew, who showed him considerable kindness. With Jewish help Layard reached Safed, fifteen miles to the north, where for the journey to Damascus he was provided with an Arab muleteer, described as 'an ill-clad and not over-clean little fellow', though by contrast Layard (a lusty young man of twenty-two who had lived solely in male company for over a month) thought he had never seen a more beautiful woman than the muleteer's wife.

Layard and his guide reached the environs of Damascus with no worse misfortune than being robbed of money and clothing by a party of deserters from the Egyptian army. For the final entry into the city Layard was handed over to a villager, who undertook to guide him

[1] The Roman remains had obliterated all surface traces of more ancient occupation.

through the cordon round Damascus by night. When morning came they were in safety in the gardens of the city. 'Clad' (as he said) 'in scarcely more than a tattered cloak, almost shoeless, and bronzed and begrimed by long exposure to sun and weather and to the dirt of Arab tents', Layard made his way to the British Consulate.

The date for the rendezvous with Mitford had long passed, and the latter had gone on to Aleppo. Layard remained in Damascus just long enough to re-equip himself, recover from certain minor maladies, and buy a mare. When he set out, he could not, despite his being already overdue, resist making a detour to visit the ruins of Baalbek on the way, and finally reached Aleppo to find Mitford on the point of departure. The two men ultimately set out for Baghdad on 18th March, 1840.

Eight months had now gone by since they had left England, and they were still scarcely more than a third of their way towards Ceylon. The next section of their journey, along the northern arc of the fertile crescent, was completed more expeditiously. Passing through Urfa, the ancient Christian centre of Edessa and the most easterly point under Egyptian control, they moved on with the assistance of a Kurdish chief to Mardin, where they were once again under a Turkish administration. Avoiding every temptation to linger (Layard comments surprisingly 'we had no time to spare'), they pushed on and by early April were in Mosul.

Mesopotamia and Persia

Mosul (the name means 'Junction') is a great trading city which grew up on the west bank of the Tigris at the place where the east-west and north-south trade routes cross. Opposite, on the east bank, are the most extensive and massive ruins in north Iraq, called Kuyun-jik, now known to be the ruins of mighty Nineveh. These ruins affected Layard powerfully, as they have many travellers before and since; 'I was', he says, 'deeply moved . . . by their desolate and solitary grandeur'.[1] Layard and Mitford stayed in Mosul as guests of William Francis Ainsworth, a medical man who had travelled extensively in the east and published *Researches in Assyria, Babylonia and Chaldaea* (1838), and of Christian Rassam, a native Christian who had been appointed British Vice-Consul in Mosul. Layard spent much of his stay upon the mound of Kuyunjik, 'taking measurements and searching for fragments of marble and bricks with cuneiform inscriptions,

[1] *Autobiography*, vol. I, 305.

which were then occasionally found amongst the ruins'.[1] Ainsworth and Rassam also took Layard and Mitford into the desert to see the ruins of Hatra, a great Parthian city, and of Kalah Shergat, now known to be the remains of the ancient Assyrian city of Ashur (*Genesis* x. 11). This journey was the occasion upon which Layard first caught sight of Nimrud, which he was later to excavate with such remarkable results. 'I saw for the first time the great conical mound of Nimrud rising against the clear evening sky. . . . The impression that it made upon me was one never to be forgotten'.[2]

Layard was far from being the first man to interest himself in the ruins and inscriptions of Mesopotamia. From the Middle Ages to Layard's own times occasional European travellers had visited the lands of Assyria and Babylonia and rightly or wrongly identified various mounds with ancient cities. Layard's great merit was that he was the first investigator with the pertinacity to overcome all obstacles, the understanding of Eastern peoples by which he could replace suspicion by collaboration, and the combination of technical skills and art appreciation to enable him to dig in the ruins to good effect and to record and interpret his results.

When Layard first set eyes on Kuyunjik and Nimrud in 1840, very little, beyond the biblical records and occasional references in classical authors, was known of ancient Assyria. When, eleven years later, internationally renowned at the age of thirty-four, he left the region for ever, Assyria had, after an obscurity of two and a half millennia, begun to take its place with the other great empires of the past, its records uncovered, its kings known, its art visible to all in its barbaric vigour in the British Museum.

Layard's discoveries and his fame still lay in the future. At the moment he was no more than a penniless young lawyer in search of employment in Ceylon. The immediate task of Layard and Mitford was to reach Baghdad, where they might hope to obtain the necessary letters and authorizations and join a caravan into Persia. The journey from Mosul to Baghdad was made by *kelek*, a very ancient but efficient type of raft, consisting of a platform supported by inflated goat skins; the same means of transport was to be used, years later, for moving the great stone colossi which Layard found at Nimrud.[3]

In Baghdad the first call was upon Colonel Taylor, Agent of the

[1] *Autobiography*, vol. I, 306.
[2] *Autobiography*, vol. I, 311.
[1] See below, pp. 275–281.

East India Company and a noted scholar of Arabic. Layard received considerable help and encouragement from the Colonel, who put both his learning and library at Layard's disposal, and encouraged him to take lessons in Persian.

After a month and a half in Baghdad Layard and Mitford attached themselves to a caravan to Kermanshah; after the usual oriental delays it finally set out from Baghdad on the 20th June.[1] For this part of the journey Layard had adopted Persian dress, with a view to reducing liability to insult and annoyance from strangers. He had, however, overlooked the members of the caravan with which he was travelling, mainly pilgrims returning from the holy city of Kerbela. 'All', reports Layard in his journal, 'were profiting much from their visit to the sacred places and . . . looked upon us with more or less contempt. The women pulled their veils down as we approached and even the little children ran away in terror. But the most prominent of all our enemies was a cholzmullah, from Meshed, a place redolent with sanctity. This good man employed the greater part of the day and whole of the night in preaching a crusade against the infidel, . . . devoting our souls and bodies to eternal perdition with as much confidence and as frequently as any Evangelical preacher.'[2]

The holy man's damnation had little effect on Layard, who in his journal continued to display a voracious appetite for everything relating to the history and customs of the East. During the journey to Kermanshah we find him discussing with himself such matters as the pronunciation of a place name, shells (not marine shells, as Ainsworth had claimed) near Mosul, Turkish justice, and Greek and Sassanian inscriptions, some of which he copied, claiming to have improved on the published copies in some instances.[3] He was constantly on the alert for ruins, and at this period and later frequently referred to the memoir by Major H. C. Rawlinson on western Persia.

Rawlinson is the one man entitled to share with Layard the honour of establishing both the science of Assyriology and the British Museum assyriological collection. The son of a member of the old landed gentry, Rawlinson had received the usual education of his class, which left him, unlike Layard, an excellent classical scholar but quite

[1] Not the 29th, as stated by Layard in *Early Adventures,* vol. I, 204; see 39092B, 2.

[2] 39092B, 12 (3rd July). The gist of this is reproduced in *Early Adventures,* vol. I, 226–7, but the humorous comparison of Muslim and Evangelical intolerance is dropped. In 1887, when *Early Adventures* was published, Evangelical preachers were no longer a proper subject of fun.

[3] 39092B, 2–3, 7–9.

insensitive to any art other than that deriving from Greek forms. He was, according to his brother, 'six feet high, broad-chested, strong limbed, with excellent thews and sinews, . . . and a nerve that few of his co-mates equalled'.[1] Seven years Layard's senior, he had received a cadetship in the East India Company in 1827. Although as an officer in the army he fully entered into the life of a sportsman, he also applied himself seriously to the study of oriental languages, including Persian. This latter circumstance gave the subsequent direction to his career.

In the 1820's Persia had suffered disastrous defeats at the hands of Russia, and in the ensuing period Persian policy principally centred upon the attempt to balance British against Russian influence. In connection with this policy, a military mission from the Indian army was called for to help in the reorganization of the Shah's fighting forces. Rawlinson, put in charge of the contingent sent, in March 1835 found himself at Kermanshah. About twenty miles east-north-east of Kermanshah there is a celebrated trilingual cuneiform inscription on a great cliff known as Bisitun; Rawlinson set himself to copy the texts, finally achieving results which eventually made possible the decipherment of the languages written in cuneiform. He also travelled in the areas west and south of Kermanshah in search of ruins and inscriptions, subsequently publishing his results in the paper which was to be of such value to Layard.

On arrival at Kermanshah, Layard found the situation less favourable than it has been for Rawlinson five years before. East of Persia lay Herat, with its dependency Seistan to the south, both of them previously provinces of Persia, but now parts of independent Afghan kingdoms. Persia was now attempting to recover these provinces, and in this attempt received Russian support. In view of the latter circumstance, the British government feared that the return of Herat to Persia would open the way for a Russian drive towards India, and consequently adopted the policy of building a strong anti-Russian Afghan state in this area. This aroused anti-British feeling in Persia, which ultimately, after expelling the British military mission, invaded Herat in 1837. The British government responded by the occupation in the following year of the island of Karak (Kharg) in the Persian Gulf, from where an invasion of south Persia could have been mounted. This had the desired effect of bringing about a Persian withdrawal from Herat. In 1839 a British army entered Afghanistan, and although

[1] G. Rawlinson, *A memoir of Major-General Sir Henry Creswicke Rawlinson* (1898), 15.

Herat was not occupied this caused a further strain between Great Britain and Persia, and diplomatic relations were broken off.

This situation inevitably had its repercussions upon the journey planned by Layard and Mitford. On arrival at Kermanshah they were summoned by the Governor and informed that they could not proceed further without specific permission from the Shah, who was with his tatterdemalion army a little to the east, between Kermanshah and Hamadan. The travellers came up with the Shah's forces encamped not far from the latter city.

At Hamadan the two men applied for the necessary firmans and were eventually introduced to the Prime Minister: it was, and remains, a principle of oriental administration that no decision but the simplest could be made at any but the top level. When Layard and Mitford explained that they wished to travel through Yezd and the Seistan, the Prime Minister's suspicions were immediately aroused. His attitude was not as unreasonable as Layard's accounts in his journal and *Early Adventures* might suggest. Seistan was a province formerly Persian, more recently under the suzerainty of Herat, and still in disputed possession: indeed, the problem of Seistan was not settled until a boundary commission partitioned it between Persia and Afghanistan in 1872. Meanwhile, there must have seemed no legitimate reason for two Englishmen to intrude into the area, which enjoys few natural advantages to recommend it to tourists. A recent handbook describes Persian Seistan (the more fertile part of the whole of Seistan) in the following terms: 'The wind is tempestuous and persistent from about the end of May until late September. It blows from the north-north-west often with a velocity of seventy miles an hour. ... Blizzards may occur from December to March from the same direction and are severe enough to cause death to camels; in one of these an average wind velocity of eighty-eight miles an hour was recorded over sixteen hours. ... [Many old houses] have had their bases undercut by wind erosion. ... Some villages have been buried by sand; the process continues today. ... In rare periods of calm during summer there are plagues of midges and mosquitoes, horse-flies, and other insects. There are also poisonous snakes.'[1] It was a reasonable conclusion that men wishing to travel in such an uninviting area must have some sinister motive. The two men belonged to a country on bad terms with Persia and believed to be preparing an invasion from the east,

[1] Naval Intelligence Division, Geographical Handbook Series B.R. 525, *Persia* (1945), 118.

and owing to an unfortunate lack of tact on the part of Layard they had already been discovered acting as bearers of letters from disaffected Persians exiled to Baghdad. These factors, added to the remoteness of Seistan and its unresolved international status, made the proposed journey by these two Englishmen a matter of grave suspicion. They might well, the Prime Minister could reasonably have thought, be spies, seeking a route across an unprotected frontier by which British armies could enter Persia from Afghanistan.

Layard still had much to learn of Oriental psychology. When the Prime Minister offered to let them take the route proposed provided they would sign a document declaring that they had taken the road contrary to his advice and acting upon their own responsibility, Layard (though not the more experienced and prudent Mitford) at once consented. This put the unfortunate Prime Minister in the embarrassing position of doing what no well-bred oriental cares to do even today, that is, of giving a point-blank refusal to a request. He left the travellers free, however, to proceed towards India either by the normal northern route or through Shiraz to Bushire and the Persian Gulf, and firmans were promised to enable them to continue their journey.

The promised firmans were not forthcoming for several weeks. Meanwhile, Layard was engaged in examining the antiquities of the Hamadan district and copying inscriptions. The city, which has never yet been excavated, was (and remains) of considerable potential interest to archaeologists, since it occupies the site of Ecbatana, the ancient Median capital.

Layard's enforced stay in Hamadan gave him a very poor impression of the Persian attitude towards strangers, which contrasted ill with the hospitality of Turks and Arabs. He complained in his diary: 'During my short stay I have received more insults and more ill treatment than during the whole of my journey thro' Turkey, Syria and amongst the Arabs.'[1] Both Layard and Mitford, exasperated by their treatment in Hamadan, were more than ready to leave the city. Layard, however, still had hopes of proceeding by the route originally planned, but Mitford was now prepared to forego this as impracticable and wished only to get on to India. The time had therefore come for the two men to separate. The firmans having been delivered, Layard recorded: 'Saturday 8th [August] ... I took leave of Mitford having been a year and one month his travelling companion. I am

[1] 39092B, 21.

22

now alone and about to undertake the most arduous part of our proposed journey.'[1]

Layard's firman permitted him to go south-east to Isfahan, and thence through Luristan to the Persian Gulf. Part of the journey would take Layard through the territory of the great Bakhtiyari tribe, and he was therefore also provided with a letter from the Prime Minister to Mohammed Taki Khan, the paramount chief of the Bakhtiyari. The eventual meeting between the two men was to have important consequences for both.

The passage quoted from Layard's journal indicates that at this stage he had certainly not yet admitted to himself the possibility of not fulfilling his original plan of reaching India. If he hoped to find an opportunity of circumventing the Prime Minister's ban and proceeding on the route originally planned through Yezd and Seistan, his next major centre had to be Isfahan. Yet although this was in fact his nominal destination, and the one he finally reached, he deliberately avoided taking the direct route to it. When, accompanied by a *ghulam* (soldier) provided by the Persian government, and a Lur servant, he set out from Hamadan, it was to strike off on a little known route leading into the mountains of Luristan. Layard was interested in seeing this province, parts of which were still unexplored, and had in fact obtained the Prime Minister's authorization to travel across it to Shushter and from there to Isfahan. Part of the attraction was to visit the ruins of the biblical Shushan,[2] which was known to be in the vicinity of Shushter, though the exact site was still a matter of dispute.

As the party began to penetrate into Luristan they found signs of increasing prosperity. 'I had rarely seen', writes Layard in his *Early Adventures*, 'a country so densely populated and with so prosperous and flourishing an appearance. We were evidently entering upon a district whose inhabitants had not been exposed to the oppressive rule of the Persian Government, with its attendant suffering and misery'. The situation had, however, its disadvantages for Layard. His protection was the authority of the Shah, and in the districts before him, where the inhabitants might give scant heed to the Shah's authority, the party might well come into serious danger. This circumstance, added to the summer heat (it was mid-August) and attacks of malaria and dysentery, finally induced Layard to abandon his attempt to cross Luristan. He returned to the high road for Isfahan.

[1] 39092B, 22–23.
[2] *Nehemiah* i.L., *Esther* ii.8, etc.

Two days after his arrival in Isfahan Layard presented himself to the Governor, to whom he had letters of introduction from the Prime Minister. The Governor of Isfahan, otherwise known as the Matamet, was the Strong Man of Persia. By birth a Christian Georgian, he had been sold as a slave in childhood and made a eunuch. Entering the public service, he had risen by his abilities to the highest rank. Even Layard, who later came to have good cause to dislike him, conceded, writing many years afterwards, that though 'he was hated and feared for his cruelty, . . . it was generally admitted that he ruled justly, that he protected the weak from oppression by the strong, and that where he was able to enforce his authority life and property were secure'. Layard gives some instances of tortures the Matamet had devised for punishing criminals. 'A tower still existed near Shiraz which he had built of three hundred living men belonging to . . . a tribe . . . which had rebelled against the Shah. They were laid in layers of ten, mortar being spread between each layer, the heads of the unhappy victims being left free. . . . At that time few nations, however barbarous, equalled—none probably exceeded—the Persian in the shocking cruelty, ingenuity, and indifference with which death or torture was inflicted.'

Layard applied afresh to the Matamet for permission to proceed to the Seistan, but received so definite a refusal that he recognized the necessity for postponing any such plan. Meanwhile the Matamet raised no objection to Layard's travelling in the mountains west of Isfahan, and assured him that with a competent guide he would have no difficulty in reaching Shushter. It happened that at this time there was in Isfahan a brother of Mohammed Taki Khan, on his way to Teheran as a hostage for the chief's loyalty to the Shah. His escort, which would shortly be returning to Bakhtiyari country, included another chief, Shefir Khan, and it was arranged that Layard should travel with his party.

It was some five weeks before Shefir Khan's party left Isfahan. For Layard, though eager to be entering new spheres of interest and exasperated by the delay, the time was not wholly passed in idleness. He continued to learn Persian, and spent much time both enquiring about antiquities in the Bakhtiyari area and examining those within his immediate access. He also found opportunity for social life during the five weeks in Isfahan, ranging from political and religious controversy with French and Italian Roman Catholic missionaries, to attendance at drunken orgies with dancing girls in the house of a friend of Shefir Khan.

With the Bakhtiyaris

Layard finally set out for the mountains with about fifty Bakhti-yaris on the 23rd September [1840], at Shefir Khan's suggestion wearing Bakhtiyari costume. He was in high spirits, and, as he said, 'much elated by the prospect of being able to visit a country hitherto unexplored by Europeans, and in which I had been led to suppose I should find important ancient monuments and inscriptions'.

Shefir Khan's personal guarantee of safety was essential, for in the Bakhtiyari mountains neither life nor property was secure. Except in the outer parts of the mountains it was with great difficulty, and at rare intervals, that the Shah was able to make his authority felt, and there were many villages prepared to deny him even nominal allegi-ance. More generally respected in the depths of the mountains was the authority of Mohammed Taki Khan, but even his power to control the region was limited. Thus even though the leader of the caravan Layard was accompanying was a Bakhtiyari chief closely linked with Mohammed Taki Khan, their route was dictated by the necessity of avoiding certain hostile tribes, whilst on this very journey Layard himself was a witness of cattle raids. Petty theft at the hands of the tribes through whose villages the travellers passed was common. Layard records: 'Sunday 4th [October]. Several things were again stolen last night, amongst them my coverlet. Fortunately the weather is warm and agreeable and even the nights not cold. Even the Arabs never rob their guests.'[1]

It is amusing to notice that in the published version in the *Early Adventures* Layard alters a detail to make his complaint more pungent. 'On waking in the morning I found that my quilt had been stolen. This was a severe loss, for although the weather was still mild during the day, the nights were cold, as it was October 3.'[2]

The foregoing discrepancy could have resulted from a mere hasty misreading of his own journal. None the less, there are a few instances where such an explanation will not serve and where the general impression given by the published *Early Adventures* is not that of the original journal. There are other passages indicating that Layard was a little given to editing his published narrative to suggest a greater rapport between himself and the natives, particularly the ladies, than one would suspect to have existed from the plain entry in the journal. Under the guidance of Shefir Khan the caravan had to cross the

[1] 39092B, 31.
[2] *Early Adventures*, vol. I, 361.

Bakhtiyari mountains towards Khuzistan, their destination being Mohammed Taki Khan's castle, Kala Tul, about two-thirds of the way from Isfahan to Shushter. They arrived there on October the 5th. The transhumant tribesmen had just moved down to their winter headquarters from the summer pastures in the mountains. Taki Khan himself was temporarily absent.

Layard's first concern on arrival at Kala Tul was to examine the area for ruins. This order of priorities is not made clear in the *Early Adventures*, where he records: 'My reputation as a Frank physician had preceded me, and I had scarcely arrived at the castle when I was surrounded by men and women asking for medicines. . . . Shortly afterwards the chief's principal wife sent to ask me to see her son, who, I was told, was dangerously ill. . . . The lady sat unveiled in a corner, watching over her child, a boy of ten years of age . . . As I entered she rose to meet me, and I was at once captivated by her sweet and kindly expression. . . . She entreated me, with tears, to save the boy, as he was her eldest son, and greatly beloved by his father. I found the child in a very weak state from a severe attack of intermittent fever. I had suffered so much myself during my wanderings from this malady that I had acquired some experience in its treatment. . . . Returning to the castle I sent her some doses of quinine; but before giving them to the child she thought it expedient to consult the two physicians who had been summoned to Kala Tul. Fearing that if their patient passed into my hands they would lose the presents they expected, they advised that it would be dangerous to try my remedies. Their opinion was confirmed by a mulla, who, upon all such important occasions, was employed to consult the Koran in the usual way by opening the leaves at random. The oracle was unfavourable, and my medicine was put aside for the baths of melon juice and Shiraz wine'.[1]

The account of the same incident in the journal, though differing in no essential fact, gives a markedly different picture of Layard's response to Mohammed Taki Khan's wife. The young Layard of 1840, not yet subject to the late Victorian convention requiring him to be 'at once captivated by [the] sweet and kindly expression' of the noble native lady, took a tougher line: 'Wednesday 7th [October]. I took another look at the ruins this morning and could not discover any of more ancient date than those I have mentioned. . . . I returned alone this morning to Kala Tul. The rest of the day was employed in administering medicines and as soon as the arrival of a Firinji was

[1] *Early Adventures*, vol. I, 369–70.

known there were few who had not some imaginary ills. The children of Mehemet Taki Khan were also afflicted with fever. A Sayyid, who enjoyed the name of Hakim [Doctor] had been sent for from Shuster to cure them. But after a month's residence in the castle appears to have had little success. His mode of treatment indeed does not promise much, his medicine consisting of cold water, wine, and lemonade. I gave the women such medicines as I judged necessary and as the fevers were simply intermittent I hoped within a day or two to effect a cure. But the Sayyid fearful lest a Christian should be more successful than he, a descendant of the prophet, induced the mother to throw the medicines to the dogs. I determined to leave the matter in the hands of the holy man with his wine and lemonade.

'Thursday 8th [October] . . . Last night at 11 o'clock my thermometer stood at 72 and I slept in the open air with no other covering than a cloak. The little son of Mehemet Taki being a little worse today he was again brought to me but I referred his mother to the Sayyid. The women, however, entreated me to save him and promised horses and all manner of presents should I be successful. I gave them medicine but it was not taken as on consulting the horoscope the hour was not considered propitious. The rice in [illegible place-name] . . . has not yet been gathered in whilst that of Lourdagan and the neighbourhood was gathered in a week ago.'[1]

The fate of the lady and her son was to the Layard of 1840 of little more interest than the rice crop or the weather and of considerably less than the ruins of Khuzistan.

Whilst waiting for the Khan's return, Layard was tracing and examining some of the more accessible of the antiquities reported by Rawlinson, including those at Mal Amir and Susan, the latter wrongly identified by Rawlinson with the biblical 'Shushan the palace'.

When the Khan eventually arrived, his first concern was for his son. According to the *Early Adventures*: 'He had scarcely entered the enderun of the castle, to which his wife had removed, than he sent for me. I found him sobbing and in deep distress. . . . The child was believed to be at the point of death. The father appealed to me in heartrending terms, offering me gifts of horses and anything that I might desire if I would only save the life of his son. The skilful physicians, he said, for whom he had sent, had now declared that they could do nothing more for the boy, and his only hope was in me.

'I could not resist Mehemet Taki Khan's entreaties, and after

[1] 39092B, 32–33.

reminding him that the medicines I had already prescribed had not been given, I consented to do all in my power to save the child's life, on condition that the native doctors were not allowed to interfere. Although he was willing to agree to all I required, he could not, as a good Musulman, allow the boy to take my remedies until the mulla, who resided in the castle and acted as secretary and chaplain to the chief, could consult the Koran and his beads. The omen was favourable, and I was authorised to administer my medicines, but they were to be mixed with water which had served to wash off from a cup a text from the Koran. . . .

'The child was in high fever, which I hoped might yield to Dover's powder and quinine. I administered a dose of the former at once, and prepared to pass the night in watching its effect. I was naturally in great anxiety as to the result. If the boy recovered I had every reason to hope that I should secure the gratitude of his father, and be allowed to carry out my plan of visiting the ruins and monuments which were said to exist in the Bakhtiyari Mountains, and which it was the main object of my journey to reach. If, on the other hand, he were to die, his death would be laid at my door, and the consequences might prove very serious, as I should be accused by my rivals, the native physicians, of having poisoned the child.'[1]

Once again the journal presents the situation as rather less dramatic. There is no question of the child dying, and Layard shows cynical scepticism as to the value of Mohammed Taki Khan's professions of gratitude:

'Friday 22nd [October]. The Khan arrived this evening accompanied by a large body of horsemen. The illness of his son who had been long under the care of the Sayyid Ibrahim seemed to be his first thought. . . . The Hakim [Doctor] had given the child over for several days and had refused to administer medicines. I was called and my opinion asked. I did not hesitate to say that the Sayyid having refused to give the child any more medicine was the most fortunate thing that could have occurred, his mode of treatment being considerably more to be feared than the disease. At the same time I assured the Khan that the child was in no immediate danger and that I would willingly administer medicines and did not despair of effecting a cure in a few days. The Khan protested that the castle and all its contents were mine should I prove successful. I know the value of Persian promises and therefore attach small value to his of horses and other presents.

---

[1] *Early Adventures*, vol. I, 376–8.

The Mullah . . . having uttered a short prayer opened the [Koran]—the passage . . . was read out and the result declared most favourable —it was immediately determined that I should give the child such medicine as I thought proper, which I only consented to do on condition that the Sayyid should not be allowed in any manner to interfere. It was decided that I should commence on the morrow morning.

'Saturday 23rd. I was summoned to the Anderun in the middle of the night, the Khan having determined that medicine should be administered immediately. I accordingly gave the child a powder and remained the greater part of the night with it, the father and mother being in the greatest anxiety. Today the child was much better—the Khan renewed his promises—I scarcely left the Anderun during the day.'[1]

During the following month Kala Tul was Layard's base for a number of journeys into the Bakhtiyari mountains and the Khuzistan plain. This was an area covered by Rawlinson's memoir, and Layard's time was spent in examing ruins and investigating the geography of the country. His journeys enabled him to make additions and corrections to Rawlinson's information, not only upon archaeological sites but also upon details of tribal territories and their sub-divisions.

The nature of some of the entries in Layard's journals at this period provides clear evidence that by this time (late Autumn 1840) he had formed the plan of publishing a book of travels, with the usual kind of miscellaneous information and anecdotes woven around the account of his adventures. Layard had every opportunity of obtaining information about the Bakhtiyari, since, after his success with Mohammed Taki Khan's son, his advice was now valued by the Khan in matters not only medical but also political. The Khan now decided to use Layard as an agent in an attempt to secure British support against the Shah.

Though virtually autonomous in the Bakhtiyari mountains, Mohammed Taki Khan nominally recognized the authority of the Shah. The Shah's advisers were, however, under no delusions as to the quality of the Khan's loyalty: in the event of war with either Turkey or England, Mohammed Taki Khan would certainly attempt to benefit by the situation, and it was known that he was already in contact with dissident Persian political leaders in exile in Baghdad. The Shah was therefore preparing to force Mohammed Taki Khan's

[1] 38975, 39.

hand by pressing for payment of taxes, never easy to extract from tribesmen. Fiscal administration amongst the Bakhtiyari was only rudimentary, and Mohammed Taki Khan, having virtually no tribal treasury, had either to refuse payment, thereby proclaiming himself in rebellion, or take unpopular measures to extract dues from reluctant tribesmen, which would undermine the fragile and shifting support on which his own semi-independent position rested. It was in this dilemma that the Khan turned to the British.

It was widely believed that the British occupation of Karak in the Persian Gulf in 1838 foreboded an attack upon the Persian mainland. Mohammed Taki Khan now asked Layard to go to Karak as emissary, to sound the possibility of an understanding with the British authorities.

Layard reached Karak without untoward incident, only to be frankly told by the British authorities that Mohammed Taki Khan had nothing to hope from British military intervention. The British attitude is summed up in a letter written later by Sir Justin Sheil, Secretary of the British Legation in Persia, who told Layard: 'I hope for his own sake [Mohammed Taki Khan] will moderate his ambition and content himself with his actual state which only wants the name to make him a nearly independent ruler. You may be assured he deceives himself if he thinks himself capable of emancipating his country from the slight control which is now exercised over it by the Persian government ... his destruction would be certain ... I hope his energy and talent will be directed to the improvement of his tribe, and to the encouragement of commerce. ... Mohammed Tekkee Khan will confer benefit on Persia and England by giving security to traffic, and by encouraging the increase of the exportable products of his country.'[1]

Layard's intentions as to his future seem at this time to have been vague. There are indications, however, that he was not without hope that his special knowledge of south-west Persia might gain him employment either with the British Government or the East India Company: in the event of trade being established with the Bakhtiyari region through Shushter, the services of a consul would become necessary. He was taking every opportunity of gaining accurate information, and was frequently able to supplement or correct the published statements of Rawlinson, the accepted authority on the area. Layard had obtained figures from Mohammed Taki Khan as to

[1] 38975, 33–34.

his war potential, and many pages of his journal are devoted to an analysis and description of the Bakhtiyari tribes of the mountain area and of the Arab tribes of the Khuzistan plain.[1] He also collected detailed economic information which would have been of considerable value to a merchant attempting to establish trade.[2]

Whilst at Karak, Layard seized the chance of bringing his existence and special qualifications to the notice of the business community in Bombay, who were informed by an intermediary that 'should any suggestions be offer'd—or requisitions on [Mr. Layard's] time or labours, with a view of obtaining commercial or other information from the various countries he is now visiting . . . he will be but too happy to comply with them.'[3]

The reference to Layard's proposed visits to 'various countries' indicates, in the context of a letter offering information to merchants in Bombay, that he was no longer thinking of proceeding to India and Ceylon. A letter from Colonel Taylor in Baghdad gives a clue to the new plans forming in Layard's mind: 'Baghdad: 10 March, 1841. . . . I think you could enter Arabia [i.e. the Arab countries] as favourably from Basra as from any other point and if you should determine upon it I shall be happy to . . . give you every aid in my power to meet your wishes.'[4]

Layard arrived back at Kala Tul on 1st February 1841 to find that the Shah was forestalling any treasonable activity on the part of Mohammed Taki Khan by sending the Matamet to the area with an army. As was the intention, the Matamet's presence rapidly brought about the disintegration of the fragile tribal confederation to which Mohammed Taki Khan had owed his ability to withstand the Shah. Layard meanwhile continued undisturbed with his archaeological researches, less concerned about the political problems of Mohammed Taki Khan than his *Early Adventures* might suggest. His journal entry reads: 'The Mautamet and M. T. Khan remained about forty days in the plain of Mal Amir. During this time I discovered two other bass reliefs.' A detailed description of the reliefs followed.[5] Layard also mentioned a second visit to Susan, which he was now able to examine with minuteness, and an expedition to a site called Kul Fara (or Faraon), which he described as 'the most remarkable place I have yet

[1] 39092B, 62ff.
[2] 39093, 50; 39092B, 91–93.
[3] 38975, 30.
[4] 38975, 31–32.
[5] 39092B, 51.

seen in the Baktiyari mountains',[1] having thirty-four figures in rock reliefs and a long cuneiform inscription in a perfect state of preservation.

Whilst Layard was engaged on his archaeological researches, the Matamet's machinations were eroding Bakhtiyari support for Mohammed Taki Khan. By early summer Mohammed Taki Khan had been deposed and made prisoner. Layard's loyalty to the Khan now proved stronger than his respect for the legal Persian government, and led him into activities which might have had serious consequences.

One gallant but ill-advised exploit was to join in a night attack on the camp of the Persian army to attempt to rescue the captive Khan. The attack failed in its main objective. An attempt by one of Mohammed Taki Khan's brothers, accompanied by Layard, to reach the headquarters of a possible source of protection, the Qashqa tribe near Shiraz, ended with the brother's capture and murder by a hostile tribe and Layard's narrow escape. Alone in the mountains, he had little alternative to returning to Shushter, where the Matamet—not without justification—put him under open arrest (July 1841).

Return to Baghdad

In his *Early Adventures* Layard makes this the point at which he formally gave up any idea of proceeding to India and decided to return to Baghdad. 'I had been able to collect much political, geographical, and commercial information [about Khuzistan] which I believed might prove useful. . . . I was still not without hope that I might persuade some English merchants at Baghdad . . . to enter into commercial relations with the Bakhtiyari and Arab tribes of Khuzistan, and that in this case the little influence I had acquired among them might prove of advantage'. But it is clear, from Layard's general course of action and from several comments in his journals, that he had effectively abandoned the Ceylon plan months before this.

After a month of open arrest in Shushter Layard managed to escape. August, with the shade temperature rising to 120°F—a hypothetical value since shade is virtually absent—, is not the most favourable time for travelling in the Khuzistan plain, but there was no prospect of a better opportunity for leaving. He finally arrived at Basra, in Turkish territory, in late August [1841], and was hospitably received by the agent of the East India Company.

Layard, anxious to reach Baghdad, set out on horseback in the

[1] 39092B, 52.

32

company of one of the postmen employed by the East India Company. The route to Baghdad was notorious for robbers, and the two men were in fact intercepted and robbed, and Layard left, without horse or shoes, clad only in tarbush, shirt, and abba. Almost within sight of Baghdad they were waylaid a second time and Layard forced to surrender even his tarbush and abba. Clad only in his shirt, and the ragged abba which one of the thieves had left in exchange for Layard's own, he staggered with bare and bleeding feet up to the city walls shortly after sunrise. As the city gates were opened, there emerged a cavalcade from the English Residency. By good chance there rode at the rear an old acquaintance of Layard, Dr. John Ross,[1] to whom he was able to make himself known.

Layard, now twenty-four, had been away from England for over two years. The net gain of his wanderings was a good[2] command of several dialects of Persian, some facility in Arabic, an intimate acquaintance with remote parts of the Luristan mountains, and a detailed knowledge of tribal organization amongst both the tribes of the mountains and the Arabs of Khuzistan. He also had personal acquaintance with many of the principal men of the Shushter and Bakhtiyari regions. He was not unreasonable in hoping that such qualifications might have a market value.

Whilst awaiting communications from home (an answer to a letter might well at that time take up to three months) he took the opportunity, provided by the East India Company steamers patrolling the Tigris between Baghdad and Basra, to make several further journeys to the south of Mesopotamia and from there into the neighbouring region of Persia.

His present interest in south-western Persia was three-fold: to learn the fate of Mohammed Taki Khan, to examine the antiquities in the area, and to investigate further the possibilities of trade. On his principal visit Layard made his way into the mountains beyond Shushter to the castle of a certain Jaffir Kuli Khan, now, with the fall of Mohammed Taki Khan, effectively the principal Bakhtiyari leader. Though a notorious robber, he received Layard warmly. 'You were', Layard reported him as saying, 'the friend of Mehemet Taki Khan,

---

[1] This gentleman, a physician who finally died of alcoholism in 1849 (38778, 369), is to be distinguished from the merchant H. J. Ross (see below, pp. 75, 292), who assisted Layard in his excavations.

[2] But not perfect. His friend Burgess in Tabriz had occasion (39093, 101) to chide Layard for a solecism in a letter in Persian which Layard had sent for transmission to Mohammed Taki Khan.

and when he fled ... you ... followed him, whilst we Bakhtiyari went against him and aided his enemies. ... I wish to be the friend of one who had thus shown himself a better man than us Mussulmans.'

Layard took the opportunity of Jaffir Kuli Khan's protection to visit a number of rock inscriptions and carvings in the mountains, and subsequently returned to Shushter by the beginning of December [1841]. There he was allowed to visit Mohammed Taki Khan, whom he found chained by the hands, feet and neck in a small dark room in the castle.

Layard also visited Mohammed Taki Khan's womenfolk. They were in miserable circumstances, but there was little he could do to assist the women in their plight. He had already had experience of the hopelessness of attempting to intercede for the womenfolk of men in disfavour with the Persian government. When in Shushter in the summer he had come upon another such group, and hoping to gain them some relief had applied to the Armenian general with whom he was residing. The answer filled Layard with indignation that spilled over into his journal. It was, he wrote, 'such as none but a Persian or the most vile and depraved of human being could have given—and Good God! that man was a Christian or assumes the name. ... "If they are women", said he, "and they are young, they will have no difficulty in finding employment in a Persian camp. If they are old and have sons, they will not amongst Persian troops want bread".'[1]

The other principal object of Layard's journey was to examine the ruins at Shush near Dizful, commonly (and, as it later proved, correctly) identified with the Shushan of the Bible, though Rawlinson had proposed another site.[2] Layard satisfied himself beyond doubt that this was indeed ancient Shushan (Susa) but seems otherwise to have been disappointed in the remains. In a letter Mitford comments, 'You did not say whether you had discovered anything of Shushan the palace. Rawlinson who seems to have heard of your proceedings told me he was disappointed that you have not found more extensive and interesting ruins'.[3]

[1] 39093, 17.
[2] Rawlinson had summarized his views in *J.R.G.S.* IX (1839), 85: 'I believe, then, that in ancient times, there were two cities of the name of Súsan, or Susa, in the province of Susiāna—the more ancient, which is the Shushan of Scripture, being situated at Súsan on the Kivan, or Eulaeus; the other, the Susa of the Greeks, at Sús, near the Kerkhah, or Choaspes. ... With regard to Súsan—the very expression of Scripture, "Shushan the palace" [*Daniel* viii.2], would appear indicative of a distinction from some other city of the same name.'
[3] 38975, 56.

The reference to Rawlinson indicates that by this period Layard was becoming known, and his activities treated as more than mere wander-lust, by some of the people best qualified to form an opinion. The quality of Layard's work is shown in a memoir on Khuzistan, which he completed during this period though it was not published in the *Journal of the Royal Geographical Society* until 1846.[1]

By the time of Layard's return to Baghdad from the visit to Jaffir Kuli Khan, he was beginning to have some success in interesting at least one of the British merchants there (a Mr. Alexander Hector), in the possibility of trade with Khuzistan. But the condition to which the Matamet's depredations had reduced Khuzistan made the commercial prospects insufficiently attractive for them to be taken up on any large scale at this time in Baghdad, although Mr. Hector, supported by his principal Mr. Stirling in Sheffield, did continue the attempt for some years. There is reason to think that Layard had hoped that a project to open trading relations with Khuzistan, officially backed by the British Government, would have led to the appointment of a consular agent in Shushter, an appointment for which he would have been the obvious candidate. When it became clear that such a move was not in prospect, Layard's expectations of official employment in the Near East faded, and he at last prepared to return home, after an absence of three years.

The bad relations between the Ottoman and Persian empires, mainly over border disputes, was having adverse effects on British interests, and Colonel Taylor wished the British Ambassador at Istanbul, Sir Stratford Canning, to be fully informed of details. As no-one had a better recent first-hand knowledge of the area concerned in the dispute than Layard, Taylor took the opportunity, as the route home lay through Istanbul, of entrusting him with letters for Canning, with the understanding that he should, if required, put himself at

---

[1] *J.R.G.S.* XVI (1846), 1–105, A. H. Layard, Esq., *A description of the Province of Khúzistán*, communicated by Lord Aberdeen. A summary of Layard's activities was given in *J.R.G.S.* as early as 1842: 'Mr. Layard has forwarded to us a paper in which he reports his success in reaching and examining with some minuteness the Bachtiari Moun-tains. He crossed the highest part of the great Chain Mungasht, and, having reached Cala Tul, proceeded to Manjanik, where he did not find the mounds mentioned by Major Rawlinson, but ruins similar to those of other Sassanian cities. . . . The Shekaft-Salman of Major Rawlinson [a natural cave] is to the west of Mel Amir, and not on the road to Susan. Mr. Layard copied a cuneiform inscription of a tablet adjoining the natural cave, it being the only one of four that was not completely effaced. . . . At Susan there are scarcely any remains which would indicate the site of a large city. . . . Mr. Layard heard of another Susan in the mountains to the N.E. of the place he visited. . . .'

35

Canning's disposal to provide further detailed information orally. Layard set out on his journey to Istanbul in the company of a Tatar, or dispatch-bearer of the Ottoman Government. At Mosul, official business detained the Tatar for three days, a fortunate circumstance for the later science of Assyriology, for Layard employed this time in the company of a certain Paul-Emile Botta. Botta, then forty years of age, had previously been French Consul in Alexandria and the Yemen, and had just been sent to fill a similar position in Mosul. France had, from the time of Napoleon's expedition to Egypt, displayed a creditable interest in the antiquities of the Near East, and this had been heightened in some influential quarters by the fact that the British Museum was in possession of the most important collection of Mesopotamian antiquities yet brought to Europe.[1] There was therefore an understanding between Botta and certain French authorities that he should use the opportunity provided by his appointment at Mosul to make archaeological investigations in the area, the huge mounds of which, with their traditional identification with ancient Nineveh, offered the possibility of spectacular results.

Botta, unlike some of his fellow-countrymen at this time and subsequently had, according to Layard, no scholarly jealousy, and when he learnt that Layard took a serious interest in antiquities and ancient history he treated him with the greatest courtesy and attention, escorting him over the great mounds of Kuyunjik (ancient Nineveh) and Nebi Yunus opposite Mosul. Botta had already opened some trenches at Kuyunjik, but with little success, mainly because, as Layard later realised, the nature of the site was such that the trenches required to be much deeper. The lack of immediate results led Botta to abandon Kuyunjik (which Layard was later to excavate), and to transfer his work to a site some 14 miles to the north-east known as Khorsabad.[2] There, in 1843, he began to uncover magnificent Assyrian sculptures, which, in the interest they aroused, had eventual repercussions upon Layard's career.

Istanbul

At the time of this first encounter with Botta, Layard's future career still lay in considerable doubt. He obviously had hopes of using the friendship of Colonel Taylor, and his expected acquaintanceship with Sir Stratford Canning, to his advantage in securing him entry into the

[1] The collection of Claudius J. Rich.
[2] See below, pp. 69, 140, 147.

36

diplomatic or consular service, but there were few solid grounds for expectations in this direction, and such as there were must have been dashed by his first reception at the British Embassy in Istanbul. The rebuff he received is reflected in a letter of protest to Canning:

'Sir,
I had the honour of calling at your Excellency's on Saturday last with a letter from Col^l. Taylor. . . . From the manner in which I was received I cannot suppose that that letter was delivered into your Excellency's hands. It was at Col^l. Taylor's particular request that I waited on your Excellency and that I undertook at much inconvenience a long land journey for that purpose. The subject of Col^l. Taylor's letter in no way personally interests me. I have only flattered myself that I might have been able to afford your Excellency some information upon a portion of the Turkish Empire and its frontiers very little known to Europeans and in which I have dwelt for nearly two years. I still believe that that part of Turkey and Persia offers a new field for the establishment of British interests and for British commercial enterprise and I still take the liberty of offering to your Excellency all the information of which I am possessed.

'I do not believe that my treatment at the British Embassy on Saturday was authorised by your Excellency, to whose affability and condescension all travellers bear a willing testimony. . . . After suffering considerable hardships for three years my face may be somewhat bronzed and my dress after a long absence from Europe might not be within the rules of fashionable elegance but I cannot admit that my outward appearance could warrant the insolent contempt with which I had the honor to be treated by the servant and other individuals at the Embassy . . .'[1]

Canning reacted with an invitation to the Embassy, where Layard was conscious of making a favourable impression on the Ambassador. Seeing in this fortunate development some hope of achieving his ambition of an official appointment, Layard decided to postpone his return to England.

Layard's interest in archaeology was temporarily in eclipse. His hope of finding his way into the diplomatic service is reflected in a letter from his friend Edward Burgess, writing from Tabriz on 30th August [1842]: 'I hope next to hear from you after you are well settled

[1] 38975, 51.

in England; pray don't turn diplomatist—it is a dirty trade—worse than a lawyers . . .'[1]

For the present no diplomatic post was available, but Canning, not wishing to lose the services of this potentially valuable young informant, devised a specific assignment for Layard. It was not, as Layard might reasonably have hoped, one which would make use of his expertise in Persian affairs. Instead, the Ambassador invited him to go on a fact-finding mission to Serbia and Bosnia (today part of eastern Yugoslavia) where disturbances threatening to involve the European powers had taken place. Canning made it clear to Layard that his journey must be as a private traveller with no official status.

Layard's investigations in the European provinces of Turkey appear to have been at least as much commercial as political. We find him writing from Salonica on 23rd August [1842], giving Canning detailed tables of the agricultural products of Macedonia and Thessaly, and pointing out a gradual rise in the price of wheat from 1832 to 1840.

Correspondence in the latter half of 1842 reflects Layard's continued hope of obtaining a diplomatic or consular appointment, and by implication his lack of any plans for archaeological work. Hector, writing from Baghdad on 8th October, comments: 'I have some idea that you would forward your views sooner by going home, more particularly now you have the right side of the Ambassador. . . . Where I want to see you employed is with a permanent appointment at Shushter—for the protection of Commerce . . .'[2]

Another correspondent whose letters reflect Layard's confidence in obtaining some official post was Mitford. The latter was able to give Layard the assurance that in at least one respect his course of action had been the right one, and that he had lost nothing by failing to fulfil his original intention of going to Ceylon to practise Law: 'I can tell you that you could have done nothing here in the Law, those out already are starving.'[3]

Through Burgess, Layard was able to obtain up-to-date information about his old friend Mohammed Taki Khan, deposed paramount chief of the Bakhtiyari, and to attempt to correspond with him. Mohammed Taki Khan's lot proved to be less grim than Layard had feared when he last met the chief laden with chains in Shushter. In March 1843 Burgess wrote:

[1] 38975, 68.
[2] 38940, 8–9.
[3] 38940, 24–25.

'. . . You will be glad to hear that your friend Taki Khan Bakhtiyari won the chief prize at the Tehran races, some time ago. The Khan's horse . . . nearly distanced all the others, altho' the best horses in Tehran were there, among them the pick of the Shah's and the Hadji's stables. When he had come in Mohomed Taki Khan took him by the bridle, dismounted his jockey, and leading the horse before the Shah presented him. H.M. would not take him, saying "such a horse as that you ought never to part with, he is without price, keep him, and may you mount him when you are striking down the Shah's enemies, he cannot be in better hands." All this is very pretty is it not but the poor Khan is still . . . under "surveillance" and not allowed to leave Tehran, tho' except this he is well treated.'[1]

As a consequence of the border dispute between Turkey and Persia, the two countries had accepted Anglo–Russian mediation, and it was planned that a British Commissioner and Assistant should be sent. With his specialist knowledge of the area Layard had some hope that he might be nominated. However, for the time being Layard was passed over in connection with the arbitration commission, despite the support of Canning. Layard, who had been under open arrest in Persia for anti-government political activities, was hardly likely to be trusted as an impartial arbitrator by the Persian authorities.

It will be apparent that to this point it had been politics, and not archaeology, which had been occupying Layard's interest since his arrival in Istanbul. Now, however, various circumstances concurred to direct his attention towards archaeology once again. His hopes of diplomatic office had for the present received a check; whilst on the other hand a Mr. Stirling, a wealthy and influential merchant in the Midlands and a potential patron, was showing some interest in archaeology.[2] But the principal factor was probably that Botta had, at the end of 1842, begun excavation at Kuyunjik (Nineveh) opposite Mosul, and in March 1843 in Khorsabad. At the latter site Botta almost immediately met with spectacular success, finding numerous bas-reliefs and inscriptions on stone slabs. Very generously Botta sent Layard a private account of some of his initial results, so that in early April Layard was able to whet the interest of the Ambassador—known as a patron of antiquities—in the ruins of Mesopotamia. 'I enclose for your Excellency's perusal a note from M. Botta which as it contains

[1] 38975, 73.
[2] See 38975, 201, postscript about the site of Susiana.

an account of his labours amongst the ruins of Nineveh may probably interest you'.[1]

Layard appears to have kept alive the Ambassador's interest in the antiquities of the Mosul area, for three months later Canning is thanking him for sending 'the Mosul drawings'.[2] There is, however, no suggestion in the correspondence at this time that either Canning or Layard had any plans for undertaking excavations themselves; Layard's main hope (and indeed a hope which his subsequent distinction as a pioneer archaeologist never quenched) was still to obtain a diplomatic or at the least a consular appointment.

Meanwhile Layard lived on a salary he received as Canning's private secretary. Circumstances had prevented him from publishing the account of his Persian adventures, but he still had hopes of making his name in print. During his early months in Constantinople he had, in addition to his other occupations, been exercising his talents privately in writing a work on the Nestorians, the ancient Christian people of the mountains of Iraq, who in 1843 were the victims of a brutal massacre; but his attempt to get the work published was at this time without success, and the main part of it was subsequently incorporated in *Nineveh and its remains* (see pp. 189–191 below).

Lacking occasion to undertake diplomatic activity in an official capacity, Layard attempted to make his own private opportunities for influencing the course of political affairs. By 1844 he was involved in the ambitious enterprise of supporting a newspaper in Malta—the *Malta Times*—to foster British interests in the eastern Mediterranean. Layard, backed by Canning, not only exercised an overriding control over editorial policy, but also contributed personally to the journal. His contributions included, at the beginning of 1845, articles dealing with Botta's excavations, which attracted attention as far afield as London and Baghdad.

In Baghdad, Colonel Taylor had at the end of 1843 been superseded as British Resident and Consul by Henry Creswicke Rawlinson. This had significant consequences for the development of Assyriology, since it gave Rawlinson the opportunity of resuming the researches, which he had begun in 1835, into the cuneiform writing system. Rawlinson had already been acquainted with Layard by name as early as 1842. In early 1845, partly prompted by the articles in the *Malta*

[1] 38975, 212.
[2] 38975, 263.

Times and partly because of notes on inscriptions which Layard had left with Colonel Taylor, Rawlinson took the first step in what was to prove a most fruitful collaboration. He wrote to Layard: 'I have long wished to commence a correspondence with you. . . . The subject which at present engrosses all my leisure and on which I am therefore most anxious to communicate with you refers to the cuneiform Inscriptions. I want particularly to know what inscriptions you have copied and what still remain uncopied in Elymeus. Also whether they are in the Babylonian character alone as on the broken obelisk at Sus or whether they are trilingual as at Bisitun and Persepolis.

'. . . Hitherto I have not taken up the Babylonian writing in earnest[1] being anxious in the first place to exhaust the Persian branch of the enquiry and to proceed from that to the Median, but I have still, thanks to the Bisitun key, identified the phonetic powers of some 30 of the Babylonian characters and I hope in time to complete the alphabet.[2] . . . The Persian writing you are aware is closely allied to the Sanscrit and is intelligible throughout.'[3]

Botta, Layard and Rawlinson were by no means the only people interested in Mesopotamian antiquities. Amongst the immediate circle of Layard and Rawlinson, the merchant Alexander Hector in Baghdad was keen to undertake excavation, and was hoping for his correspondent in England, Mr. Stirling, to provide funds for such an attempt. He writes (Mosul, 20th April, 1845): 'I should like very much to have a dig in some of the mounds here, for Antiquities. Nimroud 9 hours below this must be the Rezen you say to be looked for . . . if I had money I would do it at once . . .'[4]

It is interesting that, despite Layard's later claim[5] that he had had it in mind since 1840 to excavate Nimrud, Hector, who had been closely acquainted with Layard since at least 1841, writes as though

[1] The words 'in earnest' are added as an afterthought above the line.

[2] Rawlinson's researches into the Babylonian writing system were for some years hampered by the belief that it was alphabetic, a view he had not completely rejected as late as 1850. In his *A commentary on the cuneiform inscriptions of Babylonia and Assyria; including readings of the inscription of the Nimrud Obelisk* (transcription of a paper read at the Royal Asiatic Society on 19th January and 16th February 1850), he refers to 'many of the Assyrian signs, which sometimes represent phonetically a complete syllable, and sometimes one only of the sounds of which the syllable is composed'. (The present writer would suggest that, in a strictly limited type of instances, such as the final sign in Assyrian writings of the form conventionally transcribed *ap-ti-qi-di* (for expected *aptiqid*), Rawlinson was right.)

[3] 38976, 158–9.

[4] 38976, 171.

[5] See p. 68.

recognition of the importance of this site was his own idea. Whilst he and Layard had obviously discussed archaeological topics in relationship to the Mosul area, there is a clear implication that Hector had never heard Layard express interest specifically in Nimrud.

This suggests that the first recognition of the importance of Nimrud as a site was due to Hector rather than Layard.[1] Every circumstance indicates, however, that Hector, who appears to have been a man of somewhat naive and ill-balanced judgment, with little general education or knowledge of the world, and certainly no ability to handle Ottoman officialdom, could never have carried through the excavation to the success achieved by Layard. Fortunately, Hector's own rashness in innocently though illegally importing arms for a certain Ahmed Pasha, a potential rebel against the Ottoman Government, gave him several months of severe anxiety and put all thoughts of antiquity-hunting out of his head.

Rawlinson in Baghdad was becoming anxious that the French should not be left with a monopoly in the field of Mesopotamian archaeology. He had no time for major excavations himself, though he was accustomed, as opportunity permitted, to undertake excavations on a small scale in Babylonia (South Iraq).[2] He therefore began to urge that something should be done, writing to Layard: 'I should be exceedingly glad indeed if the Ambassador and through him the Govt. could be induced to take an interest in the antiquities of this country. It pains me grievously to see the French monopolize the field, for the fruits of Botta's labours, already achieved and still in progress, are not things to pass away in a day but will constitute a nation's glory in future ages.'[3]

[1] Another claimant for the credit was the missionary George Percy Badger, who writes (*The Nestorians and their remains* (1852), vol. I, 86) 'there is reason to believe [that my visit to Nimrud] had some influence in setting on foot the work of successful excavation'. He paid a visit in March 1844 and sent Sir Stratford Canning a written report on 26th October of the same year (*op. cit.*, 71). But Layard was already interesting the Ambassador in Mesopotamian archaeology in April 1844 (see above, page 39) and the choice of Nimrud as the initial site of excavation was Layard's, not the Ambassador's. Badger's claim was simply another aspect of the self-conceit which led Alexander Hector to say of him 'Mr. Badger I think puts too much consequence on himself and his position to do much good in these countries as a missionary' (38975, 364 of 6th March 1844). Badger's evident pomposity is reflected in his book. Canning's opinion of Badger, whom on the latter's own evidence Canning knew as a missionary in Mesopotamia, is reflected in the Ambassador's specific injunction to Layard (see below, p. 43) 'to keep clear . . . as much as possible of missionaries'.

[2] 38976, 241.

[3] 38976, 234.

'A traveller, fond of antiquities'

This was written on the 15th October [1845]. Rawlinson was un-aware that Layard had already succeeded in persuading Canning to take action of the kind he proposed, and that the Ambassador had decided to subsidize Layard for a limited period to attempt excavation in Mesopotamia. A memorandum from Canning on the 9th October recapitulates the arrangements already agreed orally between Layard and the Ambassador:

'I rely upon Mr. Layard's obliging attention to the following points:

1. To keep me informed of his operations, and of any objects of sufficient interest and curiosity which he may see or discover.

2. To keep clear of political and religious questions, and as much as possible of missionaries, or native chiefs in tribes regarded with enmity or jealousy by the Turkish authorities.

3. To cultivate the good will of the Pashas and others of the Sultan's functionaries by all becoming means.

4. To bear in mind that his professed character will be that of a traveller, fond of antiquities, of picturesque scenery, and of the manners peculiar to Asia.

5. Not to start on his return without a previous communication with me subsequent to his first enquiries and attempts at discovery.

6. In case of success to give me early and exact information as to the nature of the objects discovered, and the best means of removal etc. with an estimate of cost, doing what he can to obtain the necessary permission on the spot. . . .

'I reckon on Mr. Layard's reaching Moussul towards the end of October, and being able to complete a fair experiment of discovery in the most probable spots during the two ensuing months. Should he have reasons for adding another ten days or fortnight, he is at liberty to follow his own discretion. . . .'[1]

Rawlinson, writing on November 12th, expressed himself 'equally surprised and delighted' at hearing of Layard's arrival in Mosul, and the object of his visit. He went on to make some observations as to the potentialities of various sites: 'I almost fear Nimrood is too far from the mountains to possess marble palaces like those of Khorsabad, but you can hardly fail to find inscriptions and other relics that will repay your labor. Nebi Yunis itself I expect to be one of the most promising

---

[1] 38976, 231–3.

sites in the vicinity of Moosul, but its sanctity I fear is not to be invaded.'[1]

Layard began digging at Nimrud on 9th November and met with immediate success. He was able to write to Canning: 'Having opened a trench in a part of the mound in which a block of stone projected from the ground I came at once upon a chamber 25 feet long and 14 broad, formed by slabs of marble $8\frac{1}{2}$ feet in length, also each slab containing an inscription in the cuneiform character. I opened one part of the chamber to the flooring, which I found to be of marble and covered with inscriptions. . . . Other trenches brought me on other walls—all with inscriptions. As yet I had not found sculptures, but from several fragments . . . I had every reason to think that figures existed. Indeed, I have found an old man here who pretends to have buried, about fifty years ago, slabs similar to those of Khorsabad, which he discovered when digging for building-bricks. He has promised to show me the spot. . . . After four days' labor a slight fever . . . compelled me to return to Mosul. I left the excavations under the charge of my cawass, with orders to clear the chamber.'[2]

By November 28th Rawlinson was writing to congratulate Layard, adding a few generalizations about the relative merits of inscriptions and sculptures and thereby revealing his markedly inferior sensitivity to Layard in matters of art appreciation: 'I regard inscriptions as of infinitely greater value than sculptures—the latter may please virtuosi —they have no doubt a certain degree of intrinsic interest but the tablets[3] are bona fide histories and very shortly I feel perfectly certain they will be completely intelligible.'[4]

Layard appeared to have found a veritable mine of antiquities. At the end of November he discovered a splendid series of bas-reliefs (see below, pp. 86 ff.). In December he was able to report to Canning the finding of 'two winged bulls of great size'[5]—limestone monsters standing some fourteen feet high and weighing twenty tons apiece. Soundings were going on simultaneously at other sites, some of which yielded further encouraging evidence of Assyrian remains.

---

[1] 38976, 240. To this day Nebi Yunis remains inaccessible to excavation for the same reason. Occasional chance finds of antiquities during building operations justify Rawlinson's view of the promise of the site.

[2] 40637, 8–9.

[3] As used by Rawlinson and his contemporaries, 'tablet' usually meant an inscribed slab of stone. In modern Assyriological usage the word denotes a small inscribed block of baked or unbaked clay.

[4] 40637, 8–9.

[5] 40637, 33.

Layard's initial excavations were of doubtful legality, no authorization of such work having been obtained from the Ottoman government.[1] This gave Layard considerable anxiety, for he had reason to

[1] Sir E. A. W. Budge's statement (*The rise and progress of Assyriology* (1925), 69) that Layard left Constantinople 'with a *faramân* empowering him to dig anywhere and everywhere in the Pâshâlik of Môṣul' is imaginative but completely untrue. No statement of Budge about Layard should be received without careful examination; see Dr. R. D. Barnett in G. Waterfield, *Layard of Nineveh*, 487.

One demonstrably false statement about Layard for which Budge is responsible is that he failed to recognize, and so brought about the loss of, many inscribed clay tablets. Budge writes (*op. cit.*, 83): 'The fact is that many tablets were found both at Ḳuyûnjiḳ and Nimrûd by Layard. . . . The natives thought were bits of pottery decorated in an unusual manner; and Dr. Birch told me that Layard thought the same until 1849, when he brought home a few specimens of the "strange pottery" and showed them to him. When Birch told him what they were, and showed him the plates in Rich's "Second Memoir", Layard sent out to Ḳuyûnjiḳ and ordered Mr. Christian Rassam to collect all the pieces of the "strange pottery" he could find, and to put them in baskets until his return to Môṣul. Similar orders were sent to Nimrûd, but it was too late; for the tablets and fragments had been thrown out on the piles of earth that had been excavated, and had since been carried away by the natives to make top-dressing for their fields.'

Despite its apparently circumstantial nature, this whole story is a pack of lies. Layard was not in England at all during 1849, since he left in November 1848 and did not return again until 1851. Budge's inaccuracy cannot however be reduced to a mere mistake in date, for there are other errors: (i) The agent who carried on work for Layard at Kuyunjik and Nimrud after his departure in 1847 was not Christian Rassam but H. J. Ross; (ii) When Layard returned to England in 1847 he knew (judging by Rawlinson's correspondence with him and his evident respect for his opinions) almost as much about the various types of cuneiform writing as Rawlinson himself, whilst Birch, who had seen only a small fraction of the inscriptions examined by Layard and Rawlinson, can hardly in 1847 have been in a position to give either man much instruction in this field; (iii) In view of the evidence from Layard's papers of his zeal in obtaining and assiduously studying, from 1839 onwards, all publications relating to Middle Eastern antiquities (see above, p. 8), it is unreasonable to suppose that he had never noticed the plates in Rich's *Second Memoir* until they were pointed out to him by Birch in 1848; (iv) The piles of earth which had been excavated at Nimrud were not, as Budge implies, taken away by native farmers; some of the excavated earth was used to re-bury those sculptures which Layard was unable to remove (see below, p. 282), whilst the remainder of the dumps were still, a century later, substantially as Layard left them (M. E. L. Mallowan, *Nimrud and its remains* (1966), vol. I, 36).

There is also evidence against Budge's story in A. H. Layard, *Inscriptions in the Cuneiform Character from Assyrian Monuments* (1851). In the preface to this work Edward Hawkins writes: 'The first forty-nine pages of this work were revised by Mr. Layard before he quitted England in 1849 [actually November 1848]; the remainder by Mr. Birch . . .' On page 30 of the work (and thus included in the part for which Layard was responsible) is a thirty-seven line inscription described as being from 'a small oblong tablet of clay, from Koujunjik'. It is unreasonable to suppose that Layard would have been entrusted with the publication of an inscription of a type which the British Museum authorities knew he had, a month or two previously, not only been unfamiliar with but had even failed to recognize as a writing system at all.

Furthermore, Layard specifically refers to writing on clay, in *Nineveh and its remains* (1849 edition, vol. II, 185–7): 'The most common mode of keeping records in Assyria believe that the French were striving to obtain excavation rights for themselves at Nimrud. Canning intended at a suitable opportunity to seek a firman, but, having already obtained substantial concessions for antiquarian work elsewhere, considered it expedient, as he put it, to 'postpone saying anything at the Porte as long as I can.' Meanwhile he relied upon Layard's tact and powers of diplomacy in dealing with Ottoman officials on the spot. Such dubious procedures hardly commended themselves to the legalistic Rawlinson, who felt it was time for Canning to take some positive action: 'I see every prospect now if the Ambassador will bestir himself and obtain you a strong Firman of our being in the field before the French.'[1]

However, the French in Mosul—particularly Botta's successor as Consul, M. Rouet—had been beforehand, and had already prevailed upon the Pasha of Mosul to take measures to bring Layard's work to a halt.[2] On hearing the news, Canning displayed annoyance: 'the Pasha's interference is untimely, not to say malicious. . . . If the said Pasha knew how easily I could send him to the Devil, and how well I know that he deserves it, he would be more on his guard, perhaps.'[3]

---

[1] Sources for this paragraph: 38976, 222 and 274.
[2] See below, pp. 87–88.
[3] 38976, 277 and 279 (21st December 1845).

---

and Babylonia was on prepared bricks, tiles, or cylinders of clay, baked after the inscription was impressed. . . . Of such records we have many specimens. The most remarkable are two hexagonal cylinders, one in the possession of Colonel Taylor, late political agent at Baghdad, and the other given by me to the British Museum. . . . In many public and private collections there are inscriptions on tiles, and on barrel-shaped cylinders of baked clay. On a tile formerly in the possession of Dr. Ross of Baghdad, and afterwards, I believe, in that of the late Mr. Steuart, there are many lines of writing, accompanied by the impression of seals, probably of attesting witnesses.' Before Layard ever began excavation he had been in close contact both with Colonel Taylor and Dr. Ross, and enjoyed free use of the library of the former, and had left some of his own notes on inscriptions deposited with Colonel Taylor (38976, 185, letters from H. C. Rawlinson dated 28th May 1845). It seems unreasonable to suppose that Layard did not see Colonel Taylor's inscribed clay cylinder before the former left Baghdad in 1842, and if he had seen this cylinder he would certainly not have taken inscribed terra-cotta tablets for 'bits of pottery decorated in an unusual manner'.

One may also refer to the statement in *Nineveh and its remains* (see below, p. 289) that Layard found and brought back to the British Museum 'several small oblong tablets of dark unbaked clay, having a cuneiform inscription over the sides'. Had these been broken pieces of baked terra-cotta tablets, it might have been possible for Budge to dispute this evidence with the argument that Layard had brought them home as examples of pottery with an odd decoration, and only identified them as inscribed tablets after consultation with Birch. But it is absurd to suppose that a man of Layard's experience in *objets d'art* should mistake regularly shaped pieces of unbaked clay for fragments of pottery, irrespective of the interpretation he may have given to the markings they bore.

In the outcome, Canning's intervention proved unnecessary, for news had already reached Mosul that the Ottoman government had taken action against the corrupt and oppressive Pasha, Keritli Oglu. After a Christmas at Baghdad, where for the first time he met Rawlinson in person, Layard returned to Mosul to find himself free to resume excavations.

Within a few days of resuming operations, Layard had found a fine winged bull in the centre of the part of the mound he now designated the South-West Palace. A second was found, after another interruption in Layard's work (see below, pp. 92–3), in mid-February, to be joined by a further collection of bas-reliefs (pp. 95 ff.), some still bearing traces of paint. But the find which caused the greatest excitement—graphically described on pp. 98 ff. below—was that of a stone head in human form five feet high, belonging to a bull colossus but taken by some of the superstitious Arabs to be the remains of Nimrod himself. The sensation this produced in Mosul again brought Layard's work to a halt.

Canning had still obtained no formal permission for Layard's excavations, and since they were therefore only permitted through the personal goodwill of the Governor, they remained subject to stoppages arising from local feeling or French intrigue. Canning himself had his own problems. He had undertaken to support Layard's excavations for two to two and a half months, and already this time had passed, with an end not in sight. He wanted tangible museum-worthy results, but expected them cheaply. He had no conception of the sheer size of Nimrud, a mound some sixty acres in extent and rising to an average height of forty feet above the plain. This lack of appreciation of the size of the problem cannot wholly be blamed upon Canning. Layard himself, in the first flush of his enthusiasm, failed to comprehend the immensity of the task he had undertaken. During the week following his first soundings he sent to the Ambassador an astounding under-estimate of the time required for the work at Nimrud: 'If the whole mound covers, as the fragments of marble, stone, brick and pottery scattered over it seem to indicate, one large palace, Your Excellency may form some idea of the vast size of the edifice. It will take some time, at least a month, to make satisfactory experiments in all parts.'[1] This estimate was on the basis of the employment of thirty workmen. Layard's successor, Professor Sir Max Mallowan, who worked at Nimrud between 1949 and 1963 with up to

[1] 40637, 10–11 (17th November 1845).

200 workmen, is still able to speak of 'wide expanses of untouched ground' inviting 'many seasons of work'.[1] If Layard himself did not recognize the size of the undertaking, Canning can hardly be blamed for failing to understand.

Despite worries as to the future, the threat of interruption, and the isolation of Nimrud, life had its compensations for Layard. He was no celibate by principle, and the social conventions of Mesopotamia at that time, Muslim country though it was, were not such as to force celibacy upon him. His friend Charles Alison, Oriental Secretary at the Embassy in Istanbul, writes in mock admonishment: 'You shock me beyond measure by your description of morals in Mesopotamia: but it must be a great resource on the whole to a youth of your complexion labouring and in other privations—and beneficial to your general health. We all continue to be very good here, whether we like it or no: virtuous upon mere compulsion.'[2]

Layard's efforts to record, safeguard and interpret the striking discoveries made by him during this period—the friezes, the inscriptions, and the colossal stone lions and bulls—is clear from his own account and need not to be anticipated here. But Layard did not confine his work merely to the considerable task of organizing the actual dig, drawing the sculptures, and copying the inscriptions. He was also active in what Alison called 'the decyphering line'. Rawlinson himself, who at this time was well in advance of anyone else in work on the cuneiform writing systems and was never slow in telling others when they were wrong, treated Layard's views with respect, and sought his opinion on the inscriptions.

Rawlinson gave such practical assistance to Layard as he could, arranging for one of the East India Company steamers to move up the Tigris to Nimrud to take off the excavated antiquities, though in the event navigational difficulties made this abortive. He was also willing to involve himself in the financial aspects of the dig, and was becoming increasingly impatient at what he felt was, on the part of Canning, niggardly or tardy financial support for Layard. He comments: 'The money business fairly puzzles me. I would myself willingly place a sum at your disposal for excavation, if I were to get a share

---

[1] *Nimrud and its remains* (1966), vol. II, 608.
[2] 38976, 317. Alison enjoyed a somewhat bawdy sense of humour, well illustrated in the account he sent Layard of how some friends of theirs, out for a night in Istanbul, went 'to a bawdy house at Galata where they all three went to bed with each other by mistake—as drunk as pipers—luckily for their virtue' (38976, 291).

of the marbles[1]—but Sir Stratford would certainly think this an improper interference ... Consider this and if you can in fairness to Sir Stratford admit me to a participation in the spoils, draw on me at Mosul for 5000 Francs as a commencement.'[2]

Layard had every reason to avoid any action likely to give offence to Sir Stratford, for he was still without any official status and wholly dependent upon Canning for financial and personal support. Layard and most of his friends still regarded his archaeological work as no more than a temporary though fascinating diversion to occupy him whilst arrangements were made for his serious career. Alison, answering a letter from Layard full of enthusiasm for his discoveries, remarked that he would rather see his friend engaged in a sphere 'in which I can better appreciate your usefulness, viz., that of politics.'[3] Rawlinson, though more sympathetic towards excavations, certainly did not at this time regard such work as constituting a career, and was clearly pleased when he was able to tell Layard (misleadingly, as it proved): 'Williams says your appointment to the frontier commission is *positive* and he must evidently have this information from the Ambassador himself.'[4]

Canning, despite his procrastination in the matter of putting Layard's excavations on a formal footing with the Ottoman authorities, was enthusiastic about the result of the work so far, and the public sensation it was likely to create. He encouraged Layard in his sketching with the view that 'the more drawings the better, as they strike the eye and interest folks in England',[5] and he held out as a further inducement to Layard's efforts that 'if you can make out a cuneiform alphabet, you will be as immortal as M. Botta.'[6] Canning's departure for home leave was now imminent, and it was his intention to take up with the Prime Minister the question of governmental support for Layard.

In order to protect Layard's work during his absence, Canning was

---

[1] This is relevant to the later criticism of Layard that he considered his archaeologica finds as available to him to dispose of as he would. Clearly Rawlinson at this time shared the same view.

[2] 38976, 339–40.

[3] 38976, 329.

[4] 38976, 340.

[5] 38976, 347. See also *op. cit.*, 358, in which Canning asked Layard to send 'more drawings and a few copies of inscriptions, and anything else which may enable me to inspire into others the interest which we ourselves take in this enterprise'.

[6] 38976, 345. Rawlinson was also at this time thinking in terms of an alphabet; see p. 57.

now driven to abandon his former caution and to make some kind of formal application on Layard's behalf. By May [1846] he had obtained, not a firman, but a Vizirial letter, which, as Canning was at pains to point out, 'is quite as good for every practical purpose, authorizing you to excavate and export to your heart's content'.[1] The relevant part of the letter reads (following the French translation of Christian Rassam):

'Letter of the Grand Vizier to the Pasha of Mosul. 5th May, 1846.

'There are, as your Excellency knows, in the vicinity of Mosul quantities of stones and ancient remains. There is an English gentleman who has come to those parts to look for stones of this kind, and has found on the banks of the Tigris, in certain uninhabited places, ancient stones on which there are pictures and inscriptions. The British Ambassador has asked that there shall be no obstacles put in the way of the above-mentioned gentleman taking the stones which may be useful to him, including those which he may discover by means of excavations . . . , nor of his embarking them to have them transported to England.

'The sincere friendship which firmly exists between the two governments makes it desirable that such demands be accepted. Therefore no obstacle should be put in the way of his taking the stones which, in accordance with the account which has been given above, are present in desert places, and are not being utilized; or of his undertaking excavations in uninhabited places where this can be done without inconvenience to anyone; or of his taking such stones as he may wish amongst those which he has been able to discover . . .'[2]

Canning pointed out that Layard was not confined by the Vizirial letter to any one site, and suggested to him that it might 'be adviseable to secure a prior right to any very probable place of discovery at once, but not *too greedily*, and with due respect not only for the ~~rights~~ claims [alteration *sic*] of others, but in some degree for their jealousy'.[3] The 'others' were, of course, the French.

Canning's instructions have some bearing upon one of the main criticisms subsequently made of Layard's work: Layard has sometimes been blamed for having frequently left his main excavations unattended whilst he rode about the countryside making small-scale

---

[1] 38976, 355.
[2] 38976, 359–60.
[3] 38976, 355.

soundings in new sites. It is quite clear, however, that in acting in this way he was doing no more than fulfilling the Ambassador's intentions and, indeed, his specific instructions.

It may be noted that Layard's name is not mentioned in the Vizirial letter. This is of some importance in relation to another criticism subsequently made against him. Layard later adopted the practice of giving away some of the excavated antiquities privately, though there has never been any suggestion that he did this for financial gain or that he failed to give the pick of the finds to the British Museum. In later years Layard responded vigorously to criticisms on this score, saying that 'the firman which Sir Stratford had obtained for me from the Sultan ... was in my name. Consequently I might have claimed all that I found in the ruins as my own property'.[1] In writing thus, obviously in good faith, Layard was relying on memory, which played him false, not only as to the question of whether he was named, but also over the source of the permit, which was actually the Vizier and not the Sultan. But the undoubted omission of Layard's name does not settle the matter. The whole tenor of the Vizirial letter suggests that the problem of ultimate ownership of 'the stones' was not even considered by the Ottoman authorities. It is a task for an international lawyer, not for an archaeologist, to decide what personal rights, if any, Layard had over the antiquities he excavated.

At the very time of the granting of the Vizirial letter in early May, an incident occurred which threatened to bring Layard's excavations permanently to a halt. Losing his temper at an insult by the Mufti of Mosul, a Muslim leader with about the same social and religious prestige as a bishop in an Italian city, Layard—whose grandfather the Dean had left him with scant respect for ecclesiastical dignitaries— disregarded the holy man's sanctity and broke his head with a stick.[2] Understandably no reference is made to this fracas in *Nineveh and its remains*. Public feeling in Mosul became highly inflamed, and the incident had repercussions in Baghdad and even in Constantinople. Rawlinson took a very grave view of the matter and even Alison, though more sympathetic, was not without anxiety as to the outcome: 'I was very much grieved to hear of your affray with the man of God. I should likely have done the same thing had I been in your place but it was an unfortunate necessity and I trust it will have no evil results.'[3]

---

[1] *Autobiography*, vol. II, 136.
[2] For Layard's account of the incident see *Autobiography*, vol. II, 168–72.
[3] 38976, 393–4.

It was not until the middle of June that Layard was able to report to Rawlinson that events had taken a satisfactory turn.

Meanwhile, news of Layard's work, and of its potential interest in throwing light on Old Testament history, was spreading abroad. A pious American friend wrote to him at this time: 'You can scarcely dream of the importance which your solitary labors may have upon the right understanding of the Historical and Prophetical parts of the Holy Word'[1] and more in like vein. It is difficult to see why the pious writer should have supposed the implications of the Nimrud discoveries to have been less evident to Layard than to himself, and in fact the Biblical relevance was plain enough even to those who cared little for it. Alison, writing from Istanbul at the end of the summer, comments 'The interest about your stones is very great, I hear—and if you can as I before said attach a Biblical importance to your discoveries you will come the complete dodge over this world of fools and dreamers: you can get some religious fellow to inspire you with the necessary cant, for which I won't think a bit the worse of you.'[2]

In Baghdad Rawlinson was continuing work on the decipherment of Assyro–Babylonian cuneiform but still lacked the key.[3] His researches went on throughout the summer of 1846, despite intense heat and an epidemic of cholera which drove him to move his establishment from Baghdad to Ctesiphon, twenty miles down the Tigris. He worked to such good effect that in the autumn he was able to inform Layard that he had translated the inscription on the bricks from Babylon, and that it read as follows: 'Nebuchadnezzar the *great* king, the *ruler* of the *land of the Chaldees*, the son of Nabu*Na*ssar the *great* king'.[4] The parts here italicised were in fact incorrect, but to have made out even half the inscription accurately was a considerable achievement at this time. Rawlinson was still handicapped by working under the impression that he was dealing with an alphabet: though he was beginning to accept that some signs might be syllograms,[5] he had

[1] 38976, 373.

[2] 38977, 45–46.

[3] In May 1846 Rawlinson was expressing the view (which proved ultimately to be correct) that the language of the Assyro-Babylonian cuneiform inscriptions was basically Semitic (38976, 376), though by late June he had reverted to the opinion that the language was utterly unknown and without cognates in any available speech, Semitic, Aryan or Scythic (38976, 398).

[4] 38977, 58.

[5] On 11th November 1846 Rawlinson wrote to Layard (38977, 92): 'The name which occurs so frequently ⟶𝖄𝖄✕𝖄 is I am almost sure, the proper title of Assyria *as.r.a.* [It is actually the royal name Ashur-naṣir-pal]. It is optional at all times to employ

not yet recognized that Assyro–Babylonian cuneiform writing was (except for its ideograms) wholly syllabic and not alphabetic at all.

During the early summer, Layard succeeded—as he describes on page 140 below—in embarking the first of the sculptures on a raft and having them floated down to Baghdad. He attempted to continue excavation at both Nimrud and Kuyunjik, but the heat of the summer and the state of his health compelled him to leave for the mountains (see below, pp. 138–9). Chapters VI–IX of Layard's book, which contain matter of considerable interest to the general reader and of importance for the study of the Yezidis and Nestorians, are presented in the context of this period in the mountains, though in fact they are in large part based on a manuscript prepared in Constantinople three years before (see above, p. 40).

Agent of the British Museum

On his return to Mosul in the autumn, Layard found that, as a result of the steps Canning had taken in London to stimulate public and official interest in the excavations, he was now the agent of the British Museum with official funds for further excavations at his disposal. Canning wrote with some self-satisfaction: 'The British Museum undertakes Nimrood in my stead. The Treasury allows £2000. You are the agent. You will have £500 for yourself, besides £100 for your expenses home. My outlay will be repaid. A sum between £1000 and £1100 will be applicable to the continuation of your works, including the embarkation of the spoils. You are to finish all by the end of next June.'[1]

Unlike Canning, Layard was far from satisfied with the sum provided. He wrote to the Trustees of the British Museum suggesting that instead of giving him £500 for himself they should add this sum to the money available for excavation. He further pointed out: 'The sum given is small when compared with the magnitude of the work contemplated and will scarcely be sufficient for the proper examination of even half the mound of Nimroud', and he doubted whether it would 'be worth while to make any outlay on experiment in other parts of the country'.[2] It is only fair to say that the thousand pounds

---

[1] 38977, 47 (7th September 1846).
[2] 38977, 95 (16th November 1846).

---

or suppress the vowels and in the usual reading the *u* is thus omitted [*i.e.* Rawlinson took the writing to represent *as* < *u* > *ra*]—but I have actually found the vowel *u* sometimes interposed between the *as* and the *r*.'

or so available purely for the dig represented, in terms of what it could do in Mesopotamia, at least eight times that amount today, and in modern archaeological work £8000 for the dig itself would by many people be considered a handsome sum. Against this, Layard wished to do far more than eight times as much as any present-day archaeologist would dream of attempting in one season. Following Canning's earlier instructions, he had plans for opening up a considerable number of promising sites in addition to Nimrud and Kuyunjik. Excavations were resumed in November, and as Layard now had Christian Rassam's younger brother Hormuzd to assist him, he felt himself free to leave excavations in progress whilst he went off on a survey of other sites.

Layard continued his work throughout the winter of 1846–7. Alison quotes the Ambassador as saying: 'Layard is making excellent progress and you may depend upon it that I am fully alive to his merits. . . . I have every wish to serve him in things more important than Archaeology'.[1] The most striking find during this period was an obelisk of black marble bearing on its four sides inscriptions and a number of bas-reliefs showing scenes representing the delivery of tribute to the Assyrian king (see below, pp. 230 ff.). It later proved that amongst those shown bringing tribute was the emissary of Jehu of Israel. The obelisk created great excitement amongst the Europeans of Baghdad, and earned Layard a special message of congratulations from the British Museum Trustees. It was probably this discovery which was responsible for the British Museum making a further five hundred pounds available to Layard.

Rawlinson and Layard were both concerned to beat the French in what was conceived as a race to exhibit Assyrian sculptures for the first time in Europe[2] and to decipher the script. A consignment of antiquities had been despatched by raft down the Tigris in the summer of 1846 and another in the early spring of 1847, with the assistance of Alexander Hector and his brother George. After trans-shipment at Baghdad, the first twelve slabs from Nimrud had already reached England and were on view in the British Museum by August 1847, though in what Layard later considered a very bad position. They

[1] 38977, 198 (24th February 1847).
[2] In a letter to Canning on 1st December 1845, Layard mentioned that the 'marbles sent by Botta [from the 1843–4 excavations] are still at Baghdad waiting for a ship to be transported to France. I think we might manage to transmit our sculpture to Europe as soon if not sooner than the French. This will be very important for our reputation.' (40637, 20–21).

made a considerable public impression, most gratifying to Layard. The removal of these slabs presented little difficulty, but the situation was otherwise when Layard wished to move the colossal bulls and lions weighing many tons. How this was successfully achieved is graphically described by Layard himself (see pp. 265–75 below), a stone bull and lion being finally placed on rafts and floated down the Tigris on 22nd April, 1847.[1]

When the British Museum took over the excavations in September 1846, it had been planned that they should continue until the following June only. There are indications that the Trustees might have been willing to extend the period of excavation, but Layard, suffering in health, wearying of the continuous work in remote parts of the country, and anxious to return to Constantinople or London to press for some official recognition of his efforts, preferred to adhere to the original plan.

In the midst of his successes, Layard's friends did not allow him to forget that (from the nineteenth century point-of-view) archaeology was no more than a pleasant diversion from the realities of life. Alison points out his folly in wasting his time on such matters: 'The vulgar may stare for a day at the curious vestiges: but few will appreciate them, and at the end what does one really achieve. . . . I have often thought that you ought to entertain a well defined result, in your mind. If it be a little way off, I do not see what you could do better than get an Attacheship to the Embassy: you could jump into anything from that, and I fancy Lord P[almerston] would have no difficulty in giving it to you: but, if you agree with me, you had better look to it before the Elchee [i.e. Sir Stratford Canning] leaves London'.[2]

One of Layard's last activities on his first archaeological expedition was to fulfil a plan for which he had long sought the approval and support of Canning and the British Museum. This was to stake a claim to the great mound of Kuyunjik (the ruins of ancient Nineveh, as Layard had at first thought and afterwards denied) opposite Mosul. He had previously made some minor soundings there, but on 14th June, 1847, he was able to write to the Secretary of the British Museum: 'I have carried on the excavation in Kouyunjik during the last fortnight and the experiment has been now fairly made. Eight chambers have been partly uncovered. . . . The discovery of this building and the extent to which the excavations have been carried out, I conclude

[1] 38977, 265. They arrived as far as Basra, and then remained there for two years.
[2] 38977, 190–1 (9th February 1847).

establish our claim to the future examination of the mound should the Trustees be desirous to continue the researches in this country'.[1] It was owing to this fortnight's work that the British Museum could afterwards claim the rights by which it obtained the famous collection of over twenty thousand cuneiform tablets and fragments from Kuyunjik upon which Assyriology is based.

By early July [1847] Layard has left Nimrud, taking with him Hormuzd Rassam, who was to be educated in England. His departure did not involve relinquishment of control of archaeological affairs. Through his friend Henry Ross he continued excavation on a small scale, mainly at Kuyunjik, directing operations by post from Constantinople or London.

The anxiety expressed by Alison for the prospects of his friend proved to be unnecessary, for Canning already had matters in hand, and in July was able to write: 'I am happy to inform you that Lord Palmerston has obligingly consented to your being attached to the Embassy at Constantinople, and eventually employed in carrying out the line of the Turco–Persian boundary'.[2] Rawlinson considered the appointment quite inadequate for Layard's deserts, and entertained the hope that he would succeed him as Consul General at Baghdad if he himself, flying at higher game, became British Minister in Persia.[3]

Layard waited several months in Constantinople expecting the Ambassador's return, but this was delayed. Finally, at the end of October, he decided to return home. He reached England in time for Christmas, after showing his drawings of the Assyrian sculptures to scholars in Italy and spending several days discussing his finds with Botta and other learned antiquarians in Paris.

Rawlinson meanwhile had been renewing his endeavours to solve the riddle of the Assyro–Babylonian script. During the winter of 1846–7, exchange of letters had continued between Layard and Rawlinson, revealing substantial advances in the understanding both of the writing system and of the historical framework in which the finds were set. Layard made new inscriptions available to Rawlinson as soon as they appeared. But the best key available for decipherment still lay in the great trilingual inscription at Bisitun, of which Rawlinson had examined and copied the Old Persian and Elamite sections about ten years before. Rawlinson had already deciphered

[1] 38977, 300.
[2] 38977, 322 (20th July 1847).
[3] 38978, 26.

the script and language of the Old Persian version with considerable accuracy, and so had an assured text of considerable length as a basis for the translation of the parallel Babylonian version. In the summer of 1847 he took the opportunity of making several further visits to Bisitun in an attempt to obtain as exact a copy as possible of the text of the less accessible Babylonian version of the inscription. He was finally successful, writing to Layard from Bisitun in September: 'When I was here in July I could make nothing of the Babylonian writing—indeed I gave up in despair the possibility of recovering any portion of it—but I was then sick with a bilious attack. ... At the beginning of this month I returned here again and made another attempt to get hold of the Babylonian writing. Having just satisfied myself that a considerable portion of the tablet was legible, I got hoisted up on the opposite precipice and from a little nook in the scarp set to work with my telescope. The letters are only distinguishable for a couple of hours during the day. ...'[1]

In addition to the copy made through his telescope Rawlinson had also, as he put it, 'bribed two Kurds (the only two individuals in the country who could or would venture on the scarp) to take a paper impression'. Consequently he had now recovered almost half of the entire inscription and could 'make out' about a third of the whole. 'I can', he added later, 'now confidently say "Land in sight"—and despite all Hincks' pretended discoveries I can affirm that he is losing himself in a quagmire'.[2]

Despite Rawlinson's somewhat contemptuous allusion to the progress of the Irish scholar Hincks in decipherment, the latter had the clue that Rawlinson had missed, or rather dismissed,[3] and in January 1848 he was writing to Layard, in his modest fashion, showing clearly that he was interpreting the signs on correct principles, even though in most instances with partially incorrect values.[4]

Rawlinson also, however, though under a misconception as to the nature of the Babylonian syllabary, was being led by the genius of his

[1] 38977, 334.

[2] Sources for this paragraph: 38977, 334-5 (20th September 1847) and 343 (13th October 1847).

[3] 38977, 343 shows Rawlinson to have been not unfamiliar with the idea of a syllabic writing system, since he states the opinion that 'the alphabet [of the Assyrian and Babylonian inscriptions] is not so much a syllabarian as the Median.'

[4] 38978, 18 (22nd January 1848). He read 𒋡𒂍𒆷𒀀𒊑𒀀 as *Sa.má.ri.a (the asterisk representing an unpronounced determinative). The syllabic signs actually represent Šu-ba-ri-e.

intuition to a remarkably close understanding of some of the texts
with which he was dealing. At the beginning of 1848 he wrote to
Layard: 'I think I told you before that the son of Ninus first conquered Babylon in the 9th year of his reign (an event described in the
Nimrud Bull Inscriptions)'.[1] This shows a considerable insight into
one of the Nimrud texts. 'Ninus' was the mythical king whom Rawlinson identified with the ruler whose real name was later proved to be
Ashur-naṣir-pal. 'The son of Ninus' was therefore Shalmaneser III,
and his Bull Inscriptions do include the passage: 'In my ninth year of
reign ... I went to Babylon'.[2] It might be argued that Rawlinson's
conclusion involved no more than recognizing the symbol for 'nine',
the cuneiform writing for 'Babylon', and making an intelligent guess.
But to isolate this correctly from the great mass of unintelligible texts
confronting Rawlinson was a considerable achievement.

Return to England

On Layard's return to England, his friends were anxious that he
should not lose the credit and rewards due to him for his work.
Canning wrote: 'You must make the most of the Assyrian antiquities.
Do them justice, and do yourself credit, and make the public understand that they have got a prize.'[3] But Layard was well capable of
safeguarding his own interests in this field. In a memorandum sum-
marizing for the Trustees of the British Museum the points arising out
of a meeting, he left no doubt that in his view no-one could adequately
replace him in Assyria. In answer to a specific question, 'I replied', he
wrote, 'that much remained to be done in Assyria and that I had little
doubt that excavations could be successfully undertaken, but that I
am unacquainted with any fit person to superintend them'.[4] Though
Layard's suggestion that he was uniquely equipped to deal with the
problems of Mesopotamian archaeology in the mid-nineteenth century
lacked modesty, it was true. Henry Ross, who was still continuing
excavation as Layard's agent, was competent, but he lacked the rare
combination of qualities which enables Layard to accomplish so much
almost single-handed: it would indeed be difficult to name a Mesopotamian archaeologist of comparable ability with Layard in the succeeding half-century. It may be added that by the end of 1848 Layard had

[1] 38978, 25 (28th January 1848).
[2] For the original publication of the text see A. H. Layard, *Inscriptions in the Cuneiform Character* (1851), plate 15 lines 24–27 and plate 46 lines 13–15.
[3] 38978, 2 (2nd January 1848).
[4] 38978, 8 (12th January 1848).

modified his judgment and did propose Ross to the museum authorities as a suitable agent.

The Assyrian sculptures on view in the British Museum were
making a considerable impression, and Layard's name was becoming
known to the educated public. Shortly after his return to England he
was elected a member of the Athenæum, and in July the University
of Oxford bestowed on him the degree of D.C.L. But despite such
distinctions, he was still without an assured income. He had the
attacheship at Constantinople, but this was unpaid, the only probable
emolument being a future allowance of £250 in connection with
duties on the Commission to delineate the Turco–Persian frontier.
Layard had originally welcomed the appointment to the Boundary
Commission, but now cooled towards it, probably as a result of the
advice of Canning: 'I do not', said Canning, 'like the idea of your
going on this trumpery frontier work'.[1] In early September, he asked
Viscount Palmerston to accept his resignation from the Boundary
Commission, on the ground that he preferred to remain with Sir
Stratford Canning, and joined to his resignation a specific request that
the attacheship at Constantinople should become a paid appointment.
In the reply from the Foreign Office, Layard's resignation from the
Commission was accepted, but, said the letter, 'the establishment of
Paid Attaches at Constantinople is full, and Lord Palmerston sees no
sufficient reason to increase that establishment'.[2] In consequence the
allowance of £250 assigned for duties on the Boundary Commission
would lapse. Shortly afterwards Layard was ordered out to Constantinople, where he returned—as he expressed it to a friend—'an
unpaid attache without a sixpence'.

Despite his considerable achievements in the excavations of 1845–7
and the public acclaim which greeted his finds in England, and,
indeed, throughout Europe, as Layard left for the east again in November 1848 he showed no great enthusiasm to undertake a second
archaeological expedition. Archaeology, even in the moment of his
success, remained for him a hobby; for his career he still looked to the
diplomatic field. Writing from shipboard on his way eastwards
(December 1848), he told Ross that he himself had virtually declined
an invitation by the Trustees of the British Museum to undertake
further excavations, but had put forward the name of Ross. He continued: 'If you have a year to spare and would wish to put 4 or 5

[1] 38978, 75 (30th April 1848). See also 38978, 82 (14th May 1848).
[2] 38978, 172 (13th September 1848).

hundred pounds into your pocket this might be a good opportunity. If you are determined to return Eastward and to seek for a consulate you may depend upon it that your name brought before the public connected with fresh discoveries at Nimrud would be of considerable service—and would almost, I think, ensure you something'.[1] A little later (February 1849) he was telling another friend: 'I am still greatly in doubt whether I should accept any further offers for exploration of Assyrian antiquities however good, for events here [*i.e.* in Constantinople] seem to be taking a curious turn and I should not be surprised to see occurrences ere long in which there might be an opportunity of distinguishing oneself in one's profession.'[2]

At the same time that Layard was expressing his doubts as to the wisdom of participating further in archaeology, Samuel Birch of the British Museum was writing to tell him that the Government had given instructions to Canning to supply Layard's services for archaeological work in Mesopotamia. A grant for a season's excavations was being made. As part of the same development, word shortly afterwards reached Layard that he was at last to be appointed a Paid Attache with a salary of £250—a mark, as the Principal Librarian of the British Museum said in his letter of congratulation giving the news, of Her Majesty's Government's recognition of the important services Layard had rendered ancient history.[3]

Second Expedition to Assyria

The new expedition planned, and the invitation to Layard to direct it, were in part due to the public sensation occasioned by the publication of Layard's *Nineveh and its remains*, and in part to a letter he wrote to the Trustees of the British Museum at the beginning of 1849.

Layard's most celebrated book, *Nineveh and its remains*, though it achieved immediate fame and has become one of the classics of archaeology, was written hurriedly and under many disadvantages. In the first place, it was only one of three works he was completing and seeing through the press simultaneously, the other two being his *Monuments of Nineveh* (the definitive publication of his drawings of the finds from Nimrud), and his *Inscriptions in the cuneiform character* (the principal cuneiform texts found at Nimrud with a few from other sources). In addition to this pressure of work, Layard's health had

[1] 38941, 36.
[2] 38946, 2.
[3] 38978, 292–3 (28th March 1849).

suffered from long residence in the east, he was under anxiety as to his future, and the celebrity he had won through his archaeological discoveries led to many calls on the limited time at his disposal. It had originally been intended that he should proceed east again to take up the duties of his attacheship in March 1848, but fortunately for the completion of his books he was able to secure a postponement. In May he was optimistically forecasting that his 'journal' (as he then called *Nineveh and its remains*) would be out in two months, and at that time he was sufficiently confident of its success to be able rather patronisingly to promise Ross 'to aid in making [him] known' by including some of his notes. But he was still working on the book at the end of September, only a few weeks before his departure for the east, with Samuel Birch checking his classical citations. The book did not finally appear until the early days of 1849. It was an immediate success, and by February had met with so much public response that Layard was professing himself 'lost in wonder at the puffs' which had greeted it. By early May the book had gone into a third edition, and by July into a fourth. Although he professed to be disappointed with the 'puff' reviews his work received, Layard was sufficiently encouraged to be, by mid-summer, already planning a new book, which would, he hoped, be a 'better work than the last, although probably not so successful ... as the novelty will have worn off'.[1]

The other stimulus to the second Mesopotamian expedition of the British Museum was Layard's own initiative. Before leaving England he had, without committing himself specifically to undertaking further excavations in Mesopotamia, expressed himself generally willing to help the Trustees of the British Museum wherever he could in the east.[2] He reverted to the matter again in a letter written in the first days of 1849, shortly after his arrival in Turkey. He explained: 'I could not in justice to myself return to the East to superintend more excavations when the means were limited, the results uncertain and no positive reward held out either in the way of professional advancement or increased reputation'. Then followed a plan of such ambition as to make a modern archaeologist gasp. Layard proposed basically a general exploration of the whole region from the Taurus to the Persian Gulf. In addition 'the numerous important ruins in the neighbourhood of Orfa (supposed to be the ancient Ur) on the banks

<hr>

[1] Sources for this paragraph: 38939, 37, 39; 38941, 29; 38944, 1, 2; 38945, 2; 38946, 2; 38977, 333; 38978, 252.
[2] 38978, 204 (10th November 1848).

of the Khabour ..., on the Upper Euphrates, in ancient Assyria proper, Babylonia and even Susiana to be examined carefully and excavations to be made in them'. The principal objective was to be the collection of inscriptions and the drawing of important monuments. To avoid any loss of the opportunities which such an expedition might offer, its secondary objectives were to include 'all branches of natural history and physical geography ... as far as possible'. For this enormous undertaking, which he was prepared to direct, Layard asked the very modest provision of a staff consisting of 'an experienced draughtsman and a medical man', and funds of four to five thousand pounds a year for two and a half years.[1] The British nation has seldom been offered such a bargain.

The Treasury was not prepared to make funds available to the British Museum on this scale. The grant for the first season's work, £1500, fell far short of what Layard had proposed. For this reason and others already indicated, he hesitated. Finally he accepted the direction of the second dig in Mesopotamia and set off from Constantinople in late August 1849. In accordance with his own proposal the British Museum had arranged for him to have the services of an artist, a doctor, and also Hormuzd Rassam, but the provision for these people meant that when all expenses were paid the actual cash available for digging was no more than £890 'to meet all other expenses including that of transporting the Antiquities selected for the Museum to Bussorah'.[2] The financial success of *Nineveh and its remains* enabled Layard to add some money of his own, but the amount available was still inadequate to implement the extensive plans he had laid.

The account of the second expedition is given in Layard's second popular work, *Discoveries in the ruins of Nineveh and Babylon* (1853), and to deal with it would go beyond the scope of this introduction to *Nineveh and its remains*. The expedition was (notwithstanding the despondency frequently reflected in Layard's letters) a success, but it represented the end of Layard's career as an archaeologist. The additions to his staff, far from being the assistance he had hoped, proved, with the exception of Rassam, to be a weight around his neck: he complained that neither the artist, who was incapacitated by homesickness, nor the doctor, who cared for nothing but shooting, were at all qualified for an expedition of that kind, and that the whole

[1] 38978, 241.
[2] 38978, 16–18.

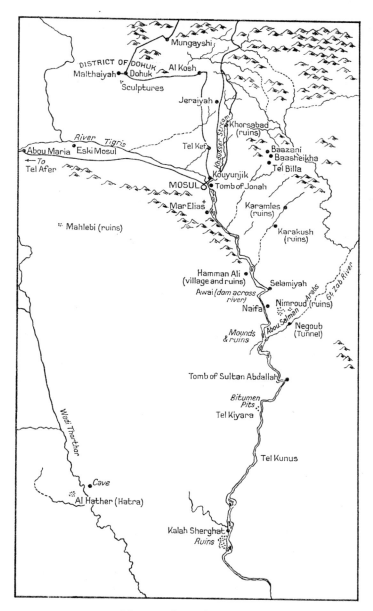

MAP 2. Central Assyria

party was achieving less than he single-handed had accomplished in the first expedition. The parsimony of the British Museum, in doling out funds inadequate to what Layard considered to be the proper performance of his operations, was a constant source of irritation. He was prevented from embarking upon some projects upon which he had set his mind—such as the thorough excavation of Babylon—by the unsettled state of the country. The cumulative effect of these annoyances, backed by the feeling that now—whilst he was high in public favour—was the time for him to carve himself a career in public affairs, led him resolutely to refuse, though invited, to lead a third expedition to Mesopotamia. He had spent twelve years almost continuously in the Near and Middle East, much of it in remote parts, under primitive conditions, and far from European society; and he had had his fill. His determination as to his future course is summed up in a letter written shortly after his return to England in 1851: 'I shall make a desperate effort not to return to the East, not even to Stamboul, which does not agree with me in any way—the climate always disagrees with me, and I can find neither books nor society. I should like to get into Parliament in England, and think that once there I could push my way'.[1]

Layard succeeded in his Parliamentary ambition. How, once there, he pushed his way, may be read in Gordon Waterfield's excellent *Layard of Nineveh* (1963). From this time forth, archaeology no longer occupied his attention, and in later life he rarely referred to it. Only as a very old man, when living in Italy, did he once again become interested in the subject, in connection with the excavations at Pompeii. Less than six months before his death in July 1894, he paid the site a last visit, and was delighted when—as they always did for distinguished visitors—the authorities put on an excavation for him.[2]

[1] 38941, 54.
[2] 38946, 345.

I [1]

DURING THE AUTUMN of 1839 and winter of 1840, I had been wandering through Asia Minor and Syria, scarcely leaving untrod one spot hallowed by tradition, or unvisited one ruin consecrated by history. I was accompanied by one no less curious and enthusiastic than myself.[2] We were both equally careless of comfort and unmindful of danger. We rode alone; our arms were our only protection; a valise behind our saddles was our wardrobe, and we tended our own horses, except when relieved from the duty by the hospitable inhabitants of a Turcoman village or an Arab tent. Thus unembarrassed by needless luxuries, and uninfluenced by the opinions and prejudices of others, we mixed amongst the people, acquired without effort their manners, and enjoyed without alloy those emotions which scenes so novel, and spots so rich in varied association, cannot fail to produce.

I look back with feelings of grateful delight to those happy days when, free and unheeded, we left at dawn the humble cottage or cheerful tent, and lingering as we listed, unconscious of distance and of the hour, found ourselves, as the sun went down, under some hoary ruin tenanted by the wandering Arab, or in some crumbling village still bearing a well-known name.

I had traversed Asia Minor and Syria, visiting the ancient seats of civilisation, and the spots which religion has made holy. I now felt an irresistible desire to penetrate to the regions beyond the Euphrates, to which history and tradition point as the birthplace of the wisdom of the West. A deep mystery hangs over Assyria, Babylonia, and Chaldaea. With these names are linked great nations and great cities dimly shadowed forth in history. After a journey in Syria the thoughts natur-

---

[1] [This abridgement is based on the original 1849 edition, with corrections and additions from the sixth edition (1854). Square brackets in the text or notes enclose additions by the editor.]

[2] [E. L. O. Mitford; see above, pp. 9 ff.]

65

ally turn eastward; and without treading on the remains of Nineveh and Babylon our pilgrimage is incomplete.

I left Aleppo, with my companion, on the 18th of March. We still travelled as we had been accustomed—without guide or servants. The road across the desert is at all times impracticable, except to a numerous and well-armed caravan, and offers no object of interest. We preferred that through Bir and Orfa. From the latter city we traversed the low country at the foot of the Kurdish hills, a country little known, and abounding in curious remains. The Egyptian frontier, at that time, extended to the east of Orfa, and the war between the Sultan and Mohammed Ali Pasha being still unfinished,[1] the tribes took advantage of the confusion, and were plundering on all sides. With our usual good fortune, we succeeded in reaching Nisibin unmolested. We entered Mosul on the 10th of April.

During a short stay in this town we visited the great ruins on the east bank of the river, which have been generally believed to be the remains of Nineveh.[2] We rode also into the desert, and explored the mound of Kalah Sherghat,[3] a vast ruin on the Tigris, about fifty miles below its junction with the Zab. As we journeyed thither we rested for the night at the small Arab village of Hammum Ali, around which are still the vestiges of an ancient city. From the summit of an artificial eminence we looked down upon a broad plain, separated from us by the river. A line of lofty mounds bounded it to the east, and one of a pyramidical form rose high above the rest. Beyond it could be faintly traced the waters of the Zab. Its position rendered its identification easy. This was the pyramid which Xenophon[4] had described, and near which the ten thousand had encamped: the ruins around it were those which the Greek general saw twenty-two centuries before, and which were even then the remains of an *ancient* city. Tradition still points to the origin of the city, and, by attributing its foundation to Nimrod,

---

[1] [Mohammed Ali, an Albanian commander in the Ottoman army, after succeeding in getting himself recognized as viceroy in Egypt, had overrun the province of Syria and crossed the Taurus into Turkey itself; see above, pp. 12 ff. He was finally forced to withdraw from Syria, but remained a virtually independent ruler in Egypt, founding the dynasty which ended with King Farouk.]

[2] These ruins include the great mounds of Kouyunjik and Nebbi Yunus. [The traditional identification of these mounds with the remains of Nineveh has proved correct.]

[3] [The ruins of ancient Ashur, the earliest Assyrian capital, subsequently excavated by the German W. Andrae between 1903 and 1914.]

[4] [Xenophon (*c.* 430–355 B.C.), an Athenian who served a Pretender in his attempt to gain the throne of Persia, extricated 10,000 Greek mercenaries from a military disaster near Babylon and led them back to Greece. The march is described in his *Anabasis.*]

whose name the ruins now bear [in the Arabic form Nimroud], connect it with one of the first settlements of the human race.

Kalah Sherghat, like Nimroud, was an Assyrian ruin: a vast, shapeless mass, now covered with grass, and showing scarcely any traces of the work of man except where the winter rains had formed ravines down its almost perpendicular sides, and had thus laid open its contents. A few fragments of pottery and inscribed bricks served to prove that it owed its construction to the people who had founded the city of which Nimroud is the remains. There was a tradition current amongst the Arabs, that strange figures carved in black stone still existed amongst the ruins; but we searched for them in vain. We passed the night in the jungle which clothes the banks of the river, and wandered during the day undisturbed by the tribes of the desert. A Cawass, who had been sent with us by the Pasha of Mosul, alarmed at the solitude, and dreading the hostile Arabs, left us in the wilderness, and turned homewards. But he fell into the danger he sought to avoid. Less fortunate than ourselves, at a short distance from Kalah Sherghat he was met by a party of horsemen, and fell a victim to his timidity.

Were the traveller to cross the Euphrates to seek for such ruins in Mesopotamia and Chaldæa as he had left behind him in Asia Minor or Syria, his search would be vain. The graceful column rising above the thick foliage of the myrtle, ilex, and oleander; the gradines of the amphitheatre covering a gentle slope, and overlooking the dark blue waters of a lake-like bay; the richly carved cornice or capital half hidden by the luxuriant herbage; are replaced by the stern shapeless mound rising like a hill from the scorched plain, the fragments of pottery, and the stupendous mass of brickwork occasionally laid bare by the winter rains. He is now at a loss to give any form to the rude heaps upon which he is gazing. Those of whose works they are the remains have left no visible traces of their civilisation, or of their arts: their influence had long since passed away. The more he conjectures, the more vague the results appear. The scene around is worthy of the ruin he is contemplating; desolation meets desolation: a feeling of awe succeeds to wonder. These huge mounds of Assyria made a deeper impression upon me, gave rise to more serious thoughts and more earnest reflection, than the temples of Balbec and the theatres of Ionia.

In the middle of April I left Mosul for Baghdad. As I descended the Tigris on a raft, I again saw the ruins of Nimroud, and had a better opportunity of examining them. It was evening as we approached the spot. The spring rains had clothed the mound with the richest verdure, and the fertile meadows, which stretched around it, were covered with flowers of every hue. Amidst this luxuriant vegetation were partly concealed a few fragments of bricks, pottery, and alabaster, upon which might be traced the well-defined wedges of the cuneiform character. A long line of consecutive narrow mounds, still retaining the appearance of walls or ramparts, stretched from the base of the ruins, and formed a vast quadrangle. The river flowed at some distance from them: its waters, swollen by the melting of the snows on the Armenian hills, were broken into a thousand foaming whirlpools by an artificial barrier, built across the stream. On the eastern bank the soil had been washed away by the current; but a solid mass of masonry still withstood its impetuosity. The Arab, who guided my small raft, gave himself up to religious ejaculations as we approached this formidable cataract, over which we were carried with some violence. Once safely through the danger, he explained to me that this unusual change in the quiet face of the river was caused by a great dam which had been built by Nimrod,[1] and that in the autumn before the winter rains, the huge stones of which it was constructed, squared, and united by cramps of iron, were frequently visible above the surface of the stream. The Arab explained the connection between the dam and the city, the vast ruins of which were then before us, and of its purpose as a causeway for the mighty hunter [Nimrod] to cross to the opposite palace, now represented by the mound of Hammum Ali. He was telling me of the histories and fate of the kings of a primitive race, still the favourite theme of the inhabitants of the plains of Shinar,[2] when the last glow of twilight faded away, and I fell asleep as we glided onward to Baghdad.

My curiosity had been greatly excited, and from that time I formed the design of thoroughly examining, whenever it might be in my power, these singular ruins.[3]

It was not until the summer of 1842 that I again passed through Mosul on my way to Constantinople. I was then anxious to reach the Turkish capital, and had no time to explore ruins. I had not, however, forgotten Nimroud.

On my arrival at Mosul, I found that M. Botta had, since my first visit, been named French Consul there; and had already commenced

---

[1] This dam is called by the Arabs, either Sukr el Nimroud [Nimrod's Dam], from the tradition, or El Awai, from the noise caused by the breaking of the water over the stones. Large rafts are obliged to unload before crossing it, and accidents frequently happen to those who neglect this precaution.

[2] [A term used in Genesis ix 2 of the plain of the Tigris–Euphrates basin.]

[3] [For possible grounds for doubting this statement, see above, p. 41f.]

excavation [on a very small scale], on the opposite side of the river, in the large mound called Kouyunjik.

Whilst detained by unexpected circumstances at Constantinople, I entered into correspondence with a gentleman in England[1] on the subject of excavations; but, with this exception, no one seemed inclined to assist or take any interest in such an undertaking. I also wrote to M. Botta, encouraging him to proceed, notwithstanding the apparent paucity of results, and particularly calling his attention to the mound of Nimroud, which, however, he declined to explore on account of its distance from Mosul and its inconvenient position. I was soon called away from the Turkish capital to the provinces; and for some months numerous occupations prevented me turning my attention to the ruins and antiquities of Assyria.

In the meanwhile M. Botta, not discouraged by the want of success which had attended his first essay, continued his excavations in the mound of Kouyunjik: and to him is due the honour of having found the first Assyrian monument. This remarkable discovery owed its origin to the following circumstances. The small party employed by M. Botta were at work on Kouyunjik, when a peasant from a distant village chanced to visit the spot. Seeing that every fragment of brick and alabaster uncovered by the workmen was carefully preserved, he asked the reason of this, to him, strange proceeding. On being informed that they were in search of sculptured stones, he advised them to try the mound on which his village was built, and in which, he declared, many such things as they wanted had been exposed on digging for the foundations of new houses. M. Botta, having been frequently deceived by similar stories, was not at first inclined to follow the peasant's advice, but subsequently sent an agent and one or two workmen to the place. After a little opposition from the inhabitants, they were permitted to sink a well in the mound; and at a small distance from the surface they came to the top of a wall which, on digging deeper, they found to be built of sculptured slabs of gypsum. M. Botta, on receiving information of this discovery, went at once to the village, which was called Khorsabad.[2] He directed a wider trench to be formed, and to be carried in the direction of the wall. He soon found that he had opened a chamber, which was connected with others, and constructed

[1] [Mr. Stirling of Sheffield; see above, p. 39.]

[2] [The ruins of Dur-Sharrukin, a military capital built by Sargon II (722–705 B.C.) and occupied in the latter part of his reign. Botta continued excavations at Khorsabad until 1844, V. Place undertook further work 1852–54, and the Oriental Institute of Chicago excavated there between 1928 and 1935.]

of slabs of gypsum covered with sculptured representations of battles, sieges, and similar events. His wonder may be easily imagined. A new history had been suddenly opened to him—the records of an unknown people were before him. He was equally at a loss to account for the age and the nature of the monument. Numerous inscriptions, accompanying the bas-reliefs, evidently contained the explanation of the events thus recorded in sculpture. They were in the cuneiform, or arrow-headed, character. The nature of these inscriptions was at least evidence that the building belonged to a period preceding the conquest of Alexander; for it was generally admitted that after the subjugation of the west of Asia by the Macedonians, the cuneiform writing ceased to be employed. It was evident that the monument appertained to a very ancient and very civilised people; and it was natural from its position to refer it to the inhabitants of Nineveh,—a city, which, although it could not have occupied a site so distant from the Tigris, must have been in the vicinity of the place. M. Botta had discovered an Assyrian edifice, the first, probably, which had been exposed to the view of man since the fall of the Assyrian empire.

M. Botta was not long in perceiving that the building, which had been thus partly excavated, unfortunately owed its destruction to fire; and that the gypsum slabs, reduced to lime, were rapidly falling to pieces on exposure to the air. No precaution could arrest this rapid decay; and it was to be feared that this wonderful monument had only been uncovered to complete its ruin. The records of victories and triumphs, which had long attested the power and swelled the pride of the Assyrian kings, and had resisted the ravages of ages, were now passing away for ever. They could scarcely be held together until an inexperienced pencil could secure an imperfect evidence of their former existence. Almost all that was first discovered thus speedily disappeared; and the same fate has befallen nearly every thing subsequently found at Khorsabad.[1]

M. Botta lost no time in communicating his remarkable discovery to the principal scientific body in France. Knowing the interest I felt in his labours, he allowed me to see his letters and drawings as they passed through Constantinople; and I was amongst the first who were made acquainted with his success. And here I gladly avail myself of the opportunity of mentioning, with the acknowledgment and praise they

[1] [V. Place was more successful in recovering monuments from Khorsabad, but most of these were lost in the Shatt al Arab in May 1855 when the rafts on which they were being sent to Basra were attacked by Arabs.]

deserve, his disinterestedness and liberality, so honourable to one engaged in the pursuit of knowledge. During the entire period of his
excavations, M. Botta regularly sent me not only his descriptions, but
copies of the inscriptions, without exacting any promise as to the use I
might make of them. That there are few who would have acted thus
liberally, those who have been engaged in a search after antiquities in
the East will not be inclined to deny.

M. Botta's communications were laid before the 'Académie' by
M. Mohl; and that body, perceiving at once the importance of the
discovery, lost no time in applying to the Minister of Public Instruction
for means to carry on the researches. Ample funds to meet the cost of
extensive excavations were at once assigned to M. Botta, and an artist
of acknowledged skill was placed under his orders to draw such parts
of the monument discovered as could not be preserved or removed.

With the exception of a few interruptions on the part of the local
authorities, who were suspicious of the objects of the excavations, the
work was carried on with activity and success, and by the beginning of
1845 the monument had been completely uncovered. The researches
of M. Botta were not extended beyond Khorsabad; and, having
secured many fine specimens of Assyrian sculpture for his country, he
returned to Europe with a rich collection of inscriptions, the most
important result of his discovery. M. Botta's results are now being
published in France, and his countrymen have not been backward in
recognising the extent and importance of his discovery, and in rewarding the zeal, discrimination, and personal sacrifices which led to it.

The advantages which I had derived from a perusal of M. Botta's
letters, and an inspection of his drawings, enabled me to call public
attention, in three letters to the *Malta Times*, to his discovery, and to
be amongst the first to hazard an opinion on the age and origin of this
remarkable monument. My knowledge of M. Botta's discoveries being
incomplete, I was led into one or two errors; but in most respects the
view taken in those letters is the one which is now generally adopted.

The success of M. Botta had increased my anxiety to explore the
ruins of Assyria. It was evident that Khorsabad could not stand alone.
It did not represent ancient Nineveh, nor did it afford us any additional
evidence as to the site of that city. My thoughts still went back to the
ruin of Nimroud, and to the traditions which attached to it. I spoke to
others, but received little encouragement. At last, in the autumn of
1845, Sir Stratford Canning mentioned to me his readiness to incur,
for a limited period, the expense of excavations in Assyria, in the hope

that, should success attend the attempt, means would be found to carry it out on an adequate scale. I received with joy the offer of commencing and carrying on these excavations. The reader will not, I trust, be disinclined to join with me in feelings of gratitude towards one who, whilst he has maintained so successfully the honour and interests of England by his high character and eminent abilities, has acquired for his country so many great monuments of ancient civilisation and art.[1] It is to Sir Stratford Canning we are mainly indebted for the collection of Assyrian antiquities with which the British Museum will be enriched.

The enlightened and liberal spirit shown by M. Botta is unfortunately not generally shared. It was, consequently, deemed most prudent and most conducive to the success of the undertaking, that I should leave Constantinople without acquainting any one with the object of my journey. I was only furnished with the usual documents given to travellers when recommended by the Embassy, and with strong letters of introduction to the authorities at Mosul and in the neighbourhood. My preparations were soon completed, and I started from Constantinople by steamer to Samsoun in the middle of October. Anxious to reach the end of my journey, I crossed the mountains of Pontus and the great steppes of the Usun Yilak as fast as post-horses could carry me, descended the high lands into the valley of the Tigris, galloped over the vast plains of Assyria, and reached Mosul in twelve days.

---

[1] I need scarcely remind the reader that it is to Sir S. Canning we owe the marbles of Halicarnassus now in the British Museum. I can testify to the efforts and labour which were necessary for nearly three years before the repugnance of the Ottoman government could be overcome, and permission obtained to extract the sculptures from the walls of a castle, which was more jealously guarded than any similar edifice in the empire. Their removal was most successfully effected by Mr. Alison. The Elgin marbles, and all other remains from Turkey or Greece now in Europe, were obtained with comparative ease.

II

MY FIRST STEP on reaching Mosul was to present my letters to the governor of the province. Mohammed Pasha, being a native of Candia,[1] was usually known as Keritli Oglu (the son of the Cretan), to distinguish him from his celebrated predecessor of the same name. The appearance of his Excellency was not prepossessing, but it matched his temper and conduct. Nature had placed hypocrisy beyond his reach. He had one eye and one ear; he was short and fat, deeply marked by the small-pox, uncouth in gestures and harsh in voice. His fame had reached the seat of his government before him. On the road he had revived many good old customs and impositions, which the reforming spirit of the age had suffered to fall into decay. He particularly insisted on *dish-parassi*[2]; or a compensation in money, levied upon all villages in which a man of such rank is entertained, for the wear and tear of his teeth in masticating the food he condescends to receive from the inhabitants. On entering Mosul, he had induced several of the principal Aghas who had fled from the town on his approach, to return to their homes; and, having made a formal display of oaths and protestations, cut their throats to show how much his word could be depended upon. At the time of my arrival, the population was in a state of terror and despair. Even the appearance of a casual traveller led to hopes, and reports were whispered about the town of the deposition of the tyrant. Of this the Pasha was aware, and hit upon a plan to test the feelings of the people towards him. He was suddenly taken ill one afternoon, and was carried to his harem almost lifeless. On the following morning the palace was closed, and the attendants answered inquiries by mysterious motions, which could only be interpreted in one fashion. The doubts of the Mosuleans gradually gave way to general rejoicings; but at mid-day his Excellency, who had

---

[1] [The town in north Crete now known as Heracleion.]
[2] Literally, "tooth-money".

posted his spies all over the town, appeared in perfect health in the market-place. A general trembling seized the inhabitants. His vengeance fell principally upon those who possessed property, and had hitherto escaped his rapacity. They were seized and stripped on the plea that they had spread reports detrimental to his authority.

The villages, and the Arab tribes, had not suffered less than the townspeople. The Pasha was accustomed to give instructions to those who were sent to collect money, in three words—'Go, destroy, eat;'[1] and his agents were not generally backward in entering into the spirit of them. The tribes, who had been attacked and plundered, were retaliating upon caravans and travellers, or laying waste the cultivated parts of the Pashalic. The villages were deserted, and the roads were little frequented and very insecure.

Such was the Pasha to whom I was introduced two days after my arrival by the British Vice-Consul, Mr. Rassam.[2] He read the letters which I presented to him, and received me with that civility which a traveller generally expects from a Turkish functionary of high rank. His anxiety to know the object of my journey was evident, but his curiosity was not gratified for the moment.

There were many reasons which rendered it necessary that my plans should be concealed, until I was ready to put them into execution. Although I had always experienced from M. Botta the most friendly assistance, there were others who did not share his sentiments[3]; from the authorities and the people of the town I could only expect the most decided opposition. On the 8th of November, having secretly procured a few tools,[4] and engaged a mason at the moment of my departure, and carrying with me a variety of guns, spears, and other

[1] To eat money, *i.e.* to get money unlawfully or by pillage, is a common expression in the East.

[2] [Mr. Christian Rassam, a native Christian of the Assyrian (Nestorian) sect. His wife Matilda, the sister of the missionary George Percy Badger (see above, page 42, note 1), became a close friend and correspondent of Layard. His younger brother Hormuzd subsequently became Layard's assistant at Nimrud and was taken by him to Istanbul and England to complete his education.]

[3] [Layard had in mind particularly Botta's successor, a M. Rouet; see also his allusions to opposition from an unstated source on pages 82 and 88. It may be noted that, although Layard frequently complained to Canning of Rouet's opposition, on 24th January 1846 he informed the Ambassador, at the time of Rouet's departure from Mosul: 'I was at all times on the best terms with him, and perhaps the interference of which I have to complain is more to be attributed to his Dragoman, who is, I fear, a worthless person, than to himself. At any rate should your Excellency see M. Rouet, I trust you will not think it necessary to let him know that I suspected him.' (40637, 39).]

[4] [These were made in Rassam's workshop; see 40637, 5.]

formidable weapons, I declared that I was going to hunt wild boars in a neighbouring village, and floated down the Tigris on a small raft constructed for my journey. I was accompanied by Mr. Ross,[1] a British merchant of Mosul, my Cawass, and a servant.

At this time of the year more than five hours are required to descend the Tigris, from Mosul to Nimroud. It was sunset before we reached the Awai, or dam across the river. We landed and walked to the village of Naifa. No light appeared as we approached, nor were we even saluted by the dogs, which usually abound in an Arab village. We had entered a heap of ruins. I was about to return to the raft, upon which we had made up our minds to pass the night, when the glare of a fire lighted up the entrance to a miserable hovel. Through a crevice in the wall, I saw an Arab family crouching round a heap of half-extinguished embers. The dress of the man, the ample cloak and white turban, showed that he belonged to one of the Arab tribes, which cultivate a little land on the borders of the desert, and are distinguished, by their more settled habits, from the Bedouins. Near him were three women, lean and haggard, their heads almost concealed in black handkerchiefs, and the rest of their persons enveloped in the striped aba. Some children, nearly naked, and one or two mangy greyhounds completed the group. As we entered all the party rose, and showed some alarm at the sudden appearance of strangers. The man, however, seeing that we were Europeans, bid us welcome, and spreading some corn-sacks on the ground, invited us to be seated. The women and children retreated into a corner of the hut. Our host, whose name was Awad or Abd-Allah, was a sheikh of the Jehesh. His tribe had been plundered by the Pasha, and was now scattered in different parts of the country; he had taken refuge in this ruined village. He told us that owing to the extortions and perfidy of Keritli Oglu, the villages in the neighbourhood had been deserted, and that the Arab tribe of Abou Salman had joined with the Tai in marauding excursions into the country on this side of the river. The neighbourhood, he said, was consequently insecure, and the roads to Mosul almost closed. Awad had learnt a little Turkish, and was intelligent and active. Seeing, at once, that he would be useful, I

[1] Mr. Ross will perhaps permit me to acknowledge in a note, the valuable assistance I received from him, during my labours in Assyria. His knowledge of the natives, and intimate acquaintance with the resources of the country, enabled him to contribute much to the success of my undertaking; whilst to his friendship I am indebted for many pleasant hours, which would have passed wearily in a land of strangers. [This was Henry James Ross, whose *Letters from the East 1837–1857* were edited by his wife and published in 1902.]

acquainted him with the object of my journey; offering him the prospect of regular employment in the event of the experiment proving successful, and assigning him regular wages as superintendent of the workmen. He had long been acquainted with the ruins, and entertained me with traditions connected with them. 'The palace,' said he, 'was built by Athur, the Kiayah, or lieutenant of Nimrod. Here the holy Abraham, peace be with him! cast down and brake in pieces the idols which were worshipped by the unbelievers. The impious Nimrod sought to slay Abraham, and waged war against him. But the prophet prayed to God, and said, "Deliver me, O God, from this man, who worships stones, and boasts himself to be the lord of all beings," and God said to him, "How shall I punish him?" And the prophet answered, "To Thee armies are as nothing, and the strength and power of men likewise. Before the smallest of thy creatures will they perish." And God was pleased at the faith of the prophet, and he sent a gnat, which vexed Nimrod night and day, so that he built himself a room of glass in yonder palace, that he might dwell therein, and shut out the insect. But the gnat entered also, and passed by his ear into his brain, upon which it fed, and increased in size day by day, so that the servants of Nimrod beat his head with a hammer continually, that he might have some ease from his pain; but he died after suffering these torments for four hundred years.'[1]

Awad volunteered to walk, in the middle of the night, to Selamiyah, a village three miles distant, and to some Arab tents in the neighbourhood, to procure men to assist in the excavations.

I slept little during the night. The hovel in which we had taken shelter, and its inmates, did not invite slumber; but such scenes and companions were not new to me: they could have been forgotten, had my brain been less excited. Visions of palaces underground, of gigantic monsters, of sculptured figures, and endless inscriptions, floated before me. After forming plan after plan for removing the earth, and extricating these treasures, I fancied myself wandering in a maze of chambers from which I could find no outlet. Then again, all was reburied, and I was standing on the grass-covered mound. Exhausted, I was at length sinking into sleep, when hearing the voice of Awad, I rose from my

---

[1] This and similar traditions are found in a work called Kusset el Nimroud (Stories of Nimrod), which Rich represents the inhabitants of the villages near the ruins as reading during the winter nights. Although there is no one in these days within some miles of the place who possesses the work, or could read it if he did, the tales it contains are current amongst the Arabs of the neighbourhood.

carpet, and joined him outside the hovel. The day already dawned; he had returned with six Arabs, who agreed for a small sum to work under my direction.

The lofty cone and broad mound of Nimroud broke like a distant mountain on the morning sky. But how changed was the scene since my former visit! The ruins were no longer clothed with verdure and many-coloured flowers; no signs of habitation, not even the black tent of the Arab, was seen upon the plain. The eye wandered over a parched and barren waste, across which occasionally swept the whirlwind, dragging with it a cloud of sand.

Twenty minutes' walk brought us to the principal mound. The absence of all vegetation enabled me to examine the remains with which it was covered. Broken pottery and fragments of bricks, both inscribed with the cuneiform character, were strewed on all sides. The Arabs watched my motions as I wandered to and fro, and observed with surprise the objects I had collected. They joined, however, in the search, and brought me handfuls of rubbish, amongst which I found with joy the fragment of a bas-relief. The material on which it was carved had been exposed to fire, and resembled, in every respect, the burnt gypsum of Khorsabad. Convinced from this discovery that sculpture remains must still exist in some part of the mound, I sought for a place where excavations might be commenced with a prospect of success. Awad led me to a piece of alabaster which appeared above the soil. We could not remove it, and on digging downward, it proved to be the upper part of a large slab. I ordered all the men to work around it, and they shortly uncovered a second slab to which it had been united. Continuing in the same line, we came upon a third; and, in the course of the morning, laid bare ten more, the whole forming a square, with one stone missing at the N.W. corner. It was evident that the top of a chamber had been discovered, and that the gap was its entrance.[1] I now dug down the face of the stones, and an inscription in the cuneiform character was soon exposed to view. Similar inscriptions occupied the centre of all the slabs, which were in the best preservation; but plain, with the exception of the writing. Leaving half the workmen to uncover as much of the chamber as possible, I led the rest to the S.W. corner of the mound, where I had observed many fragments of calcined alabaster.

I dug at once into the side of the mound, which was here very steep, and thus avoided the necessity of removing much earth. We came

[1] This was the chamber marked A on plan 3.

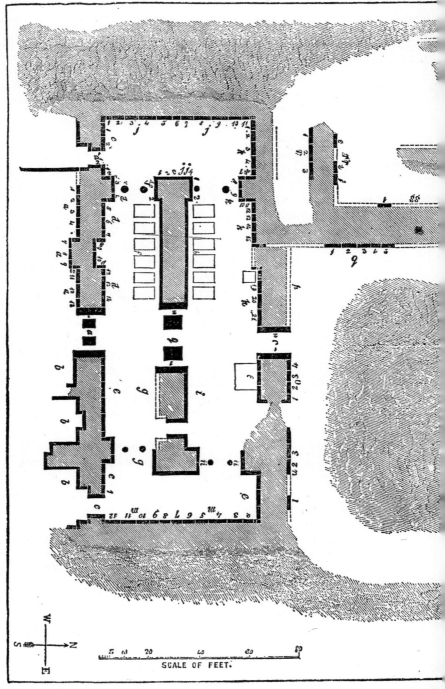

SCALE OF FEET.

PLAN 2. South-W

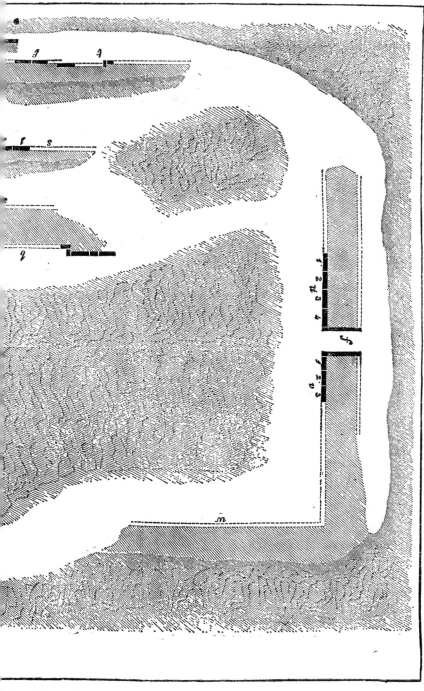

uin, Nimroud

almost immediately to a wall,[1] bearing inscriptions in the same character as those already described; but the slabs had evidently been exposed to intense heat, were cracked in every part, and, reduced to lime, threatened to fall to pieces as soon as uncovered.

Night interrupted our labours. I returned to the village well satisfied with their result. It was now evident that buildings of considerable extent existed in the mound; and that although some had been destroyed by fire, others had escaped the conflagration. As there were inscriptions, and as the fragment of a bas-relief had been found, it was natural to conclude that sculptures were still buried under the soil. I determined to follow the search at the N.W. corner, and to empty the chamber partly uncovered during the day.

On returning to the village, I removed from the crowded hovel in which we had passed the night. With the assistance of Awad, who was no less pleased than myself with our success, we patched up with mud the least ruined house in the village, and restored its falling roof. We contrived at least to exclude, in some measure, the cold night winds; and to obtain a little privacy for my companion and myself.

Next morning my workmen were increased by five Turcomans from Selamiyah, who had been attracted by the prospect of regular wages. I employed half of them in emptying the chamber partly uncovered on the previous day, and the rest in following the wall at the S.W. corner of the mound. Before evening, the work of the first party was completed, and I found myself in a room built of slabs about eight feet high, and varying from six to four feet in breadth, placed upright and closely fitted together. One of the slabs had fallen backwards from its place; and was supported, in a slanting position, by the soil behind. Upon it was rudely inscribed, in Arabic characters, the name of Ahmed Pasha, one of the former hereditary governors of Mosul. A native of Selamiyah remembered that some Christians were employed to dig into the mount about thirty years before, in search of stone for the repair of the tomb of Sultan Abd-Allah, a Mussulman Saint, buried on the left bank of the Tigris, a few miles below its junction with the Zab. They uncovered this slab; but being unable to move it, they cut upon it the name of their employer, the Pasha.

The bottom of the chamber was paved with smaller slabs than those employed in the construction of the walls. They were covered with inscriptions on both sides, and on removing one of them, I found that it had been placed upon a layer of bitumen which must have been in a

[1] Back of wall *j*, plan 2.

liquid state, for it had retained, with remarkable distinctness and accuracy, an impression of the characters carved upon the stone.

In the rubbish near the bottom of the chamber, I found several ivory ornaments, upon which were traces of gilding; amongst them was the figure of a man in long robes, carrying in one hand the Egyptian crux ansata, part of a crouching sphinx, and flowers designed with great taste and elegance. Awad, who had his own suspicions of the object of my search, which he could scarcely persuade himself was limited to mere stones, carefully collected all the scattered fragments of gold leaf he could find in the rubbish; and, calling me aside in a mysterious and confidential fashion, produced them wrapped up in a piece of dingy paper. 'O Bey,' said he, 'Wallah! your books are right, and the Franks know that which is hid from the true believer. Here is the gold, sure enough, and, please God, we shall find it all in a few days. Only don't say anything about it to those Arabs, for they are asses and cannot hold their tongues. The matter will come to the ears of the Pasha.' The Sheikh was much surprised, and equally disappointed, when I generously presented him with the treasures he had collected, and all such as he might hereafter discover. He left me, lost in conjectures as to the meaning of these strange proceedings.

On the third day, I opened a trench in the high conical mound, and found nothing but fragments of inscribed bricks. I also dug at the back of the north end of the chamber first explored, in the expectation of discovering other walls beyond, but unsuccessfully. As my chief aim was to prove the existence, as soon as possible, of sculptures, all my workmen were moved to the S.W. corner, where the many ramifications of the building already identified, promised speedier success. I continued the excavations in this part of the mound until the 13th, still uncovering inscriptions, but finding no sculptures.

Some days having elapsed since my departure from Mosul, and the experiment having been now sufficiently tried, it was time to return to the town and acquaint the Pasha, who had, no doubt, already heard of my proceedings, with the object of my researches. I started, therefore, early in the morning of the 14th, and galloped to Mosul in about three hours.

I found the town in great commotion. In the first place, his Excellency had, on the day before, entrapped his subjects by the reports of his death, in the manner already described. In the second, the British Vice-Consul having purchased an old building in which to store his stock in trade, the Cadi, a fanatic, and a man of the most infamous character, on the pretence that the Franks had formed a design of buying up the whole of Turkey, was endeavouring to raise a riot, which was to end in the demolition of the Consulate and other acts of violence. I called on the Pasha, and, in the first place, congratulated him on his speedy recovery; a compliment which he received with a grim smile of satisfaction. He then introduced the subject of the Cadi, and the disturbance he had created. 'Does that ill-conditioned fellow,' exclaimed he, 'think that he has Sherif Pasha (his immediate predecessor) to deal with, that he must be planning a riot in the town? When I was at Siwas the Ulema[1] tried to excite the people because I encroached upon a burying-ground. But I made them eat dirt! Wallah! I took up every gravestone and built up the castle walls with them.' He pretended at first to be ignorant of the excavations at Nimroud; but subsequently thinking that he would convict me of prevarication in my answers to his questions as to the amount of treasure discovered, pulled out of his writing-tray a scrap of paper, as dingy as that produced by Awad, in which was also preserved an almost invisible particle of gold leaf. This, he said, had been brought to him by the commander of the irregular troops stationed at Selamiyah, who had been watching my proceedings. I suggested that he should name an agent to be present as long as I worked at Nimroud, to take charge of all the precious metals that might be discovered. He promised to write on the subject to the chief of the irregulars; but offered no objection to the continuation of my researches.

Reports of the wealth extracted from the ruins had already reached Mosul and had excited the cupidity and jealousy of the Cadi and principal inhabitants of the place. Others, who well knew my object, and might have spared me any additional interruption without a sacrifice of their national character, were not backward in fanning the prejudices of the authorities and natives of the town. It was evident that I should have to contend against a formidable opposition; but as the Pasha had not, as yet, openly objected to my proceedings, I hired several Nestorian Chaldæans, who had left their mountains for the winter to seek employment in Mosul, and sent them to Nimroud. At the same time I engaged agents to explore several mounds in the neighbourhood of the town, hoping to ascertain the existence of sculptured buildings in some part of the country, before steps were taken to interrupt me. The mounds which I directed to be opened were those of Baasheikha (of

---

[1] [The Ulema was the body of theologians who gave authoritative decisions on points of Islamic law and theology.]

considerable size), Baazani, Karamles, Karakush, Yara, and Jeraiyah.

Whilst at Mosul, Mormous, an Arab of the tribe of Haddedeen, informed me that figures had been accidentally uncovered in a mound near the village of Tel Kef. As he offered to take me to the place we rode out together; but he only pointed out the site of an old quarry, with a few rudely hewn stones. Such disappointments were daily occurring; and I wearied myself in scouring the country to see remains which generally proved to be the ruin of some modern building, or an early tombstone inscribed with Arabic characters.

Having finished my arrangements in Mosul, I returned to Nimroud on the 19th. During my absence, the workmen, under the direction of my Cawass, had carried the excavations along the back of the wall c, in plan 2, and had discovered the entrance d. Being anxious to make as much progress as possible, I increased my party to thirty men, and distributed them in three sets over the S.W. corner of the mound. By opening long trenches at right angles in various directions, we came upon the top of wall m, built of slabs with inscriptions similar to those already described. One, however (No. 10), was reversed, and was covered with characters, exceeding in size any I had yet seen. On examining the inscription carefully, it was found to correspond with those of the chamber in the N.W. corner [of the mound]. The edges of this, as well as of all the other slabs hitherto discovered in the S.W. ruins, had been cut away, several letters of the inscriptions being destroyed, in order to make the stones fit into the wall. From these facts it was evident that materials taken from another building had been used in the construction of the one we were now exploring. But as yet it could not be ascertained whether the face or the back of the slabs had been uncovered. Neither the plan nor the nature of the edifice could be determined until the heap of rubbish and earth under which it was buried had been removed. The excavations were now carried on but slowly. The soil, mixed with sun-dried and kiln-burnt bricks, pottery and fragments of alabaster, offered considerable resistance to the tools of the workmen; and when loosened, had to be removed in baskets and thrown over the edge of the mound. The Chaldæans from the mountains, strong and hardy men, could alone wield the pick; the Arabs were employed in carrying away the earth. The spade could not be used, and there were no other means, than those I had adopted, to clear away the rubbish from the ruins.

The Abou Salman and Tai Arabs continuing their depredations in the plains of Nimroud and surrounding country, I deemed it prudent to remove from Naifa, where I had hitherto resided, to Selamiyah. The latter village is built on a rising ground near the Tigris, and was formerly a place of some importance. It probably occupied an ancient site, and in a line of mounds now at a considerable distance from the village, but enclosing it, can be traced the original walls. Even five years ago Selamiyah was a flourishing place, and could furnish 150 well-armed horsemen. The Pasha had, however, plundered it; and the inhabitants had fled to the mountains or into the Baghdad territories. Ten miserable huts now stood in the midst of the ruins of bazaars and streets surrounding a kasr or palace, belonging to the family of the old hereditary Pashas, well built of Mosul alabaster, but rapidly falling into decay. I had intended to take possession of this building, but the rooms were in such a dilapidated condition that the low mud hut of the Kiayah[1] appeared to be both safer and warmer. I accordingly spread my carpet in one of its corners, and giving the owner a few piastres to finish other dwelling-places which he had commenced, established myself for the winter. The premises, which were speedily completed, consisted of four hovels, surrounded by a wall built of mud, and covered in with reeds and boughs of trees plastered over with the same material. I occupied half of the largest habitation, the other half being appropriated for various domestic animals,—cows, bullocks, and other beasts of the plough. We were separated by a wall; in which, however, numerous apertures served as a means of communication. These I studiously endeavoured for some time to block up. A second hut was devoted to the wives, children, and poultry of my host; a third served as kitchen and servants' hall: the fourth was converted into a stall for my horses. In the enclosure formed by the buildings and the outer wall, the few sheep and goats which had escaped the rapacity of the Pasha congregated during the night, and kept up a continual bleating and coughing until they were milked and turned out to pasture at day-break.

The roofs not being constructed to exclude the winter rains now setting in, it required some exercise of ingenuity to escape the torrent which descended into my apartment. I usually passed the night on these occasions crouched up in a corner, or under a rude table which I had constructed. My Cawass, who was a Constantinopolitan, complained bitterly of the hardships he was compelled to endure, and I had some difficulty in prevailing upon my servants to remain with me.

The present inhabitants of Selamiyah, and of most of the villages in

---

[1] [The official in charge of a village.]

this part of the Pashalic of Mosul, are Turcomans, descendants of tribes brought by the early Turkish Sultans from the north of Asia Minor, to people a country which had been laid waste by repeated massacres and foreign invasions. In this portion of the Ottoman Empire, except in Mosul and the mountains, there is scarcely a vestige of the ancient population. The tribes which inhabit the desert were brought from the Jebel Shammar, in Nedjd, almost within the memory of man. The inhabitants of the plains to the east of the Tigris are mostly Turcomans and Kurds, mixed with Arabs, or with Yezidis, who are strangers in the land, and whose origin cannot easily be determined. A few Chaldæans and Jacobite Christians, scattered in Mosul and the neighbouring villages, or dwelling in the most inaccessible part of the mountains, are probably the only descendants of that great people which once swayed, from these plains, the half of Asia.

The Yuz-bashi, or captain of the irregular troops, one Daoud Agha, a native of the north of Asia Minor, came to call upon me as soon as I was established in my new quarters. Like most men of his class, acknowledged freebooters[1], he was frank and intelligent. He tendered me his services, entertained me with his adventures, and planned hunting expeditions. A few presents[2] secured his adherence, and he proved himself afterwards a very useful and faithful ally.

I had now to ride three miles every morning to the mound; and my workmen, who were afraid, on account of the Arabs, to live at Naifa, returned, after the day's labour, to Selamiyah.

The excavations were still carried on as actively as the means at my disposal would permit. But still no sculptures had been discovered; nor could any idea be yet formed of the relative position of the walls. I ordered a trench to be opened obliquely from the entrance (d) into the interior of the mound, presuming that we should ultimately find the opposite side of the chamber. After removing a large accumulation of

[1] The irregular cavalry (Hytas as they are called in this part of Turkey), are collected from all classes and provinces. A man, known for his courage and daring, is named Hyta-bashi, or chief of the Hytas, and is furnished with *teskeres* (orders for pay and provisions), for so many horsemen, from four or five hundred to a thousand or more. He collects all the vagrants and freebooters he can find to make up his number. The best Hytas are Albanians and Lazes. Their pay at Mosul is small, amounting to about eight shillings a month; in other provinces it is considerably more. They are quartered on the villages, and are the terror of the inhabitants, whom they plunder and ill-treat as they think fit. When a Hyta-bashi has established a reputation for himself, his followers are numerous and devoted. He wanders about the provinces, and sells his services, and those of his troops, to the Pasha who offers most pay, and the best prospects of plunder.

[2] [In his private communication to Canning, Layard more bluntly used the word 'bribe' (40637, 36).]

earth mixed with charcoal, charred wood, and broken bricks, we reached the top of wall f, on the afternoon of the 28th November. In order to ascertain whether we were in the inside of a chamber, the workmen were directed to clear away the earth from both sides of the slabs. The south face was unsculptured, but the first stroke of the pick on the opposite side disclosed the top of a bas-relief. The Arabs were no less excited than myself by the discovery; and notwithstanding a violent shower of rain, working until dark, they completely exposed to view two slabs (Nos. 1 and 2).

On each slab were two bas-reliefs, separated from one another by a band of inscriptions. The subject on the upper part of No. 1 was a battle scene. I observed with surprise the elegance and richness of the ornaments, the faithful and delicate delineation of the limbs and muscles, both in the men and horses, and the knowledge of art displayed in the grouping of the figures, and the general composition. In all these respects, as well as in costume, this sculpture appeared to me not only to differ from, but to surpass, the bas-reliefs of Khorsabad. I traced also, in the character used in the inscription, a marked difference from that found on the monuments discovered by M. Botta. Unfortunately, the slab had been exposed to fire, and was so much injured that its removal was hopeless. The edges had, moreover, been cut away, to the injury of some of the figures and of the inscription.

The lower bas-relief on No. 1 represented the siege of a castle or walled city. To the left were two warriors, each holding a circular shield in one hand, and a short sword in the other. The foremost warrior was ascending a ladder placed against the castle. Three turrets, with angular battlements, rose above walls similarly ornamented. In the first turret were two warriors, one in the act of discharging an arrow, the other raising a shield and casting a stone at the assailants, from whom the besieged were distinguished by their head-dress,—a simple fillet binding the hair above the temples. Their beards, at the same time, were less carefully arranged. The second turret was occupied by a slinger preparing his sling. In the interval between this turret and the third, and over an arched gateway, was a female figure, known by her long hair descending upon the shoulders in ringlets. Her right hand was raised as if in the act of asking for mercy. In the third turret were two more of the besieged, the first discharging an arrow, the second elevating his shield, and endeavouring with a torch to burn an instrument resembling a catapult, which had been brought up to the wall by an inclined plane apparently built on a heap of boughs and rubbish.

These figures were out of all proportion when compared with the size of the building. A warrior with a pointed helmet, bending on one knee, and holding a torch in his right hand, was setting fire to the gate of the castle, whilst another in full armour was forcing the stones from its foundations with an instrument, probably of iron, resembling a blunt spear. Between them was a wounded man falling headlong from the walls.

No. 2 was a corner-stone very much injured, the greater part of the relief having been cut away to reduce it to convenient dimensions. The upper part was occupied by two warriors, one riding a horse, the other standing in a chariot. The horses had been destroyed, and the marks of the chisel were visible on many parts of the slab, the sculpture having been in some places carefully defaced. The lower bas-relief represented a singular subject. On the battlements of the castle, two stories high, and defended by many towers, stood a woman tearing her hair to show her grief. Beneath the walls by the side of a stream, figured by numerous undulating lines, crouched a fisherman drawing from the water a fish he had caught. This slab had been exposed to fire like that adjoining, and had sustained too much injury to be removed.

As I was meditating in the evening over my discovery, Daoud Agha entered, and seating himself near me, delivered a long speech, to the effect that he was a servant of the Pasha, who was again the slave of the Sultan; and that servants were bound to obey the commands of their master, however disagreeable and unjust they might be. I saw at once to what this exordium was about to lead, and was prepared for the announcement that he had received orders from Mosul to stop the excavations by threatening those who were inclined to work for me. On the following morning, therefore, I rode to the town, and waited upon his Excellency. He pretended to be taken by surprise, disclaimed having given any such orders, and directed his secretary to write at once to the commander of the irregular troops, who was to give me every assistance rather than throw impediments in my way. He promised to let me have the letter in the afternoon before I returned to Selamiyah; but an officer came to me soon after, and stated that as the Pasha was unwilling to detain me he would forward it in the night. I rode back to the village, and acquainted Daoud Agha with the result of my visit. About midnight, however, he returned to me, and declared that a horseman had just brought him more stringent orders than any he had yet received, and that on no account was he to permit me to carry on the work.

Surprised at this inconsistency, I returned to Mosul early next day, and again called upon the Pasha. 'It was with deep regret,' said he, 'I learnt, after your departure yesterday, that the mound in which you are digging had been used as a burying-ground by Mussulmans, and was covered with their graves; now you are aware that by the law it is forbidden to disturb a tomb, and the Cadi and Mufti have already made representations to me on the subject.' 'In the first place,' replied I, 'being pretty well acquainted with the mound, I can state that no graves have been disturbed; in the second, after the wise and firm "*politica*" which your Excellency exhibited at Siwas, grave-stones would present no difficulty. Please God, the Cadi and Mufti have profited by the lesson which your Excellency gave to the ill-mannered Ulema of that city.' 'In Siwas,' returned he, immediately understanding my meaning, 'I had Mussulmans to deal with, and there was *tanzimat*[1], but here we have only Kurds and Arabs, and, Wallah! they are beasts. No, I cannot allow you to proceed; you are my dearest and most intimate friend; if any thing happens to you, what grief should I not suffer! your life is more valuable than old stones; besides, the responsibility would fall upon my head.' I pretended to acquiesce in his answer, and requested that a Cawass of his own might be sent with me to Nimroud, as I wished to draw the sculptures and copy the inscriptions which had already been uncovered. To this he consented, and ordered an officer to accompany me. Before leaving Mosul, I learnt with regret from what quarter the opposition to my proceedings chiefly came.

On my return to Selamiyah there was little difficulty in inducing the Pasha's Cawass to countenance the employment of a few workmen to *guard* the sculptures during the day; and as Daoud Agha considered that this functionary's presence relieved him from any further responsibility, he no longer interfered with any experiment I might think proper to make. Wishing to ascertain the existence of the graves, and also to draw one of the bas-reliefs, which had been uncovered, I rode to the ruins on the following morning, accompanied by the Hytas and their chief, who were going their usual rounds in search of plundering Arabs. Daoud Agha confessed to me on our way that he had received orders to make graves on the mound, and that his troops had been employed for two nights in bringing stones from distant villages for that purpose.[2] 'We have destroyed more real tombs of the true Believers,'

---

[1] The reformed system introduced into most provinces of Turkey, but which had not yet been extended to Mosul and Baghdad.

[2] In Arabia, the graves are merely marked by large stones placed upright at the head and feet, and in a heap over the body.

said he, 'in making sham ones, than you could have defiled between the Zab and Selamiyah. We have killed our horses and ourselves in carrying those accursed stones.'

In the evening Daoud Agha brought back with him a prisoner and two of his followers severely wounded. He had fallen in with a party of Arabs under Sheikh Abd-ur-rahman of the Abou Salman, whose object in crossing the Zab had been to plunder me as I worked at the mound. After a short engagement, the Arabs were compelled to recross the river.

I continued to employ a few men to open trenches by way of experiment, and was not long in discovering other sculptures. Near the western edge we came upon the lower part of several gigantic figures, uninjured by fire.[1] At the foot of the S.E. corner was found a crouching lion, rudely carved in basalt. In the centre of the mound we uncovered part of a pair of gigantic winged bulls, the head and half the wings of which had been destroyed. Their length was fourteen feet, and their height must have been originally the same. A pair of small winged lions, the heads and upper part destroyed, were also discovered.[2] They appeared to form an entrance into a chamber, were admirably designed and very carefully executed. Finally, a bas-relief representing a human figure, nine feet high, the right hand elevated, and carrying in the left a branch with three flowers, resembling the poppy, was found in wall k (plan 2). I uncovered only the upper part of these sculptures, satisfied with proving their existence, without exposing them to the risk of injury, should my labours be at any time interrupted. Still no conjecture could be formed as to the nature of the buildings I was exploring.

The experiment had been fairly tried; there was no longer any doubt of the existence not only of sculptures and inscriptions, but even of large edifices in the interior of the mound of Nimroud. I lost no time, therefore, in acquainting Sir Stratford Canning with my discovery, and in urging the necessity of a Firman, or order from the Porte, which would prevent any future interference on the part of the authorities, or the inhabitants of the country.

It was now nearly Christmas, and as it was desirable to remove from the mound all the tombs which had been made by the Pasha's orders, and others, more genuine, which had since been found, I came to an understanding on the subject with Daoud Agha. I covered over the

---

[1] Wall t, in plan 2.
[2] Entrance to chamber BB, plan 3. [These lions were originally misreported to Canning as bulls; see 40637, 33 and 46.]

sculptures brought to light, and withdrew altogether from Nimroud, leaving an agent at Selamiyah.

On entering Mosul on the morning of the 18th of December, I found the whole population in a ferment of joy. A Tatar had that morning brought from Constantinople the welcome news that the Porte, at length alive to the wretched condition of the province, and to the misery of the inhabitants, had disgraced the governor, and had named Ismail Pasha, a young Major-General of the new school, to carry on affairs until Hafiz Pasha, who had been appointed to succeed Keritli Oglu, could reach his government.

Ismail Pasha, who had been for some time in command of the troops at Diarbekir, had gained a great reputation for justice among the Mussulmans, and for tolerance amongst the Christians. Consequently his appointment had given much satisfaction to the people of Mosul, who were prepared to receive him with demonstration. However, he slipped into the town during the night, some time before he had been expected. On the following morning a change had taken place at the Serai, and Mohammed Pasha, and his followers, were reduced to extremities. The dragoman of the Consulate, who had business to transact with the late Governor, found him sitting in a dilapidated chamber, through which the rain penetrated without hindrance. 'Thus it is,' said he, 'with God's creatures. Yesterday all those dogs were kissing my feet; to-day every one, and every thing, falls upon me, even the rain!'[1]

During these events the state of the country rendered the continuation of my researches at Nimroud almost impossible. I determined, therefore, to proceed to Baghdad, to make arrangements for the removal of the sculptures at a future period, and to consult generally with Major Rawlinson, from whose experience and knowledge I could derive the most valuable assistance. A raft having been constructed, I started with Mr. Hector, a gentleman from Baghdad, who had visited me at Nimroud, and reached that city on the 24th of December.

---

[1] [This was only a temporary reverse in the affairs of Keritli Oglu. In September 1847 Layard wrote to H. J. Ross from Constantinople, mentioning 'that scamp Cretli Oglu, who is here, reinstated in his dignities' (38941, 13).]

III

ON MY RETURN to Mosul in the beginning of January [1846], I found Ismail Pasha installed in the government. He received me with courtesy, offered no opposition to the continuation of my researches at Nimroud, and directed the irregular troops stationed at Selamiyah to afford me every assistance and protection. The change since my departure had been as sudden as great. A few conciliatory acts on the part of the new Governor, an order from the Porte for an inquiry into the sums unjustly levied by the late Pasha, with a view to their repayment, and a promise of a diminution of taxes, had so far reassured and gained the confidence of those who had fled to the mountains and the desert, that the inhabitants of the villages were slowly returning to their homes; and even the Arab tribes, which were formerly accustomed to pasture their flocks in the districts of Mosul, were again pitching their tents on the banks of the Tigris. The diminished population of the province had been so completely discouraged by the repeated extortions of Keritli Oglu, that the fields had been left untilled. The villagers were now actively engaged, although the season was already far advanced, in sowing grain of various kinds. The palace was filled with Kurdish chiefs and Arab Sheikhs, who had accepted the invitation of the new Pasha to visit the town, and were seeking investiture as heads of their respective tribes.

During my absence my agents had not been inactive. Several trenches had been opened in the great mound of Baasheikha; and fragments of sculpture and inscriptions, with entire pottery and inscribed bricks, had been discovered there. At Karamles a platform of brickwork had been uncovered, and the Assyrian origin of the ruin was proved by the inscription on the bricks, which contained the name of the Khorsabad king.

I rode to Nimroud on the 17th of January, having first engaged a party of Nestorian Chaldæans to accompany me.

The change that had taken place in the face of the country during my absence, was no less remarkable than that which I had found in the political state of the province. To me they were both equally agreeable and welcome. The rains, which had fallen almost incessantly from the day of my departure for Baghdad, had rapidly brought forward the vegetation of spring. The mound was no longer an arid and barren heap; its surface and its sides were covered with verdure. From the summit of the pyramid my eye ranged, on one side, over a broad level, enclosed by the Tigris and the Zab; on the other, over a low undulating country bounded by the snow-capped mountains of Kurdistan; but it was no longer the dreary waste I had left a month before; the landscape was clothed in green, the black tents of the Arabs chequered the plain of Nimroud, and their numerous flocks pastured on the distant hills. The Jehesh and Shemutti Arabs had returned to their villages, and were now engaged in cultivating the soil. Even on the mound the plough opened its furrows, and corn was sown over the palaces of the Assyrian kings.

Security had been restored, and Nimroud offered a more convenient and more agreeable residence than Selamiyah. Hiring, therefore, from the owners three huts, which had been hastily built in the outskirts of the village, I removed to my new dwelling place. A few rude chairs, a table, and a wooden bedstead, formed the whole of my furniture. The servants constructed a rude kitchen, and the grooms shared the stalls with the horses. Mr. Hormuzd Rassam, the brother of the British Vice-Consul, came to reside with me, and undertook the daily payment of the workmen and the domestic arrangements.

I had now uncovered [parts of five walls] belonging to the palace in the S.W. corner of the mound (plan 2). In the centre of the mound I had discovered the remains of the two winged bulls[1]; in the N.W. palace (plan 3), the great hall Y, the chamber A, and the two small winged lions forming the entrance to chamber BB. The only additional bas-reliefs were two [from the S.W. palace]. The slab on which these bas-reliefs occurred had been reduced in size, to the injury of the sculpture, and had evidently belonged to another building. The slabs on either side of it bore the usual inscription, and the whole had been so much injured by fire that they could not be moved.

My labours had scarcely been resumed when I received information

---

[1] [This is not quite accurately stated. Layard found the first bull between 19th and 24th January (40637, 37), but did not discover the second until 9th February, after the stoppage occasioned by the Cadi, still to be related (40637, 42).]

that the Cadi of Mosul was endeavouring to stir up the people against me, chiefly on the plea that I was carrying away treasure; and, what was worse, finding inscriptions which proved that the Franks once held the country and upon the evidence of which they intended immediately to resume possession of it, exterminating all true believers. These stories, however absurd they may appear, rapidly gained ground in the town. A representation was ultimately made by the Ulema to Ismail Pasha; and as he expressed a wish to see me, I rode to Mosul. He was not, he said, influenced by the Cadi or the Mufti, nor did he believe the absurd tales[1] which they had spread abroad. I should shortly see how he intended to treat these troublesome fellows; but he thought it prudent at present to humour them, and made it a personal request that I would, for the time, suspend the excavations. I consented with regret; and once more returned to Nimroud without being able to gratify the ardent curiosity I felt to explore further the extraordinary building, the nature of which was still a mystery to me.

The Abou Salman Arabs, who encamp around Nimroud, are known for their thieving propensities, and might have caused me some annoyance. Thinking it prudent, therefore, to conciliate their chief, I rode over one morning to their principal encampment. Sheikh Abd-ur-rahman received me at the entrance of his capacious tent of black goat-hair, which was crowded with his relations, followers, and strangers, who were enjoying his hospitality. He was one of the handsomest Arabs I ever saw; tall, robust, and well-made, with a countenance in which intelligence was no less marked than courage and resolution. On his head he wore a turban of dark linen, from under which a many-coloured handkerchief fell over his shoulders; his dress was a simple white shirt, descending to the ankles, and an Arab cloak thrown loosely over it. Unlike Arabs in general, he had shaved his beard; and, although he could scarcely be much beyond forty, I observed that the little hair which could be distinguished from under his turban was grey. He received me with every demonstration of hospitality, and led me to the upper place, divided by a goat-hair curtain from the harem. The tent was capacious; half was appropriated for the women, the rest formed the place of reception, and was at the same time occupied by two favourite mares and a colt. A few camels were kneeling on the grass around and the horses of the strangers were tied by the halter to the tent-pins. From the carpets and cushions, which were spread for me,

---

[1] [For fuller details of these 'absurd tales' see Layard's letter to Canning of 26th January 1846 (40637, 40–41).]

stretched on both sides a long line of men of the most motley appearance, seated on the bare ground. The Sheikh himself, as is the custom in some of the tribes, to show his respect for his guest, placed himself at the furthest end; and could only be prevailed upon, after many excuses and protestations, to share the carpet with me. In the centre of the group, near a small fire of camel's dung, crouched a half-naked Arab, engaged alternately in blowing up the expiring embers, and in pounding the roasted coffee in a copper mortar, ready to replenish the huge pots which stood near him.

After the customary compliments had been exchanged with all around, one of my attendants beckoned to the Sheikh, who left the tent to receive the presents I had brought to him,—a silk gown and a supply of coffee and sugar. He dressed himself in his new attire, and returned to the assembly. 'Inshallah,' said I, 'we are now friends, although scarcely a month ago you came over the Zab on purpose to appropriate the little property I am accustomed to carry about me.' 'Wallah, Beh,' he replied, 'you say true, we are friends; but listen: the Arabs either sit down and serve his Majesty the Sultan, or they eat from others, as others would eat from them. These lands were given [to my tribe] in return for the services we rendered the Turks in keeping back the Tai and the Shammar, who crossed the rivers to plunder the villages. All the great men of the Abou Salman perished in encounters with the Bedouin, and Injeh Bairakdar, Mohammed Pasha, upon whom God has had mercy, acknowledged our fidelity, and treated us with honour. When that blind dog, the son of the Cretan (May curses fall upon him!) came to Mosul, I waited upon him, as it is usual for the Sheikh; what did *he* do? Did he give me the cloak of honour? No; he put me, an Arab of the tribe of Zobeide, a tribe which had fought with the Prophet, into the public stocks. For forty days my heart melted away in a damp cell, and I was exposed to every variety of torture. Look at these hairs,' continued he, lifting up his turban, 'they turned white in that time, and I must now shave my beard, a shame amongst the Arabs. I was released at last; but how did I return to the tribe?—a beggar, unable to kill a sheep for my guests. He took my mares, my flocks, and my camels, as the price of my liberty. Now tell me, O Bey, in the name of God, if the Osmanlis have eaten from me and my guests, shall I not eat from them and theirs?'

The fate of Abd-ur-rahman had been such as he described it; and so had fared several chiefs of the desert and of the mountains. It was not surprising that these men, proud of their origin, and accustomed to the independence of a wandering life, had revenged themselves upon the unfortunate inhabitants of the villages, who had no less cause to complain than themselves.

It was nearly the middle of February[1] before I thought it prudent to make fresh experiments among the ruins. A trench was first opened at right angles to the centre of wall *k* [in the S.W. palace] (plan 2), and we speedily found the wall *q*. All the slabs were sculptured, and uninjured by fire; but unfortunately had been half destroyed by long exposure to the atmosphere. It was evident from the costume, the ornaments, and the nature of the relief, that these sculptures did not belong either to the same building, or to the same period as those previously discovered. I recognised in them the style of Khorsabad, and in the inscriptions particular forms in the character, which were used in the inscriptions of that monument. Still the slabs were not *in situ*: they had been brought from elsewhere, and I was even more perplexed than I had hitherto been.

The most perfect of the bas-reliefs (No. 1) was in many respects interesting. It represented a king, distinguished by his high conical tiara, standing over a prostrate warrior; his right hand elevated, and the left supported by a bow. The figure at his feet, probably a captive enemy or rebel, wore a pointed cap. An eunuch holds a fly-flapper or fan over the head of the king, who appears to be conversing or performing some ceremony with a figure standing in front of him; probably his vizir or minister.[2] Behind this personage, who differs from the King by his head-dress,—a simple fillet round the temple,—are two attendants, the first an eunuch, the second a bearded figure, half of which was continued on the adjoining slab. This bas-relief was separated from a second above, by a band of inscriptions; the upper sculpture was almost totally destroyed, and I could with difficulty trace upon it the forms of horses, and horsemen. The rest of the wall, which had completely disappeared in some places, had been composed of gigantic winged figures, sculptured in low relief. They were almost entirely defaced.

Several trenches carried to the west of wall *q*, and at right angles with it, led me to walls *s* and *t*. The sculptured slabs, of which they were built, were not better preserved than others in this part of the mound. I could only distinguish the lower part of gigantic figures; some had been purposely defaced by a sharp instrument; others, from long

---

[1] [9th February, 1846; see 40637, 42–43.]

[2] I shall in future always designate this figure, which frequently occurs in the Assyrian bas-reliefs, the King's Vizir or Minister.

exposure, had been worn almost smooth. Inscriptions were carried across the slabs over the drapery, but were interrupted when a naked limb occurred, and resumed beyond it. Such is generally the case when, as in the older palace of Nimroud, inscriptions are engraved over a figure.

No sculptures had hitherto been discovered in a perfect state of preservation, and only one or two could bear removal. I determined, therefore, to abandon [the building in] this corner, and to resume excavations [in the north-west of the mound] near the chamber first opened (chamber A, plan 3), where the slabs had in no way been injured.

As these ruins occurred on the edge of the mound, it was probable that they had been more exposed than the rest, and consequently had sustained more injury than other parts of the building. As there was a ravine running far into the mound, apparently formed by the winter rains, I determined to open a trench in the centre of it. In two days the workmen reached the top of a slab which appeared to be both well preserved, and to be still standing in its original position. On the south side I discovered, to my great satisfaction, two human figures, considerably above the natural size, sculptured in low relief, and still exhibiting all the freshness of a recent work. In a few hours the earth and rubbish were completely removed from the face of the slab, no part of which had been injured. The figures appeared to represent divinities, presiding over the seasons, or over particular religious ceremonies. The limbs were delineated with peculiar accuracy, and the muscles and bones faithfully, though somewhat too strongly, marked. An inscription ran across the sculpture.

To the west of this slab, and fitting to it, was a corner-stone ornamented with flowers and scroll-work, tastefully arranged, and resembling in detail those graven on the injured tablet, near entrance _d_ of the south-west building.[1] I recognised at once from whence many of the sculptures, employed in the construction of that edifice, had been brought; and it was evident that I had at length discovered the earliest palace of Nimroud.

The corner stone led me to a figure of singular form.[2] A human body clothed in robes similar to those of the winged men already described, was surmounted by the head of an eagle or of a vulture. The curved beak, of considerable length, was half open, and displayed a narrow

[1] [See above, p. 83.]
[2] No. 32, chamber B, plan 3. [For Layard's drawing of the figure, see opposite.]

Eagle-headed figure

pointed tongue, which was still coloured with red paint. On the shoulders fell the usual curled and bushy hair of the Assyrian images, and a comb of feathers rose on the top of the head. Two wings sprang from the back, and in either hand was the square vessel and fir-cone.

On all these figures paint could be faintly distinguished, particularly on the hair, beard, eyes, and sandals. The slabs on which they were sculptured had sustained no injury, and could be without difficulty packed and moved to any distance. There could no longer be any doubt that they formed part of a chamber, and that, to explore it completely, I had only to continue along the wall, now partly uncovered.

On the morning following these discoveries,[1] I rode to the encampment of Sheikh Abd-ur-rahman, and was returning to the mound, when I saw two Arabs of his tribe urging their mares to the top of their speed. On approaching me they stopped. 'Hasten, O Bey,' exclaimed one of them—'hasten to the diggers, for they have found Nimrod himself. Wallah, it is wonderful, but it is true! we have seen him with our eyes. There is no God but God;' and both joining in this pious exclamation, they galloped off, without further words, in the direction of the tents.

On reaching the ruins I descended into the new trench, and found the workmen, who had already seen me as I approached, standing near a heap of baskets and cloaks. Whilst Awad advanced and asked for a present to celebrate the occasion, the Arabs withdrew the screen they had hastily constructed, and disclosed an enormous human head sculptured in full out of the alabaster of the country. They had uncovered the upper part of a figure, the remainder of which was still buried in the earth. I saw at once that the head must belong to a winged lion or bull, similar to those of Khorsabad and Persepolis. It was in admirable preservation. The expression was calm, yet majestic, and the outline of the features showed a freedom and knowledge of art, scarcely to be looked for in the works of so remote a period. The cap had three horns, and, unlike that of the human-headed bulls hitherto found in Assyria, was rounded and without ornament at the top.

I was not surprised that the Arabs had been amazed and terrified at this apparition. This gigantic head, blanched with age, thus rising from the bowels of the earth, might well have belonged to one of those fearful beings which are pictured in the traditions of the country, as appearing to mortals, slowly ascending from the regions below. One of the workmen, on catching the first glimpse of the monster, had thrown

[1] [20th February, 1846; see 40637, 47.]

Discovery of gigantic Head

down his basket and had run off towards Mosul as fast as his legs could carry him. I learnt this with regret, as I anticipated the consequences.

Whilst I was superintending the removal of the earth, which still clung to the sculpture, and giving directions for the continuation of the work, a noise of horsemen was heard, and presently Abd-ur-rahman, followed by half his tribe, appeared on the edge of the trench. When they beheld the head they all cried together, 'There is no God but God, and Mohammed is his Prophet!' It was some time before the Sheikh could be prevailed upon to descend into the pit, and convince himself that the image he saw was of stone. 'This is not the work of men's hands,' exclaimed he, 'but of those infidel giants of whom the Prophet

H   99

—peace be with him!—has said that they were higher than the tallest date tree; this is one of the idols which Noah—peace be with him!—cursed before the flood.' In this opinion, the result of a careful examination, all the bystanders concurred.

I now ordered a trench to be dug due south from the head, in the expectation of finding a corresponding figure, and before night-fall reached the object of my search about twelve feet distant. Engaging two or three men to sleep near the sculptures, I returned to the village, and celebrated the day's discovery by a slaughter of sheep, of which all the Arabs near partook. As some wandering musicians chanced to be at Selamiyah, I sent for them, and dances were kept up during the greater part of the night. On the following morning Arabs from the other side of the Tigris, and the inhabitants of the surrounding villages, congregated on the mound. Even the women could not repress their curiosity, and came in crowds, with their children, from afar. My Cawass was stationed during the day in the trench, into which I would not allow the multitude to descend.

As I had expected, the report of the discovery of the gigantic head, carried by the terrified Arab to Mosul, had thrown the town into commotion. He had scarcely checked his speed before reaching the bridge. Entering breathless into the bazaars, he announced to everyone he met that Nimrod had appeared. The news soon got to the ears of the Cadi, who, anxious for a fresh opportunity to annoy me, called the Mufti and the Ulema together, to consult upon this unexpected occurrence. Their deliberations ended in a procession to the Governor, and a formal protest, on the part of the Mussulmans of the town, against proceedings so directly contrary to the laws of the Koran. The Cadi had no distinct idea whether the bones of the mighty hunter had been uncovered, or only his image; nor did Ismail Pasha very clearly remember whether Nimrod was a true-believing prophet, or an Infidel. I consequently received a somewhat unintelligible message from his Excellency, to the effect that the remains should be treated with respect, and be by no means further disturbed; that he wished the excavations to be stopped at once, and desired to confer with me on the subject.

I called upon him accordingly, and had some difficulty in making him understand the nature of my discovery. As he requested me to discontinue my operations until the sensation in the town had somewhat subsided, I returned to Nimroud, and dismissed the workmen, retaining only two men to dig leisurely along the walls without giving cause for further interference. I ascertained by the end of March, the

Winged Human-headed lion

existence of a second pair of winged human-headed lions[1], differing
from those previously discovered in form, the human shape being
continued to the waist and furnished with arms. They were about
twelve feet in height, and the same number in length. The body and
limbs were admirably portrayed; the muscles and bones, although
strongly developed to display the strength of the animal, showed at
the same time a correct knowledge of its anatomy and form. Expanded
wings sprang from the shoulder and spread over the back; a knotted
girdle, ending in tassels, encircled the loins. These sculptures, forming
an entrance, were partly in full and partly in relief. The head and fore-

[1] Entrance to chamber B, plan 3.

part, facing the chamber, were in full; but only one side of the rest of the slab was sculptured, the back being placed against the wall of sun-dried bricks. That the spectator might have both a perfect front and side view of the figures, they were furnished with five legs; two were carved on the end of the slab to face the chamber, and three on the side. The relief of the body and three limbs was high and bold, and the slab was covered, in all parts not occupied by the image, with inscriptions in the cuneiform character. These magnificent specimens of Assyrian art were in perfect preservation; the most minute lines in the details of the wings and in the ornaments had been retained with their original fresh-ness. Not a character was wanting in the inscriptions.

I used to contemplate for hours these mysterious emblems, and muse over their intent and history.

During the month of March I received visits from the principal Sheikhs of the Jebour Arabs, whose tribes had now partly crossed the Tigris, and were pasturing their flocks in the neighbourhood of Nim-roud, or cultivating millet on the banks of the river. Their encamping grounds are on the banks of the Khabour, from its junction with the Euphrates to its source at Ras-el-Ain. They were suddenly attacked and plundered a year or two ago by the Aneyza; and being compelled to leave their haunts, took refuge in the district around Mosul. The Pasha, at first, received them well; but learning that several mares of pure Arab blood still remained with the Sheikhs, he determined to seize them; and a body of irregular troops was accordingly sent for the purpose. A conflict ensued, in which the Pasha's horsemen were com-pletely defeated. A more formidable expedition, including regular troops and artillery, now marched against them. But the Arabs were again victorious, and repulsed the Turks with considerable loss. They fled, nevertheless, to the desert, where they had since been wandering in great misery, joining with the Shammar and other tribes in plunder-ing the villages of the Pashalic. On learning the policy pursued by Ismail Pasha, dying with hunger, they had returned to arable lands on the banks of the river; where, by an imperfect and toilsome fashion of irrigation, they could during the summer months raise a small supply of millet to satisfy their immediate necessities.

The Jebour were at this time divided into three branches, obeying different Sheikhs. The names of the three chiefs were Abd'rubbou, Mohammed Emin, and Mohammed ed Dagher. Although all three visited me at Nimroud, it was the first with whom I was best acquainted, and who rendered me most assistance. I thought it necessary to give them each small presents, a silk dress, or an embroidered cloak, with a pair of capacious boots, as in case of any fresh disturbances in the country it would be as well to be on friendly terms with the tribe. The intimacy, however, which sprang from these acts of generosity, was not in all respects of the most desirable or convenient nature. The Arab compliment of 'my house is your house' was accepted more literally than I had intended, and I was seldom free from a large addition to my establishment. A Sheikh and a dozen of his attendants were generally installed in my huts, whilst their mares were tied at every door. My fame even reached the mountains, and one day on returning from Mosul, I found a Kurdish chief, with a numerous suite, in the full enjoyment of my premises. The whole party were dressed in the height of fashion. Every colour had received due consideration in their attire. Their arms were of very superior design and workmanship, their turbans of adequate height and capacity. The chief enjoyed a multiplicity of titles, political, civil, and ecclesiastical: he was announced as Mullah Ali Effendi Bey[1]; and brought, as a token of friendship, a skin of honey and cheese, a Kurdish carpet, and some horse trappings.

He had evidently some motives sufficiently powerful to overcome his very marked religious prejudices—motives which certainly could not be traced to disinterested friendship. Like Shylock, he would have said, had he not been of too good breeding, 'I will buy with you, sell with you, talk with you, walk with you, and so following; but I will not eat with you, drink with you, nor pray with you'; for he sat in solitary sanctity to eat his own pillaf, drank out of a reserved jar, and sought the dwellings of the true believers to spread his prayer-carpet.

As my guest was the chief of a large tribe of nomad Kurds who inhabit the mountains in the neighbourhood of Rowandiz during the summer, and the plains around Arbela in winter, I did not feel the necessity of conciliating him as I had done the Arab Sheikhs encamping near Nimroud, nor did I desire to encourage visits from persons of his sanctity and condition. I allowed him therefore to remain without making any return for his presents, or understanding the hints on the subject he took frequent occasion to drop. At length, on the second evening, his secretary asked for an interview. 'The Mullah Effendi,' said he, 'will leave your Lordship's abode to-morrow. Praise be to God, the most disinterested and sincere friendship has been established between you, and it is suitable that your Lordship should take this opportunity of

---

[1] These double titles are very common amongst the Kurds, as Beder Khan Bey, Mir Nur Ullah Bey, etc.

giving a public testimony of your regard for his Reverence. Not that he desires to accept anything from you, but it would be highly gratifying to him to prove to his tribe that he has met with a friendly reception from so distinguished a person as yourself, and to spread through the mountains reports of your generosity.' 'I regret,' answered I, 'that the trifling differences in matters of religion which exist between us, should preclude the possibility of the Effendi's accepting anything from me; for I am convinced that, however amiable and friendly he may be, a man of his sanctity would not do anything forbidden by the law. I am at a loss, therefore, to know how I can meet his wishes.' 'Although,' he rejoined, 'there might perhaps be some difficulty on that score, yet it could be, I hope, overcome. Moreover, there are his attendants; they are not so particular as he is, and, thank God, we are all one. To each of them you might give a pair of yellow boots and a silk dress; besides, if you chance to have any pistols or daggers, they would be satisfied with them. As for me, you might show your approbation of my devotedness to your service, by giving me white linen for a turban, and a pair of breeches. The Effendi, however, would not object to a set of razors, because the handles are of ivory and the blades of steel; and it is stated in the Hadith that those materials do not absorb moisture[1]; besides, he would feel himself obliged if you could lend him a small sum—five purses, for instance, for which he would give you a note of hand.' 'It is very unfortunate,' I replied, 'that there is not a bazaar in the village. I will make a list of all the articles you specify as proper to be given to the attendants and to yourself. But these can only be procured in Mosul, and two days would elapse before they could reach me. I could not think of taking up so much of the valuable time of the Mullah Effendi, whose absence must already have been sorely felt by his tribe. With regard to the money, for which, God forbid that I should think of taking any note of hand (praise be to God! we are on much too good terms for such formalities), and to the razors, I think it would give more convincing proofs of my esteem for the Effendi, if I were myself to return his welcome visit, and be the bearer of suitable presents.' Finding that a more satisfactory answer could not be obtained, the secretary retired with evident marks of disappointment in his face. After staying four days, the Mullah Effendi Bey and his attendants,

---

[1] Some sects make a distinction between those things which may be used or touched by a Mussulman after they have been in the hands of a Christian, and those which may not; this distinction depends upon whether they be, according to their doctors, absorbents or non-absorbents. If they are supposed to absorb moisture, they become unclean after contact with an unbeliever.

about twenty in number, mounted their horses and rode away. I was no more troubled with visits from Kurdish chiefs.

The middle of March in Mesopotamia is the brightest epoch of spring. A new change had come over the face of the plain of Nimroud. Its pasture lands, known as the 'Jaif', are renowned for their rich and luxuriant herbage. In times of quiet, the studs of the Pasha and of the Turkish authorities, with the horses of the cavalry and of the inhabitants of Mosul, are sent here to graze. Day by day they arrived in long lines. The Shemutti and Jehesh left their huts, and encamped on the greensward which surrounded the villages. The plain, as far as the eye could reach, was studded with the white pavilions of the Hytas and the black tents of the Arabs. Picketed around them were innumerable horses in gay trappings, struggling to release themselves from the bonds, which restrained them from ranging over the green pastures.

Flowers of every hue enamelled the meadows; not thinly scattered over the grass as in northern climes, but in such thick and gathering clusters that the whole plain seemed a patchwork of many colours. The dogs, as they returned from hunting, issued from the long grass dyed yellow, or blue, according to the flowers through which they had last forced their way.

The villages of Naifa and Nimroud were deserted, and I remained alone with Said and my servants. The houses now began to swarm with vermin; we no longer slept under the roofs, and it was time to follow the example of the Arabs. I accordingly encamped on the edge of a large pond on the outskirts of Nimroud. Said accompanied me; and Salah, his young wife, a bright-eyed Arab girl, built up his shed, and watched and milked his diminutive flock of sheep and goats.

I was surrounded by Arabs, who had either pitched their tents, or, too poor to buy the black goat-hair cloth of which they are made, had erected small huts of reeds and dry grass.

In the evening after the labour of the day, I often sat at the door of my tent, and giving myself up to the full enjoyment of that calm and repose which are imparted to the senses by such scenes as these, gazed listlessly on the varied groups before me. As the sun went down behind the low hills which separate the river from the desert—even their rocky sides had struggled to emulate the verdant clothing of the plain—its receding rays were gradually withdrawn, like a transparent veil of light, from the landscape. Over the pure, cloudless sky was the glow of the last light. The great mound threw its dark shadow far across the plain. In the distance, and beyond the Zab, Keshaf, another venerable ruin, rose indistinctly into the evening mist. Still more distant, and still more indistinct, was a solitary hill overlooking the ancient city of Arbela. The Kurdish mountains, whose snowy summits cherished the dying sunbeams, yet struggled with the twilight. The bleating of sheep and lowing of cattle, at first faint, became louder as the flocks returned from their pastures, and wandered amongst the tents. Girls hurried over the greensward to seek their fathers' cattle, or crouched down to milk those which had returned alone to their well-remembered folds. Some were coming from the river bearing the replenished pitchers on their heads or shoulders; others, no less graceful in their form, and erect in their carriage, were carrying the heavy load of long grass which they had cut in the meadows. Sometimes a party of horsemen might have been seen in the distance slowly crossing the plain, the tufts of ostrich feathers which topped their long spears showing darkly against the evening sky. They would ride up to my tent, and give me the usual salutation, 'Peace be with you, O Bey,' or, 'Allah Aienak, God help you.' Then driving the end of their lances into the ground, they would spring from their mares, and fasten their halters to the still quivering weapons. Seating themselves on the grass, they related deeds of war and plunder, or speculated on the site of the tents of Sofuk, until the moon rose, when they vaulted into their saddles, and took the way of the desert.

The plain now glittered with innumerable fires. As the night advanced, they vanished one by one, until the landscape was wrapped in darkness and in silence, only disturbed by the barking of the Arab dog.

Abd-ur-rahman rode to my tent one morning, and offered to take me to a remarkable cutting in the rock, which he described as the work of Nimrod, the Giant. The Arabs call it 'Negoub', or, The Hole. We were two hours in reaching the place, as we hunted gazelles and hares by the way. A tunnel, bored through the rock, opens by two low arched outlets upon the river. It is of considerable length, and is continued for about a mile by a deep channel, also cut out of the rock, but open at the top. I suspected at once that this was an Assyrian work, and, on examining the interior of the tunnel, I discovered a slab covered with cuneiform characters, which had fallen from a platform, and had been wedged in a crevice of the rock. With much difficulty I succeeded in ascertaining that an inscription was also cut on the back of the tablet. From the darkness of the place, I could scarcely copy even the few characters which had resisted the wear of centuries. Some days after, others who had casually heard of my visit, and conjectured that some

Assyrian remains might have been found there, sent a party of workmen to the spot; who, finding the slab, broke it into pieces, in their attempt to displace it. This wanton destruction of the tablet is much to be regretted; as, from the fragment of the inscription copied, I can perceive that it contained an important, and, to me, new genealogical list of kings. I had intended to remove the stone carefully, and had hoped, by placing it in a proper light, to ascertain accurately the forms of the various characters upon it. This was not the only loss I had to complain of, from the jealousy and competition of rivals.

The tunnel of Negoub is undoubtedly a remarkable work. Its object is rather uncertain[1]. It may have been cut to lead the waters of the Zab into the surrounding country for irrigation; or it may have been the termination of the great canal, which is still to be traced by a double range of lofty mounds, near the ruins of Nimroud, and which may have united the Tigris with the neighbouring river, and thus fertilised a large tract of land. In either case the level of the two rivers must have changed considerably since the period of its construction. At present Negoub is above the Zab, except at the time of the highest flood in the spring, and then water is only found in the mouth of the tunnel; all other parts having been much choked up with rubbish and river deposits.

[1] [On this tunnel, in relation to the irrigation of ancient Kalḫu (Calah), see most recently D. Oates, *Studies in the ancient history of Northern Iraq* (1968), 46–47.]

IV

THE OPERATIONS AT Nimroud having been completely suspended until orders could be received from Constantinople, I thought the time not inopportune to visit Sofuk, the Sheikh of the great Arab tribe of Shammar, which occupies nearly the whole of Mesopotamia. He had lately left the Khabour, and was now encamped near the western bank of the Tigris below its junction with the Zab, and consequently not far from Nimroud. I had two objects in going to his tents; in the first place I wished to obtain the friendship of the chief of a large tribe of Arabs, who would probably cross the river in the neighbourhood of the excavations during the summer, and might indulge, to my cost, in their plundering propensities; and, at the same time, I was anxious to visit the remarkable ruins of Al Hather, which I had only examined very hastily on my former journey.

Mr. Rassam (the Vice-Consul) and his wife, with several native gentleman of Mosul, Mussulmans and Christians, were induced to accompany me; and, as we issued from the gates of the town, I found myself at the head of a formidable party. Our tents, obtained from the Pasha, and our provisions and necessary furniture, were carried by a string of twelve camels. Mounted above these loads, and on donkeys, was an army of camel-drivers, tent-pitchers, and volunteers, ready for all services. There were, moreover, a few irregular horsemen, the Cawasses, the attendants of the Mosul gentlemen, the Mosul gentlemen themselves, and our own servants, all armed to the teeth. Ali Effendi, chief of the Mosul branch of the Omeree, or descendants of Omar, which had furnished several Pashas to the province, was our principal Mussulman friend. He was mounted on the Hedban, a well-known white Arab, beautiful in form and pure in blood, but now of great age. Close at his horse's heels followed a confidential servant; who, perched on a pack-saddle, seemed to roll from side to side on two small barrels, the use of which might have been an enigma, had they not emitted a very strong smell of raki. A Christian gentleman was wrapped up in cloaks and furs, and appeared to dread the cold, although the thermometer was at 100. The English lady[1] was equipped in riding-habit and hat. The two Englishmen, Mr. Ross and myself, wore a striking mixture of European and oriental raiments. Mosul ladies, in blue veils, their faces concealed by black horse-hair sieves, had been dragged to the top of piles of carpets and cushions, under which groaned their unfortunate mules. Greyhounds in leashes were led by Arabs on foot; whilst others played with strange dogs, who followed the caravan for change of air. The horsemen galloped round and round, now dashing into the centre of the crowd, throwing their horses on their haunches when at full speed, or discharging their guns and pistols into the air. A small flag with British colours was fastened to the top of a spear, and confided to a Cawass. Such was the motley caravan which left Mosul by the Bab el Top, where a crowd of women had assembled to witness the procession.

We took the road to the ruins of the monastery of Mar Elias, a place of pilgrimage for the Christians of Mosul, which we passed after an hour's ride. Evening set in before we could reach the desert, and we pitched our tents for the night on a lawn near a deserted village, about nine miles from the town.

On the following morning we soon emerged from the low limestone hills; which, broken into a thousand rocky valleys, form a barrier between the Tigris and the plains of Mesopotamia. We now found ourselves in the desert, or rather wilderness; for at this time of the year, nature could not disclose a more varied scene, or a more luxuriant vegetation. We trod on an interminable carpet, figured by flowers of every hue. Nor was water wanting; for the abundant rains had given reservoirs to every hollow, and to every ravine. Their contents, owing to the nature of the soil, were brackish, but not unwholesome. Clusters of black tents were scattered, and flocks of sheep and camels wandered over the plain. Those of our party who were well mounted urged their horses through the meadows, pursuing the herds of gazelles, or the wild boar, skulking in the long grass. Although such scenes as these may be described, the exhilaration caused by the air of the desert in spring, and the feeling of freedom arising from the contemplation of its boundless expanse, must have been experienced before they can be understood.

The first object we had in view was to discover the tents of Sofuk.

[1] [Matilda Rassam.]

The Sheikh had been lately exposed to demands on the part of the governors of Mosul and Baghdad; and, moreover, an open hostility to his authority had arisen amongst the Shammar tribes. He was consequently keeping out of sight, and seeking the most secluded spots in the desert to pitch his tents. We asked our way of the parties of Arab horsemen, whom we met roving over the plain; but received different answers from each. Some were ignorant; others fancied that our visit might be unacceptable, and endeavoured to deceive us.

About mid-day we found ourselves in the midst of extensive herds of camels. They belonged to the Haddedeen. The sonorous whoop of the Arab herdsmen resounded from all sides. A few horsemen were galloping about, driving back the stragglers, and directing the march of the leaders of the herd. Shortly after we came up with some families moving to a new place of encampment, and at their head I recognised my old antiquity hunter, Mormous. He no sooner perceived us than he gave orders to those who followed him, and of whom he was the chief, to pitch their tents. About fifteen tents were soon raised. A sheep was slaughtered in front of the one in which we sat; large wooden bowls of sour milk and platters of fresh butter were placed before us; fires of camel's dung were lighted; decrepit old women blew up the flames; the men cut the carcass into small pieces, and capacious cauldrons soon sent forth volumes of steam.

Mormous tended the sheep of Ali Effendi, our travelling companion, as well as his own.[1] The two were soon in discussion, as to the amount of butter and wool produced. Violent altercations arose on the subject of missing beasts. Heavy responsibilities, which the Effendi did not seem inclined to admit, were thrown upon the wolves. Some time elapsed before these vital questions were settled to the satisfaction of both parties; ears having been produced, oaths taken, and witnesses called, with the assistance of wolves and the rot, the diminution in the flocks was fully accounted for.

The sheep was now boiled. The Arabs pulled the fragments out of the cauldron, and laid them on wooden platters with their fingers. We helped ourselves after the same fashion. The servants succeeded to the dishes, which afterwards passed through the hands of the camel drivers

---

[1] It is customary for the inhabitants of Mosul possessing flocks to confide them to the Haddedeen Arabs, who take them into the desert during the winter and spring, and pasture them in the low hills to the east of the town during the summer and autumn. The produce of the sheep, the butter and wool, is divided between the owner and the Arab in charge of them; the sour milk, curds, etc., are left to the latter. In case of death the Arab brings the ears, and takes an oath that they belong to the missing animal.

and tent pitchers; and at last, denuded of all apparently edible portions, reached a strong party of expectant Arabs. The condition of the bones by the time they were delivered to a crowd of hungry dogs may easily be imagined.

We resumed our journey in the afternoon, preceded by Mormous, who volunteered to accompany us. As we rode over the plain, we fell in with the Sheikh of the Haddedeen, mounted on a fine mare, and followed by a large concourse of Arabs, driving their beasts of burden loaded with tents and furniture. He offered to conduct us to a branch of the Shammar, whose encampment we could reach before evening. We gladly accepted his offer, and he left his people to ride with us.

Before nightfall we came to a large encampment, and recognised in its chief one Khalaf, an Arab who frequently came to Mosul. His tribe, although a branch of the Shammar, usually encamp near the town; and avoid, if possible, the broils which divide their brethren. Strong enough to defend themselves against the attacks of other Arabs, and generally keeping at a sufficient distance from Mosul to be out of reach of the devastating arm of its governors, they have become comparatively wealthy. Their flocks of sheep and camels are numerous, and their Sheikhs boast some of the finest horses and mares in Mesopotamia.

Sheikh Khalaf received us with hospitality; sheep were immediately slaughtered, and we dismounted at his tent. Even his wives, amongst whom was a remarkably pretty Arab girl, came to us to gratify their curiosity by a minute examination of the Frank lady. As the intimacy, which began to spring up, was somewhat inconvenient, we directed our tents to be pitched at a distance from the encampment, by the side of a small stream. It was one of those calm and pleasant evenings, which in spring make a paradise of the desert. The breeze, bland and perfumed by the odour of flowers, came calmly over the plain. As the sun went down, countless camels and sheep wandered to the tents, and the melancholy call of the herdsmen rose above the bleating of the flocks. The Arabs led their prancing mares to the water; the colts, as they followed, played and rolled on the grass. I spread my carpet at a distance from the group, to enjoy uninterrupted the varied scene.

We had now reached the pasture-grounds of the Shammar, and Sheikh Khalaf declared that Sofuk's tents could not be far distant. We started early in the morning, and took the direction pointed out by Khalaf. Our view was bounded to the east by a rising ground. When we reached the summit, we looked down upon a plain, which appeared to swarm with moving objects. We had come upon the main body of the Shammar. We soon found ourselves in the midst of wide-spreading flocks of sheep and camels. As far as the eye could reach, to the right, to the left, and in front, still the same moving crowd. Long lines of asses and bullocks laden with black tents, huge cauldrons and variegated carpets; aged women and men, no longer able to walk, tied on the heap of domestic furniture; infants crammed into saddle-bags, their tiny heads thrust through the narrow opening, balanced on the animal's back by kids or lambs tied on the opposite side; young girls clothed only in the close-fitting Arab shirt, which displayed rather than concealed their graceful forms; mothers with their children on their shoulders; boys driving flocks of lambs; horsemen armed with their long tufted spears, scouring the plain on their fleet mares; riders urging their dromedaries with their short hooked sticks, and leading their high-bred steeds by the halter; colts galloping amongst the throng; high-born ladies seated in the centre of huge wings, which extend like those of a butterfly from each side of the camel's hump, and are no less gaudy and variegated. Such was the motley crowd through which we had to wend our way for several hours.

It was mid-day before we found a small party that had stopped, and were pitching their tents. A young chestnut mare belonging to the Sheikh, was one of the most beautiful creatures I ever beheld. Her limbs were in perfect symmetry; her ears long, slender and transparent; her nostrils, high, dilated and deep red; her neck gracefully arched, and her mane and tail of the texture of silk. We all involuntarily stopped to gaze at her. 'Say Masha-Allah,' exclaimed the owner, who seeing, not without pride, that I admired her, feared the effect of an evil eye. 'That I will,' answered I, 'and with pleasure; for, O Arab, you possess the jewel of the tribe.' He brought us a bowl of camel's milk, and directed us to the tents of Sofuk.

We had still two hours' ride before us, and when we reached the encampment of the Shammar Sheikh, our horses, as well as ourselves, were exhausted by the heat of the sun, and the length of the day's journey. The tents were pitched on a broad lawn in a deep ravine; they were scattered in every direction, and amongst them rose the white pavilions of the Turkish irregular cavalry. Ferhan, the son of Sofuk, and a party of horsemen, rode out to meet us as we approached, and led us to the tent of the chief, distinguished from the rest by its size, and the spears which were driven into the ground at its entrance. Sofuk advanced to receive us; he was followed by about three hundred

Arabs, including many of the principal Sheikhs of the tribe. In person he was short and corpulent, more like an Osmanli than an Arab; but his eye was bright and intelligent, his features regular, well formed and expressive. His dress differed but in the quality of the materials from that of his followers. A thick kerchief, striped with red, yellow, and blue, and fringed with long platted cords, was thrown over his head, and fell down his shoulders. It was held in its place, above the brow, by a band of spun camel's wool, tied at intervals by silken threads of many colours. A long white shirt, descending to the ankles, and a black and white cloak over it, completed his attire.

He led Rassam and myself to the top of the tent, where we seated ourselves on well-worn carpets. When all the party had found places, the words of welcome, which had been exchanged before we dismounted, were repeated. 'Peace be with you, O Bey! upon my head you are welcome; my house is your house,' exclaimed the Sheikh, addressing the stranger nearest to him. 'Peace be with you, O Sofuk! may God protect you!' was the answer, and similar compliments were made to every guest and by every person present. Whilst this ceremony, which took nearly half an hour, was going on, I had leisure to examine those who had assembled to meet us. Nearest to me was Ferhan, the Sheikh's son, a young man of handsome appearance and intelligent countenance, although the expression was neither agreeable nor attractive. From beneath the handkerchief thrown over his head hung his long black tresses platted into many tails. His teeth were white as ivory, like those of most Arabs. Beyond him sat a crowd of men of the most ferocious and forbidding exterior—warriors who had passed their lives in war and rapine, looking upon those who did not belong to their tribe as natural enemies, and preferring their wild freedom to all the riches of the earth.

The compliments having been at length finished, we conversed upon general topics. Coffee, highly drugged with odoriferous roots found in the desert, and with spices, a mixture for which Sofuk has long been celebrated, was handed round before we retired to our own tents.

Sofuk was descended from the Sheikhs, who brought the tribe from Nedjd. At the commencement of his career he had shared the chiefship with his uncle, after whose death he became the great Sheikh of the Shammar. From an early period he had been troublesome to the Turkish governors of the provinces on the Tigris and Euphrates; but gained the applause and confidence of the Porte by a spirited attack which he made upon the camp of Mohammed Ali Mirza, governor of Kirmanshah, when that prince was marching upon Baghdad and Mosul. After this exploit, to which was mainly attributed the safety of the Turkish cities, Sofuk was invested as Sheikh of the Shammar. At times, however, his tribes were accustomed to indulge their love of plunder, to sack villages and pillage caravans. He thus became formidable to the Turks, and was known as the King of the Desert. When Mehemet Reshid Pasha led his successful expedition into Kurdistan and Mesopotamia, Sofuk was amongst the chiefs whose power he sought to destroy. He knew that it would be useless to attempt it by force, and he consequently invited the Sheikh to his camp, on the pretence of investing him with the customary robe of honour. He was seized, and sent a prisoner to Constantinople. Here he remained some months, until, deceived by his promises, the Porte permitted him to return to his tribes. From that time his Arabs had generally been engaged in plunder, and all efforts to subdue them had failed. However, Nejris, the son of Sofuk's uncle, had appeared as his rival, and many branches of the Shammar had declared for the new Sheikh. This led to dissensions in the tribe; and, at the time of our visit, Sofuk, who had forfeited his popularity by many acts of treachery, was almost deserted by the Arabs. In this dilemma, he had applied to the Pasha of Mosul, and had promised to serve the Porte and to repress the depredations of the tribes, if he were assisted in re-establishing his authority. This state of things accounted for the presence of the white tents of the Hytas in the midst of the encampment.

His intercourse with the Turkish authorities, who must be conciliated by adequate presents before assistance can be expected from them; and the famine, which for the last two years had prevailed in the countries surrounding the desert, were not favourable to the domestic prosperity of Sofuk. The wealth and display, for which he was once renowned amongst the Arabs, had disappeared. A few months before, he had even sent to Mosul the silver ankle-rings of his favourite wife—the last resource—to be exchanged for corn. The furred cloaks, and embroidered robe, which he once wore, had not been replaced. The only carpet in his tent was the rag on which sat his principal guests; the rest squatted on the grass, or on the bare ground. He led the life of a pure Bedouin, from the commonest of whom he was only distinguished by the extent of his female establishment—always a weak point with the Sheikh. But even in his days of greatest prosperity, the meanest Arab looked upon him as his equal, addressed him as 'Sofuk',

View of Kala Tul

Procession of the Bull Beneath the Mound of Nimroud

and seated himself unbidden in his presence. Although the Arabs for convenience recognise one man as their chief; yet any unpopular or oppressive act on his part at once dissolves their allegiance; and they seek, in another, a more just and trustworthy leader. The chief is consequently always unwilling to risk his authority by asking for money or horses from those under him. He can only govern as long as he has the majority in his favour. He moves his tent; and others, who are not of his own family, follow him if they think proper. If his ascendency be great, and he can depend upon his majority, he may commit acts of bloodshed and oppression, becoming an arbitrary ruler; but such things are not forgotten by the Arabs, or seldom in the end go unpunished. Of this Sofuk himself was, as it will be seen hereafter, an example.

The usual Arab meal was brought to us soon after our arrival—large wooden bowls and platters filled with boiled fragments of mutton swimming in melted butter, and sour milk.

When our breakfast was removed, the chief of the Hytas called upon us. I had known him at Mosul; he was the commander of the irregular troops stationed at Selamiyah, and had been the instrument of the late Pasha in my first troubles, as he now good-humouredly avowed. He was called Ibrahim Agha, Goorgi Oglu, or the son of the Georgian, from his Christian origin. In his person he was short; his features were regular, and his eyes bright; his compressed brow, and a sneer, which continually curled his lip, well marked the character of the man. In appearance he was the type of his profession; his loose jacket, tight under vest, and capacious shalwars, were covered with a mass of gold embroidery; the shawls round his head and waist were of the richest texture and gayest colours; the arms in his girdle of the costliest description, and his horses and mares were renowned. His daring and courage had made him the favourite of Mohammed Pasha; and he was chiefly instrumental in reducing to obedience the turbulent inhabitants of Mosul and Kurdistan, during the struggle between that governor and the hereditary chiefs of the province. One of his exploits deserves notice. Some years ago there lived in the Island of Zakko, formed by the river Khabour, and in a castle of considerable strength, a Kurdish Bey of great power and influence. His resistance to the authority of the Porte called for the interference of Mohammed Pasha, but all attempts to seize him and reduce his castle had failed. At the time of my first visit to Mesopotamia he still lived as an independent chief, and I enjoyed for a night his hospitality. He was one of the last in this part of

Kurdistan who kept up the ancient customs of the feudal chieftains. His spacious hall, hung around with arms of all kinds, with the spreading antlers of the stag and the long knotted horns of the ibex, was filled every evening with guests and strangers. After sunset the floor was covered with dishes overflowing with various messes. The Bey sat on cushions at the top of the hall, and by him were placed the most favoured guests. After dinner he retired to his harem; every one slept where it was most convenient to himself, and rising at daybreak, went his way without questions from his host. The days of the chief were spent in war and plunder, and half the country had claims of blood against him. 'Will no one deliver me from that Kurdish dog?' exclaimed Mohammed Pasha one day in his salamlik, after an ineffectual attempt to reduce Zakko; 'By God and his Prophet, the richest cloak of honour shall be for him who brings me his head.' Ibrahim Agha, who was standing amongst the Pasha's courtiers, heard the offer and left the room. Assembling a few of his bravest followers, he took the road to the mountains. Concealing all his men, but six or eight, in the gardens outside the small town of Zakko, he entered after nightfall the castle of the Kurdish chief. He was received as a guest, and the customary dishes of meat were placed before him. After he had eaten he rose from his seat, and advancing towards his host, fired his long pistol within a few feet of the breast of the Bey, and drawing his sabre, severed the head from the body. The Kurds, amazed at this unparalleled audacity, offered no resistance. A signal from the roof was answered by the men outside; the innermost recesses of the castle were rifled, and the Georgian returned to Mosul with the head and wealth of the Kurdish chieftain.

But this is not the last deed of daring of Ibrahim Agha: Sofuk himself, now his host, was destined likewise to become his victim.

After the Hyta-bashi had retired, Sofuk came to our tents and remained with us the greater part of the day. He was dejected and sad. He bewailed his poverty, and confessed, with tears, that his tribe was fast deserting him. Whilst conversing on these subjects, two Sheikhs rode into the encampment, and hearing that the chief was with us, they fastened their high-bred mares at the door of our tent and seated themselves on our carpets. They had been amongst the tribes to ascertain the feeling of the Shammar towards Sofuk, of whom they were the devoted adherents. One was a man of forty, blackened by long exposure to the desert sun, and of a savage and sanguinary countenance. His companion was a youth, his features were so delicate and feminine, and his eyes so bright, that he might have been taken for a woman; the deception would not have been lessened by a profusion of black hair which fell, platted into numerous tresses, on his breast and shoulders. The young man's enthusiasm and devotedness knew no bounds. He threw himself upon Sofuk, and clinging to his neck covered his cheek and beard with kisses. When the chief had disengaged himself, his follower seized the edge of his garment, and sobbed violently as he held it to his lips. 'I entreat thee, O Sofuk!' he exclaimed, 'say but the word; by thine eyes, by thy beard, by the Prophet, order it, and this sword shall find the heart of Nejris, whether he escape into the farthest corner of the desert, or be surrounded by all the warriors of the tribe.' But it was too late, and Sofuk saw that his influence in the tribe was fast declining.

Mrs. Rassam, [who had been taken to the tent of the women,] having returned from her visit, described her reception. I must endeavour to convey to the reader some idea of the domestic establishment of a great Arab Sheikh. Sofuk, at the time of our visit, was the husband of three wives. It was one of Sofuk's weaknesses, arising either from a desire to impress the Arabs with a notion of his greatness and power, or from a partiality to the first stage of married life, to take a new partner nearly every month; and at the end of that period to divorce her, and marry her to one of his attendants. The happy man thus lived in a continual honeymoon. Of the three ladies now forming his harem, the chief was Amsha, a lady celebrated in the song of every Arab of the desert, for her beauty and noble blood. She was daughter of Hassan, Sheikh of the Tai, a tribe tracing its origin from the remotest antiquity. Sofuk had carried her away by force from her father; but had always treated her with great respect. From her rank and beauty she had earned the title of 'Queen of the Desert.' Her form, traceable through the thin shirt which she wore like other Arab women, was well proportioned and graceful. She was tall in stature, and fair in complexion. Her features were regular, and her eyes dark and brilliant. She had undoubtedly claims to more than ordinary beauty; to the Arabs she was perfection, for all the resources of their art had been exhausted to complete what nature had begun. Her lips were dyed deep blue, her eyebrows were continued in indigo until they united over the nose, her cheeks and forehead were spotted with beauty-marks, her eyelashes darkened by kohl; and on her legs and bosom could be seen the tattooed ends of flowers and fanciful ornaments, which were carried in festoons and network over her whole body. Hanging from each ear, and reaching to her waist, was an enormous earring of gold, terminating in a tablet of the same material, carved and ornamented with four turquoises. Her nose was also adorned with a prodigious gold ring, set with jewels, of such ample dimensions that it covered the mouth, and was to be removed when the lady ate. Ponderous rows of strung beads, Assyrian cylinders, fragments of coral, agates, and parti-coloured stones, hung from her neck; loose silver rings encircled her wrists and ankles, making a loud jingling as she walked. Over her blue shirt was thrown, when she issued from her tent, a coarse striped cloak, and a common black handkerchief was tied round her head.

Her ménage combined, if the old song be true, the domestic and the queenly, and was carried on with a nice appreciation of economy. The immense sheet of black goat-hair canvass, which formed the tent, was supported by twelve or fourteen stout poles, and was completely open on one side. Between the centre poles were placed, upright and close to one another, large goat-hair sacks, filled with rice, corn, barley, coffee, and other household stuff; their mouths being, of course, upwards. Upon them were spread carpets and cushions, on which Amsha reclined. Around her, squatted on the ground, were some fifty handmaidens, tending the wide cauldron, baking bread on the iron plates heated over the ashes, or shaking between them the skins suspended between three stakes, and filled with milk, to be thus churned into butter. It is the privilege of the head wife to prepare in her tent the dinners of the Sheikh's guests. The fires, lighted on all sides, sent forth a cloud of smoke, which hung heavily under the folds of the tent, and would have long before dimmed any eyes less bright than those of Amsha. As supplies were asked for by the women she lifted the corner of her carpet, untied the mouths of the sacks, and distributed their contents. Everything passed through her hands. To show her authority and rank she poured continually upon her attendants a torrent of abuse, and honoured them with epithets of which I may be excused attempting to give a translation; her vocabulary equalling, if not exceeding, in richness, that of the highly educated lady of the city.[1]

Amsha, as I have observed, shared the affections, though not the tent of Sofuk—for each establishment had a tent of its own—with two other ladies. Amsha, however, always maintained her sway, and the others could not sit, without her leave, in her presence. To her alone were confided the keys of the larder—supposing Sofuk to have had

---

[1] It may not perhaps be known that the fair inmate of the harem, whom we picture to ourselves conversing with her lover in language too delicate and refined to be expressed by anything else but flowers, uses ordinarily words which would shock the ears of even the most depraved amongst us.

A Shammar lady on a camel

either keys or larder—and there was no appeal from her authority on all subjects of domestic economy.

Mrs. Rassam informed me that she was received with great ceremony by the ladies. To show the rank and luxurious habits of her husband, Amsha offered her guest a glass of 'eau sucrée,' which Mrs. Rassam, who is over-nice, assured me she could not drink, as it was mixed by a particularly dirty negro, in the absence of a spoon, with his fingers, which he sucked continually during the process.

When the tribe is changing its pastures, the ladies of the Sheikhs are placed on the backs of dromedaries in the centre of the most extraordinary contrivance that man's ingenuity, and a love of the picturesque, could have invented. A light framework, varying from sixteen to twenty feet in length, stretches across the hump of the camel. It is brought to a point at each end, and the outer rods are joined by distended parchment; two pouches of gigantic pelicans seem to spring from the sides of the animal. In the centre, and over the hump, rises a small pavilion, under which is seated the lady. The whole machine, as well as the neck and body of the camel, is ornamented with tassels and fringes of worsted of every hue, and with strings of glass beads and shells. It sways from side to side as the beast labours under the unwieldy burthen;

looking, as it appears above the horizon, like some stupendous butterfly skimming slowly over the plain.

Al Hather was about eighteen miles from Sofuk's encampment. He gave us two well-known horsemen to accompany us to the ruins. Their names were Dathan and Abiram. The former was a black slave, to whom the Sheikh had given his liberty and a wife—two things, it may be observed, which are in the desert perfectly consistent. He was the most faithful and brave of all the adherents of Sofuk, and the fame of his exploits had spread through the tribes of Arabia. As we rode along, I endeavoured to obtain from him some information concerning his people, but he would only speak on one subject. 'Ya Bej,'[1] said he, 'the Arab only thinks of two things, war and love: war, Ya Bej, every one understands; let us, therefore, talk of love;' and he dwelt upon the beauties of Arab maidens in glowing language, and on the rich reward they offered to him who has distinguished himself in the foray or the fight. He then told me how a lover first loved, and how he made his love known. An Arab's affections are quickly bestowed upon any girl that may have struck his fancy as she passed him, when bearing water from the springs, or when moving to fresh pastures. Nothing can equal the suddenness of his first attachment, but its ardour. He is ready to die for her, and gives himself up to desperate feats, or to deep melancholy. The maiden, or the lady of his love, is ignorant of the sentiment she has unconsciously inspired. The lover therefore seeks to acquaint her with his passion. He speaks to a distant relation, or to a member of the tribe who has access to the harem of the tent which she occupies; and after securing his secrecy by an oath, he confesses his love, and entreats his confidant to arrange an interview. If the person addressed consents to talk to the woman, he goes to her when she is alone, and gathering a flower or a blade of grass, he says to her, 'Swear by him who made this flower and us also, that you will not reveal to any one that which I am about to unfold to you.' If she be not disposed to encourage the addresses of any lover, or if in other cases she be virtuous, she refuses and goes her way, but will never disclose what has passed; otherwise she answers, 'I swear by him who made the leaf you now hold and us,' and the man settles a place and time of meeting. Oaths taken under these circumstances are seldom, if ever, broken.

The Shammar women are not celebrated for their chastity. Some time after our visit to Sofuk, Mohammed Emin, Sheikh of the Jebour, was a guest at his tents. Some altercation arising between him and Ferhan, he

---

[1] *I.e.* 'O my Lord'; he so prefaced every sentence.

called the son of the chief 'a liar.' 'What manner of unclean fellow art thou,' exclaimed Sofuk, 'to address thus a Sheikh of the Shammar? Dost thou not know that there is not a village in the pashalic of Mosul in which the Arab name is not dishonoured by a woman of the Jebour?' 'That may be,' replied the indignant chief; 'but canst thou point out, O Sofuk, a man of the Nejm[1] who can say that his father is not of the Jebour?' This reproach so provoked Sofuk, that he sprang upon his feet, and drawing his sword, would have murdered his guest had not those who sat in the tent interposed.

The system of marriages, and the neglect with which women are treated, cannot but be productive of bad results. If an Arab suspects the fidelity of his wife, and obtains such proof as is convincing to him, he may kill her on the spot; but he generally prefers concealing his dishonour from the tribe, as an exposure would be looked upon as bringing shame upon himself. Sometimes he merely divorces her, which can be done by thrice repeating a certain formula. The woman has most to fear from her own relations, who generally put her to death if she has given a bad name, as they term it, to the family.

A dark thunder-cloud rose behind the time-worn ruins of Al Hather as we approached them. The sun, still throwing its rays upon the walls and palace, lighted up the yellow stones until they shone like gold.[2] Mr. Ross and myself, accompanied by an Arab, urged our horses onwards, that we might escape the coming storm; but it burst upon us in its fury ere we reached the palace. The lightning played through the vast buildings, the thunder re-echoed through its deserted halls, and the hail compelled us to rein up our horses, and turn our backs to the tempest. It was a fit moment to enter such ruins as these. On my previous visit, the first view I obtained of Al Hather was perhaps no less striking. We had been wandering for three days in the wilderness without seeing one human habitation. On the fourth morning a thick mist hung over the place. We had given up the search, when the vapours were drawn up like a curtain, and we saw the ruins before us.

We pitched our tents in the great court-yard, in front of the palace, and near the entrance to the inner inclosure. During the three days we remained amongst the ruins I had ample time to take accurate measurements, and to make plans of the various buildings still partly standing

---

[1] [A branch of the Shammar tribe.]

[2] The rich golden tint of the limestone, of which the great monuments of Syria are built, is known to every traveller in that country. The ruins of Al Hather have the same bright colour; they look as if they had been steeped in the sunbeams.

within the walls. The walls of the city, flanked by numerous towers, form almost a complete circle, in the centre of which rises the palace, an edifice of great magnificence solidly constructed of squared stones and elaborately sculptured with figures and ornaments. It dates probably from the reign of one of the Sassanian Kings of Persia, certainly not prior to the Arsacian dynasty, although the city itself was, I have little doubt, founded at a very early period.[1]

With the exception of occasional alarms in the night, caused by thieves attempting to steal the horses, we were not disturbed during our visit. The Arabs from the tents in the neighbourhood brought us milk, butter, and sheep. We drank the water of the Thathar, which is, however, rather salt; and our servants and camel-drivers filled during the day many baskets with truffles.

On our return we crossed the desert, reaching Wadi Ghusub the first night, and Mosul on the following morning. Dathan and Abiram, who had both distinguished themselves in recent foraging parties, and had consequently accounts to settle with the respectable merchants of the place, the balance being very much against them, could not be prevailed upon to enter the town, where they were generally known. We had provided ourselves with two or three dresses of Damascus silk, and we invested our guides as a mark of satisfaction for their services. Dathan grinned a melancholy smile as he received his reward. 'Ya Bej,' he exclaimed, as he turned his mare towards the desert; 'may God give you peace! Wallah, your camels shall be as the camels of the Shammar. Be they laden with gold, they shall pass through our tents, and our people shall not touch them.'

A year after our visit the career of Sofuk was brought to its close. I have mentioned that Nejris, Sofuk's rival, had obtained the support of nearly the whole tribe of Shammar. In a month Sofuk found himself nearly alone. His relations and immediate adherents, amongst whom were Dathan and Abiram, still pitched their tents with him, but he feared the attacks of his enemies, and retreated for safety into the territory of Beder Khan Bey, to the East of the Tigris, near Jezirah. He sent his son Ferhan with a few presents, and with promises of more substantial gifts in case of success, to claim the countenance and support

---

[1] [Hather was a Parthian city which enjoyed its main period of prosperity in the second and third centuries A.D. Excavations at the site were undertaken by a German expedition in 1906-11, and from 1951 by the Iraqi Department of Antiquities, which is now engaged in the restoration of the principal buildings. In the course of the latter work evidence of an Assyrian village settlement (not further excavated nor published) was found, confirming Layard's supposition as to the early period of occupation of the site.]

of Nejib Pasha of Baghdad, under whose authority the Shammar are supposed to be. The Pasha honoured the young Sheikh with his favour, and invested him as chief of the tribe, to the exclusion of Sofuk, whom he knew to be unpopular; but who still, it was understood, was to govern as the real head of the Shammar. He also promised to send a strong military force to the assistance of Ferhan, to enable him to enforce obedience amongst the Arabs.

The measures taken by Nejib Pasha had the effect of bringing back a part of the tribe to Sofuk, who now proposed to Nejris, that they should meet at his tents, forget their differences, and share equally the Sheikhship of the Shammar. Nejris would not accept the invitation; he feared the treachery of a man, who had already forfeited his good name as an Arab. Sofuk prevailed upon his son to visit his rival. He hoped, through the means of the young chief, who was less unpopular and more trusted than himself, to induce Nejris to accept the terms he had offered, and to come to his encampment. Ferhan refused, and was only persuaded to undertake the mission after his father had pledged himself, by a solemn oath, to respect the laws of hospitality. He rode to the tents of Nejris, who received him with affection, but refused to trust himself in the power of Sofuk, until Ferhan had given his own word that no harm should befall him. 'I would not have gone,' said he, 'to the tents of Sofuk, had he sworn a thousand oaths; but to show you, Ferhan, that I have confidence in your word, I will ride with you alone'; and, mounting his mare, unaccompanied by any of his attendants, he followed Ferhan to the encampment of Sofuk.

His reception showed him at once that he had been betrayed. Sofuk sat in gloomy silence, surrounded by several of the most desperate of his tribe. He rose not to receive his guest, but beckoned him to a place by his side. Ferhan trembled as he looked on the face of his father; but, Nejris, undaunted, advanced into the circle, and seated himself where he had been bidden. Sofuk at once upbraided him as a rebel to his authority, and sought the excuse of a quarrel. As Nejris answered boldly, the occasion was not long wanting. Sofuk sprang to his feet, and drawing his sword, threw himself upon his rival. In vain Ferhan appealed to his father's honour, to the laws of hospitality, so sacred to the Arab; in vain he entreated him not to disgrace his son by shedding the blood of one whom he had brought to his tents. Nejris sought protection of Hajar, the uncle of Sofuk, and clung to his garments; but he was one of the most treacherous and bloodthirsty of the Shammar. Upon this man's knee was the head of the unfortunate Sheikh held down, whilst Sofuk slew him as he would have slain a sheep. The rage of the murderer was now turned against his son, who stood at the entrance of the tent tearing his garments, and calling down curses upon the head of his father. The reeking sword would have been dipped in his blood, had not those who were present interfered.

The Shammar were amazed and disgusted by this act of perjury and treachery. The hospitality of an Arab tent had been violated, and disgrace had been brought upon the tribe. A deed so barbarous and so perfidious had been unknown. They withdrew a second time from Sofuk, and placed themselves under a new leader, a relation of the murdered Sheikh. Sofuk again appealed to Nejib Pasha, justifying his treachery by the dissensions which would have divided the tribe, and would have led to constant disorders in Mesopotamia had there still been rival candidates for the Sheikhship. Nejib pretended to be satisfied, and agreed to send out a party of irregular troops to assist Sofuk in enforcing his authority throughout the desert.

The commander of the troops sent by Nejib was Ibrahim Agha, the son of the Georgian, whom we met on our journey into the desert. Sofuk received him with joy, and immediately marched against the tribe; but he himself was the enemy against whom the Agha was sent. He had scarcely left his tent, when he found that he had fallen into a snare which he had more than once set for others. In a few hours after, his head was in the palace of the Pasha of Baghdad.

V

ON MY RETURN to Mosul I hastened back to Nimroud. During my absence little progress had been made, as only two men had been employed in removing the rubbish from the upper part of the chamber to which the great human-headed lions formed an entrance.

In clearing the earth from this entrance, and [nearby], many ornaments in copper, two small ducks in baked clay, and tablets of alabaster inscribed on both sides were discovered. Amongst the copper mouldings were the head of a ram or bull[1], several hands (the fingers closed and slightly bent), and a few flowers. The heads of the ducks, for they resemble that bird more than any other, are turned and rest upon the back, which bears an inscription in cuneiform characters. Objects somewhat similar have been found in Egypt. It is difficult to determine the original site of the small tablets. The inscription upon them resembled that on all the slabs in the north-west palace.

As several of the principal Christian families of Mosul were anxious to see the sculptures, I was desirous of gratifying their curiosity before the heat of summer had rendered the plain of Nimroud almost uninhabitable. An opportunity at the same time presented itself of securing the good-will of the Arab tribes encamping near the ruins, by preparing an entertainment which might gratify all parties. The Christian ladies, who had never before been out of sight of the walls of their houses, were eager to see the wonders of Nimroud, and availed themselves joyfully of the permission, with difficulty extracted from their husbands, to leave their homes. The French consul and his wife, and Mr. and Mrs. Rassam, joined the party. On the day after their arrival I issued a general invitation to all the Arabs of the district, men and women.

White pavilions, borrowed from the Pasha, had been pitched near

---

[1] This head may have belonged to the end of a chariot pole, or to a throne such as that represented in one of the sculptures.

the river, on a broad lawn still carpeted with flowers. These were for the ladies, and for the reception of the Sheikhs. Black tents were provided for some of the guests, for the attendants and for the kitchen. An open space was left in the centre of the group of tents for dancing, and for various exhibitions provided for the entertainment of the company.

Early in the morning came Abd-ur-rahman, mounted on a tall white mare. He had adorned himself with all the finery he possessed. Over his keffiah, or head-kerchief, was folded a white turban, edged with long fringes which fell over his shoulders, and almost concealed his handsome features. He wore a long robe of red silk and bright yellow boots, an article of dress much prized by Arabs. He was surrounded by horsemen carrying spears tipped with tufts of ostrich feathers.

As the Sheikh of the Abou-Salman approached the tents I rode out to meet him. A band of Kurdish musicians, hired for the occasion, advanced at the same time to do honour to the Arab chief. As they drew near to the encampment, the horsemen, led by Schloss, the nephew of Abd-ur-rahman, urged their mares to the utmost of their speed, and engaging in mimic war, filled the air with their wild war-cry. Their shoutings were, however, almost drowned by the Kurds, who belaboured their drums, and blew into their pipes with redoubled energy. Sheikh Abd-ur-rahman, having dismounted, seated himself with becoming gravity on the sofa prepared for guests of his rank; whilst his Arabs picketted their mares, fastening the halters to their spears driven into the ground.

The Abou-Salman were followed by the Shemutti and Jehesh, who came with their women and children on foot, except the Sheikhs, who rode on horseback. They also chanted their peculiar war-cry as they advanced. When they reached the tents, the chiefs placed themselves on the divan, whilst the others seated themselves in a circle on the greensward.

The wife and daughter of Abd-ur-rahman, mounted on mares, and surrounded by their slaves and hand-maidens, next appeared. They dismounted at the entrance of the ladies' tents, where an abundant repast of sweetmeats, halwa, parched peas, and lettuces had been prepared for them.

Fourteen sheep had been roasted and boiled to feast the crowd that had assembled. They were placed on large wooden platters, which, after the men had satisfied themselves, were passed on to the women. The dinner having been devoured to the last fragment, dancing succeeded. Some scruples had to be overcome before the women would join, as there were other tribes, besides their own, present. Those who did not take an active share in the amusements seated themselves on the grass, and formed a large circle round the dancers. The Sheikhs remained on the sofas and divans. In the dance of the Arabs, the Debkè, as it is called, those who perform in it form a circle, holding one another by the hand, and, moving slowly round at first, go through a shuffling step with their feet, twisting their bodies into various attitudes. As the music quickens, their movements are more active; they stamp with their feet, yell their war-cry, and jump as they hurry round the musicians. The motions of the women are not without grace; but as they insist on wrapping themselves in their coarse cloaks before they join in the dance, their forms, which the simple Arab shirt so well displays, are entirely concealed.

When those who formed the Debkè were completely exhausted by their exertions, they joined the lookers-on, and seated themselves on the ground. Two warriors of different tribes, furnished with shields and drawn scimitars, then entered the circle, and went through the sword-dance. As the music quickened, the excitement of the performers increased. The bystanders at length were obliged to interfere, and to deprive the combatants of their weapons, which were replaced by stout staves. With these they belaboured one another unmercifully to the great enjoyment of the crowd. On every successful hit, the tribe, to which the one who dealt it belonged, set up their war-cry and shouts of applause, whilst the women deafened us with the shrill 'tahlehl', a noise made by a combined motion of the tongue, throat, and hand vibrated rapidly over the mouth. When an Arab or a Kurd hears this tahlehl he almost loses his senses through excitement, and is ready to commit any desperate act.

A party of Kurdish jesters from the mountains entertained the Arabs with performances and imitations, more amusing than refined. They were received with shouts of laughter. The dances were kept up by the light of the moon, the greater part of the night.

On the following morning Abd-ur-rahman invited us to his tents, and we were entertained with renewed Debkès and sword-dances. The women, undisturbed by the presence of another tribe, entered more fully into the amusement, and danced with greater animation. The Sheikh insisted upon my joining with him in leading off a dance, in which we were joined by some five hundred warriors, and Arab women. His admiration of the beauty of the French lady who accompanied us exceeded all bounds, and when he had ceased dancing, he sat gazing upon her from a corner of the tent. 'Wallah,' he whispered to me, 'she is the sister of the Sun! what would you have more beautiful than that? Had I a thousand purses, I would give them all for such a wife. See!—her eyes are like the eyes of my mare, her hair is as bitumen, and her complexion resembles the finest Busrah dates. Any one would die for a Houri like that.' The Sheikh was almost justified in his admiration.

The festivities lasted three days,[1] and made the impression I had anticipated. They earned me a great reputation and no small respect, the Arabs long afterwards talking of their reception and entertainment. When there was occasion for their services, I found the value of the feeling towards me, which a little show of kindness to these ill-used people had served to produce.

Hafiz Pasha, who had been appointed to succeed the last governor, having received a more lucrative post, the province was sold to Tahyar Pasha. He made his public entry into Mosul early in May, and I rode out to meet him. He was followed by a large body of troops, and by the Cadi, Mufti, Ulema, and principal inhabitants of the town, who had been waiting for him at some distance from the gates to show their respect. He was a venerable old man, bland and polished in his manners, courteous to Europeans, and well informed on subjects connected with the literature and history of his country. He was a perfect specimen of the Turkish gentleman of the old school, of whom few are now left in Turkey. I had been furnished with serviceable letters of introduction to him[2]; he received me with every mark of attention, and at once permitted me to continue the excavations[3]. As a matter of form, he named a Cawass, to superintend the work on his part. I willingly concurred in this arrangement, as it saved me from any further inconvenience on the score of treasure; for which, it was still believed, I was successfully searching. This officer's name was Ibrahim Agha. He had been many years with Tahyar, and was a kind of favourite. He served me during my residence in Assyria, and on my subsequent journey to Con-

---

[1] [At the beginning of May 1846, Alison in Constantinople was given an account and replied: 'I have received your letter of the 4th May with the account of your jollifications. You seem to me to conduct these things on a highly extravagant scale to say nothing of the highly immoral features of the entertainment. If the lark, however, can manage to stop when modesty requires it there is not much harm' (38976, 380).]

[2] [By Sir Stratford Canning; see 40637, 72.]

[3] [Layard explained to Canning (40637, 72) that he had deliberately avoided asking for permission to excavate and had simply 'asked him for a Boyourouldi to *continue* my labours'.]

stantinople, with great fidelity; and, as is very rarely the case with his fraternity, with great honesty.

The support of Tahyar Pasha relieved me from some of my difficulties; for there was no longer cause to fear any interruption on the part of the authorities. But my means were very limited, and my own resources did not enable me to carry on the excavations as I wished. I returned, however, to Nimroud, and formed a small but effective body of workmen, choosing those who had already proved themselves equal to the work.

The heats of summer had now commenced, and it was no longer possible to live under a white tent. The huts were equally uninhabitable, and still swarmed with vermin. In this dilemma I ordered a recess to be cut into the bank of the river, where it rose perpendicularly from the water's edge. By screening the front with reeds and boughs of trees, and covering the whole with similar materials, a small room was formed. I was much troubled, however, with scorpions and other reptiles, which issued from the earth forming the walls of my apartment; and later in the summer by the gnats and sandflies, which hovered on a calm night over the river. Similar rooms were made for my servants. They were the safest that could be invented, should the Arabs take to stealing after dark. My horses were picketted on the edge of the bank above, and the tents of my workmen were pitched in a semi-circle behind them.

The change to summer had been as rapid as that which ushered in the spring. The verdure of the plain had perished almost in a day. Hot winds, coming from the desert, had burnt up and carried away the shrubs; flights of locusts, darkening the air, had destroyed the few patches of cultivation, and had completed the havoc commenced by the heat of the sun. The Abou-Salman Arabs, having struck their black tents, were now living in ozailis, or sheds, constructed of reeds and grass along the banks of the river. The Shemutti and Jehesh had returned to their villages, and the plain presented the same naked and desolate aspect that it wore in the month of November. The heat, however, was now almost intolerable. Violent whirlwinds occasionally swept over the face of the country. They could be seen as they advanced from the desert, carrying along with them clouds of sand and dust. Almost utter darkness prevailed during their passage, which lasted generally about an hour, and nothing could resist their fury. On returning home one afternoon after a tempest of this kind, I found no traces of my dwellings; they had been completely carried away. Ponderous wooden frameworks had been borne over the bank, and hurled some hundred yards distant; the tents had disappeared, and my furniture was scattered over the plain. When on the mound, my only secure place of refuge was beneath the fallen lion, where I could defy the fury of the whirlwind: the Arabs ceased from their work, and crouched in the trenches, almost suffocated and blinded by the dense cloud of fine dust and sand which nothing could exclude.[1]

Although the number of my workmen was small, the excavations were carried on as actively as possible. The two human-headed lions, forming the entrance d[2], led into another chamber, with sculptured walls. All the slabs, except one, were broken, but the sculpture had been well preserved.

On the slabs Nos. 2 and 3 was represented the king, accompanied by his attendants. These figures were about eight feet high; the relief very low, and the ornaments rich and elaborately carved. The bracelets, armlets, and weapons they bore were all adorned with the heads of bulls and rams; colour still remained on the hair, beard, and sandals.

No. 1, forming a corner wall, was a slab of enormous dimensions; it had been broken in two: the upper part was on the floor, the lower was still standing in its place. It was only after many ineffectual attempts that I succeeded in raising the fallen part sufficiently to ascertain the nature of the sculpture. It was a winged figure, with a three-horned cap, carrying the fir cone and square utensil; its dimensions were gigantic, the height being about sixteen feet and a half, but the relief was low.

The first slab on the other side of the entrance contained a vizir and his attendant, similar to No. 3. The succeeding slabs were occupied by figures, differing altogether in costume from those previously discovered, and apparently representing people of another race; some carrying presents or offerings, consisting of armlets, bracelets, and earrings on trays; others elevating their clenched hands, either in token of submission, or in the attitude still peculiar to Easterns when they dance. One figure was accompanied by two monkeys, held by ropes; the one raising itself on its hind legs in front, the other sitting on the shoulders of the man, and supporting itself by placing its fore paws on

---

[1] Storms of this nature are frequent during the early part of summer throughout Mesopotamia, Babylonia, and Susiana. They appear suddenly and without any previous sign, and seldom last above an hour. It was during one of them that the Tigris steamer, under the command of Colonel Chesney, was wrecked in the Euphrates; and so darkened was the atmosphere that, although the vessel was within a short distance of the bank of the river, several persons who were in her are supposed to have lost their lives from not knowing in what direction to swim.

[2] Chamber B, plan 3.

Lowering the Great Winged Bull

Bridge of Boats at Mosul

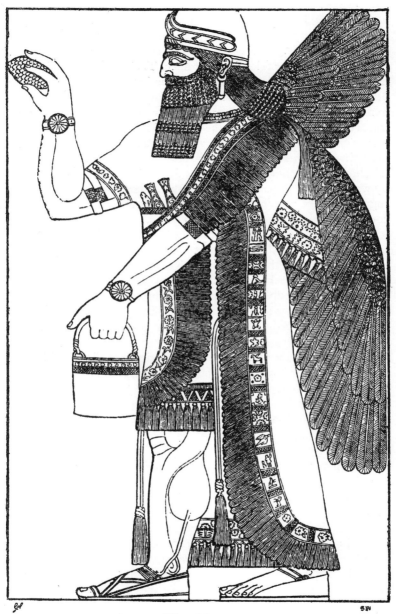

Winged figure

K

his head. The dresses of all these figures were singular. They had high boots turned up at the toes, somewhat resembling those still in use in Turkey and Persia. Their caps, although conical, appear to have been made up of bands, or folds of felt or linen. Their tunics varied in shape from those of the high-capped warriors and attendants represented in other bas-reliefs. The figure with the monkeys wore a tunic descending to the calf of the leg. His hair was simply fastened by a fillet. There were traces of black colour all over the face, and it is not improbable that it was originally painted to represent a negro; although the features were in no way characteristic of one of that race, but were of the usual form: it is, however, possible that the paint of the hair had been washed down by water over other parts of the sculpture. These peculiarities of dress suggest that the persons represented were captives from some distant country, bringing tribute to the conquerors.

In chamber B the wall was continued to the south. The sun-dried brick wall, against which sculptured slabs had been placed, was still distinctly visible to the height of twelve or fourteen feet; and I could trace, by the accumulation of ashes, the places where beams had been inserted to support the roof or for other purposes. This wall served as my guide in digging onwards, as, to the distance of 100 feet, the slabs had all fallen. I was unwilling to raise them at present, as I had neither the means of packing nor moving them.

The first sculpture still standing in its original position, which was uncovered after following the wall, was a winged human-headed bull of yellow limestone. On the previous day the detached head, now in the British Museum, had been found. The bull, to which it belonged, had fallen against the opposite sculpture, and had been broken by the fall into several pieces. I lifted the body with difficulty; and, to my surprise, discovered under it sixteen copper lions, admirably designed, and forming a regular series, diminishing in size from the largest, which was above one foot in length, to the smallest, which scarcely exceeded an inch. To their backs was affixed a ring, giving them the appearance of weights.

Beyond the winged bull the slabs were still entire, and occupied their original positions. On one were represented three warriors, probably escaping from the enemy, swimming across the stream; two of them on inflated skins, in the mode practised to this day by the Arabs inhabiting the banks of the rivers of Assyria and Mesopotamia; except that, in the bas-relief, the swimmers were pictured as retaining the aperture, through which the air is forced, in their mouths. The third, pierced by

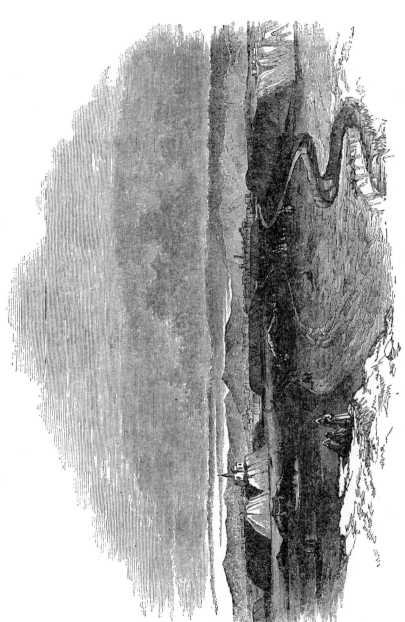

The Tomb of Jonah [left] and Kouyunjik [right], opposite Mosul.

arrows, was struggling, without the support of a skin, against the current.

Upon the third [and fourth slabs] were [scenes of] the king hunting the lion [and the bull]. The lion hunt is probably the finest specimen of Assyrian art in existence.

On the flooring, below the sculptures, were discovered considerable remains of painted plaster still adhering to the sun-dried bricks, which had fallen in masses from the upper part of the wall. The colours, particularly the blues and reds, were as brilliant and vivid when the earth was removed from them, as they could have been when first used. On exposure to the air they faded rapidly. The designs were elegant and elaborate. It was found almost impossible to preserve any portion of these ornaments, the earth crumbling to pieces when any attempt was made to raise it.

About this time I received the vizirial letter procured by Sir Stratford Canning, authorizing the continuation of the excavations and the removal of such objects as might be discovered. I was sleeping in the tent of Sheikh Abd-ur-rahman, who had invited me to hunt gazelles with him before dawn on the following morning, when an Arab awoke me. He was the bearer of letters from Mosul, and I read by the light of a small camel-dung fire, the document which secured to the British nation the records of Nineveh, and a collection of the earliest monuments of Assyrian art.

The vizirial order was as comprehensive as could be desired; and having been granted on the departure of the British ambassador, was the highest testimony the Turkish government could give of their respect for the character of Sir Stratford Canning, and of their appreciation of the eminent services he had rendered them.[1]

One of the difficulties was now completely removed. Still, however, pecuniary resources were wanting, and in the absence of the necessary means, extensive excavations could not be carried on. I hastened, nevertheless, to communicate the letter of the Grand Vizir to the Pasha, and to make arrangements for pursuing the researches as effectually as possible.

Not having yet examined the great mound of Kouyunjik, which, as it has already been observed, has generally been believed by travellers to mark the true site of Nineveh, I determined to open trenches in it. I had not previously done so, as the vicinity of the ruins to Mosul would have enabled the inhabitants of the town to watch my movements, and

[1] [See above, p. 50.]

to cause me continual interruptions before the sanction of the authorities could be obtained to my proceedings. Excavations were commenced on the southern face, where the mound was highest; as sculptures, if any still existed, would probably be found in the best state of preservation under the largest accumulation of rubbish.

The only opposition I received was from the French Consul, who claimed the ruins as French property. The claim not being recognised, he also dug into the mound, but in another direction. We both continued our researches for about a month without much success. A few fragments of sculpture and inscriptions were discovered, which enabled me to assert with some confidence that the remains were those of a building contemporary, or nearly so, with Khorsabad, and consequently of a more recent epoch than the most ancient palace of Nimroud. All the bricks dug out bore the name of the same king, but I could not find any traces of his genealogy.

On my return to Nimroud, [my excavations] led me into a new chamber (G in plan 3), remarkable for the elaborate and careful finish of its sculptures, and the size of its slabs. I uncovered the northern wall, and the eastern as far as the entrance *e*. Each slab, except the cornerstones, was occupied by two figures about eight feet in height. Nos. 2, 3, and 4 formed one group. On the centre slab (No. 3) was the king seated on a stool or throne of most elegant design and careful workmanship. His feet were placed upon a footstool supported by lions' paws. In his elevated right hand he held a cup; his left rested upon his knee. Upon his breast, and forming a border with fringes attached, were graved a variety of religious emblems and figures, like those found upon cylinders and seals of Assyria and Babylon. Amongst them were men struggling with animals, winged horses, gryphons, the sacred tree, and the king himself engaged in the performance of religious ceremonies. All these were represented in the embroidery of the robes. They were lightly cut, and it is not improbable that they were originally coloured. The bracelets, armlets, and other ornaments were equally elegant and elaborate in design. In front of the king stood an eunuch, holding in one hand and above the cup, a fly-flapper; and in the other the cover, or case of the cup, which was in the hand of the king. A piece of embroidered linen, or a towel, thrown over the eunuch's shoulder, was ready to be presented to the king, as is the custom to this day in the East, after drinking or performing ablutions. Behind the eunuch was a winged figure wearing the horned cap, and bearing the fir-cone and basket. At the back of the throne were two eunuchs, carrying the arms of the king, followed by a second winged human figure. The garments and ornaments of all these persons were as richly embroidered and adorned as those of the monarch. The colours still adhered to the sandals, brows, hair, and eyes. The sculptures were in the best state of preservation; the most delicate carvings were still distinct, and the outline of the figures retained its original sharpness. Across the slabs ran the usual inscription.

The Arabs marvelled at these strange figures. As each head was uncovered they showed their amazement by extravagant gestures, or exclamations of surprise. If it was a bearded man, they concluded at once that it was an idol or a Jin, and cursed or spat upon it. If an eunuch, they declared that it was the likeness of a beautiful female, and kissed or patted the cheek. They soon felt as much interest as I did in the objects discovered, and worked with renewed ardour when their curiosity was excited by the appearance of a fresh sculpture. On such occasions they would strip themselves almost naked, throw the kerchief from their heads, and letting their matted hair stream in the wind, rush like madmen into the trenches, to carry off the baskets of earth, shouting, at the same time, the war cry of the tribe.

I was now anxious to embark and forward to Baghdad, or Busrah, for transport to Bombay, such sculptures as I could move with the means at my disposal. Major Rawlinson had obligingly proposed that for this purpose the Nitocris, the small steamer navigating the lower part of the Tigris, should be sent up to Nimroud, and I expected the most valuable assistance, both in removing the slabs and in plans for future excavations, from her able commander, Lieutenant Jones. It was found, however, that the machinery of the Nitocris was either too much out of repair, or not sufficiently powerful, to impel the vessel over the rapids, which occur in some parts of the river. After ascending some miles above Tekrit the attempt was given up, and she returned to her station.

Without proper materials it was impossible to move either the gigantic lions, or even the large sculptures of chamber G. The few ropes to be obtained in the country were so ill-made that they could not support any considerable weight. I determined, therefore, to displace the slabs in chamber B, [which were smaller]; then to saw off the sculptures, and to reduce them as much as possible by cutting from the back. The inscriptions being a mere repetition of the same formula I did not consider it necessary to preserve them, as they added to the weight. With the help of levers of wood, I was enabled to turn them into the centre of the trench, where they were sawn by marble-cutters from Mosul. When the bas-reliefs were thus prepared, there was no difficulty in dragging them out of the trenches. One of the winged figures from chamber G, and an eagle-headed divinity, were also successfully moved.

After having been removed from the trenches, the sculptures were packed in felts and matting, and screwed down in roughly made cases. They were transported from the mound to the river upon rude buffalo carts belonging to the Pasha, and then placed upon a raft formed of inflated skins and beams of poplar wood.[1] They floated down the Tigris as far as Baghdad, were there placed on board boats of the country, and reached Busrah in the month of August.

Whilst I was moving these sculptures Tahyar Pasha visited me, accompanied by a large body of regular and irregular troops, three guns, and all the dignitaries of the household. I entertained this large company for two days. The Pasha visited the ruins, and expressed no less wonder at the sculptures than the Arabs; nor were his conjectures as to their origin and the nature of the subjects represented, much more rational than those of the sons of the desert. The gigantic human-headed lions terrified, as well as amazed, his Osmanli followers. 'These are the idols of the infidels,' said one, more knowing than the rest. 'I saw many such when I was in Italia. Wallah, they have them in all the churches, and the Papas (priests) kneel and burn candles before them.' 'No, my lamb,' exclaimed a more aged and experienced Turk. 'I have seen the images of the infidels in the churches of Beyoglu; and although some of them have wings, none have a dog's body and a tail; these are the works of the Jin, whom the holy Solomon, peace be upon him! reduced to obedience and imprisoned under his seal.' 'I have seen something like them in your apothecaries' and barbers' shops,' said I, alluding to the well-known figure, half woman and half lion, which is met with so frequently in the bazaars of Constantinople. 'Istafer Allah (God forbid),' piously ejaculated the Pasha; 'that is the sacred emblem of which true believers speak with reverence, and not the handywork of infidels.' 'May God curse all infidels and their works!' observed the Cadi's deputy, who accompanied the Pasha; 'what comes from their hands is of Satan: it has pleased the Almighty to let them be more powerful and ingenious than the true believers in this world, that their punishment and the reward of the faithful may be greater in the next.'

The heat had now become so intense that my health began to suffer

---

[1] [For a detailed description of this type of craft, called a *kelek*, see below, p. 277.]

from continual exposure to the sun, and from the labour of super-intending the excavations, drawing the sculptures, and copying the inscriptions. In the trenches, where I daily passed many hours, the thermometer generally ranged from 112° to 115° in the shade, and on one or two occasions even reached 117°. The hot winds swept over the desert; they were as blasts from a furnace during the day, and even at night they drove away sleep. I resolved, therefore, to take refuge for a week in the sardaubs or cellars of Mosul; and, in order not to lose time, to try further excavations in the mound of Kouyunjik. Leaving a superintendent, and a few guards to watch over the uncovered sculptures, I rode to the town.

The houses of Baghdad and Mosul are provided with underground apartments, in which the inhabitants pass the day during the summer months. They are generally ill-lighted, and the air is close and oppressive. Many are damp and unwholesome; still they offered a welcome retreat during the hot weather, when it was almost impossible to sit in a room. At sunset the people emerge from these subterraneous chambers and congregate on the roofs, where they spread their carpets, eat their evening meal, and pass the night.

After endeavouring in vain for some time to find any one who had seen the bas-relief, described by Rich[1] as having been found in one of the mounds forming the large quadrangle in which are included Nebbi Yunus and Kouyunjik, an aged stone-cutter presented himself, and declared that he had not only been present when the sculpture was discovered, but that he had been employed to break it up. He offered to show me the spot, and I opened a trench at once into a high mound which he pointed out in the northern line of ruins. The workmen were not long in coming upon fragments of sculptured alabaster, and after two or three days' labour an entrance was discovered, formed by two winged figures, which had been purposely destroyed. The legs and the lower part of the tunic were alone preserved. The proportions were gigantic, and the relief higher than that of any sculpture hitherto discovered in Assyria. This entrance led into a chamber, of which slabs about five feet high and three broad alone remained standing. There were marks of the chisel over them all; but from their size it appeared doubtful whether figures had ever been sculptured upon them. It is probable that the upper part of the walls was constructed of kiln-burnt bricks, with which the whole chamber was filled up, and which indeed formed the greater part of the mound. On the sides of many of them

---

[1] *Residence in Kurdistan and Nineveh*, [1836], vol. II, p. 39.

was an inscription, containing the name of the king who built the edifices of which Kouyunjik and Nebbi Yunus are the remains. The pavement was of limestone. After tracing the walls of one chamber, I renounced a further examination, as no traces of sculpture were to be found, and the accumulation of rubbish was very considerable.

The comparative rest obtained in Mosul so far restored my strength, that I returned to Nimroud in the middle of August, and again attempted to renew the excavations. [After uncovering parts of chambers H, I, and R (plan 3), and discovering further bas-reliefs and inscriptions,] the state of my health again compelled me to renounce for the time my labours at Nimroud. As I required a cooler climate, I determined to visit the Tiyari mountains, inhabited by the Chaldæan Christians, and to return to Mosul in September, when the violence of the heat had abated.

VI

THE PREPARATIONS FOR my departure for the Tiyari mountain were completed by the 28th August, and on that day I started from Mosul. My party consisted of Mr. Hormuzd Rassam, Ibraham Agha, two Albanian irregulars, a servant, a groom, and one Ionian, or Ionunco, as he was familiarly called, a half-witted Nestorian, who was enlisted into our caravan for the amusement of the company. We rode our own horses. As Ionunco pretended to know all the mountain roads, and volunteered to conduct us, we placed ourselves under his guidance. I was provided with Bouyourouldis, or orders, from the Pasha to the authorities as far as Amadiyah, and with a letter to Abd-ul-Summit By, the Keurdish chief of Berwari, through whose territories we had to pass. Mar Shamoun, the Patriarch, furnished me with a very strong letter of recommendation to the meleks and priests of the Nestorian districts.

As I was anxious to visit the French excavations at Khorsabad on my way to the mountains, I left Mosul early in the afternoon, notwithstanding the great heat of the sun. It was the sixth day of Ramazan, and the Mahommedans were still endeavouring to sleep away their hunger when I passed through the gates, and crossed the bridge of boats. Leaving my baggage and servants to follow leisurely, I galloped on with the Albanians, and reached Khorsabad in about two hours.

The mound is about fourteen miles N.N.E. of Mosul. A village formerly stood on its summit, but the houses were purchased and removed by M. Botta, when the excavations were undertaken by the French Government. It has been rebuilt in the plain at the foot of the mound. The Khausser, a small stream issuing from the hills of Makloub, is divided into numerous branches as it approaches the village, and irrigates extensive rice-grounds. The place is consequently very unhealthy, and the few squalid inhabitants who appeared, were almost speechless from ague. During M. Botta's excavations, the workmen suffered greatly from fever, and many fell victims to it.

The mode of carrying on the excavations resembled that which I adopted at Nimroud; and the general plan of construction is the same as in the Assyrian edifices already described. There are, however, more narrow passages in this building than at Nimroud, and the chambers are inferior in size. At the same time the slabs used in their construction are in general higher, though narrower. The relief in the larger figures is more bold, in the smaller there is little difference. The human-headed bulls differ principally in the head-dress from those of the earliest buildings at Nimroud; the three-horned cap is higher, and is not rounded off, the top being richly ornamented. The head-dress, in fact, is like that of similar winged animals at Persepolis. The faces of several of the bulls were turned inwards, which gave them an awkward and unsightly appearance.

Since M. Botta's departure the chambers had been partly filled up by the falling in of the trenches; the sculptures were rapidly perishing; and, shortly, little will remain of this remarkable monument. Scarcely any part of the building had escaped the fire which destroyed it, and consequently very few sculptures could be removed. Of exterior architecture I could find no trace except a flight of steps, flanked by solid masonry, which appears to have led up to a small temple of black stone or basalt, a few traces of which still remain.

The subjects of the sculptures, and the characters used in the inscriptions, have a general resemblance to those of Nimroud.

Khorsabad, or Khishtabad, is mentioned by the early Arab geographers. It is described as a village occupying the site of an ancient Assyrian city called 'Saraoun,' or 'Saraghoun;' and Yakuti declares, that soon after the Arab conquest considerable treasures were found amongst the ruins.[1] It was generally believed at Mosul that it was in consequence of this notice, and in the hopes of further riches, that M. Botta excavated in the mound—hence much of the opposition encountered from the authorities.

I had finished my examination of the ruins by the time the baggage reached the village. The sun had set, but being unwilling to expose my party to fever by passing the night on this unhealthy spot, I rode on to a small hamlet about two miles distant. It was dark when we reached it, and we found ourselves in the midst of a marsh, even more extensive than that of Khorsabad. As there was no village beyond, I was obliged

---

[1] [Since the ancient Assyrian name was Dur-sharrukin (see above, p. 69, n. 2), local tradition had retained a reliable memory of the name for over two millennia.]

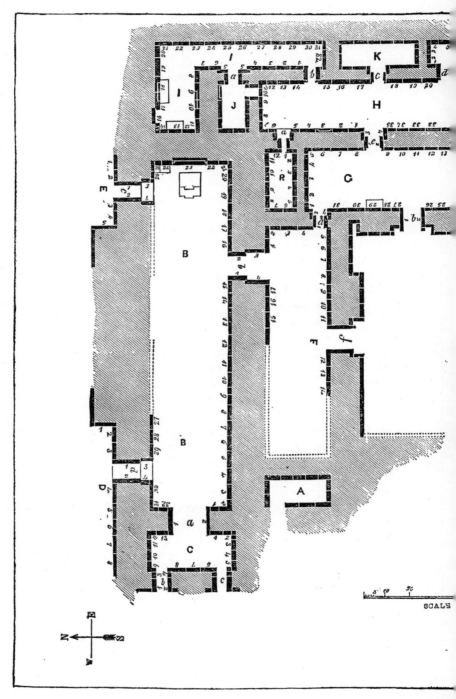

SCALE

PLAN 3. North-W

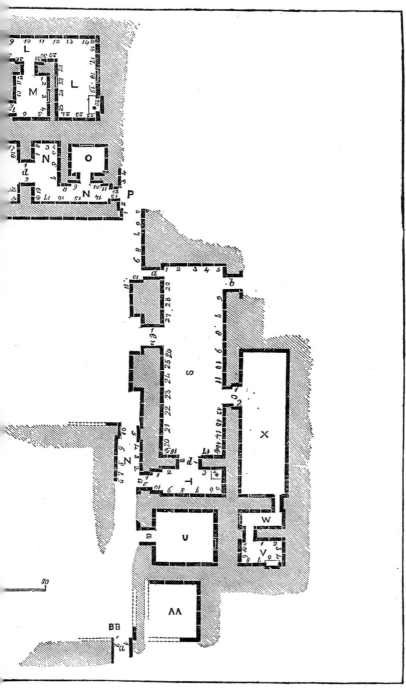

ce, Nimroud

to stop here; and clambering up to a platform, formed of branches of trees and elevated upon poles, I passed the night free from the attacks of the swarms of gnats which infested the stagnant water below.

We left the hamlet long before sunrise. Our road crossed the northern spur of Jebel Maklub, and then stretched over an extensive level to the first range of the Kurdish hills. The heat soon became intense, the plain was parched and barren; a few mud-built walls marked here and there the ruins of a village, and the silence and solitude were only broken by parties of Kurds, who were lazily driving before them, towards Mosul, donkeys heavily laden with rich clusters of grapes from the mountains.

A weary ride brought us to the Yezidi village of Ain Sifni. Its white houses and conical tombs had long been visible on the declivity of a low hill; its cleanliness was a relief after the filth of Mussulman and Christian habitations. I had expected to find here Sheikh Nasr, the religious chief of the Yezidis. As he was absent I continued my journey, after partaking of the hospitality of the chief of the village, to the tomb of Sheikh Adi. After a further ride of two hours through a pleasant valley, watered by a mountain torrent, whose banks were concealed by flowering oleanders, we reached a well-wooded basin, in the centre of which rose the white spire of the tomb of the great Yezidi saint.

I was soon stretched by a fountain in the cool shade, flung over the tomb by a cluster of lofty trees, and gave myself up to a full flow of gratitude at this sudden change from the sultry heat and salt streams of the plains, to the verdure and sweet springs of the Kurdish hills. The guardians of the tomb, and a few wanderers from a neighbouring village, gathered round me, and satisfied my curiosity as far as their caution and prejudices would allow. We passed the night on the roof of one of the buildings within the precincts of the sacred edifice, and continued our journey at dawn on the following morning.

Quitting the Yezidi district, we entered the mountains inhabited by the large Kurdish tribe of Missouri. The valleys were well-wooded; many-shaped rocks towered above our heads, or hung over the streams of the Gomel, which almost cut off our passage through the narrow defiles. In four hours we reached the large village of Kaloni, or Kalah-oni, built amongst vineyards, and hanging over the bed of the Gomel. The houses, well constructed of stone, were empty. Huge horns of the ibex ornamented the lintels of the gateways, and the corners of the buildings. The inhabitants were at some distance, on the banks of the stream, living under the trees in their temporary sheds, built of branches of trees as their summer habitations.

These Kurds were of the Badinan branch of the Missouri tribe. Their chief, whose hut was in the midst of this group of simple dwellings, was absent; but his wife received me with hospitality. Carpets, the work of her own women, were spread under a mulberry tree; and large bowls of milk and cream, wooden platters filled with boiled rice, slices of honey-comb, and baskets of new-gathered fruit, were speedily placed before us. The men sat at a respectful distance, and readily gave me such information as I asked for. The women, unembarrassed by the veil, brought straw to our horses, or ran to and fro with their pitchers. Their hair fell in long tresses down their backs, and their foreheads were adorned with rows of coins and beads; many were not unworthy the reputation for beauty which the women of Missouri enjoy.

The spot was rich in natural beauties. The valley, shut in by lofty rocks, was well wooded with fruit trees—the mulberry, the peach, the fig, the walnut, the olive, and the pomegranate; beneath them sprang the vine, or were laid out plots of Indian corn, sesame, and cotton. The sheds were built of boughs; and the property of the owners, carpets, horse-cloths, and domestic utensils, were spread out before them. From almost every door, mingling with the grass and flowers, stretched the many-coloured threads of the loom, at which usually sat one female of the family. There was a cleanliness, and even richness, in the dresses of both women and men, an appearance of comfort and industry, which contrasted strikingly with the miserable state of the people of the plain; and proved that these Kurds had been sufficiently fortunate to escape the notice of the last governor of Mosul, and were reserved for some more scrutinising Pasha.

I acknowledged the hospitality of the Kurdish lady by a present to her son, and rode up to the small Chaldæan village of Bebozi, standing on the summit of a high mountain. The ascent was most precipitous, and the horses could with difficulty reach the place. We found a group of ten houses, built on the edge of a cliff overhanging the valley, at so great a height, that the stream below was scarcely visible. The in-habitants were poor, but received us with unaffected hospitality. I visited the small church. The people of Bebozi are amongst those Chaldæans who have very recently become Catholics, and are but a too common instance of the mode in which such proselytes are made. In the church I saw a few miserable prints, dressed up in all the horrors of red, yellow, and blue, miracles of saints and of the blessed Virgin, and a hideous infant in swaddling clothes, under which was written 'l'Iddio, bambino.' They had recently been stuck up against the bare walls. 'Can you understand these pictures?' I asked. 'No,' was the reply; 'we did not place them here; when our priest (a Nestorian) died a short time ago, Mutran Yusuf, the Catholic bishop, came to us. He put up these pictures, and told us that we were to adore them. We pulled them down again; but for doing so our Kiayahs (heads of the village) were bastinadoed by Mahmoud Agha, the chief of Missouri, and we got our heads broken. We now, therefore, leave them where they are. And as the Kurds have been bribed not to allow a Nestorian priest to come to the village, we are compelled to hear the Catholic priest, whom Mutran Yusuf occasionally sends us.' On the altar and reading-desk, were a few books—forms of prayer, rituals, and the scriptures used by the Chaldæans. They had not been changed, only the name of Nestorius had been carefully blotted out with a pen, and the Sunday worship of the new proselytes, with the exception of a few prostrations to the pictures, remained as it was before their conversion.

I returned to the house at which I had alighted, and endeavoured to sleep. Ionunco, however, had engaged in a controversy on the merits of their respective creeds with some Chaldæans, strangers from a neighbouring village, whose conversion was of a more ancient date, and more complete, than that of the people of Bebozi. I was fain to cover my face with my cloak, and to lie and listen. The dispute waxed warm. Ionunco brought to bear all the texts he had gathered during a prolonged residence with the patriarch, and other dignitaries of his Church. The converts quoted the arguments which had turned them from their errors. Those of Bebozi listened in admiration to a learned discussion on the distinction of the persons. The strangers then insisted on the advantage of recognising and being under the Pope. 'The Pope,' exclaimed the irritated Ionunco, 'may be very useful; but, as far as I am concerned, I would not change him against my donkey!' This irreverent sally would have been the signal for a general commencement of hostilities, had I not interfered. Ionunco was ordered to saddle his mare, and we resumed our journey.

After crossing a range of hills, covered by a forest of dwarf oak, we descended into the valley of Cheloki, and reached about sunset the large Kurdish village of Spandareh, so called from its poplar trees, 'spandar.' The inhabitants, alarmed at the formidable appearance of our party, were inclined to shirk the duties of hospitality; and it required a few stringent measures before we could convince them that ours was a friendly, not a hostile, invasion.

We were now separated from the valley of Amadiyah by a range of high and well-wooded mountains called Ghara. This we crossed by a road little frequented, and of so precipitous a nature that our horses could scarcely keep their footing—one, indeed, carrying part of our baggage, suddenly disappeared over the edge of a rock, and was found some hundred feet below, on his back, firmly wedged between two rocks; how he got there with nothing but the bone of his tail broken, was a mystery beyond the comprehension of our party. The valley of Amadiyah, chiefly a sandstone deposit, is cut up into innumerable ravines by the torrents, which rush down the mountains and force their way to the river Zab. It is, however, well wooded with oaks, producing in abundance the galls for which this district is celebrated. The peasants were picking them at the time of our journey; and as this year the crop was abundant, I had an opportunity of distinguishing between the trees which produce them, and those which do not.

It was nearly mid-day ere we reached the foot of the lofty isolated rock on which the town and fort of Amadiyah are built. The plain of Amadiyah contains many Chaldæan villages, which were formerly very flourishing. Most of them have now been deserted, and the inhabitants have taken refuge in the higher mountains from the violence and tyranny of Kurds and Turkish governors, and from the no less galling oppression of proselytising bishops.

Some half-clothed fever-stricken Albanians were slumbering on the stone benches as we entered the gates of the fort, which certainly during the season of Ramazan, if not at all others, might be taken by surprise by a few resolute Kurds. We found ourselves in the midst of a heap of ruins—porches, bazaars, baths, habitations, all laid open to their inmost recesses. We had some difficulty in finding our way to a crumbling ruin, honoured with the name of Serai—the Palace. Here the same general sleep prevailed. Neither guards nor servants were visible, and we wandered through the building until we reached the room of the governor. His hangers-on were indulging in comfort and sleep upon the divans, and we had some trouble in rousing them. We were at length taken to a large room, in a tower built on the very edge of the rock, and overlooking the whole valley—the only remnant of the state of the old hereditary Pashas of Amadiyah. A refreshing breeze came down from the mountain, the view was extensive and beautiful, and I forgot the desolation and misery which reigned around.

The Albanian irregulars were to leave me here, as the authority of the Pasha of Mosul did not extend beyond. We were now to enter the territories of Kurdish chiefs, who scarcely admitted any dependence upon the Porte. I determined upon sending all my horses, except one, with the Albanians to Dohuk, there to await my return, and to hire mules for the rest of my journey.

It was the hour of afternoon prayer before Selim Agha, the Mute-sellim or governor, emerged from his harem; which, however, as far as the fair sex were concerned, was empty.

The old gentleman, who was hungry, half asleep, and in the third stage of the ague, hurried through the ordinary salutations, and asked at once for quinine. His attendants exhibited illustrations of every variety of the fever; some shivered, others glowed, and the rest sweated. He entreated me to go with him into the harem; his two sons were buried beneath piles of cloaks, carpets, and grain-sacks, but the whole mass trembled with the violence of their shaking. I dealt out emetics and quinine with a liberal hand, and returned to the Salamlik, to hear from Selim Agha a most doleful history of fever, diminished revenues, arrears of pay, and rebellious Kurds. He was a native of Zillah, in Asia Minor, where he had been Nefous Emini, a kind of public registrar and tax-gatherer, and had followed in the train of the late Pasha to seek his fortunes in the south. He sighed as he talked of his native place, a flourishing, healthy market town; and the tears ran down his cheeks as he recapitulated his manifold misfortunes, and entreated me to inter-cede with the governor of Mosul for his advancement or recall. I left him with his watch in his hand, anxiously looking for sunset, that he might console himself with a dose of tartar emetic.

Amadiyah was formerly a place of considerable importance and strength, and contained a very large and flourishing population. It was governed by hereditary Pashas—feudal chiefs, who traced their descent from the Abbasid Caliphs, and were always looked up to, on that account, with religious respect by the Kurds. The ladies of this family were no less venerated, and enjoyed the very peculiar title for a woman of 'Khan.' The last of these hereditary chiefs was Ismail Pasha; who long defied, in his almost inaccessible castle, the attempts of Injeh Bairakdar Mohammed Pasha to reduce him. A mine was at length sprung under a part of the wall, which, from its position, the Kurds had believed safe from attack, and the place was taken by assault. Ismail Pasha was sent a prisoner to Baghdad, where he still remains; and his family, amongst whom was his beautiful wife, Esma Khan, not un-known to the Europeans of Mosul,[1] long lived upon the bounty of

[1] [In the context of a Muslim family, this allusion seems to hint at some scandal in-volving the lady and European residents, but no amplification has been found in the Layard Papers.]

Mr. Rassam. Amadiyah is frequently mentioned by the early Arab geographers and historians, and its foundation dates, most probably, from a very early epoch. The only remains that I could discover about the town were a defaced bas-relief on the rock near the northern gate, of which sufficient alone was distinguishable to enable me to assign to it an approximate date—the time of the Arsacian kings[1]; and some excavations in the rock within the walls, which appear to have been used at an early period as a Christian church. Amadiyah is proverbially unhealthy, notwithstanding its lofty and exposed position. At this time of the year the inhabitants leave the town for the neighbouring mountains, in the valleys of which they construct 'ozailis,' or sheds, with boughs. The population has greatly diminished since the reduction of the place by the Turks. The castle is considered of great importance as a key to Kurdistan, and is defended by 300 Albanians and a small party of artillerymen with three guns.

I made my way through the deserted streets to a small enclosure, in which were the quarters of the Albanians. The disposable force may have consisted of three men; the rest were stretched out on all sides, suffering under every stage of fever, amidst heaps of filth and skins of water-melons, showing the nature and extent of their commissariat. One of their chiefs boasted that he had braved the fever, and insisted upon my drinking coffee, and smoking a narguileh of no very prepossessing appearance with him. He even indulged so far in mirth and revelry, that he disturbed a shivering youth basking in the last rays of the sun, and brought him to play upon a santour, which had lost the greater number of its strings. An air of his native mountains brought back his melancholy, and he dwelt upon the miseries of an irregular's life, when there was neither war nor plunder. The evening gun announced sunset whilst I was sitting with the chief; and I left the garrison as they were breaking their fast on donkey-loads of unripe water-melons.

On my return to the Serai, I found the governor recovering from the effects of his emetic, and anxious for his dinner. As the month of Ramazan is one of festivity and open house, Ismail Agha (the Albanian chief in command of the garrison), the Cadi, and one or two others came as guests. Our meal gave undoubted proofs either of the smallness of the means of Selim Agha, or of the limited resources of the country. When the dinner was over, I introduced a theological subject as becoming the season, and the Cadi entered deeply into the subject of

[1] [The Parthian ruling dynasty, who controlled this area from the middle of the second century B.C. to the end of the second century A.D.]

predestination and free will. The reckless way in which the Albanian threw himself into the argument astonished the company, and shocked the feelings of the expounder of the law. His views of the destinies of man were bold and original; he appealed to me for a confirmation of his opinions, and assuming that I fully concurred with him, he finished by asking me to breakfast.

Next morning, after some difficulty I found my way to the quarters of Ismail Agha. They were in a small house, the only habitable spot in the midst of a heap of ruins. His room was hung round with guns, swords, and yataghans, and a few dirty Albanians, armed to the teeth, were lounging at the door. The chief had adorned himself most elaborately. His velvet jacket was covered with a maze of gold embroidery, his arms were of the most costly description, and ample fur cloaks were spread over the dingy divans. It was a strange display of finery in the midst of misery. He received me with a great cordiality; and when he found that I had been to his old haunts in his native land, and had known his friends and kindred, his friendship exceeded all reasonable bounds. 'We are all brothers, the English and the Tosques,' exclaimed he, endeavouring to embrace me; 'we are all Framasouns[1]; I know nothing of these Turks and their Ramazan, thank God! Our stomachs were given us to be filled, and our mouths to take in good things.' He accompanied these words with a very significant signal to one of his followers, who was at no loss to understand its meaning, and set about forming a pyramid of cushions, on the top of which he mounted at the imminent risk of his neck, and reached down from a shelf a huge bottle of wine, and a corresponding pitcher of raki. Ismail Agha then dived into the recesses of a very capacious but ill-looking purse, out of which he pulled twenty paras[2], its sole contents, and despatched without delay one of his attendants to the stall of a solitary grocer, who was apparently the only commercial survivor in the wreck around him. The boy soon returned with a small parcel of parched peas, a few dates, and three lumps of sugar, which were duly spread on a tray and placed before us as zests to the wine and brandy. It was evident that Ismail Agha had fully made up his mind to a morning's debauch, and my position was an uncomfortable one. After drinking a few glasses of raki in solitary dignity, he invited his followers to join

[1] The term Framasoun (or Freemason), as well as Protestant, are in the East, I am sorry to say, equivalent to infidel. The Roman Catholic missionaries have very industriously spread the calumny.
[2] About one penny.

him. Messengers were despatched in all directions for music; a Jew with the ague, the band of the regiment, consisting of two cracked dwarf kettledrums, and a fife, and two Kurds with a fiddle and a santour, were collected together. I took an opportunity of slipping out of the room unseen, amidst the din of Albanian songs and the dust of Palicari dances.

On my return to the Serai I found mules ready, the owners having been at length brought to understand that it was my intention to pay for their hire. Every thing being settled, and the animals loaded, I wished the Mutesellim good day, and promised to bring his miserable condition to the notice of the Pasha.

We left Amadiyah by the opposite gate to that by which we had entered. We were obliged to descend on foot the steep pathway leading to the valley below. Crossing some well-cultivated gardens, we commenced the ascent of the mountains through a wooded ravine, and came suddenly upon the Yilaks, or summer quarters of the population of Amadiyah. The spot was well chosen. The torrent was divided into a thousand streams, which broke over the rocks, falling in cascades into the valley below. Fruit and forest trees concealed the sheds and tents, and creepers of many hues almost covered the sides of the ravine. All our party enjoyed the delicious coolness and fragrance of the place; and we did not wonder that the people of Amadiyah had left the baneful air of the town for these pleasant haunts. An hour's ride brought us to the summit of the pass, from which a magnificent view of the Tiyari mountains opened upon us. Ionunco became eloquent when he saw his native Alps before him. He named one by one the lofty peaks which sprang out of the confused heap of hills; that of Asheetha and several others were covered with snow. Below us was the extensive valley of Berwari, which separates the range of Amadiyah from the Nestorian country. We reached Hayis, a Nestorian hamlet, about sunset. There were only four families in the place, so poor that we could only procure a little boiled meal, and some dried mulberries for our supper. The poor creatures, however, did all they could to make us comfortable, and gave us what they had.

The valley of Berwari is well wooded with the gall-bearing oak; and the villages, which are numerous, are surrounded by gardens and orchards. The present chief of the district is a fanatic, and has almost ruined the Christian population. In all the villages through which we passed, we saw the same scene and heard the same tale of wretchedness. Yet the land is fruitful, water plentiful, and the means of cultivation easy. Fruit trees of many descriptions abound; and tobacco, rice, and grain of various kinds could be raised to any extent. Even the galls afford but a scanty gain to the villagers, as Abd-ul-Summit Bey has monopolised them, and those who pick are compelled to deliver them to the chief at a very small price. The villages are partly inhabited by Kurds and partly by Nestorian Chaldæans; there are no Catholics amongst them. Many of the Christian villages have been reduced to no more than five or six houses, and some have only two or three. We stopped at several during our day's journey. The men, with the priests, were generally absent picking galls; the women were seated in circles under the trees, clipping the grapes and immersing them in boiling water previous to drying them for raisins. We were everywhere received with the same hospitality, and everywhere found the same poverty.

The waters of the mountain torrents collected in the valley, form a branch of the Khabour[1], and the river is sufficiently deep, during the rainy season and spring, to admit of rafts being floated from Berwari to the Tigris. At that time of the year poplars, oaks, and other trees, are thus sent to Mosul. The most important produce of the valley is the gall nut, which abounds. Were agriculture encouraged, the inhabitants might carry on a lucrative trade with Mosul in many useful articles; but at present the Christians are too much exposed to the rapacity of the Kurds, and the Mohammedans are too idle, to cultivate the land to any extent. The district is very insecure; and Abd-ul-Summit Bey loses no opportunity of shedding the blood of the Christians of the mountains. During the massacre in Tiyari[2] many of those who succeeded in making their escape, were put to death by his orders, when passing through his territories. Zeinel Bey, the blood-thirsty agent of Beder Khan Bey, is a cousin of this chief.

The castle of Kumri or Gumri, the residence of Abd-ul-Summit Bey, stands on the pinnacle of a lofty isolated rock, and may be seen from most parts of the valley of Berwari. It is a small mud fort, but is looked upon as an impregnable place by the Kurds. The chief had evidently received notice of my approach, and probably suspected that the object of my visit was an inspection, for no friendly purposes, of his stronghold; for as we came near to the foot of the hill, we saw him hastening down a precipitous pathway on the opposite side, as fast as his horse could carry him. A mullah, one of his hangers on, having been sent to meet us on the road, informed us that his master had left

[1] [To be distinguished from the similarly-named major tributary of the Euphrates.]
[2] [See below, pp. 156 ff.]

the castle early in the morning, for a distant village, whither we could follow him. Not having any particular wish to make a closer inspection of Kalah[1] Kumri, I struck into the hills, and took the pathway pointed out by the mullah.

We rode through several Kurdish villages, surrounded by gardens and well watered by mountain streams. A pass of some elevation had to be crossed before we could reach the village of Mia, our quarters for the night. Near its summit we found a barren plain on which several Kurdish horsemen, who had joined us, engaged with my own party in the Jerid. The mimic fight soon caused general excitement, and old habits getting the better of my dignity, I joined the *mêlée*. A severe kick in the leg from a horse soon put an end to my manœuvres, and the party was detained until I was sufficiently recovered from the effects of the blow to continue our journey. It was sunset consequently before we reached Mia. There are two villages of this name; the upper, inhabited by Mohammedans, the lower by Nestorian Chaldæans. A Kurd met us as we were entering the former, with a message from Abd-ul-Summit Bey, to the effect that, having guests, he could not receive us there, but had provided a house in the Christian village, where he would join us after his dinner. I rode on to the lower Mia, and found a party of Kurds belabouring the inhabitants, and collecting old carpets and household furniture. Finding that these proceedings were partly meant as preparations for our reception, though the greater share of the objects collected was intended for the comfort of the Bey's Mussulman guests, I at once put a stop to the pillaging, and released the sufferers. We found a spacious and cleanly roof; and with the assistance of the people of the house, who were ready enough to assist when they learnt we were Christians, established ourselves for the night.

Soon after dark another messenger came from Abd-ul-Summit Bey to say that as the Cadi and other illustrious guests were with him, he could not visit me before the morning. I had from the first suspected that these delays and excuses had an object, and that the chief wished to give a proof of his dignity to the Kurds, by treating me in as unceremonious a manner as possible; so, calling the Kurd and addressing him in a loud voice, that the people who had gathered round the house might hear, I requested him to be the bearer of a somewhat uncivil answer to his master, and took care that he should fully understand its terms. Ionunco's hair stood on end at the audacity of this speech, and the Nestorians trembled at the results. Ibrahim Agha tittered with

[1] [Kalah == 'castle'.]

delight; and pushing the Kurd away by the shoulders, told him to be particular in delivering his answer. The message had the effect I had anticipated; an hour afterwards, shuffling over the house-tops at the great risk of his shins, and with a good chance of disappearing down a chimney, came the Bey. He was enveloped in a variety of cloaks; he wore, after the manner of the Bohtan chiefs, a turban of huge dimensions, about four feet in diameter, made up of numberless kerchiefs and rags of every hue of red, yellow, and black; his jacket and wide trowsers were richly embroidered; and in his girdle were all manner of weapons. In person he was tall and handsome; his eyes were dark, his nose aquiline, and his beard black; but the expression of his face was far from prepossessing. I left him to open the conversation, which he did by a multiplicity of excuses and apologies for what had passed, not having, by the Prophet, been aware, he said, of the rank of the guest by whose presence he had been honoured. I pointed out to him one or two fallacies in his assertions; and we came to a distinct understanding on the subject, before we proceeded to general topics. He sat with me till midnight, and entered, amongst other things, into a long justification of his conduct towards Christians, which proved that his authority was not established as well as he could desire. In dealing with a Kurd, you are generally safe as long as you can make him believe that you are his superior, or his equal.

In the morning the Bey sent me a breakfast and a party of Kurdish horsemen to accompany us as far as the Tiyari frontier, which was not far distant. Beyond Mia we passed through Bedou, the largest and most populous Kurdish village I had seen. The valley was generally well cultivated; the chief produce appeared to be tobacco and rice, with 'garas' and 'uthra,' two kinds of grain, of the English names of which I am ignorant. The garas is, I think, millet.

Our guards would not venture into the territories of the Tiyari, between whom and the Kurds there are continual hostilities, and quitted us in a narrow desolate valley, up which our road to Asheetha now led. I lectured my party on the necessity of caution during our future wanderings; and reminded my Cawass and Mohammedan servants that they had no longer the quiet Christians of the plains to deal with. Resigning ourselves to the guidance of Ionunco, who now felt that he was on his own soil, we made our way with difficulty over the rocks and stones with which the valley is blocked up, and struck into what our guide represented to be a short cut to Asheetha. The pathway might certainly, on some occasions, have been used by the mountain goats;

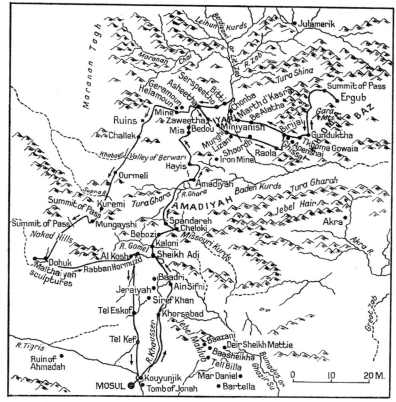

MAP 3. Layard in Kurdistan, August – September 1846

but the passage of horses and mules was a miracle. After a most tedious walk, we reached the top of the pass and looked down on the village. From this spot the eye rested upon a scene of great beauty. In front rose the lofty peak, with its snows and glaciers, visible even from Mosul. At our feet the village spread over the whole valley; and detached houses, surrounded by garden and orchards, were scattered over the sides of the mountains. To the right ran the valley which leads to the Zab. We had little difficulty in descending through the loose stones and detritus which cover the face of the mountain, although both our mules and ourselves had frequent falls. On reaching the entrance of the valley, we rode at once to the house of Yakoub, the rais or chief of Asheetha, who received us with grateful hospitality.

155

VII

WE HAD NO sooner reached the house of Yakoub Rais, than a cry
of 'The Bey is come,' spread rapidly through the village, and I was
surrounded by a crowd of men, women, and boys. My hand was kissed
by all, and I had to submit for some time to this tedious process. As for
my companion, he was almost smothered in the embraces of the girls,
nearly all of whom had been liberated from slavery after the great
massacre, or had been supported by his brother for some months in
Mosul.[1] Amongst the men were many of my old workmen, who were
distinguished from the rest of the inhabitants of Asheetha by their gay
dresses and arms, the fruits of their industry during the winter. They
were anxious to show their gratitude, and their zeal in my service. The
priests came too; Kasha Ghioorghis, Kasha Hormuzd, and others. As
they entered the room, the whole assembly rose; and lifting their
turbans and caps reverentially from their heads, kissed the hand extended to them. In the mean while the girls had disappeared; but soon
returned, each bearing a platter of fruit, which they placed before me.
My workmen also brought large dishes of boiled garas swimming in
butter. There were provisions enough for the whole company.

The first inquiries were after Mar Shamoun, the Patriarch. I produced
his letter, which the priests first kissed and placed to their foreheads.
They afterwards passed it to the principal men, who went through the

---

[1] In 1843 Beder Khan Bey invaded the Tiyari districts, massacred in cold blood nearly
10,000 of their inhabitants, and carried away as slaves a large number of women and
children. It is perhaps not generally known, that the release of the greater part of the
captives was obtained through the humane interference and generosity of Sir Stratford
Canning, who prevailed upon the Porte to send a commissioner into Kurdistan, for
the purpose of inducing Beder Khan Bey and other Kurdish Chiefs to give up the slaves
they had taken, and advanced, himself, a considerable sum towards their liberation.
Mr. Rassam also obtained the release of many slaves, and maintained and clothed at
his own expense, and for several months, not only the Nestorian Patriarch, who had
taken refuge in Mosul, but many hundred Chaldaeans who had escaped from the mountains.

same ceremony. Kasha Ghioorghis then read the letter aloud, and those present renewed their expressions of welcome to us.

The village was in the greatest alarm at a threatened invasion from Beder Khan Bey. The district of Tkhoma, which had escaped the former massacre, was now the object of his fanatical vengeance. He was to march through Asheetha, and orders had already been sent to the inhabitants to collect provisions for his men. As his expedition was not to be undertaken before the close of Ramazan, there was full time to see the proscribed districts before the Kurds entered them.

A Nestorian House in the district of Tiyari

On the morning following our arrival, I went with Yakoub Rais to visit the village. The trees and luxuriant crops had concealed the desolation of the place, and had given to Asheetha, from without, a flourishing appearance. As I wandered, however, through the lanes, I found little but ruins. A few houses were rising from the charred heaps; still the greater part of the sites were without owners, the whole family having perished. Yakoub pointed out, as we went along, the former dwellings of wealthy inhabitants, and told me how and where they had been murdered. A solitary church had been built since the massacre, the foundations of others were seen amongst the ruins. The pathways were still blocked up by the trunks of trees cut down by the Kurds.

Watercourses, once carrying fertility to many gardens, were now empty and dry; and the lands which they had irrigated were left naked and unsown. I was surprised at the proofs of the industry and activity of the few surviving families, who had returned to the village, and had already brought a large portion of the land into cultivation.

The houses of Asheetha, like those of the Tiyari districts[1], are not built in a group, but are scattered over the valley. Each dwelling stands in the centre of the land belonging to its owner; consequently, the village occupies a much larger space than would otherwise be required, but has a cheerful and pleasing appearance. The houses are simple, and constructed so as to afford protection and comfort, during winter and summer. The lower part is of stone, and contains two or three rooms inhabited by the family and their cattle during the cold months. Light is admitted by the door, and by small holes in the wall. There are no windows, as in the absence of glass, a luxury as yet unknown in Kurdistan, the cold would be very great during the winter, when the inhabitants are frequently snowed up for many days together. The upper floor is constructed partly of stone, and partly of wood, the whole side facing the south being open. Enormous beams, resting on wooden pillars and on the walls, support the roof. This is the summer habitation, and here all the members of the family reside. During July and August, they usually sleep on the roof, upon which they erect stages of boughs and grass resting on high poles. By thus raising themselves as much above the ground as possible, they avoid the vermin which swarms in the rooms, and catch the night wind which carries away the gnats. Sometimes they build these stages in the branches of high trees around the houses. The winter provision of dried grass and straw for the cattle is stacked near the dwelling, or is heaped on the roof.

As this was the first year that the surviving inhabitants of Asheetha, about 200 families, had returned to the village and had cultivated the soil, they were almost without provisions of any kind. We were obliged to send to Zaweetha for meat and rice; and even milk was scarce, the flocks having been carried away by the Kurds. Garas was all we could find to eat. They had no corn, and very little barley. Their bread was made of this garas, and upon it alone they lived, except when on holidays they boiled the grain, and soaked it in melted butter.

The men were now busy in irrigating the land; and seemed to be

---

[1] Asheetha and Zaweetha were formerly looked upon as half-independent districts, each having its own Rais or head. They were neither within the territories nor under the authority of the Meleks of Tiyari.

rewarded by the promise of ample crops of their favourite grain, and of wheat, barley, rice, and tobacco. The boys kept up a continued shrill shriek or whistle to frighten away the small birds, which had been attracted in shoals by the ripe corn. When tired of this exercise, they busied themselves with their partridges. Almost every youth in the country carries one of these birds at his back, in a round wicker cage. Indeed, whilst the mountains and the valleys swarm with wild partridges, the houses are as much infested by the tame. The women, too, were not idle. The greater part of them, even the girls, were beating out the corn, or employed in the fields. A few were at the doors of the houses working at the loom, or spinning wool for the clothes of the men. I never saw more general or cheerful industry; even the priests took part in the labours of their congregation.

Yakoub Rais, who was naturally of a lively and jovial disposition, could not restrain his tears as he related to me the particulars of the massacre [perpetrated by the Kurds in 1843]. He had been amongst the first seized by Beder Khan Bey; and having been kept by the chief as a kind of hostage, he had been continually with him, during the attack on the Tiyari, and had witnessed all the scenes of bloodshed which he so graphically described. The descent upon Asheetha was sudden and unexpected. The greater part of the inhabitants fell victims to the fury of the Kurds, who endeavoured to destroy every trace of the village. We walked to the church, which had been newly constructed by the united exertions and labour of the people. The door was so low, that a person, on entering, had to perform the feat of bringing his back to the level of his knees. The entrances to Christian churches in the East are generally so constructed, that horses and beasts of burthen may not be lodged there by the Mohammedans. A few rituals, a book of prayer, and the Scriptures, all in manuscript, were lying upon the rude altar; but the greater part of the leaves were wanting, and those which remained were either torn into shreds, or disfigured by damp and water. The manuscripts of the churches were hid in the mountains, or buried in some secure place, at the time of the massacre; and as the priests, who had concealed them, were mostly killed, the books have not been recovered. A few English prints and handkerchiefs from Manchester were hung about the walls; a bottle and a glass, with a tin plate for the sacrament, stood upon a table; a curtain of coarse cloth hung before the inner recess, the Holy of Holies; and these were all the ornaments and furniture of the place.

I visited my former workmen, the priests, and those whom I had seen at Mosul; and as it was expected that I should partake of the hospitality of each, and eat of the dishes they had prepared for me—generally garas floating in melted rancid butter, with a layer of sour milk above—by the time I reached Yakoub's mansion my appetite was abundantly satisfied. At the door, however, stood Sarah, and a bevy of young damsels with baskets of fruits mingled with ice, fetched from the glacier: nor would they leave me until I had tasted of everything.

We lived in a patriarchal way with the Rais. My bed was made in one corner of the room. The opposite corner was occupied by Yakoub, his wife and unmarried daughters: a third was appropriated to his son and daughter-in-law, and all the members of his son's family: the fourth was assigned to my companion: and various individuals, whose position in our household could not be very accurately determined, took possession of the centre. We slept well nevertheless, and no one troubled himself about his neighbour.

Yakoub volunteered to accompany me during the rest of my journey through the mountains; and as he was generally known, was well acquainted with the by-ways and passes, and a very merry companion withal, I eagerly accepted his offer. We left part of our baggage at his house, and it was agreed that he should occasionally ride one of the mules. He was a very portly person, gaily dressed in an embroidered jacket and striped trowsers, and carrying a variety of arms in his girdle.

The country through which we passed, after leaving Asheetha [on our way to Zaweetha in the same valley], can scarcely be surpassed in the beauty and sublimity of its scenery. The patches of land on the declivities of the mountains were cultivated with extraordinary skill and care. I never saw greater proofs of industry. We forgot the toils and dangers of the way in gazing upon the magnificent prospect before us. The stream formed by the eternal snows above Asheetha forces its way to the Zab. On the sides of the mountains is the most populous and best cultivated district in Tiyari. The ravine below Asheetha is too narrow to admit of the road being carried along the banks of the torrent: and we were compelled to climb over an immense mass of rocks, rising to a considerable height above it. Frequently the footing was so insecure that it required the united force of several men to carry the mules along by their ears and tails. We, who were unaccustomed to mountain paths, were obliged to have recourse to the aid of our hands and knees.

I had been expected at Zaweetha; and before we entered the first gardens of the village, a party of girls, bearing baskets of fruit, advanced to meet me. Their hair, neatly platted and adorned with flowers, fell down their backs. On their heads they wore coloured handkerchiefs loosely tied, or an embroidered cap. Many were pretty, and the prettiest was Aslani, a liberated slave, who had been for some time under the protection of Mrs. Rassam; she led the party, and welcomed me to Zaweetha. My hand having been kissed by all, they simultaneously threw themselves upon my companion, and saluted him vehemently on both cheeks; such a mode of salutation, in the case of a person of my rank and distinction, not being, unfortunately, considered either respectful or decorous. The girls were followed by the Rais and the principal inhabitants, and I was led by them into the village.

The Rais of Zaweetha had fortunately rendered some service to Beder Khan Bey, and on the invasion of Tiyari his village was spared. It had not even been deserted by its inhabitants, nor had its trees and gardens been injured. It was consequently, at the time of my visit, one of the most flourishing villages in the mountains. The houses, neat and clean, were still overshadowed by the wide-spreading walnut-tree; every foot of ground which could receive seed, or nourish a plant, was cultivated. Soil had been brought from elsewhere, and built up in terraces on the precipitous sides of the mountains. A small pathway amongst the gardens led us to the house of the Rais.

We were received by Kasha Kana of Lizan, and Kasha Yusuf of Siatha; the first, one of the very few learned priests left among the Nestorian Chaldæans. Our welcome was as unaffected and sincere as it had been at Asheetha. Preparations had been made for our reception, and the women of the family of the chief were congregated around huge cauldrons at the door of the house, cooking an entire sheep, rice, and garas. The liver, heart, and other portions of the entrails were immediately cut into pieces, roasted on ramrods, and brought on these skewers into the room. The fruit, too, melons, pomegranates, and grapes, all of excellent quality, spread on the floor before us, served to allay our appetites until the breakfast was ready.

Mar Shamoun's letter was read with the usual solemnities by Kasha Kana, and we had to satisfy the numerous inquiries of the company. Their Patriarch was regarded as a prisoner in Mosul, and his return to the mountains was looked forward to with deep anxiety. Everywhere, except in Zaweetha, the churches had been destroyed to their foundations, and the priests put to death. Some of the holy edifices had been rudely rebuilt; but the people were unwilling to use them until they had been consecrated by the Patriarch. There were not priests enough indeed to officiate, nor could others be ordained until Mar Shamoun himself performed the ceremony. These wants had been the cause of great irregularities and confusion in Tiyari; and the Nestorian Chaldæans, who are naturally a religious people, and greatly attached to their churches and ministers, were more alive to them than to any of their misfortunes.

Kasha Kana was making his weekly rounds to the villages which had lost their priests. He carried under his arm a bag full of manuscripts, consisting chiefly of rituals and copies of the Scriptures; but he had also one or two volumes on profane subjects which he prized highly; amongst them was a grammar by Rabba Iohannan bar Zoabee, to which he was chiefly indebted for his learning. He read to us—holding as usual the book upside down—a part of the introduction treating of the philosophy and nature of languages. A taste for the fine arts seemed to prevail generally in the village, and the walls of the Rais's house were covered with sketches of wild goats and snakes in every variety of posture. The young men were eloquent on the subject of the chase, and related their exploits with the wild animals of the mountains. A cousin of the chief, a handsome youth very gaily dressed, had shot a bear a few days before, after a hazardous encounter, and he brought me the skin, which measured seven feet in length. The two great subjects of complaint I found to be the Kurds and the bears, both equally mischievous; the latter carrying off the fruit both when on the trees and when laid out to dry; and the former, the provisions stored for the winter. In some villages in Berwari the inhabitants pretended to be in so much dread of the bears, that they would not venture out alone after dark.

The Rais, finding that I would not accept his hospitality for the night, accompanied us, followed by all the inhabitants, to the outskirts of the village. His frank and manly bearing, and simple kindness, had made a most favourable impression upon me, and I left him with regret. Kasha Kana, too, fully merited the praises which he received from all who knew him. His appearance was mild and venerable; his beard, white as snow, fell low upon his breast; but his garments were in a very advanced stage of rags. I gave him a few handkerchiefs, some of which were at once gratefully applied to the bettering of his raiment; the remainder being reserved for the embellishment of his parish church. The Kasha is looked up to as the physician, philosopher, and sage of Tiyari, and is treated with great veneration by the people. As we walked through the village, the women left their thresholds and the boys their sports to kiss his hand—a mark of respect, however, which is invariably shown to the priesthood.

We had been joined by Mirza, a confidential servant of Mar Shamoun, and our party was further increased by several men returning to villages on our road. Yakoub Rais kept every one in good humour by his anecdotes, and the absurdity of his gesticulations. Ionunco, too, dragging his mare over the projecting rocks, down which he generally contrived to tumble, added to the general mirth, and we went laughing through the valley.

From Zaweetha to the Zab, there is almost an unbroken line of cultivation on both sides of the valley. The two villages of Miniyanish and Murghi are buried in groves of walnut-trees, and their peaceful and flourishing appearance deceived me, until I wandered amongst the dwellings, and found the same scenes of misery and desolation that I had witnessed at Asheetha. Yakoub pointed out a spot where above three hundred persons had been murdered in cold blood, and all our party had some tale of horror to relate. We found an old priest, blind and grey, bowed down by age and grief, the solitary survivor of six or eight of his order. He was seated under the shade of a walnut-tree, near a small stream. Some children of the village were feeding him with grapes, and on our approach his daughter ran into the half-ruined cottage, and brought out a basket of fruit and a loaf of garas bread. I endeavoured to glean some information from the old man as to the state of his flock; but his mind wandered to the cruelties of the Kurds, or dwelt upon the misfortunes of his Patriarch, over whose fate he shed many tears.

Our road lay through the gardens of the villages, or through the forest of gall-bearing oaks which clothe the mountains above the line of cultivation. But it was everywhere equally difficult and precipitous, and we tore our way through the matted boughs of overhanging trees, or the thick foliage of creepers which hung from every branch. Innumerable rills, led from the mountain springs into the terraced fields, crossed our path, and rendered our progress still more tedious. We reached Lizan, however, early in the afternoon, descending to the village through scenery of extraordinary beauty and grandeur.

Lizan stands on the river Zab, which is crossed by a rude bridge. I need not weary or distress the reader with a description of desolation and misery, hardly concealed by the most luxuriant vegetation. We rode to the graveyard of a roofless church slowly rising from its ruins—

the first edifice in the village to be rebuilt. We spread our carpets amongst the tombs; for as yet there were no inhabitable houses. The Melek, with the few who had survived the massacre, was living during the day under the trees, and sleeping at night on stages of grasses and boughs, raised on high poles, fixed in the very bed of the Zab. By this latter contrivance they succeeded in catching any breeze that might be carried down the narrow ravine of the river, and in freeing themselves from the gnats and sandflies abounding in the valley.

It was near Lizan that occurred one of the most terrible incidents of the massacre; and an active mountaineer offering to lead me to the spot, I followed him up the mountain. Emerging from the gardens we found ourselves at the foot of an almost perpendicular detritus of loose stones, terminated, about one thousand feet above us, by a wall of lofty rocks. Up this ascent we toiled for above an hour, sometimes clinging to small shrubs whose roots scarcely reached the scanty soil below; at others crawling on our hands and knees. We soon saw evidences of the slaughter. At first a solitary skull rolling down with the rubbish; then heaps of blanched bones; further up fragments of rotten garments. As we advanced, these remains became more frequent—skeletons, almost entire, still hung to the dwarf shrubs. I was soon compelled to renounce an attempt to count them. As we approached the wall of rock, the declivity became covered with bones, mingled with the long platted tresses of the women, shreds of discoloured linen, and well-worn shoes. There were skulls of all ages, from the child unborn to the toothless old man. We could not avoid treading on the bones as we advanced, and rolling them with the loose stones into the valley below. 'This is nothing,' exclaimed my guide, who observed me gazing with wonder on these miserable heaps; 'they are but the remains of those who were thrown from above, or sought to escape the sword by jumping from the rock. Follow me!' He sprang upon a ledge running along the precipice that rose before us, and clambered along the face of the mountain overhanging the Zab, now scarcely visible at our feet. I followed him as well as I was able to some distance; but when the ledge became scarcely broader than my hand, and frequently disappeared for three or four feet altogether, I could no longer advance. The Tiyari, who had easily surmounted these difficulties, returned to assist me, but in vain. I was still suffering severely from the kick received in my leg four days before; and was compelled to return, after catching a glimpse of an open recess or platform covered with human remains.

164

When the fugitives who had escaped from Asheetha spread the news of the massacre through the valley of Lizan, the inhabitants of the villages around collected such part of their property as they could carry, and took refuge on the platform I have just described and on the rock above; hoping thus to escape the notice of the Kurds, or to be able to defend, against any numbers, a place almost inaccessible. Women and young children, as well as men, concealed themselves in a spot which the mountain goat could scarcely reach.[1] Beder Khan Bey was not long in discovering their retreat; but being unable to force it, he surrounded the place with his men, and waited until they should be compelled to yield. The weather was hot and sultry; the Christians had brought but small supplies of water and provisions. After three days, the first began to fail them, and they offered to capitulate. The terms proposed by Beder Khan Bey, and ratified by an oath on the Koran, were the surrender of their arms and property. The Kurds were then admitted to the platform. After they had taken the arms from their prisoners, they commenced an indiscriminate slaughter; until, weary of using their weapons, they hurled the few survivors from the rocks into the Zab below. Out of nearly one thousand souls, who are said to have congregated here, only one escaped.

We had little difficulty in descending to the village; a moving mass of stones, skulls, and rubbish carried us rapidly down the declivity. The Melek, who had but recently been raised to that rank, his predecessor having been killed by the Kurds, prepared a simple meal of garas and butter—the only provisions that could be procured. The few stragglers who had returned to their former dwellings collected round us, and made the usual inquiries after their Patriarch, or related their misfortunes. As I expressed surprise at the extent of land already cultivated, they told me that the Kurds of some neighbouring villages had taken possession of the deserted property, and had sown grain and tobacco in the spring, which the Tiyari were now compelled to irrigate and look after.

The sun had scarcely set, when I was driven by swarms of insects to

---

[1] When amongst the Bakhtiyari I saw a curious instance of the agility of the women of the mountains. I occupied an upper room in a tower, forming one of the corners in the yard of the chief's harem. I was accustomed to lock my door on the outside with a padlock. The wife of the chief advised me to secure the window also. As I laughed at the idea of any one being able to enter by it, she ordered one of her handmaidens to convince me, which she did at once, dragging herself up in the most marvellous way by the mere irregularities of the bricks. After witnessing this feat, I could believe any thing of the activity of the Kurdish women.

one of the platforms in the river. A slight breeze came from the ravine and I was able to sleep undisturbed.

The bridge across the Zab at Lizan is of basket-work. Stakes are firmly fastened together with twigs, forming a long hurdle, reaching from one side of the river to the other. The two ends are laid upon beams, resting upon piers on the opposite banks. Both the beams and the basket-work are kept in their places by heavy stones heaped upon

A wicker bridge across the Zab near Lizan

them. Animals, as well as men, are able to cross over this frail structure, which swings to and fro, and seems ready to give way at every step. These bridges are of frequent occurrence in the Tiyari mountains.

As some of the beams had been broken, the bridge of Lizan formed an acute angle with the stream below, and was scarcely to be crossed by a man on foot. We had consequently to swim the mules and horses, a labour of no slight trouble and difficulty, as the current was rapid, and the bed of the river choked with rocks. More than an hour was wasted in finding a spot sufficiently clear of stones, and in devising means to induce the animals to enter the water. We resumed our journey on the opposite side of the valley. But before leaving Lizan I must mention the heroic devotion of ten Tiyari girls, who, as they were led across the bridge by the Kurds, on their return from the great massacre,—preferring death to captivity and conversion,—threw themselves simultaneously into the Zab, and were drowned in its waters.

We now entered a valley formed by a torrent which joins the Zab below Lizan. We passed through the small Chaldæan village of Shoordh, now a heap of ruins, into a wild and rocky ravine, leading to the once rich and populous valley of Raola.

We were nearly two hours in reaching the house of the Melek.[1] Melek Khoshaba[2] had been apprised of my intended visit; for he met us with the priests and principal inhabitants at some distance from his dwelling. I was much struck by his noble carriage and handsome features. He wore, like the other chiefs, a dress of very gay colours, and a conical cap of felt, slightly embroidered at the edges, in which was stuck an eagle's feather. The men who accompanied him were mostly tall and well made, and were more showily dressed than the inhabitants of other villages through which we had passed. Their heads were shaved, as is customary amongst the Tiyari tribes, a small knot of hair being left uncut on the crown, and allowed to fall in a plait down the back. This tail, with the conical cap, gives them the appearance of Chinese. The boys, in addition to their inseparable partridges, carried cross-bows, with which they molested every small bird that appeared, and almost every one had an eagle's feather in his cap.

We followed the Melek to his house, which stood high above the torrent, on the declivity of the mountain. The upper or summer room was large enough to contain all the party. The Melek and priests sat on my carpets; the rest ranged themselves on the bare floor against the walls. The girls brought me, as usual, baskets of fruit, and then stood at the entrance of the room. Many of them were very pretty; but the daughter of the chief, a girl of fourteen, excelled them all. I have seldom seen a more lovely form. Her complexion was fair; her features regular; her eyes and hair as black as jet; a continual smile played upon her mouth; and an expression of mingled surprise and curiosity stole over her face, as she examined my dress or followed my movements. Her tresses, unconfined by the coloured handkerchief bound loosely round her head, fell in disorder down her back, reaching to her waist. Her dress was more gay, and neater, than that of the other women, who evidently confessed her beauty and her rank. I motioned to her to sit down; but that was an honour only reserved for the mother of the

[1] Literally, King, the title given to the chiefs of Tiyari.
[2] A corruption of *Khath Shaba*, Sunday.

Melek, who occupied a corner of the room. At length she approached timidly to examine more closely a pocket compass, which had excited the wonder of the men.

The threatened invasion of Tkhoma by Beder Khan Bey, was the chief subject of conversation, and caused great excitement amongst the inhabitants of Raola. They calculated the means of defence possessed by the villagers of the proscribed district; but whilst wishing them success against the Kurds, they declared their inability to afford them assistance; for they still trembled at the recollection of the former massacre, and the very name of the Bohtan chief struck terror into the hearts of the Tiyari. They entreated me to devise some mode of delivering them from the danger. Several men, whose wives and daughters were still in slavery, came to me, thinking that I could relieve them in their misfortune; and there was scarcely any one present who had not some tale of grief to relate.

Whilst we were discussing these matters the women left the room, and I observed them, shortly after, performing their ablutions by a rill in a garden below. They stripped themselves without restraint of all their garments, and loosed their hair over their shoulders. Some stood in the stream, and poured water over one another out of wooden bowls; others combed and plaited the long tresses of their companions, who crouched on the grass at their feet. They remained thus for above an hour, unnoticed by the men, and as unmindful of their presence as if they bathed in some secluded spot, far distant from any human habitation.

The Melek insisted upon accompanying us, with the priests and principal inhabitants, to the end of the valley. As we passed through the village we saw the women bathing at almost every door; nor did they appear at all conscious that we were near them. This simple and primitive mode of washing is thus publicly practised amongst all the Chaldæan tribes, particularly on the Saturday. The men neither heed nor interfere, and their wives and daughters are not the less virtuous or modest.

Although all this district is known as Raola, yet its length has rendered distinct names for various parts of the village necessary. The houses are scattered over the sides of the mountains, and surrounded by gardens and vineyards. A torrent, rising at the head of the valley, is divided into innumerable watercourses carried along the sides of the hills to the most distant plots of cultivation. Its waters are consequently entirely absorbed, except during the period of winter rains, when they seek an outlet in the Zab. The gardens are built up in terraces, and are sown with tobacco, rice, and such vegetables and grains as are peculiar to the mountains. The valley is well wooded with fruit trees, amongst which are the walnut, fig, pomegranate, apple, and mulberry.

Melek Khoshaba accompanied me to a rude monument raised over the bodies of fifty prisoners, who had been murdered at the time of the invasion, and left me at the entrance of the village. We had to pass through a narrow and barren ravine, and a rocky gorge, before entering the district of Tkhoma. This was the only road by which we could reach Tkhoma, without crossing the lofty ranges of rocks surrounding it on all other sides. A resolute body of men might have held the ravine against any numbers. This was one of the most dangerous tracks we had to traverse during our journey. On the heights above are one or two villages, inhabited by the Apenshai Kurds, who are always engaged in hostilities with the Tiyari, and fall upon such as are crossing the frontiers of Tkhoma. My party was numerous and well armed, and keeping close together we travelled on without apprehension.

We emerged suddenly from this wilderness, and saw a richly cultivated valley before us. Flocks of sheep and goats were browsing on the hill sides, and herds of cattle wandered in the meadows below. These were the first domestic animals we had seen in the Chaldæan country, and they showed that hitherto Tkhoma had escaped the hand of the spoiler. Two villages occupied opposite sides of the valley; on the right, Ghissa, on the left, Birijai. We rode to the latter. The houses are built in a cluster, and not scattered amongst the gardens, as in Tiyari. We were surrounded by the inhabitants as soon as we entered the streets, and they vied with one another in expressions of welcome and offers of hospitality. Kasha Hormuzd, the principal priest, prevailed upon me to accompany him to a house he had provided, and on the roof of which carpets were speedily spread. The people were in great agitation at the report of Beder Khan Bey's projected march upon Tkhoma. They immediately flocked round us, seeking for news. The men were better dressed than any Nestorian Chaldæans I had yet seen. The felt cap was replaced by turbans of red and black linen, and these two favourite colours of the Kurds were conspicuous in their ample trowsers, and embroidered jackets. As they carried pistols and daggers in their girdles, and long guns in their hands, they could scarcely be distinguished from the Mussulman inhabitants of the mountains. The women wore small embroidered scull-caps, from beneath which their hair fell loose or in plaits. Their shirts were richly embroidered, and round their necks and bosoms were hung coins and beads. They were happy in having escaped so long the fanaticism and rapacity of the Kurds. But they foresaw their fate. All was bustle and anxiety; the women were burying their ornaments and domestic utensils in secure places; the men preparing their arms, or making gunpowder. I walked to the church, where the priests were collecting their books and the holy vessels, to be hid in the mountains. Amongst the manuscripts I saw many ancient rituals, forms of prayer, and versions of the Scripture, some on vellum, evidently of a very early period.

I was much touched by the unaffected hospitality and simple manners of the two priests, Kashas Hormuzd, and Khoshaba, who entertained me; a third was absent. Their dress, torn and soiled, showed that they were poorer than their congregation. They had just returned from the vineyards, where they had been toiling during the day; yet they were treated with reverence and respect; the upper places were given to them, they were consulted on all occasions; and no one drew nigh without kissing the hand, scarred by the plough and the implements of the field.

Almost every house furnished something towards our evening repast; and a long train of girls and young men brought us in messes of meat, fowls, boiled rice, garas, and fruit. The priests and the principal inhabitants feasted with us, and there remained enough for my servants, and for the poor who were collected on the roof of a neighbouring house. After our meal many of the women came to me, and joined with the men in debating on their critical position, and in forming schemes for the security of their families, and the defence of their village. It was past midnight before the assembly separated.

The following day being Sunday, we were roused at dawn to attend the service of the church. The two priests officiated in white surplices. The ceremonies were short and simple; a portion of Scripture was read and then interpreted by Kasha Hormuzd in the dialect in use in the mountains—few understanding the Chaldæan of the books. His companion chanted the prayers—the congregation kneeling or standing, and joining in the responses. The people used the sign of the cross when entering, and bowed when the name of Christ occurred in the prayers. The Sacrament was administered to all present—men, women, and children partaking of the bread and wine, and my companion receiving it amongst the rest. They were disposed to feel hurt at my declining to join them, until I explained that I did not refuse from any religious prejudice. When the service was ended the congregation embraced one another, as a symbol of brotherly love and concord[1], and left the church. I could not but contrast these simple and primitive rites with the senseless mummery, and degrading forms, adopted by the converted Chaldæans of the plains—the unadorned and imageless walls, with the hideous pictures and monstrous deformities which encumber the churches of Mosul.

The vestibule of the church was occupied by a misshapen and decrepit nun. Her bed was a mat in the corner of the building, and she was cooking her garas on a small fire near the door. She inquired, with many tears, after Mar Shamoun, and hung round the neck of my companion when she learnt that he had been living with him. Vows of chastity are very rarely taken amongst the Nestorian Chaldæans; and this woman, whose deformity might have precluded the hope of marriage, was the sole instance we met with in the mountains. Convents for either sex are unknown.

Birijai contained, at the time of my visit, nearly one hundred houses, and Ghissa forty. The inhabitants were comparatively rich, possessing numerous flocks, and cultivating a large extent of land. There were priests, schools, and churches in both villages.

Melek Putros, one of the Meleks of the tribe, came early from Tkhoma Gowaia[2], the principal village in the district, to welcome me to his mountains, and to conduct me to his house. He was a stout jovial fellow, gaily dressed and well armed. He explained that as it was Sunday the Chaldæans did not travel, and consequently the other Meleks and the principal inhabitants had not been able to meet me. We took leave of the good people of Birijai, and followed Melek Putros up the valley.

An uninterrupted line of gardens brought us to the church of Tkhoma Gowaia, standing in the midst of scattered houses, this village being built like those of Tiyari. Here we found almost the whole tribe assembled, and in deep consultation on the state of affairs. We sat in a loft above the church during the greater part of the day, engaged in discussion on the course to be pursued to avoid the present difficulties, and to defend the valley against the expected attack of Beder Khan Bey. The Kurds, who inhabited two or three hamlets in Tkhoma, had also assembled. They expressed sympathy for the Christians, and offered to

---

[1] This custom, it will be remembered, prevailed generally amongst the primitive Christians. The Roman Catholic Church has retained the remembrance of it in the 'Pax'.

[2] *i.e.* middle or centre Tkhoma.

arm in their behalf. After much debate it was resolved to send at once a deputation to the Pasha of Mosul, to beseech his protection and assistance. Two priests, two persons from the families of the Meleks, and two of the principal inhabitants, were chosen; and a letter was written by Kasha Bodaca, one of the most learned and respectable priests in the mountains. It was a touching appeal, setting forth that they were faithful subjects of the Sultan, had been guilty of no offence, and were ready to pay any money, or submit to any terms that the Pasha might think fit to exact. The letter, after having been approved by all present, and sealed with the seals of the chiefs, was delivered to the six deputies, who started at once on foot for Mosul. At the same time no precaution was to be omitted to place the valley in a state of defence, and to prepare for the approach of the Kurds.

We passed the night on the roof of the church, and rose early to continue our journey to Baz. The valley and pass, separating Tkhoma from this district, being at this time of the year uninhabited, is considered insecure, and we were accompanied by a party of armed men, furnished by the Meleks. The whole valley up to the rocky barrier closing it towards the east, is an uninterrupted line of cultivation. Rice and flax are very generally cultivated, and fruit-trees abound.

We stopped for a few minutes at Gunduktha, the last village in Tkhoma, to see Kasha Bodaca, whom we found preparing, at the request of his congregation, to join the deputation to the Pasha of Mosul. We took leave of him, and he started on his journey. He was an amiable, and, for the mountains, a learned man, much esteemed by the Chaldæan tribes. Being one of the most skilful penmen of the day, his manuscripts were much sought after for the churches. He was mild and simple in his manners; and his appearance was marked by the gentleness and unassuming dignity, which I had found in more than one of the Nestorian Chaldæan priests.[1]

The torrent enters the valley of Tkhoma by a very narrow gorge, through which a road, partly constructed of rough stones piled up in the bed of the stream, is with difficulty carried. In the winter, when the rain has swollen the waters, this entrance must be impracticable; and even at this time, we could scarcely drag our mules and horses over the rocks, and through the deep pools in which the torrent abounds. All

---

[1] Mr. Ainsworth observes that he resembled in his manners and appearance an English clergyman. [Few readers under fifty will have had the privilege of knowing the admirable type of English clergyman—usually a gentleman and often a classical scholar as well —which Ainsworth and Layard had in mind. H.W.F.S.]

signs of cultivation now ceased. Mountains rose on all sides, barren and treeless. Huge rocks hung over the road, or towered above us. On their pinnacles, or in their crevices, a few goats sought a scanty herbage. The savage nature of the place was heightened by its solitude.

Soon after entering the ravine, we met a shepherd-boy, dragging after him a sheep killed by the bears; and a little beyond we found the reeking carcase of a bullock, which had also fallen a victim to these formidable animals, of whose depredations we heard continual complaints. I observed on the mountain-sides several flocks of ibex, and some of our party endeavoured to get within gun-shot; but after sun-rise their watchfulness cannot be deceived, and they bounded off to the highest peaks, long before the most wary of our marksmen could approach them.

We were steadily making our way over the loose stones and slippery rocks, when a party of horsemen were seen coming towards us. They were Kurds, and I ordered my party to keep close together, that we might be ready to meet them in case of necessity. As they were picking their way over the rough ground like ourselves, to the evident risk of their horses' necks as well as of their own, I had time to examine them fully as they drew near. In front, on a small, lean, and jaded horse, rode a tall gaunt figure, dressed in all the tawdry garments sanctioned by Kurdish taste. A turban of wonderful capacity, and almost taking within its dimensions horse and rider, buried his head, which seemed to escape by a miracle being driven in between his shoulders by the enormous pressure. From the centre of this mass of many-coloured rags rose a high conical cap of white felt. This load appeared to give an unsteady rolling gait to the thin carcase below, which could with difficulty support it. A most capacious pair of claret-coloured trowsers bulged out from the sides of the horse, and well nigh stretched from side to side of the ravine. Every shade of red and yellow was displayed in his embroidered jacket and cloak; and in his girdle were weapons of extraordinary size, and most fanciful workmanship. His eyes were dark and piercing, and overshadowed by shaggy eyebrows; his nose aquiline, his cheeks hollow, his face long, and his beard black and bushy. Notwithstanding the ferocity of his countenance, and its unmistakeable expression of villany, it would have been difficult to repress a smile at the absurdity of the figure, and the disparity between it and the miserable animal concealed beneath. This was a Kurdish dignitary of the first rank; a man well-known for deeds of oppression and blood; the Mutesellim, or Lieutenant-Governor under Nur-Ullah Bey, the Chief of Hakkiari. He was followed by a small body of well-armed men, resembling their master in the motley character of their dress. The cavalcade was brought up by an individual differing considerably from those who had preceded. His smooth and shining chin, and the rich glow of raki[1] upon his cheeks, were undoubted evidences of Christianity. He had the accumulated obesity of all his companions; and rode, as became him, upon a diminutive donkey, which he urged over the loose stones with the point of a claspknife. His dress did not differ much from that of the Kurds, except that, instead of warlike weapons, he carried an ink-horn in his girdle. This was Bircham, the *goulama d'Mira,*[2] as he was commonly called,—a half renegade Christian, who was the steward, banker, and secretary of the Hakkiari chief.

I saluted the Mutesellim, as we elbowed each other in the narrow pass; but he did not seem inclined to return my salutation, otherwise than by a curl of the lip, and an indistinct grunt, which he left me to interpret in any way I thought proper. It was no use quarrelling with him, so I passed on. We had not proceeded far, when one of his horsemen returned to us, and called away Yakoub Rais, Ionunco, and one of the men of Tkhoma. Looking back, I observed them all in deep consultation with the Kurdish chief, who had dismounted to wait for them. I rode on, and it was nearly an hour before the three Chaldæans rejoined us. Ionunco's eyes were starting out of his head with fright, and the expression of his face was one of amusing horror. Even Yakoub's usual grin had given way to a look of alarm. The man of Tkhoma was less disturbed. Yakoub began by entreating me to return at once to Tkhoma and Tiyari. The Mutesellim, he said, had used violent threats; declaring that as Nur-Ullah Bey had served one infidel who had come to spy out the country, and teach the Turks its mines, alluding to Schultz[3], so he would serve me; and had sent off a man to the Hakkiari chief to apprise him of my presence in the mountains. 'We must turn back at once,' exclaimed Yakoub, seizing the bridle of my horse, 'or, Wallah! that Kurdish dog will murder us all.' I had formed a different plan; and, calming the fears of my party as well as I was able, I continued my journey toward Baz. Ionunco, however, raked his brain for every murder that had been attributed to Nur-Ullah Bey; and at each new tale of horror Yakoub turned his mule, and vowed he would go back to Asheetha.

[1] Ardent spirits, extracted from raisins or dates.
[2] *i.e.* The servant of the Prince.
[3] This traveller was murdered by Nur-Ullah Bey.

We rode for nearly four hours through this wild, solitary valley. My people were almost afraid to speak, and huddled together as if the Kurds were coming down upon us. Two or three of the armed men scaled the rocks, and ran on before us as scouts; but the solitude was only broken by an eagle soaring above our heads, or by a wild goat which occasionally dashed across our path.

It was mid-day before we reached the foot of the mountain dividing us from the district of Baz. The pass we had to cross is one of the highest in the Chaldæan country, and at this season there was snow upon it. The ascent was long, steep, and toilsome. We were compelled to walk, and even without our weight, the mules could scarcely climb the acclivity. But we were well rewarded for our labour when we gained the summit. A scene of extraordinary grandeur opened upon us. At our feet stretched the valley of Baz,—its villages and gardens but specks in the distance. Beyond the valley, and on all sides of us, was a sea of mountains—peaks of every form and height, some snow-capped, others bleak and naked; the furthermost rising in the distant regions of Persia. I counted nine distinct mountain ranges. Two vast rocks formed a kind of gateway on the crest of the pass, and I sat between them for some minutes gazing upon the sublime prospect before us.

The descent was rapid and dangerous, and so precipitous that a stone might almost have been dropped on the church of Ergub, first visible like a white spot beneath us. We passed a rock, called the 'Rock of Butter,' from a custom, perhaps of pagan origin, existing amongst the Chaldæan shepherds, of placing upon it, as an offering, a piece of the first butter made in the early spring. As we approached the village, we found several of the inhabitants labouring in the fields. They left their work, and followed us. The church stands at some distance from the houses; and when we reached it, the villagers compelled all my servants to dismount, including Ibrahim Agha, who muttered a curse upon the infidels as he took his foot out of the stirrup. The Christians raised their turbans,—a mark of reverence always shown on these occasions.

The houses of Ergub are built in a group. We stopped in a small open space in the centre of them, and I ordered my carpet to be spread near a fountain, shaded by a cluster of trees. We were soon surrounded by the inhabitants of the village. The Melek and the priest seated themselves with me; the rest stood round in a circle. The men were well dressed and armed; and, like those of Tkhoma, they could scarcely be distinguished from the Kurds. Many of the women were pretty enough to be entitled to the front places they had taken in the crowd. They wore silver ornaments and beads on their foreheads, and were dressed in jackets and trowsers of gay colours.

After the letter of the Patriarch had been read, and the inquiries concerning him fully satisfied, the conversation turned upon the expected expedition of Beder Khan Bey against Tkhoma, and the movements of Nur-Ullah Bey, events causing great anxiety to the people of Baz. Although this district had been long under the chief of Hakkiari, paying an annual tribute to him, and having been even subjected to acts of oppression and violence, yet it had never been disarmed, nor exposed to a massacre such as had taken place in Tiyari. There was, however, cause to fear that the fanatical fury of Beder Khan Bey might be turned upon it as well as upon Tkhoma; and the only hope of the inhabitants was in the friendly interference of Nur-Ullah Bey, whose subjects they now professed themselves to be. They had begun to conceal their church-books and property, in anticipation of a disaster.

Both the Melek and the priest pressed me to accept their hospitality. I preferred the house of the latter, to which we moved in the afternoon. My host was suffering much from the ague, and was moreover old and infirm. I gave him a few medicines to stop his fever, for which he was very grateful.

After the events of the morning I had made up my mind to proceed at once to Nur-Ullah Bey, whose residence was only a short day's journey distant; but on communicating my intention to Mr. Hormuzd Rassam, he became so alarmed, and so resolutely declared that he would return alone rather than trust himself in the hands of the Mir of Hakkiari, that I was forced to give up my plan. In the present state of the mountains there were only two courses open to me, either to visit the chief, who would probably, after learning the object of my journey, receive and assist me; or to retrace my steps without delay. I decided upon the latter with regret. I did not, however, communicate my plans to any one; but learning that there were two of Nur-Ullah Bey's attendants in the village, I sent for them, and induced them, by a small present, to take a note to their master. I instructed them to report that it was my intention to visit him on the following day, and sent a Christian to see that they took the road to Julamerik. The treachery and daring of Nur-Ullah Bey were so well known, that I thought it most prudent to deceive him, in case he might wish to waylay me on my return to Tkhoma. I started therefore before day-break without any one in the village being aware of my departure, and took the road by which we had reached Baz the day before.

The district of Baz contains five large villages; it is well cultivated and well watered, producing tobacco, flax, rice, and grain of various kinds. We crossed the pass as quickly as we were able, hurried through the long barren valley, and reached Gunduktha, without meeting any one during our journey: to the no small comfort of my companions, who could not conceal their alarm during the whole of our morning's ride.

We stopped to breakfast at Gunduktha, and saw the Meleks at Tkhoma Gowaia. The people of this village had felt much anxiety on our account, as the Mutesellim had passed the night there, and had used violent threats against us. I learnt that Bircham had been sent to Tkhoma by Nur-Ullah Bey to withdraw his family and friends; 'for this time,' said the chief, 'Beder Khan Bey intends to finish with the Christians, and will not make slaves for consuls and Turks to liberate.'

Being unwilling to return to Asheetha by the villages I had already visited, I determined—notwithstanding the account given by the people of Tkhoma of the great difficulty of the passes between us and the Zab—to cross the mountain of Khouara, which rises at the back of Birijai. I found that their descriptions had not been exaggerated. We were two hours dragging ourselves over the loose stones, and along the narrow ledges, and reached the summit weary and breathless. From the crest we overlooked the whole valley of Tkhoma, with its smiling villages, bounded to the east by the lofty range of Kareetha; to the west I recognised the peaks of Asheetha, the valley of the Zab, Chal, and the heights inhabited by the Apenshai Kurds.

An hour's rapid descent brought us to the Tiyari village of Be-Alatha,—a heap of ruins on the opposite sides of a valley. The few surviving inhabitants were in extreme poverty, and the small-pox was raging amongst them. The water-courses destroyed by the Kurds had not been repaired and the fields were mostly uncultivated. Even the church had not yet been rebuilt; and as the trees which had been cut down were still lying across the road, and the charred timber still encumbered the gardens, the place had a most desolate appearance. We were hospitably received by a Shamasha, or deacon; whose children, suffering from the prevailing disease, and covered with discoloured blains, crowded into the only small room of the wretched cottage. Women and children, disfigured by the malignant fever, came to me for medicines; but it was beyond my power to relieve them. Our host, as well as the rest of the inhabitants, was in extreme poverty. Even a little garas, and rancid butter, could with difficulty be collected by contributions from all the houses, and I was at a loss to discover how the people of Be-Alatha lived. Yet the deacon was cheerful and contented, dwelling with resignation upon the misfortunes that had befallen his village, and the misery of his family.

On leaving the village, now containing only ten families, I was accosted by an old priest, who had been waiting until we passed, and who entreated me to eat bread under his roof. As his cottage was distant I was compelled to decline his hospitality, though much touched by his simple kindness, and mild and gentle manners. Finding that I would not go with him, he insisted upon accompanying us to the next village, and took with him three or four sturdy mountaineers, to assist us on our journey; for the roads, he said, were nearly impassable.

Without the assistance of the good priest our attempt to reach Marth d'Kasra would certainly have been hopeless. More than once we turned back in despair, before the slippery rocks and precipitous ascents. Ibrahim Agha, embarrassed by his capacious boots, which, made after the fashion of the Turks, could have contained the extremities of a whole family, was more beset with difficulties than all the party. When he attempted to ride a mule, unused to a pack-saddle, he invariably slid over the tail of the animal, and lay sprawling on the ground, to the great amusement of Yakoub Rais. If he walked, either his boots became wedged into the crevices of the rocks, or filled with gravel, to his no small discomfort. At length, in attempting to cross a bed of loose stones, he lost all presence of mind, and remained fixed in the middle, fearful to advance or retreat. The rubbish yielded to his grasp, and he looked down into a black abyss, towards which he found himself gradually sinking with the avalanche he had put in motion. There was certainly enough to frighten any Turk, and Ibrahim Agha clung to the face of the declivity—the picture of despair. 'What's the Kurd doing?' cried a Tiyari, with whom all Mussulmans were Kurds, and who was waiting to pass on; 'Is there anything here to turn a man's face pale? This is dashta, dashta' (a plain, a plain). Ibrahim Agha, who guessed from the words Kurd and dashta, the meaning of which he had learnt, the purport of the Christian's address, almost forgot his danger in his rage and indignation. 'Gehannem with your dashta!' cried he, still clinging to the moving stones, 'and dishonour upon your wife and mother. Oh! that I could only get one way or the other to show this infidel what it is to laugh at the beard of an Osmanli, and to call him a Kurd in the bargain!' With the assistance of the mountaineers he was at length rescued from his perilous position, but not restored to good humour. By main force the mules were dragged over this and similar places; the Tiyaris seizing them by the halter and tail, and throwing them on their sides.

We were two hours struggling through these difficulties before reaching Marth d'Kasra, formerly a large village, but now containing only forty houses.[1] Its appearance, however, was more flourishing than that of Be-Alatha; and the vineyards, and gardens surrounding it, had been carefully trimmed and irrigated. I rode to the house of a priest, and sat there whilst the mules were resting.

As we were engaged in conversation, Ibrahim Agha, who had not yet recovered his composure, entered the room labouring under symptoms of great indignation. The cause of his anger was some women who had commenced their ablutions, in the manner I have already described, near the spot where he had been sitting. 'When I told them to go to a greater distance,' said he, 'they replied, that if I did not wish to see them, I might turn my head the other way. If these infidels have no modesty,' continued he, 'let them at least know that we Mussulmans have. Mohammed Pasha, upon whom God has had mercy! declared of the Arabs, that the men were without religion, the women without drawers, and the horses without bridles; but these unbelievers are verily little better than the beasts of the field.' Having calmed the wrath of the Cawass, I reasoned with the priest on the impropriety of this habit; but he did not appear at all sensible of it, only observing that the custom was general in the mountains.

The road between Marth d' Kasra and Chonba was no less difficult and dangerous than that we had taken in the morning. The gardens of the former village extend to the Zab, and we might have followed the valley; but the men who were with us preferred the shorter road over the mountain, that we might reach Chonba before night-fall.

The villages in the valley of the Zab had suffered more from the Kurds than any other part of Tiyari. Chonba was almost deserted; its houses and churches a mass of ruins, and its gardens and orchards uncultivated and neglected. It was here that Beder Khan Bey, after the great massacre, received Melek Ismail, when delivered a prisoner into his hands. Yakoub, who had been present at the murder of the unfortunate chief of Tiyari, thus described the event. Melek Ismail, his thigh broken by a musket-ball, was carried by a few followers to a cavern in a secluded ravine; where he might have escaped the search of his enemies, had not a woman, to save her life, betrayed his retreat. He

---

[1] The village contains two churches and two priests.

was dragged down the mountain with savage exultation, and brought before Beder Khan Bey. Here he fell upon the ground. 'Wherefore does the infidel sit before me?' exclaimed the ferocious chief, who had seen his broken limb, 'and what dog is this that has dared to shed the blood of true believers?' 'O Mir,' replied Melek Ismail, still undaunted, and partly raising himself, 'this arm has taken the lives of nearly twenty Kurds; and, had God spared me, as many more would have fallen by it.' Beder Khan Bey rose and walked to the Zab, making a sign to his attendants that they should bring the Melek to him. By his directions they held the Christian chief over the river, and, severing his head from his body with a dagger, cast them into the stream.

All the family of the Melek had distinguished themselves, at the time of the invasion, by their courage. His sister, standing by his side, slew four men before she fell mortally wounded.

Over the spring, where we had alighted, formerly grew a cluster of gigantic walnut-trees, celebrated in Tiyari for their size and beauty. They had been cut down by the Kurds, and their massive trunks were still stretched on the ground. A few smaller trees had been left standing, and afforded us shelter. The water, gushing from the foot of an overhanging rock, was pure and refreshing; but the conduits, which had once carried it into the fields, having been destroyed, a small marsh had been formed around the spring. The place consequently abounded in mosquitoes, and we were compelled to keep up large fires during the night, to escape their attacks.

On the following morning we ascended the valley of the Zab, for about three miles, to cross over the river.

A bridge of wicker-work at this part of the river was in better repair than that of Lizan, and we crossed our mules without difficulty. Descending along the banks of the Zab for a short distance, we struck into the mountains; and passing through Kona Zavvi and Bitti, two Kurdish villages buried in orchards, reached Serspeetho about mid-day. We sat for two hours in the house of the priest, who received us very hospitably. Out of eighty families thirty have alone survived; the rest having been utterly destroyed. The two churches were still in ruins, and but a few cottages had as yet been rebuilt.

In the afternoon we resumed our journey, and crossing a high and barren mountain, descended into the valley of Asheetha.

I spent a day in the village, to give rest to our mules; for they stood in great need of it, after crossing the mountains of Tiyari. As I was desirous of visiting some copper mines, described to me by the people of the district, I engaged Kasha Hormuzd, and one Daoud, who had been a workman at Nimroud, to accompany me. We left Asheetha, followed by Yakoub, the priests, and principal inhabitants, who took leave of us at some distance from the village. We chose a different road from that we had followed on entering the mountains, and thus avoided a most precipitous ascent. We entered the mountains to the right, and, after a rapid ascent, found ourselves in a forest of oaks. Our guides were some time in finding the mouth of the mine, which was only known to a few of the mountaineers. At a distance from the entrance, copper ores were scattered in abundance amongst the loose stones. I descended with some difficulty, and discovered many passages running in various directions, all more or less blocked up with rubbish and earth, much of which we had to remove before I could explore the interior of the mine. The copper runs in veins of bright blue; in small crystals, in compact masses, and in powder which I could scrape out of the cracks of the rocks with a knife. I recognised at once in the latter the material used to colour the bricks and ornaments in the Assyrian Palaces. The mine had evidently been opened, and worked at a very remote period. In the Tiyari mountains, particularly in the heights above Lizan, and in the valley of Berwari, mines of iron, lead, copper, and other minerals abound. Both the Kurds and the Chaldæans make their own weapons and implements of agriculture, and cast bullets for their rifles,—collecting the ores, which are scattered on the declivities, or brought down by the torrents.

Leaving the district of Helamoun and Geramoun to our right, we entered a deep valley, and rode for five hours through a thick forest of oak, beech, and other mountain trees, until we reached Challek. By the roadside, as we descended to this place, I observed an extensive ruin, of substantial masonry of square stones. It was evidently a very ancient work, and may have been an Assyrian fort to command the entrance into the mountains.

Challek is a large village, inhabited partly by Chaldæans and partly by Kurds. There are about fifteen families of Christians, who have a church and a priest. The gardens are very extensive, and well irrigated, and the houses are almost concealed in a forest of fruit trees. We passed the night in the residence of the Kiayah, and were hospitably entertained.

In the morning we rode for some time along the banks of the Khabour, and about five hours and a half from Challek forded the Supna, one of its confluents. The valley of Berwari is here broken up into numberless ravines, and is thickly wooded with the gall-bearing oak. The mountain-range separating us, at this point, from the valley of Amadiyah, is considerably lower than where we had previously crossed it. Scattered over the hills are numerous Kurdish villages, and the turreted castle of a chief may occasionally be seen, in the distance, crowning the summit of some isolated rock.

We stopped at the Kurdish village of Ourmeli during the middle of the day, and found there a Su-bashi—a kind of superintendent tax-gatherer—from Mosul, who received me in a manner worthy the dignity of both. He was dressed in an extraordinary assortment of Osmanlu and Kurdish garments, the greater part of which had been, of course, robbed from the inhabitants of the district placed under his care. He treated me with sumptuous hospitality, at the expense of the Kurds, to whom he proclaimed me a particular friend of the Vizir, and a person of very exalted worth. He brought, himself, the first dish of pillau, which was followed by soups, chicken-kibaubs, honey, yaghourt, cream, fruit, and a variety of Kurdish luxuries. He refused to be seated, and waited upon me during the repast. It was evident that all this respectful attention on the part of so great a personage, was not intended to be thrown away; and when he retired I collected a few of the Kurds, and, obtaining their confidence by paying for my breakfast, soon learnt from them that my host had dealt so hardly with the villages in his jurisdiction, that the inhabitants, driven to despair, had sent a deputation to lay their grievances before the Pasha. This might explain the fashion of my reception, which I could scarcely attribute to my own merits. As I anticipated, he came to me before I left, and commenced a discourse on the character of Kurds in general, and on the way of governing them. 'Wallah, Billah, O Bey!' said he, 'these Kurds are no Mussulmans; they are worse than unbelievers; they are nothing but thieves and murderers; they will cut a man's throat for a para. You will know what to tell His Highness when he asks you about them. They are beasts that must be driven by the bit and the spur; give them too much barley,' continuing the simile, 'and they will get fat, and vicious, and dangerous. No, no, you must take away the barley and leave them only the straw.' 'You have no doubt,' I observed, eyeing his many-coloured Kurdish cloak, 'taken care that as little be left them to fatten upon as possible.' 'I am the lowest of His Highness's servants,' he replied, scarcely suppressing a broad grin; 'but nevertheless, God knows that I am not the least zealous in his service.' It was at any rate satisfactory to find that, in the Su-bashi's system of government,

Kurds and Christians were placed on an equal footing, and that the Mussulmans themselves now tasted of the miseries they had so long inflicted with impunity upon others.

We soon crossed the valley of Amadiyah, and meeting the high road between Daoudeeya and Mosul, entered some low hills thickly set with Kurdish villages. In Kuremi, through which we passed, there dwells a holy Sheikh, who enjoys a great reputation for sanctity and miracles throughout Kurdistan. He was seated in the Iwan, or open chamber, of a very neat house; built, kept in repair, and continually white-washed by the inhabitants of the place. A beard, white as snow, fell almost to his waist; and he wore a turban and a long gown of spotless white linen. He is almost blind, and sat rocking himself to and fro, fingering his rosary. He keeps a perpetual Ramazan, never eating between dawn and sunset. Ibrahim Agha, who was not more friendly to the Kurds than the Su-bashi, treated the Sheikh to a most undignified epithet as he passed. Although I might not have expressed myself so forcibly as the Cawass, I could not but concur generally in his opinion when reflecting that this man, and some others of the same class, had been the chief cause of the massacres of the unfortunate Christians; and that, at that moment, his son, Sheikh Tahar[1], was urging Beder Khan Bey to prove his religious zeal by shedding anew the blood of the Chaldæans.

We stopped for the night in the large Catholic Chaldæan village of Mungayshi, containing above forty Christian houses, a new church, and two priests. The inhabitants carry on a considerable trade with Mosul in raisins, and their vineyards are extensive and well cultivated.

A pass, over a richly wooded range of hills, leads from Mungayshi into a fertile plain, watered by several streams, and occupied by many Kurdish villages. Beyond, the mountains are naked and most barren. We wandered for some hours amongst pinnacles, through narrow ravines, and over broken rocks of sandstone, all scattered about in the wildest confusion. Not a blade of vegetation was to be seen; the ground was parched by the sun, and was here and there blackened by volcanic action. We came to several large pools of hot, sulphurous springs, bubbling up in many parts of the valley. In the spring, both the Kurds and the people of the surrounding villages congregate near these reservoirs, and pitch their tents for nearly a month; bathing continually

---

[1] This fanatic, who was one of Beder Khan Bey's principal advisers, when entering Mosul was accustomed to throw a veil over his face that his sight might not be polluted by Christians, and other impurities in the place. He exercises an immense influence over the Kurdish population, who look upon him as a saint and worker of miracles.

in the waters, which have a great reputation for their medicinal qualities.

A long defile brought us to the town of Dohuk, formerly a place of some importance, but now nearly in ruins. It is built on an island formed by a small stream, and probably occupies an ancient site. Ismail Bey, the Mutesellim, received me very civilly, and I breakfasted with him. The son of a Kurdish chief, of some importance in the neighbourhood, was visiting the Bey. He was dressed in a most elaborately embroidered suit, had ponderous jewelled rings in his ears, carried enormous weapons in his girdle, and had stuck in his turban a profusion of marigolds and other flowers. He was a handsome, intelligent boy; but, young as he might be, he was already a precocious pupil of Sheikh Tahar; and when I put him upon a religious topic, he entered most gravely into an argument to prove the obligation imposed upon Mussulmans to exterminate the unbelievers, supporting his theological views by very apt quotations from the Koran.

My horses, which had been sent from Amadiyah, were waiting for me here; and leaving our jaded mules we rode on to the Christian village of Malthaiyah, about one hour beyond, and in the same valley as Dohuk. Being anxious to visit the rock-sculptures near this place, I took a peasant with me and rode to the foot of a neighbouring hill. A short walk up a very difficult ascent brought me to the monuments.

Four tablets have been cut in the rock. On each tablet are nine figures. The sculpture is Assyrian, and evidently of the later period, contemporary with the edifices of Khorsabad and Kouyunjik. The subjects represented in the four bas-reliefs are similar, and appear to be an adoration of the gods. Two figures, the first and the last, are those of kings; the remainder those of divinities, standing upon animals. All the tablets have suffered much from long exposure to the atmosphere, and one has been almost destroyed by the entrance into a chamber, which probably at one time served for a tomb, cut in the rock behind it.

The details in these bas-reliefs are, as far as they can be distinguished, precisely similar to those on the later Assyrian monuments. In the head-dress of the kings, in the form of the chair of the sitting divinity, and in the mode of treatment, the sculptures of Malthaiyah closely resemble those of Khorsabad.

I returned to the village after sunset. My Cawass and servants had established themselves for the night on the roof of the church; and the Kiayah had prepared a very substantial repast. The inhabitants of Malthaiyah are Catholic Chaldæans; their conversion not dating many years. The greater part joined us in the evening. My companion, who was always ready to plunge into a religious controversy, and delighted in the subtle distinctions between the Nestorian and Roman Catholic creeds, engaged them at once on these subjects; bringing about a noisy theological combat, which lasted till past midnight, without any one being convinced of his errors.

The next morning we rode over a dreary plain to Alkosh. In a defile, through the hills behind the village, I observed several rock-tombs,—excavations similar to those of Malthaiyah; some having rude ornaments above the entrance, the door-ways of others being simply square holes in the rock.

On reaching Alkosh I proceeded at once to the house of the Kiayah, but found his apartments occupied by a Su-bashi, a pompous, ill-favoured Turk; who, putting his head out of the window, asked, in a very impertinent way, who I was, whence I came, where I was going and what I wanted,—questions which were not otherwise answered than by his being speedily dislodged from his corner, and pushed by the shoulders into the street, to his no small surprise, and to the great satisfaction and delight of a crowd of by-standers, who had been all more or less the victims of his extortions. 'What dog are you,' exclaimed Ibrahim Agha, as he gave him the last push into the gutter, and made many very offensive and unwarrantable allusions to the female members of his family, 'to establish a Makiamah[1] up there, and cross-question people like his Reverence the Cadi? O you offspring of a bad breed! you shall have the Dahiakparasi[2]; but it shall be on the soles of your feet.'

Alkosh is a very considerable Christian village. The inhabitants, who were formerly pure Chaldæans, have been converted to Roman Catholicism. It contains, according to a very general tradition, the tomb of Nahum, the prophet—the Alkoshite, as he is called in the introduction to his prophecies. It is a place held in great reverence by Mohammedans and Christians, but especially by Jews, who keep the building in repair, and flock here in great numbers at certain seasons of the year. The tomb is a simple plaster box, covered with green cloth, and standing at the upper end of a large chamber. On the walls of the room are slips of paper, upon which are written, in distorted Hebrew characters, religious exhortations, and the dates and particulars of the visits of various Jewish families. The house containing the tomb is a modern

[1] Court of Justice.
[2] Literally 'stick-money', the tax on suits paid to the Cadi.

building. There are no inscriptions, nor fragments of any antiquity about the place; and I am not aware in what the tradition originated, or how long it has attached to the village of Alkosh.

After visiting the tomb I rode to the convent of Rabban Hormuzd, built on the almost perpendicular sides of lofty rocks. The spot is well suited to solitude and devotion. Half-buried in barren crags, the building can scarcely be distinguished from the natural pinnacles by which it is surrounded. There is scarcely a blade of vegetation to be seen, except a few olive trees, encouraged, by the tender solicitude of the monks, to struggle with the barren soil. Around the convent, in almost every accessible part of the mountains, are a multitude of caves or chambers in the rock, said to have once served as retreats for a legion of hermits, and from which most probably were ejected the dead, to make room for the living; for they appear to have been, for the most part, at a very remote period, places of burial.

Rabban Hormuzd, formerly in the possession of the Nestorian Chaldæans, but now appropriated by the Catholics, is said to have been founded by one of the early Chaldæan Patriarchs, in the latter part of the fourth century. The saint, after whom the convent is called, is much venerated by the Nestorians. He was, according to some traditions, the son of a king of Persia, and a Christian martyr. The convent is an extensive building, partly excavated in the rocks, and partly constructed of stones well cut and fitted together. In the chapel are the tombs of several Patriarchs of the Chaldæan Church, buried here long before its divisions, and whose titles, carved upon the monuments, are always 'Patriarch of the Chaldæans of the East.'[1] Six or eight half famished monks reside in the convent. They depend for supplies, which are scanty enough, upon the faithful of the surrounding country.

It was night before we reached the large Catholic village of Tel Kef. I had sent a horseman in the morning, to apprise the people of my intended visit; and Gouriel, the Kiayah, with several of the principal inhabitants, had assembled to receive me. As we approached they emerged from a dark recess, where they had probably been waiting for

---

[1] The seal used by Mar Shamoun bears the same title, and the Patriarch so styles himself in all public documents. It is only lately that he has been induced, on some occasions, *when addressing Europeans*, to call himself 'Patriarch of the Nestorians'; the name never having been used by the Chaldæans themselves. The Catholics have endeavoured to fix the title of Chaldæans upon the converted alone, using that of Nestorian as one of contempt and reproach, in speaking of those who have retained their ancient faith. I have termed the Nestorians 'Chaldæans' or 'Nestorian Chaldæans', and the new sect 'Catholic Chaldæans'.

some time. They carried a few wax lights, which served as an illumi-
nation. The motion of these lights, as the bearers advanced, was so
unsteady, that there could be no doubt of the condition of the deputation.

Gouriel and his friends reeled forward towards my Cawass who
chanced to be the first of the party, and believing him to be me they fell
upon him, kissing his hands and feet, and clinging to his dress. Ibrahim
Agha struggled hard to extricate himself, but in vain. 'The Bey's
behind,' roared he. 'Allah! Allah! will no one deliver me from these
drunken infidels?' Rejoicing in the mistake, I concealed myself among
the horsemen. Gouriel, seizing the bridle of Ibrahim Agha's horse, and
unmindful of the blows which the Cawass dealt about him, led him in
triumph to his residence. It was not before the wife of the Kiayah and
some women, who had assembled to cook our dinner, brought torches,
that the deputation discovered their error. I had alighted in the meanwhile unseen, and had found my way to the roof of the house, where all
the cushions that could be found in the village were piled up in front of
a small table covered with bottles of raki and an assortment of raisins
and parched peas, all prepared in my honour. I hid myself among the
pillows, and it was some time before the Kiayah discovered my retreat.
He hiccuped out excuses till he was breathless, and endeavouring to
kiss my feet, asked forgiveness for the unfortunate blunder. I would
have remonstrated with my hosts; but there was no one in a fit state to
hear advice; and I was not sorry to see them at midnight scattered over
the roof, buried in profound sleep. I ordered the horses to be loaded,
and reached Mosul as the gates opened at daybreak.

The reader may desire to learn the fate of Tkhoma. A few days after
my return to Mosul, notwithstanding the attempts of Tahyar Pasha to
avert the calamity, Beder Khan Bey marched through the Tiyari
mountains, on his way to the unfortunate district. The inhabitants of
Tkhoma, headed by their Meleks, made some resistance, but were soon
overpowered by numbers. An indiscriminate massacre took place. The
women were brought before the chief, and murdered in cold blood.
Those who attempted to escape were cut off. Three hundred women
and children, who were flying into Baz, were killed in the pass I have
described. The principal villages with their gardens were destroyed, and
the churches pulled down. Nearly half the population fell victims to the
fanatical fury of the Kurdish chief; amongst these were one of the
Meleks, and Kasha Bodaca. With this good priest, and Kasha Auraham,
perished the most learned of the Nestorian clergy; and Kasha Kana is

the last who has inherited any part of the knowledge, and zeal, which once so eminently distinguished the Chaldæan priesthood.

The Porte was prevailed upon to punish this atrocious massacre, and to crush a rebellious subject who had long resisted its authority. An expedition was fitted out under Osman Pasha; and after two engagements, in which the Kurds were signally defeated, Beder Khan Bey took refuge in a mountain-castle. The position had been nearly carried, when the chief, finding defence hopeless, succeeded in obtaining from the Turkish commander, Osman Pasha, the same terms which had been offered to him before the commencement of hostilities. Although the Turkish ministers more than suspected that Osman Pasha had reasons of his own for granting these terms, they honourably fulfilled the conditions upon which the chief, although a rebel, had surrendered. He was brought to Constantinople, and subsequently sent to the Island of Candia—a punishment totally inadequate to his numerous crimes.

After Beder Khan Bey had retired from Tkhoma, a few of the surviving inhabitants returned to their ruined villages; but Nur-Ullah Bey, suspecting that they knew of concealed property, fell suddenly upon them. Many died under the tortures to which they were exposed; and the rest, as soon as they were released, fled into Persia. This flourishing district was thus destroyed; and it will be long ere its cottages again rise from their ruins, and the fruits of patient toil again clothe the sides of its valleys.

VIII

THE ACCOUNT GIVEN in the preceding chapter, of the Chaldæan or Nestorian tribes, will probably have made the reader desirous of knowing something of the events which led to the isolation of a small Christian community in the midst of the mountains of Kurdistan.

In the first centuries of the Christian æra, the plains of Assyria Proper were still the battle-ground of the nations of the East, and the West. The doctrines of Christianity had early penetrated into the Assyrian provinces; they may even have been carried there by those who had imbibed them at their source. When, in the first part of the fifth century, the church was agitated by the dissensions of St. Cyril and Nestorius, the Patriarch of Constantinople, the Chaldæans were already recognised as one of the most extensive of the Eastern sects.

Subsequently, Babæus, [Archbishop of Seleucia 498-503,] openly declared himself in favour of the [doctrines associated with the name of Nestorius]; and from his accession may be dated the first recognised establishment of the Nestorian Church in the East, and the promulgation of its doctrines amongst the nations of central Asia.

Until the establishment of the Arab supremacy in the provinces to the east of the Tigris, the Chaldæans were alternately protected and persecuted; their condition mainly depending upon the relative strength of the Persian and Byzantine Empires. They laboured assiduously to disseminate their doctrines over the continent of Asia; and it is even asserted that one of the Persian Kings was amongst their converts. From Persia, where the Chaldæan Bishoprics were early established, they spread eastwards. We find, in the earliest annals of the Chaldæan Church, frequent accounts of missionaries sent by the Patriarchs of the East into Tatary and China, and notices of their success and of their fate.

At the time of the Arab invasion, the learning of the East was still chiefly to be found amongst the Chaldæans. We are indebted to the

189

Chaldæans for the preservation of numerous precious fragments of Greek learning; as the Greeks were, many centuries before, to the ancestors of the Chaldæans for the records of astronomy and the elements of Eastern science. In the celebrated schools of Edessa, Nisibis, and Seleucia, the early languages of the country, the Chaldee and Syriac, as well as Greek, were publicly taught; and there were masters of the sciences of grammar, rhetoric, poetry, dialectics, arithmetic, geometry, music, astronomy, and medicine, whose treatises were preserved in public libraries. The works of Greek physicians and philosophers had at an early period been translated into Chaldee. They excited the curiosity of the Caliphs, who were then the encouragers and patrons of learning; and by their orders they were translated by Nestorian Chaldæans into Arabic.

After the fall of the Caliphs[1], the power of the Chaldæan Patriarch in the East rapidly declined. The sect endured persecution from the Tatar sovereigns, and had to contend against even more formidable rivals in the Catholic missionaries, who now began to spread themselves over Asia. But it is to the merciless Tamerlane that their reduction to a few wanderers in the provinces of Assyria must be attributed. He followed them with relentless fury; destroyed their churches, and put to the sword all who were unable to escape to the almost inaccessible fastnesses of the Kurdish mountains. Those who at that time sought the heights and valleys of Kurdistan, were the descendants of the ancient Assyrians, and the remnant of one of the earliest Christian sects.

From the year 1413, the Chaldæan records contain scarcely any mention of the existence of the Nestorian church beyond the confines of Kurdistan. A few Chaldæans who still dwelt in the cities and villages of the plains, were exposed not only to the tyranny of Turkish governors, but to the machinations of Popish emissaries, and did not long retain their faith. Those alone who had found refuge in Kurdistan, and on the banks of the Lake of Oroomiah in Persia, remained faithful to their church. The former maintained a kind of semi-independence, and boasted that no conqueror had penetrated into their secluded valleys. Although they recognised the supremacy of the Sultan by the payment of an annual tribute, no governors had been sent to their districts; nor, until the invasion and massacre described in the last chapter, had any Turk, or Kurd, exercised authority in their villages.

It is only in the mountains of Kurdistan, and in the villages of the district of Oroomiah in Persia, that any remnant of this once wide-

[1] [A.D. 1258.]

spreading sect can now be discovered; unless, indeed, the descendants of those whom they converted still preserve their faith in some remote province of the Chinese Empire.

The Patriarch [of the Nestorian Chaldæans] is always chosen, if not of necessity, at least by general consent, from one family. It is necessary that the mother should abstain from meat and all animal food, some months before the birth of a child, who is destined for the high office of chief of the Chaldæan Church. The Patriarch himself never tastes meat. Vegetables and milk constitute his only nourishment. He should be consecrated by three Metropolitans, and he always receives the name of Shamoun, or Simon; whilst his rival, the Patriarch of the converted Chaldæans, in like manner, always assumes that of Usuf, or Joseph.

The language of the Chaldæans is a Shemitic dialect allied to the Hebrew, the Arabic, and the Syriac, and still bears the name of Chaldee. Most of their church books are written in Syriac, which, like the Latin in the West, became the sacred language in the greater part of the East. The dialect spoken by the mountain tribes varies slightly from that used in the villages of the plains.

The Protestants of America have, for some time past, taken a deep interest in the Chaldæans. Their missionaries have opened schools in and around Oroomiah. A printing-press has been established, and several works, including the Scriptures, have already been issued in the vernacular language of the people, and printed in a character peculiar to them. Their labours have, I believe, been successful.

It is to be hoped that the establishment of the authority of the Sultan in the mountains, and the removal of several of the most fanatical and bloodthirsty of the Kurdish chiefs, will henceforth enable the Chaldæans to profess their faith without hindrance or restraint[1]; and that, freed from fears of fresh aggression, they may, by their activity and industry, restore prosperity to their mountain districts. As the only remnant of a great nation, every one must feel an interest in their history and condition; and our sympathies cannot but be excited in favour of a long-persecuted people, who have merited the title of 'the Protestants of Asia.'

---

[1] [Layard's hopes were not realised. Another massacre of these people occurred as recently as 1933.]

IX

A FEW DAYS after my return to Mosul from the Tiyari mountains, a Cawal, or priest of the Yezidis, was sent by Sheikh Nasr, the religious chief of that remarkable sect, to invite Mr. Rassam and myself to their great periodical feast at Sheikh Adi. The Vice-consul was unable to accept the invitation; but I seized with eagerness the opportunity of being present at ceremonies not before witnessed by an European—ceremonies which have given rise, among Mussulmans and Christians, to fables ascribing to them certain midnight orgies, and every excess of debauchery and lust. The quiet and inoffensive demeanour of the Yezidis, and the cleanliness and order of their villages, do not certainly warrant these charges. Their known respect or fear for the evil principle has acquired for them the title of 'Worshippers of the Devil.' Many stories are current as to the emblems by which this spirit is represented. They are believed by some to adore a cock, by others a peacock; but their worship, their tenets, and their origin were alike a subject of mystery which I felt anxious to clear up as far as I was able.

The origin of my invitation proves that the Yezidis may lay claim to a virtue which is, unfortunately, not of frequent occurrence in the East, —I mean gratitude. When Keritli Oglu, Mohammed Pasha, first came to Mosul, this sect was amongst the objects of his cupidity and tyranny. He seized by treachery, as he supposed, their head or high-priest; but Sheikh Nasr had time to escape the plot against him, and to substitute in his place the second in authority, who was carried a prisoner to the town. Such is the attachment shown by the Yezidis to their chief, that the deceit was not revealed, and the substitute bore with resignation the tortures and imprisonment inflicted upon him. Mr. Rassam having been applied to, obtained his release from the Pasha, on the advance of a considerable sum of money, which the inhabitants of the district of Sheikhan undertook to repay, in course of time, out of the produce of their fields. They punctually fulfilled the engagement thus entered into and looked to the British Vice-consul as their protector.

It was customary for the Yezidis to meet periodically in large numbers at the tomb of their great Saint. Men and women from the Sinjar, and from the northern districts of Kurdistan, left their tents and pastures to be present at the solemnisation of their holy rites. Owing to the disturbed state of the country, and the misconduct of the late Pashas, some years had elapsed since the Yezidis had assembled at Sheikh Adi. The short rule of Ismail Pasha, and the conciliatory measures of the new governor, had so far restored confidence amongst persons of all sects, that the Worshippers of the Devil had determined to celebrate their great festival with more than ordinary solemnity and rejoicings. This year, as the roads were once more free from plunderers, it was expected that the distant tribes would again repair to the tomb of the Sheikh.

I quitted Mosul, accompanied by Hodja Toma (the dragoman of the Vice-consulate), and the Cawal, or priest, sent by Sheikh Nasr. We were joined on the road by several Yezidis, who were, like ourselves, on their way to the place of meeting. We passed the night in a small hamlet near Khorsabad, and reached Baadri early next day. This village, the residence of Sheikh Nasr, the religious, and Hussein Bey, the political chief of the Yezidis, is about five miles to the north of Ain Sifni.

On approaching the village I was met by Hussein Bey, followed by the priests and principal inhabitants on foot. The chief was about eighteen years of age, and one of the handsomest young men I ever saw. His features were regular and delicate, his eye lustrous and the long curls, which fell from under his variegated turban, of the deepest black. An ample white cloak of fine texture, was thrown over his rich jacket and robes. I dismounted as he drew near, and he endeavoured to kiss my hand; but to this ceremony I decidedly objected; and we compromised matters by embracing each other after the fashion of the country. He then insisted upon leading my horse, which he wished me to remount, and it was with difficulty that I at length prevailed upon him to walk with me into the village. He led me to his salamlik, or reception room, in which carpets and cushions had been spread. Through the centre ran a stream of fresh water derived from a neighbouring spring. The people of the place stood at the lower end of the room, and listened in respectful silence to the conversation between their chief and myself.

Breakfast was brought to us from the harem of Hussein Bey; and the crowd having retired after we had eaten, I was left during the heat of the day to enjoy the cool temperature of the salamlik.

I was awakened in the afternoon by that shrill cry of the women, which generally announces some happy event. The youthful chief entered soon afterwards, followed by a long retinue. It was evident, from the smile upon his features, that he had joyful news to communicate. He seated himself on my carpet, and thus addressed me:— 'O Bey, your presence has brought happiness on our house. At your hands we receive nothing but good. We are all your servants; and, praise be to the Highest, in this house another servant has been born to you. The child is yours: he is our first-born, and he will grow up under your shadow. Let him receive his name from you, and be hereafter under your protection.' The assembly joined in the request, and protested that this event was solely to be attributed to my fortunate visit. I was not quite aware of the nature of the ceremony, if any, in which I might be expected to join on naming the new-born chief, and I was naturally anxious to ascertain the amount of responsibility which I might incur, in standing godfather to a devil-worshipping baby. However, as I was assured that no other form was necessary than the mere selection of a name (the rite of baptism being reserved for a future day, when the child could be carried to the tomb of Sheikh Adi, and could bear immersion in its sacred waters), I thus answered Hussein Bey:— 'O Bey, I rejoice in this happy event, for which we must return thanks to God. May this son be but the first of many who will preserve, as their forefathers have done, the fame and honour of your house. As you ask of me a name for this child I could give you many which, in my language and country, are well-sounding and honourable; but your tongue could not utter them, and they would moreover be without meaning. Were it usual I would call him after his father; but such is not the custom. I have not forgotten the name of his grandfather,—a name which still brings to the memory of the Yezidis the days of their prosperity and happiness. Let him therefore be known as Ali Bey; and may he live to see the Yezidis as they were in the time of him after whom he is called.'—This oration, which was accompanied by a few gold coins to be sewn to the cap of the infant, was received with great applause; and the name of Ali Bey was unanimously adopted[1]; one of

---

[1] [The person so named died in 1913, murdered, according to some, by his wife's paramour. The editor owes this information to the kindness of Major C. J. Edmonds, to whose *A Pilgrimage to Lalish* (1967) the reader may be referred for further authoritative details of the Yezidis.]

the chief's relations hastening to the harem, to communicate it to the ladies. He returned with a carpet and some embroidery, as presents from the mother, and with an invitation to the harem to see the females of the family. I found there the chief's mother and his second wife; for he had already taken two. They assured me that the lady, who had just brought joy to the house, was even more thankful than her husband; and that her gratitude to me, as the author of her happiness, was unbounded. They brought me honey and strings of dried figs from the Sinjar, and entertained me with domestic histories until I thought it time to return to the salamlik.

The Yezidis were some years ago a very powerful tribe. Their principal strongholds were in the district which I was now visiting, and in the Jebel Sinjar, a solitary mountain rising in the centre of the Mesopotamian desert to the west of Mosul. The last independent chief of the Yezidis of Sheikhan was Ali Bey, the father of Hussein Bey. He was beloved by his tribe and sufficiently brave and skilful in war to defend them, for many years, against the attacks of the Kurds and Mussulmans of the plain. The powerful Bey of Rowandiz, who had united most of the Kurdish tribes of the surrounding mountains under his banner, and had defied for many years the Turks and the Persians, resolved to crush the hateful sect of the Yezidis. Ali Bey's forces were greatly inferior in numbers to those of his persecutor. He was defeated, and fell into the hands of the Rowandiz chief, who put him to death. The inhabitants of Sheikhan fled to Mosul. It was in spring; the river had overflowed its banks, and the bridge of boats had been removed. A few succeeded in crossing the stream; but a vast crowd of men, women, and children were left upon the opposite side, and congregated on the great mound of Kouyunjik. The Bey of Rowandiz followed them. An indiscriminate slaughter ensued; and the people of Mosul beheld, from their terraces, the murder of these unfortunate fugitives, who cried to them in vain for help—for both Christians and Mussulmans rejoiced in the extermination of an odious and infidel sect, and no arm was lifted in their defence. Hussein Bey, having been carried by his mother to the mountains, escaped the general slaughter. He was carefully brought up by the Yezidis, and from his infancy had been regarded as their chief.

It will be remembered that Mohammedans, in their dealings with men of other creeds, make a distinction between such as are believers in the sacred books, and such as have no recognised inspired works. To the first category belong Christians of all denominations, as receiving the two Testaments; and the Jews, as followers of the old. With

Christians and Jews, therefore, they may treat, make peace, and live; but with such as are included in the second class, the good Mussulman can have no intercourse. The Yezidis, not being looked upon as 'Masters of a Book,' have been exposed for centuries to the persecution of the Mohammedans. Yearly expeditions have been made by the governors of provinces into their districts; and whilst the men and women were slaughtered without mercy, the children of both sexes were carried off, and exposed for sale in the principal towns. These annual hunts were one of the sources of revenue of Beder Khan Bey; and it was the custom of the Pashas of Baghdad and Mosul to let loose the irregular troops upon the ill-fated Yezidis, as an easy method of satisfying their demands for arrears of pay. This system was still practised to a certain extent within a very few months of my visit; and gave rise to atrocities scarcely equalled in the better known slave trade. It may be hoped that the humane and tolerant policy of the Sultan, which has already conferred such great and lasting benefits upon multitudes of his subjects, will be extended to this unfortunate sect.

It was not unnatural that the Yezidis should revenge themselves, whenever an opportunity might offer, upon their oppressors. They formed themselves into bands, and were long the terror of the country. No Mussulman that fell into their hands was spared. Caravans were plundered, and merchants murdered without mercy. Christians, however, were not molested; for the Yezidis looked upon them as fellow-sufferers for religion's sake. These acts of retaliation furnished an excuse for the invasion of the Sinjar by Mehemet Reshid, and a second time by Hafiz Pasha. On both occasions there was a massacre, and the population was reduced by three-fourths. The Yezidis took refuge in caves, where they were either suffocated by fires lighted at the mouth, or destroyed by discharges of cannon. The devotion of the Yezidis to their religion is no less remarkable than that of the Jews; and I remember no instance of a person of full age renouncing his faith. They invariably prefer death, and submit with resignation to the tortures inflicted upon them. Even children of tender age, although educated in Turkish harems, and nominally professing the Mussulman religion, have frequently retained in secret the peculiar doctrines of the sect, and have been in communication with Yezidi priests.

Sheikh Nasr had already left Baadri, and was preparing for the religious ceremonies at the tomb of Sheikh Adi. I visited his wife, and was gratified by the unaffected hospitality of my reception, and by the cleanliness of the house and its scanty furniture. All the dwellings which I entered appeared equally neat and well built. Some stood in small gardens filled with flowers, and near them were streams of running water, brought from the abundant springs which issue from the hill above the village.

Late in the afternoon two horsemen arrived, as if from a long journey. Their garments were torn, and their faces bronzed and weather beaten. They were received with general demonstrations of joy by the inhabitants of the village, who crowded round them. Throwing down their guns, they kissed my hand, and then that of the chief. They had returned from a mission to a branch of the Yezidis, who had crossed the frontiers some years before, and had taken refuge from the tyranny of the Kurds in the Russian territories. They were bringing back a considerable sum of money towards the support of their clergy, and the repair of the tomb of Sheikh Adi. They described the flourishing state of those they had visited, and the wonders they had seen in Georgia.

Walking to the ruins of the fort built by Ali Bey, which crowns a hill overhanging the village, I found, on the outskirts of the houses, the women performing their ablutions in the principal stream. They were preparing for the festival of the morrow; for no one can enter the valley of Sheikh Adi on this occasion without having first purified his body and his clothes. They took no notice of me; and, although divested of all their garments, walked about unconcernedly. The men had been washing during the day in another part of the rivulet.

At dawn Hussein Bey issued from his harem, armed and dressed in his gayest robes, ready to proceed to the tomb of the saint. The principal people of the village were soon collected, and we all started together, forming a long procession, preceded by musicians with the tambourine and pipe. The women were busily employed in loading their donkeys with carpets and domestic utensils. They were to follow leisurely. Hussein Bey and I rode together, and as long as the ground permitted, the horsemen and footmen who accompanied us, engaged in mimic fight, discharging their fire-arms into the air, and singing their war-cry. We soon reached the foot of a very precipitous ascent, up which ran a steep and difficult pathway. The horsemen now rode on in single file, and we were frequently compelled to dismount and drag our horses over the rocks. We gained the summit of the pass in about an hour, and looked down into the richly wooded valley of Sheikh Adi. As soon as the white spire of the tomb appeared above the trees, all our party discharged their guns. The echoes had scarcely died away, when our signal was answered by similar discharges from below. As we descended through the thick wood of oaks, we passed many pilgrims on their way, like ourselves, to the tomb; the women seated under the trees, relieving themselves awhile from their infant burdens; the men re-adjusting the loads which the rapid descent had displaced. As each new body of travellers caught sight of the object of their journey, they fired their guns, and shouted the cry of the tribe to those below.

At some distance from the tomb we were met by Sheikh Nasr and a crowd of priests and armed men. The Sheikh was dressed in the purest white linen, as were the principal members of the priesthood. His age could scarcely have exceeded forty; his manners were most mild and pleasing; he welcomed me with warmth; and it was evident that my visit had made a very favourable impression upon all present. After I had embraced the chief and exchanged salutations with his followers, we walked together towards the sacred precincts. The outer court, as well as the avenue which led to it, was filled with people; but they made way for us as we approached, and every one eagerly endeavoured to kiss my hand.

The Yezidis always enter the inner court of the tomb barefooted. I followed the custom, and left my shoes at the entrance. I seated myself, with Sheikh Nasr and Hussein Bey, upon carpets spread under an arbour, formed by a wide-spreading vine. The Sheikhs and Cawals, two of the principal orders of the priesthood, alone entered with us, and squatted around the yard against the walls. The trees which grew amongst and around the buildings threw an agreeable shade over the whole assembly. I entered into conversation with Sheikh Nasr and the priests, and found them more communicative than I could have ex-pected. I deferred, however, until I could be alone with the chief, such questions as he might be unwilling to answer in the presence of others.

The tomb of Sheikh Adi is in a narrow valley, or rather ravine, which has only one outlet, as the rocks rise precipitously on all sides, except where a small stream forces its way into a larger valley beyond. It stands in a court-yard, and is surrounded by a few buildings, inhabited by the guardians and servants of the sanctuary. The interior is divided into three principal compartments; a large hall partitioned in the centre by a row of columns and arches, and having at the upper end a reservoir filled by an abundant spring issuing from the rock; and two smaller apartments, in which are the tombs of the saint and of some inferior personage. The water of the reservoir is regarded with peculiar venera-tion, and is believed to be derived from the holy well of Zemzem [at

Mecca]. In it children are baptized, and it is used for other sacred purposes.

The tomb of Sheikh Adi is covered, as is the custom in Mussulman sanctuaries, by a large square case or box made of clay and plastered; an embroidered green cloth being thrown over it. It is in the inner room, which is dimly lighted by a small lamp. On it is written the chapter of the Koran, called the Ayat el Courci.[1]

In the principal hall a few lamps are generally burning, and at sunset lights are placed in niches scattered over the walls.

Two white spires, rising above the building, form a pleasing contrast with the rich foliage by which they are surrounded. They are topped by gilt ornaments, and their sides are fashioned into many angles, causing an agreeable variety of light and shade. On the lintels of the doorway are rudely carved a lion, a snake, a hatchet, a man, and a comb. The snake is particularly conspicuous. Although it might be suspected that these figures were emblematical, I could obtain no other explanation from Sheikh Nasr, than that they had been cut by the Christian mason who repaired the tomb some years ago, as ornaments suggested by his mere fancy.

In the centre of the inner court, and under the vine, is a square plaster case, in which is a small recess filled with balls of clay taken from the tomb of the saint. These are sold and distributed to pilgrims, and regarded as very sacred relics—useful against diseases and evil spirits. Certain members of the priesthood and their families alone inhabit the surrounding buildings. They are chosen to watch over the sacred precincts, and are supplied with provisions, and supported by contributions from the tribe.

The outer court is enclosed by low buildings, with recesses similar to those in an Eastern bazaar. They are intended for the accommodation of pilgrims, and for the stalls of pedlars, during the celebration of the festival. Several gigantic trees throw their shade over the open space, and streams of fresh water are led around the buildings.

Around the tomb, and beneath the trees which grow on the sides of the mountain, are numerous rudely-constructed edifices, each belonging to a Yezidi district or tribe. The pilgrims, according to the place from which they come, reside in them during the time of the feast; so

[1] [Literally 'the Throne verse', which occurs in the Koran ii 256: 'God, there is no god but He, the living, the self-subsistent. Slumber takes Him not, nor sleep. His is what is in the heavens and what is in the earth. . . . His throne extends over the heavens and the earth, and it tires Him not to guard them both, for He is high and grand.' (Translation after E. H. Palmer, *The Qur'án*, Part I, p. 40).]

that each portion of the valley is known by the name of the country, or tribe, of those who resort there.

I sat till nearly mid-day with the assembly, at the door of the tomb. Sheikh Nasr then rose, and I followed him into the outer court, which was filled by a busy crowd of pilgrims. In the recesses and on the ground were spread the stores of the travelling merchants, who, on such occasions, repair to the valley. Many-coloured handkerchiefs, and cotton stuffs, hung from the branches of the trees; dried figs from the Sinjar, raisins from Amadiyah, dates from Busrah, and walnuts from the mountains, were displayed in heaps upon the pavement. Around these tempting treasures were gathered groups of boys and young girls. Men and women were engaged on all sides in animated conversation, and the hum of human voices was heard through the valley. All respectfully saluted the Sheikh, and made way for us as we approached. We issued from the precincts of the principal building, and seated ourselves on the edge of a fountain built by the road side, and at the end of the avenue of trees leading to the tomb. The slabs surrounding the basin are to some extent looked upon as sacred; and at this time only Sheikh Nasr, Hussein Bey, and myself were permitted to place ourselves upon them. The principal Sheikhs and Cawals sat in a circle round the spring, and listened to the music of pipes and tambourines.

I never beheld a more picturesque or animated scene. Long lines of pilgrims toiled up the avenue. There was the swarthy inhabitant of the Sinjar, with his long black locks, his piercing eye and regular features— his white robes floating in the wind, and his unwieldy matchlock thrown over his shoulder. Then followed the more wealthy families of the Kochers,—the wandering tribes who live in tents in the plains, and among the hills of ancient Adiabene; the men in gay jackets and varie-gated turbans, with fantastic arms in their girdles; the women richly clad in silk antaris; their hair, braided in many tresses, falling down their backs, and adorned with wild flowers; their foreheads almost con-cealed by gold and silver coins; and huge strings of glass beads, coins, and engraved stones hanging round their necks. Next would appear a poverty-stricken family from a village of the Mosul district; the women clad in white, pale and care-worn, bending under the weight of their children; the men urging on the heavily-laden donkey. Similar groups descended from the hills. Repeated discharges of fire-arms, and a well-known signal, announced to those below the arrival of every new party.

All turned to the fountain before proceeding to their allotted station, and laying their arms on the ground, kissed the hands of Sheikh Nasr, Hussein Bey, and myself. After saluting the assembled priests they continued their way up the sides of the mountains, and chose some wide-spreading oak, or the roof of a building, for a resting-place during their sojourn in the valley. They then spread their carpets, and, lighting fires with dry branches and twigs, busied themselves in preparing their food. Such groups were scattered in every direction. There was scarcely a tree without its colony.

All, before entering the sacred valley, washed themselves and their clothes in the stream issuing from it. They came thus purified to the feast. I never before saw so much assembled cleanliness in the East. Their garments, generally white, were spotless.

During the afternoon, dances were performed before the Bey and myself. They resembled the Arab Debkhè and the Kurdish Tchopee. As many young men as could crowd in the small open space in front of the fountain joined in them. Others sang in chorus with the music. Every place from which a sight could be obtained of the dancers was occupied by curious spectators. Even the branches above our heads were bending under the clusters of boys who had discovered that, from them, they could get a full view of what was going on below. The manœuvres of one of these urchins gave rise to a somewhat amusing incident, which illustrates the singular superstitions of this sect. He had forced himself to the very end of a weak bough, which was immediately above me, and threatened every moment to break under the weight. As I looked up I saw the impending danger, and made an effort, by an appeal to the Chief, to avert it. 'If that young Sheit——' I exclaimed, about to use an epithet, generally given in the East to such adventurous youths; I checked myself immediately; but it was already too late; half the dreaded word had escaped.[1] The effect was instantaneous; a look of horror seized those who were near enough to overhear me; it was quickly communicated to those beyond. The pleasant smile, which usually played upon the fine features of the young Bey, gave way to a serious and angry expression. I lamented that I had thus unwillingly wounded the feelings of my hosts, and was at a loss to know how I could make atonement for my indiscretion—doubting whether an apology to the Evil principle or to the chief was expected. I endeavoured, however, to make them understand that I regretted what had

---

[1] The term Sheitan (equivalent to Satan) is usually applied in the East to a clever, cunning, or daring fellow. [For the prohibition of this term amongst the Yezidis, see below, p. 206.]

passed; but it was some time ere the group resumed their composure, and indulged in their previous merriment.

My carpets had been spread on the roof of a building of some size, belonging to the people of Semil. Around me, but at a convenient distance, were scattered groups of pilgrims from that district. Men, women, and children were congregated round their cauldrons, preparing for their evening meal; or were stretched upon their coarse carpets, resting after the long march of the day. Near me was the chief, whose mud castle crowns the mound of the village of Semil. He was an ill-looking man, gaily dressed, and well armed. He received me with every demonstration of civility, and I sat for some time with him and his wives; one of whom was young and pretty, and had been recently selected from the Kochers, or wanderers. Her hair was profusely adorned with flowers and gold coins. They had sacrificed a sheep, and all (including the chief, whose arms, bare to the shoulder, were reeking with blood) gathered round the carcase; and, tearing the limbs, distributed morsels to the poor who had been collected to receive them.

Below the cluster of buildings assigned to the people of Semil is a small white spire, springing from a low edifice, neatly constructed, and, like all the sacred edifices of the Yezidis, kept as pure as repeated coats of whitewash can make it. It is called the sanctuary of Sheikh Shems, or the Sun; and is so built, that the first rays of that luminary should as frequently as possible fall upon it. Near the door is carved on a slab an invocation to Sheikh Shems: and one or two votive tablets are built into the walls. The interior, which is a very holy place, is lighted by a few small lamps. At sunset, as I sat in the alcove in front of the entrance, a herdsman led into a pen, attached to the building, a drove of white oxen. I asked a Cawal, who was near me, to whom the beasts belonged. 'They are dedicated,' he said, 'to Sheikh Shems, and are never slain except on great festivals, when their flesh is distributed amongst the poor.'[1] This unexpected answer gave rise to an agreeable musing; and I sat almost unconscious of the scene around me, until darkness stole over the valley.

As the twilight faded, the Fakirs, or lower order of priests, dressed in brown garments of coarse cloth, closely fitting to their bodies, and wearing black turbans on their heads, issued from the tomb, each bearing a light in one hand, and a pot of oil, with a bundle of cotton

---

[1] The dedication of the bull to the sun probably originated in Assyria, and the Yezidis may have unconsciously preserved a myth of their ancestors.

wicks, in the other. They filled and trimmed lamps placed in niches in the walls of the court-yard, and scattered over the buildings on the sides of the valley, and even on isolated rocks and in the hollow trunks of trees. Innumerable stars appeared to glitter on the black sides of the mountain, and in the dark recesses of the forest. As the priests made their way through the crowd, to perform their task, men and women passed their right hands through the flame; and, after rubbing the right eyebrow with the part which had been purified by the sacred element, they devoutly carried it to their lips. Some, who bore children in their arms, anointed them in like manner, whilst others held out their hands to be touched by those who, less fortunate than themselves, could not reach the flame.

The lamps are votive offerings from pilgrims, or from those who have appealed to Sheikh Adi in times of danger or disease. A yearly sum is given to the guardians of the tomb for oil, and for the support of the priests who tend the lamps. They are lighted every evening as long as the supplies last. In the day time the smoked walls mark the places where they are placed; and I have observed the Yezidis devoutly kissing the blackened stones. As bitumen and naphtha are both considered somewhat impure, the oil of sesame and other vegetable substances are alone used.

About an hour after sunset the Fakirs, who are the servants of the tomb, appeared with platters of boiled rice, roast meat, and fruit. They had been sent to me from the kitchen of the holy edifice. The wife of Sheikh Nasr also contributed some dishes towards the repast.

As night advanced, those who had assembled—they must now have amounted to nearly five thousand persons—lighted torches, which they carried with them as they wandered through the forest. The effect was magical; the varied groups could be faintly distinguished through the darkness; men hurrying to and fro; women, with their children, seated on the house-tops; and crowds gathering round the pedlars who exposed their wares for sale in the court-yard. Thousands of lights were reflected in the fountains and streams, glimmered amongst the foliage of the trees, and danced in the distance. As I was gazing on this extraordinary scene, the hum of human voices was suddenly hushed, and a strain, solemn and melancholy, arose from the valley. It resembled some majestic chant which years before I had listened to in the cathedral of a distant land. Music so pathetic and so sweet I had never before heard in the East. The voices of men and women were blended in harmony with the soft notes of many flutes. At measured intervals the song was broken by the loud clash of cymbals and tambourines; and those who were without the precincts of the tomb then joined in the melody.

I hastened to the sanctuary, and found Sheikh Nasr, surrounded by the priests, seated in the inner court. The place was illuminated by torches and lamps, which threw a soft light over the white walls of the tomb and green foliage of the arbour. The Sheikhs, in their white turbans and robes, all venerable men with long grey beards, were ranged on one side; on the opposite, seated on the stones, were about thirty Cawals in their motley dresses of black and white—each performing on a tambourine or a flute. Around stood the Fakirs in their dark garments, and the women of the orders of the priesthood also arrayed in pure white. No others were admitted within the walls of the court.

The same slow and solemn strain, occasionally varied in the melody, lasted for nearly an hour; a part of it was called 'Makam Azerat Esau,' or the song of the Lord Jesus. It was sung by the Sheikhs, the Cawals, and the women; and occasionally by those without. I could not catch the words; nor could I prevail upon any of those present to repeat them to me. They were in Arabic; and as few of the Yezidis can speak or pronounce that language, they were not intelligible, even to the experienced ear of Hodja Toma, who accompanied me. The tambourines which were struck simultaneously, only interrupted at intervals the song of the priests. As the time quickened they broke in more frequently. The chant gradually gave way to a lively melody, which, increasing in measure, was finally lost in a confusion of sounds. The tambourines were beaten with extraordinary energy; the flutes poured forth a rapid flood of notes; the voices were raised to their highest pitch; the men outside joined in the cry; whilst the women made the rocks resound with the shrill tahlehl. The musicians, giving way to the excitement, threw their instruments into the air, and strained their limbs into every contortion, until they fell exhausted to the ground. I never heard a more frightful yell than that which rose in the valley. It was midnight. The time and place were well suited to the occasion; and I gazed with wonder upon the extraordinary scene around me. I did not marvel that such wild ceremonies had given rise to those stories of unhallowed rites, and obscene mysteries, which have rendered the name of Yezidi an abomination in the East. Notwithstanding the uncontrollable excitement which appeared to prevail amongst all present, there were on indecent gestures nor unseemly ceremonies. When the musicians and singers were exhausted, the noise suddenly died away; the various groups resumed their previous cheerfulness, and again wandered through the valley, or seated themselves under the trees.

So far from Sheikh Adi being the scene of the orgies attributed to the Yezidis, the whole valley is held sacred; and no acts, such as the Jewish law has declared to be impure, are permitted within the sacred precincts. No other than the high priests and the chiefs of the sect are buried near the tomb. Many pilgrims take off their shoes on approaching it, and go barefooted as long as they remain in its vicinity.

Some ceremony took place before I joined the assembly at the tomb, at which no stranger can be present, nor could I learn its nature from the Cawals. Sheikh Nasr gave me to understand that their holy symbol, the Melek Taous, was then exhibited to the priests, and he declared that, as far as he was concerned, he had no objection to my witnessing the whole of their rites; but that many of the Sheikhs were averse to it, and he did not wish to create any ill feeling in the tribe.

Daylight had begun to appear before the pilgrims sought repose. Silence reigned through the valley until mid-day, when new parties of travellers reached the tomb, and again awakened the echoes by their cries and the discharge of fire-arms. Towards the evening about seven thousand persons must have assembled. The festival was more numerously attended than it had been for many years, and Sheikh Nasr rejoiced in the prospect of times of prosperity for his people. At night the ceremonies of the previous evening were repeated. New melodies were introduced; but the singing ended in the same rapid measure and violent excitement that I have described. During the three days I remained at Sheikh Adi, I wandered over the valley and surrounding mountains, visiting the various groups of pilgrims. From all I received the same simple courtesy and kindness; nor had I any cause to change the good opinion I had already formed of the Yezidis. There were no Mohammedans present, nor any Christians, except those who were with me, and a poor woman who had lived long with the sect, and was a privileged guest at their festivals. Unrestrained by the presence of strangers, the women forgot their usual timidity, and roved unveiled over the mountains. As I sat beneath the trees, laughing girls gathered round me, examined my dress or asked me of things to them strange and new. Some, more bold than the rest, would bring me the strings of beads and engraved stones hanging round their necks, and permit me to examine the Assyrian relics thus collected together; whilst others, more fearful, though not ignorant of the impression which their charms would create, stood at a distance, and weaved wild flowers into their hair.

Sheikh Nasr frequently visited me, and I had opportunities of talking to him alone on the singular tenets of his sect. From these conversations, and from such observations as I was able to make during my visit at Sheikh Adi, I noted down the following particulars.

The Yezidis recognise one Supreme Being; but, as far as I could learn, they do not offer up any direct prayer or sacrifice to him. Sheikh Nasr endeavoured to evade my questions on this subject; and appeared to shun, with superstitious awe, every topic connected with the existence and attributes of the Deity. The name of the Evil Spirit is never mentioned; and any allusion to it by others so vexes and irritates them, that it is said they have put to death persons who have wantonly outraged their feelings by its use. So far is their dread of offending the Evil principle carried, that they carefully avoid every expression which may resemble in sound the name of Satan, or the Arabic word for 'accursed.' Thus, in speaking of a river, they will not say *Shat*, because it is too nearly connected with the first syllable in *Sheitan*, the Devil; but substitute *Nahr*. Nor, for the same reason, will they utter the word *Keitan*, thread or fringe.

When they speak of the Devil, they do so with reverence, as *Melek Taous*, King Peacock, or *Melek el Kout*, the mighty angel. Sheikh Nasr distinctly admitted that they possessed a bronze or copper figure of a bird, which, however, he was careful in explaining was only looked upon as a symbol, and not as an idol. It always remains with the great Sheikh, and is carried with him wherever he may journey. When deputies are sent to any distance to collect money for the support of the tomb and the priests, they are furnished with a small image of it (I understood the Sheikh to say made in wax), which is shown to those amongst whom they go, as an authority for their mission. This symbol is called the Melek Taous, and is held in great reverence. Much doubt has prevailed amongst travellers as to its existence; but Sheikh Nasr, when I had an opportunity of speaking to him in private, so frankly admitted it, that I consider the question as completely set at rest. The admission of the Sheikh is moreover confirmed, by the answer of the guardian of the tomb, to a question which I put to him on my first visit, when he was completely off his guard.

They believe Satan to be the chief of the Angelic host, now suffering punishment for his rebellion against the Divine will, but still all-powerful, and to be restored hereafter to his high estate in the celestial hierarchy. He must be conciliated and reverenced, they say; for as he now has the means of doing evil to mankind, so will he hereafter have the power of rewarding them. Next to Satan, but inferior to him in might and wisdom, are seven arch-angels, who exercise a great influence over the world. Christ, according to them, was also a great angel, who had taken the form of man. He did not die on the cross, but ascended to heaven.

They hold the Old Testament in great reverence, and believe in the cosmogony of Genesis, the Deluge, and other events recorded in the Bible. They do not reject the New Testament, nor the Koran; but consider them less entitled to their veneration. Still they always select passages from the latter for their tombs and holy places. Mohammed they look upon as a prophet; as they do Abraham, and the patriarchs.

They expect the second coming of Christ, as well as the re-appearance of Imaum Mehdi, giving credence to the Mussulman fables relating to him.

Sheikh Adi is their great saint; but I could not learn any particulars relating to him: indeed the epoch of his existence seemed doubtful; and on one occasion Sheikh Nasr asserted that he lived before Mohammed.

It is difficult to trace their ceremonies to any particular source. They baptize in water, like the Christians; if possible, within seven days after birth. They circumcise at the same age, and in the same manner as the Mohammedans; and reverence the sun, and have many customs in common with the Sabæans. All these ceremonies and observances may indeed have had a common origin, or may have been grafted at different times on their original creed. They may have adopted circumcision to avoid detection by their Mussulman oppressors; and may have selected passages from the Koran, to carve upon their tombs and sacred places, because they were best suited to a country in which Arabic was the spoken language. They have more in common with the Sabæans than with any other sect. I have already alluded to their reverence for the sun. They are accustomed to kiss the object on which its first beams fall; and I have frequently, when travelling in their company at sunrise, observed them perform this ceremony. For fire, as symbolical, they have nearly the same reverence; they never spit into it, but frequently pass their hands through the flame, kiss them, and rub them over their right eyebrow, or sometimes over the whole face. The colour blue, to them, as to the Sabæans, is an abomination; and never to be worn in dress, or to be used in their houses. Their Kubleh, or the place to which they look whilst performing their holy ceremonies, is that part of the heavens in which the sun rises, and towards it they turn the faces of their dead.[1] In their fondness for white linen, in their cleanliness of habits, and in their frequent ablutions, they also resemble the Sabæans.

The lettuce, and some other vegetables, are never eaten by them. Pork is unlawful; but not wine, which is drunk by all. Although they assert that meat should not be eaten, unless the animal has been slain according to the Mosaic and Mohammedan law, they do not object to partake of the food of Christians.

I could not learn that there were any religious observances on marriage; nor are the number of wives limited. I was informed by the Cawals that the men and women merely presented themselves to a Sheikh, who ascertains that there is mutual consent. A ring is then given to the bride, or sometimes money instead. A day is fixed for rejoicings. They drink sherbet, and dance, but have no religious ceremonies.

Their year begins with that of the Eastern Christians, whom they follow also in the order and names of their months. Some fast three days at the commencement of the year; but this is not considered necessary. They do not observe the Mohammedan Ramazan. Wednesday is their holiday, and although some always fast on that day, yet they do not abstain from work on it, as the Christians do on the Sabbath.

Sheikh Nasr informed me that they had a date of their own, and that he believed we were then, according to their account, in the year 1550.

Their names, both male and female, are generally those used by Mohammedans and Christians, or such as are common amongst the Kurds, and not strictly of Mussulman origin. The name of *Goorgis* (George) is, however, objectionable; and is never, I believe, given to a Yezidi.

They have four orders of priesthood, the Pirs, the Sheikhs, the Cawals, and the Fakirs; and, what is very remarkable, and, I believe, unexampled in the East, these offices are hereditary, and descend to females, who, when enjoying them, are treated with the same respect and consideration as the men.

The *Pirs*[2], or saints, are most reverenced after the great Sheikh, or religious head of the sect. They are believed to have the power, not only of interceding for the people, but of curing disease and insanity. They are expected to lead a life of great sanctity and honesty; and are

---

[1] All Eastern sects appear to have had some Kubleh, or holy point, to which the face was to be turned during prayer. The Jews, it will be remembered, looked towards Jerusalem. The early Christians chose the East; Mohammed appointed the holy Kaaba of Mecca to be the Kubleh of his disciples.

[2] Pir is a Kurdish (Persian) title—it means, literally, an old man.

looked up to with great reverence. They are not confined, I believe, to any particular fashion of dress. The only Pir I knew was one Sino, who was recognised as the deputy of Sheikh Nasr, and had suffered imprisonment in his stead.

The *Sheikhs* are next in rank. They are acquainted with the hymns, and are expected to know something of Arabic, the language in which the hymns are written. Their dress should be entirely white, except the skull-cap beneath the turban, which is black. As servants of Sheikh Adi, they are the guardians of his tomb, keep up the holy fires, and bring provisions and fuel to those who dwell within its precincts, and to pilgrims of distinction. They always wear round their bodies a band of red and yellow, or red and orange plaid, as the mark of their office; with it they bind together the wood, and other supplies which they bring to the sacred edifice. The women carry the same badge, and are employed in the same services. There are always several Sheikhs residing in the valley of Sheikh Adi. They watch over the tomb, and receive pilgrims; taking charge in rotation of the offerings that may be brought, or selling the clay balls and other relics.

The *Cawals*, or Preachers, appear to be the most active members of the priesthood. They are sent by Sheikh Nasr on missions, going from village to village as teachers of the doctrines of the sect. They alone are the performers on the flute and tambourine; both instruments being looked upon, to a certain extent, as sacred. I observed that before, and after, using the tambourine they frequently kissed it, and then held it to those near them to be similarly saluted. They are taught singing at a very early age, and are skilful musicians. They dance also at festivals. Their robes are generally white, although coloured stuffs are not forbidden. Their turbans, unlike those of the Sheikhs, are black, as are also their skull-caps.

The *Fakirs* are the lowest in the priesthood. They wear coarse dresses of black, or dark brown cloth, or canvas, descending to the knee and fitting tightly to the person; and a black turban, across or over which is tied a red handkerchief. They perform all menial offices connected with the tomb, trim and light the votive lamps, and keep clean the sacred buildings.

Whilst each tribe and district of Yezidis has its own chief, Sheikh Nasr is looked up to as the religious head of the whole sect, and he is treated with great reverence and respect. His office is hereditary; but the Yezidis frequently chose, without reference to priority of claim, the one amongst the descendants of the last Sheikh most qualified by his knowledge and character, to succeed him. The father of Sheikh Nasr held the office for some years; and no one better suited to it than his son could have been chosen to fill his place.

The language in general use amongst all the Yezidis is a Kurdish dialect; and very few, except the Sheikhs and Cawals, are acquainted with Arabic. The chants and hymns—the only form of prayer, which, as far as I could ascertain, they possess—are, as I have already observed, in Arabic. They have, I believe, a sacred volume, containing their traditions, their hymns, directions for the performance of their rites, and other matters connected with their religion. It is preserved either at Baazani or Baasheikha, and is regarded with so much superstitious reverence that I failed in every endeavour to obtain a copy, or even to see it. It is considered unlawful to know how to read and write. There are only one or two persons amongst the Yezidis who can do either: even Sheikh Nasr is unacquainted with the alphabet. Those who know how to read have only been taught, in order that they may preserve the sacred book, and may refer to it for the doctrines and ceremonies of the sect.

The Yezidis have a tradition that they originally came from Busrah, and from the country watered by the lower part of the Euphrates; that, after their emigration, they first settled in Syria, and subsequently took possession of the Sinjar hill, and the districts they now inhabit in Kurdistan. This tradition, with the peculiar nature of their tenets and ceremonies, points to a Sabæan or Chaldæan origin. It is not improbable that the sect may be a remnant of the ancient Chaldees, who have, at various times, outwardly adopted the forms and tenets of the ruling people to save themselves from persecution and oppression.

The Yezidis are known amongst themselves by the name of the district, or tribe, to which they respectively belong. Tribes of Yezidis are found in the north of Syria, in Northern Kurdistan, in Bohtan, Sheikhan, and Missouri. In the plains, their principal settlements are in the villages of Baazani, Baasheikha, and Semil.

Having spent three days at Sheikh Adi, and witnessed all the ceremonies at which a stranger could be present, I prepared to return to Mosul. Sheikh Nasr, Hussein Bey, and the principal Sheikhs and Cawals, insisted upon accompanying me about three miles down the valley; as I preferred this road to the precipitous pathway over the mountains. After parting with me, the chiefs returned to the tomb to finish their festival, and I made my way to the village of Ain Sifni. Before leaving me, Sheikh Nasr placed in my hands a letter, written by

his secretary, to the inhabitants of the Sinjar. I had acquainted him with
my intention of visiting that district in company with the Pasha, and he
promised to send a Cawal to secure me the most friendly reception in
the villages. The document was couched in the following terms:—

"Peace be always to our most honoured and excellent friends, the
inhabitants of Bukrah, and to all those who are of the village, old and
young.

"Peace be also to the inhabitants of Mirkan, and to all the dwellers in
the village, old and young.

"Peace be also to the tribe of Deenah, to Murad, and to the old and
young.

"Peace be also to Fukrah Rizo, who dwells in Koulkah.

"Peace be also to the inhabitants of the town of Sinjar, old and
young.

"Peace be also to the dwellers in the mountain of Sinjar, old and
young.

"May God the most High watch over you all. Amen.

"We never forget you in our prayers before Sheikh Adi, the greatest
of all Sheikhs, and of all Khasseens[1]; our thoughts are always with you,
and ye are in our mind by day and by night.

"A beloved friend of ours is about to visit you, and we have sent him
our Cawal, Murad, in order that ye may treat him with all kindness and
honour. For, as ye receive him, so would ye receive me; and if ye do
evil unto him, so do ye evil unto me. As ye are the children of obedience,
and faithful to Sheikh Adi, the chief of all Sheikhs, disregard not these
our commands, and may God the most High watch over you always.
                              "He who intercedes for you,
                                        "Sheikh Nasr,
                                             "The Elder."

The village of Ain Sifni was almost deserted; the inhabitants having
migrated during the festival to the valley of Sheikh Adi. I urged on my
horse, and reached Mosul early in the afternoon.

Tahyar Pasha had for some time been planning an expedition into the
Sinjar, not with any hostile intention, but for the purpose of examining
the state of the country, which had been ruined by the vexations, extortions and gratuitous cruelty of the late governor of Mosul. The

---

[1] I am not aware of the exact position of the Khasseens in the hierarchy of the Yezidis,
or whether this is a general name for their saints.

arrangements of his Excellency, after numerous delays, were at length completed by the 8th October, and three o'clock of that day was declared to be the fortunate hour for leaving the town. The principal inhabitants, with the Cadi and Mufti at their head, were collected in the large square opposite the palace and without the walls, ready to accompany the Pasha, as a mark of respect, some distance from the gates. It was with difficulty that I made my way to the apartments of the governor, through the crowd of irregular troops and servants which thronged the court-yard of the Serai. Above, there was no less confusion than below. The attendants of his Excellency were hurrying to and fro laden with every variety of utensil and instrument; some carrying gigantic telescopes, or huge bowls, in leather cases; others labouring under bundles of pipe-sticks, or bending under the weight of calico bags crammed with state documents. The grey-headed Kiayah had inserted his feet into a pair of capacious boots, leaving room enough for almost any number of intruders. Round his fez, and the lower part of his face, were wound endless folds of white linen, which gave him the appearance of a patient emerging from a hospital; and he carried furs and cloaks enough to keep out the cold of the frigid zone. At the door of the harem waited a bevy of Aghas; amongst them the lord of the towel, the lord of the washing-basin, the lord of the cloak, the cheif of the coffee-makers, and the cheif of the pipe-bearers, the treasurer, and the seal-bearer. At length the Pasha approached; the Cawasses forced the crowd out of the way; and, as his Excellency placed his foot in the stirrup, the trumpets sounded as a signal for the procession to move onwards. First came a regiment of infantry, followed by a company of artillery-men with their guns. The trumpeters, and the Pasha's own standard, a mass of green silk drapery, embroidered in gold, with verses from the Koran, succeeded; behind were led six Arab horses, richly caparisoned with coloured saddle-cloths, glittering with gold embroidery. The Pasha himself then appeared, surrounded by the chiefs of the town and the officers of his household. The procession was finished by the irregular cavalry, divided into companies, each headed by its respective commander, and by the wild Suiters with their small kettle-drums fastened in front of their saddles.

I was accompanied by my Cawass and my own servants, and rode as it best suited, and amused me, in different parts of the procession. We reached Hamaydat, a ruined village on the banks of the Tigris, three caravan hours from Mosul, about sun-set. Here we had the first proofs of

---

[1] These are all offices in the household of a Turkish pasha.

the commissariat arrangements; for there was neither food for ourselves nor the horses, and we all went supperless to bed.

On the following day, after a ride of six hours through a barren and uninhabited plain, bounded to the east and west by ranges of low limestone hills, we reached a ruined village, built on the summit of an ancient artificial mound, and called Abou Maria. A most abundant spring issues from the foot of the mound of Abou Maria. The water is collected in large, well-built reservoirs. Near them is a mill, now in ruins, but formerly turned by the stream, within a few yards of its source. Such an ample supply of water, although brackish to the taste, must always have attracted a population in a country where it is scarce.

The Aneyza Arabs were known to be out on this side of the Euphrates, and during our march we observed several of their scouts watching our movements. The irregular cavalry frequently rushed off in pursuit; but the Arabs, turning their fleet mares towards the desert, were soon lost in the distance.

We passed the ruins of three further villages. The plain, once thickly inhabited, is now deserted; and the wells, formerly abundant, are filled up. The remains of buildings, and the traces of former cultivation, prove that at some period, not very remote, others than the roving Bedouins dwelt on these lands: whilst the artificial mounds, scattered over the face of the country, show that long ere the Mussulman invasion this was one of the flourishing districts of ancient Assyria.

Three hours' ride, still over the desert, brought us to Tel Afer, which we reached suddenly on emerging from a range of low hills. The place had a much more important and flourishing appearance than I could have expected. A very considerable eminence, partly artificial, is crowned by a castle, whose walls are flanked by numerous towers of various shapes. The town, containing some well-built houses, lies at the foot of the mound, and is partly surrounded by gardens well wooded with the olive, fig, and other fruit trees. Beyond this cultivated plot is the broad expanse of the desert. A spring, as abundant as that of Abou Maria, gushes out of a rock beneath the castle, supplies the inhabitants with water, irrigates their gardens, and turns their mills.

Tel Afer was once a town of some importance, being mentioned by the early Arab geographers. It has been three times besieged within a few years. On each occasion the inhabitants offered a vigorous resistance. Finally Mohammed Pasha took the place by assault. More than two-thirds of the inhabitants were put to the sword, and the property of the remainder was confiscated. The houses within the fort were destroyed, and the town was rebuilt at the foot of the mound. A small Turkish garrison now occupies the castle. Previous to its last capture, Tel Afer was almost independent of the Turkish governors of Mesopotamia. It paid a small tribute, but had its own hereditary chief, who, in league with the Bedouins of the desert and the Yezidis of the Sinjar, enriched his followers by the plunder of caravans, and by foraging expeditions into the uncultivated districts of Mosul. Great wealth is said to have been discovered in the place, on its pillage by Mohammed Pasha, who took all the gold and silver, and distributed the remainder of the spoil amongst his soldiers.

Tel Afer

The inhabitants of Tel Afer are of Turcoman origin, and speak the Turkish language. They occasionally intermarry, however, with the Arabs, and generally understand Arabic.

Towards evening I ascended the mound, and visited the castle, in which was quartered a small body of irregular troops. From the walls I had an uninterrupted view over a vast plain, stretching westwards towards the Euphrates, and losing itself in the hazy distance. The ruins of ancient towns and villages rose on all sides; and as the sun went down, I counted above one hundred mounds, throwing their dark and lengthening shadows across the plain. These were the remains of Assyrian civilisation and prosperity. Centuries have elapsed since a settled population dwelt in this district of Mesopotamia. Now, not even the tent of the Bedouin could be seen. The whole was a barren deserted waste.

We remained two days at Tel Afer. The commissariat was replenished, as far as possible, from the scanty stores of the inhabitants. The Pasha recommended forbearance and justice; but his advice was not followed; nor were his orders obeyed. The houses were broken into and a general pillage ensued. At length, on the 13th, we resumed our march, to the mountain of Sinjar, about thirty miles distant from Tel Afer.

We passed the first night on the banks of a small salt stream, near the ruins of a village, called by the people of Sinjar and Tel Afer, Zabardok; and by the Arabs simply Kharba, or the ruins. We had seen during the day several other ruins and water courses.[1] The second day we encamped in the plain, near the southern end of the Sinjar mountain, and under the village of Mirkan, the white houses of which, rising one above the other on the declivity, were visible from below. Here the Pasha was met by all the chiefs of the mountain except those of the small district in which we had halted.

Mirkan is one of the principal Yezidi settlements in the Sinjar. Its inhabitants had been exposed to great extortions, and many were put to death when Mohammed Pasha visited the mountain. They expected similar treatment at our hands. No promises could remove their fears, and they declared their intention of resolutely defending their village. The Pasha sent up an officer of his household, with a few irregular troops, to re-assure them, and to restore obedience. I accompanied him. As we entered the village we were received by a general discharge of fire-arms. Two horsemen, who had accidentally—and as I thought at the time somewhat disrespectfully—pushed forward before

---

[1] All these streams at this time of the year are nearly dry and lose themselves in the desert; but when replenished by the winter rains they find their way to the Tharthar, the small river which flows near the ruins of Al Hather, and ends in a lake to the south of them. [This is the site of the Wadi Tharthar scheme, a major engineering operation of the Iraq Government, whereby the whole Tharthar depression has been made into a reservoir for the flood waters of the Tigris.]

the officer and myself, fell dead at our feet, and several of our party were wounded. The Pasha, exasperated at this unprovoked and wanton attack, ordered an advance of the Hytas and Arab irregulars; who, long thirsting for plunder, hastened towards the village. The Yezidis had already deserted it, and had taken refuge in a narrow gorge; abounding in caverns and isolated rocks—their usual place of refuge on such occasions.

The village was soon occupied; the houses were entered, and plundered of the little property that had been left behind. A few aged women and decrepit old men, too infirm to leave with the rest, and found hiding in the small dark rooms, were murdered, and their heads severed from their bodies. Blazing fires were made in the neat dwellings, and the whole village was delivered to the flames. Even the old Pasha, with his grey hair and tottering step, hurried to and fro amongst the smoking ruins, and helped to add the torch where the fire was not doing its work.

The old Turkish spirit of murder and plunder was roused; the houses were soon burnt to the ground; but the inhabitants were still safe. When the irregulars had secured all the property they could discover, they rushed towards the gorge, scarcely believing that the Yezidis would venture to oppose them. But they were received by a steady and well-directed fire. The foremost fell almost to a man. The caverns were high up amongst the rocks, and all attempts to reach them completely failed. The contest was carried on till night; when the troops, dispirited and beaten, were called back to their tents.

In the evening the heads of the miserable old men and women, taken in the village, were paraded about the camp; and those who were fortunate enough to possess such trophies wandered from tent to tent, claiming a present as a reward for their prowess. I appealed to the Pasha, who had been persuaded that every head brought to him was that of a powerful chief, and after some difficulty prevailed upon him to have them buried; but the troops were not willing to obey his orders, and it was late in the night before they were induced to resign their bloody spoil, which they had arranged in grim array, and lighted up with torches.

On the following morning the contest was renewed; but the Yezidis defended themselves with undiminished courage. The first who ventured into the gorge was the commander of a body of irregular troops, one Osman Agha, a native of Lazistan. He advanced boldly at the head of his men. On each side of him was a Suiter, with his small kettle-drums by his side, and the tails of foxes in his cap.[1] He had scarcely entered the valley, when two shots from the rocks above killed his two supporters. The troops rushed forward, and attempted to reach the caves in which the Yezidis had taken refuge. Again they were beaten back by their unseen enemies. Every shot from the rocks told, while the Pasha's troops were unable to discover, but by the thin smoke which marked the discharge of the rifle, the position of those who defended the gorge. The contest lasted during the day, but without results. The loss of the Hytas was very considerable; not a cavern had been carried; nor a Yezidis, as far as the assailants could tell, killed, or even wounded.

On the following morning the Pasha ordered a fresh attack. To encourage his men he advanced himself into the gorge, and directed his carpet to be spread on a rock. Here he sat, with the greatest apathy, smoking his pipe, and carrying on a frivolous conversation with me, although he was the object of the aim of the Yezidis; several persons within a few feet of us falling dead, and the balls frequently throwing up the dirt into our faces. Coffee was brought to him occasionally as usual, and his pipe was filled when the tobacco was exhausted; yet he was not a soldier, but what is termed 'a man of the pen'. I have frequently seen similar instances of calm indifference in the midst of danger amongst Turks, when such displays were scarcely called for, and would be very unwillingly made by a European. Notwithstanding the example set by his Excellency, and the encouragement which his presence gave to the troops, they were not more successful in their attempts to dislodge the Yezidis than they had been the day before. One after another, the men were carried out of the ravine, dead or dying. The wounded were brought to the Pasha, who gave them water, money, or words of encouragement. The 'Ordou cadesi', or Cadi of the camp, reminded them that it was against the infidels they were fighting; that every one who fell by the enemies of the prophet was rewarded with instant translation to Paradise; while those who killed an unbeliever were entitled to the same inestimable privilege. The dying were comforted, and the combatants animated by the promises and extortions of the Cadi; who, however, kept himself well out of the way of danger behind a rock. He was a fanatic, the fellow; and his self-satisfied air and comfortable obesity, had created in me very strong feelings of indignation and disgust;—not diminished by the new prin-

---

[1] The Suiters are buffoons who precede the irregular cavalry, play on small kettle-drums, and are fantastically attired. They generally display great daring and courage.

ciples of international law which he propounded in my presence to the Pasha. 'If I swore an oath to these unbelieving Yezidis,' asked his Excellency, 'and in consequence thereof, believing their lives to be secure, they should surrender, how far am I bound thereby?' 'The Yezidis being Infidels,' replied his Reverence, smoothing down his beard, 'are in the same category as other unbelievers,'—here his eye turned on me;—'as they do not understand the true nature of God and of his prophet, they cannot understand the true nature of an oath; consequently it is not binding upon them; and therefore, as there is no reciprocity, it cannot be binding upon you. Not only *could* you put them to the sword, after they had surrendered upon the faith of your oath, but it is your duty as a good Mussulman to do so: for the unbelievers are the enemies of God and his prophet.' Here he again honoured me with a particular look. The Pasha, as soon as the expounder of the law had departed, thought it necessary to condemn the atrocious doctrines which I had heard, and to assure me that the Cadi was an ass. This fanatic was half Kurd, half Arab, and was a specimen of the religious chiefs who dwell in Kurdistan, and in the towns on its borders; and are constantly inciting the Mohammedans against the Christians, and urging them to shed their blood. I need scarcely say that the abominable opinions which they profess, are not shared by any respectable Turk or Mussulman; and will no longer, it is to be hoped,—now that the Porte has established its authority in Kurdistan,—lead to massacres of the Sultan's Christian subjects.

Attempts were made during the day to induce the Yezidis to surrender, and there was some chance of success. However, night drew near, and hostilities still continued. The regular and irregular troops were then posted at all the known places of access to the gorge. The morning came, and the attack was recommenced. No signs of defence issued from the valley. The Hytas rushed in, but were no longer met by the steady fire of the previous day. They paused, fearing some trick or ambuscade; then advanced cautiously, but still unnoticed. They reached the mouths of the caves;—no one opposed them. It was some time, however, before they ventured to look into them. They were empty. The Yezidis had fled during the night, and had left the ravine by some pathway known only to themselves, and which had escaped the watchfulness of the Turkish soldiery. In the caverns were found a few rude figures of men and goats, formed of dried figs fastened upon sticks. These were seized by the victors, and borne in triumph through the camp as the gods of the worshippers of Satan. The Pasha, having fully satisfied himself upon this point, by a reference to his reverence, the Cadi, directed the idols to be carefully packed, and sent them at once, as trophies and valuable curiosities, to Constantinople by a special Tatar.

Whilst attempts were being made to discover the retreat of the fugitives, the Turkish camp remained near the village of Mirkan. I took this opportunity of visiting other parts of the Sinjar. All the villages of the Sinjar are built upon one plan. The houses rise on the hill-sides, and are surrounded by terraces, formed of rough stones piled one above the other as walls, to confine the scanty earth. These terraces are planted with olive and fig trees; a few vineyards are found near some villages. The houses, which are flat-roofed, are exceedingly clean and neat. They frequently contain several apartments. The walls of the interior are full of small recesses, like pigeon-holes, which are partly ornamental, and partly used to keep the domestic utensils and property of the owner. They give a very singular and original appearance to the room; and the oddity of the effect is considerably increased by masses of red and black paint daubed on the white wall, in patches, by way of ornament.

The principal, and indeed now the only, trade carried on by the inhabitants of the Sinjar, is in dried figs, which are celebrated in this part of Turkey, and supply all the markets in the neighbouring provinces. The soil is fertile, and, as the means of irrigation are abundant, corn and various useful articles of produce might be raised in great plenty from the extensive tracts of arable land surrounding the villages. But the people have been almost ruined by misgovernment; they can now scarcely cultivate corn enough for their own immediate wants.

The Pasha still lingered at Mirkan; and as I was anxious to return to Mosul, to renew the excavations, I took my leave of him, and rode through the desert to Tel Afer. I was accompanied by a small body of irregular cavalry,—a necessary escort, as the Aneyza Arabs were hanging about the camp, and plundering stragglers and caravans of supplies. As evening approached, we saw, congregated near a small stream, what appeared to be a large company of dismounted Arabs, their horses standing by them. As we were already near them, and could not have escaped the watchful eye of the Bedouin, we prepared for an encounter. I placed the baggage in the centre of my small party, and spread out the horsemen as widely as possible to exaggerate our numbers. We approached cautiously, and were surprised to see that the horses still remained without their riders: we drew still nearer, when they all galloped off towards the desert. They were wild asses. We attempted to follow them. After running a little distance they stopped to gaze at us, and I got sufficiently near to see them well; but as soon as they found that we were in pursuit, they hastened their speed, and were soon lost in the distance.[1]

I reached Mosul in two days, taking the road by Kessi Kupri, and avoiding the desert beyond Abou Maria, which we had crossed on our march to the Sinjar.

---

[1] Xenophon mentions these beautiful animals, which he must have seen during his march in these very plains. 'The asses', says he, 'when they were pursued, having gained ground of the horses, stood still (for they exceeded them much in speed); and when they came up with them, they did the same thing again; so that our horsemen could take them by no other means but by dividing themselves into relays, and succeeding one another in the chase.' In fleetness they equal the gazelle; and to match them is a feat which only one or two of the most celebrated mares have been known to accomplish. The Arabs sometimes catch the foals during the spring, and bring them up with milk in their tents. I endeavoured in vain to obtain a pair. They are of a light fawn colour—almost pink. The Arabs still eat their flesh.

X

ON MY RETURN to Mosul, I received letters from England, informing me that Sir Stratford Canning had presented the sculptures discovered in Assyria, and had made over all advantages that might be derived from the order given to him by the Sultan, to the British nation; and that the British Museum had received a grant of funds for the continuation of the researches commenced at Nimroud, and elsewhere. The grant was small, and I was doubtful whether I should be able to fulfil the expectations which appeared to have been formed, as to the results of the undertaking. The sum given to M. Botta for the excavations at Khorsabad alone, greatly exceeded the whole grant to the Museum, which was to include private expenses, those of carriage, and many extraordinary outlays inevitable in the East, when works of this nature are to be carried on. I determined, however, to accept the charge of superintending the excavations, to make every exertion, and to economise as far as it was in my power—that the nation might possess as extensive and complete a collection of Assyrian antiquities as, considering the smallness of the means, it was possible to collect. The want of knowledge and experience as a draughtsman, was a drawback, indeed a disqualification, which I could scarcely hope to overcome. Many of the sculptures, and monuments discovered, were in too dilapidated a condition to be removed, and others threatened to fall to pieces as soon as uncovered. It was only by drawings that the record of them could be preserved. There was no inclination to send an artist to assist me, and I made up my mind to do the best I could; to copy as carefully and accurately as possible, that which was before me. I had therefore to superintend the excavations; to draw all the bas-reliefs discovered; to copy and compare the innumerable inscriptions; to take casts of them;[1] and to preside over the moving and

---

[1] Casts of the inscriptions and of some of the sculptures were taken with brown paper simply damped, and impressed on the slab with a hard brush. Some of these served as

packing of the sculptures. As there was no one to be trusted to over-look the diggers, I was obliged to be continually present, and fre-quently to remove the earth myself from the face of the slabs—as, through the carelessness and inexperience of the workmen, they were exposed to injury from blows of the picks. I felt that I was far from qualified to undertake these multifarious occupations. I knew, how-ever, that if persons equal to the task, and sufficiently well acquainted with the various languages of the country to carry on the necessary communications with the authorities, and to hold the requisite inter-course with the inhabitants—Arabs, Kurds, Turks, and Chaldæans—were sent out expressly from England, the whole sum granted would be expended before the excavations could be commenced. The researches would probably be then less extensive, and their results less complete than they would be if, however unqualified, I at once under-took their superintendence. I determined, therefore, to devote the whole of my time to the undertaking, and to make every sacrifice to ensure its success.

It was, in the first place, necessary to organise a band of workmen best fit to carry on the work. The scarcity of corn, resulting from the oppressive measures of Mohammed Pasha, had driven the Arab tribes to the neighbourhood of the town, where they sought to gain a liveli-hood by engaging in labours not very palatable to a Bedouin. I had no difficulty in finding workmen amongst them. There was, at the same time, this advantage in employing these wandering Arabs—they brought their tents and families with them, and, encamping round the ruins and the village, formed a very efficient guard against their brethren of the desert, who looked to plunder, rather than to work, to supply their wants. To increase my numbers I chose only one man from each family; and, as his male relations accompanied him, I had the use of their services, as far as regarded the protection of my sculptures. Being well acquainted with the Sheikhs of the Jebour, I chose my workmen chiefly from that tribe. The Arabs were selected to remove the earth—they were unable to dig; this part of the labour required stronger and more active men; and I chose for it about fifty Nestorian Chaldæans, who had sought work for the winter in Mosul, and many of whom, having already been employed, had acquired

---

moulds, and were subsequently cast in plaster of Paris in England. When intended for this purpose, the paper was made into a kind of paste, and mixed with a glutinous powder derived from a root called 'Shirais'.

some experience in excavating. They went to Nimroud with their wives and families. I engaged at the same time one Bainan, a Jacobite, or Syrian Christian, who was a skilful marble-cutter, and a very intelligent man. I had made also a valuable addition to my establishment in a standard-bearer of the irregular troops, of whose courage I had seen such convincing proofs during the expedition to the Sinjar, that I induced his commander to place him in my service. His name was Mohammed Agha; but he was generally called, from the office he held in his troop, the 'Bairakdar'. He was a native of Scio, and had been carried off at the time of the massacre, when a child, by an irregular, who had brought him up as a Mussulman. In his religious opinions and observances, however, he was as lax, as men of his profession usually are. He served me faithfully and honestly, and was of great use during the excavations. Awad still continued in my employ; my Cawass, Ibrahim Agha, returned with me to Nimroud; and I hired a carpenter and two or three men of Mosul as superintendents.

I was again amongst the ruins by the end of October. The winter season was fast approaching, and it was necessary to build a proper house for the shelter of myself and servants. I marked out a plan on the ground, on the outside of the village of Nimroud, and in a few days the habitations were complete. My workmen formed the walls of mud bricks, dried in the sun, and covered in the rooms with beams and branches of trees. A thick coat of mud was laid over the whole, to exclude the rain. Two rooms for my own accommodation were divided by an Iwan, or open apartment, the whole being surrounded by a wall. In a second court-yard were huts for my Cawass, for Arab guests, and for my servants, and stables for my horses. Ibrahim Agha displayed his ingenuity by making equidistant loopholes, of a most warlike appearance, in the outer walls; which I immediately ordered to be filled up, to avoid any suspicion of being the constructor of forts and castles, with the intention of making a permanent Frank settlement in the country. We did not neglect precautions, however, in case of an attack from the Bedouins, of whom Ibrahim Agha was in constant dread. Unfortunately, the only showers of rain that I saw during the remainder of my residence in Assyria, fell before my walls were covered in, and so saturated the bricks that they did not become again dry before the following spring. The consequence was, that the only verdure, on which my eyes were permitted to feast before my return to Europe, was furnished by my own property—the walls in the interior of the rooms being continually clothed with a crop of grass.

On the mound itself, and immediately above the great winged lions first discovered, I built a house for my Nestorian workmen and their families, and a hut, to which I could at once remove for safety any small objects discovered among the ruins. I divided my Arabs into three parties, according to the branches of the tribe to which they belonged. About forty tents were pitched on different parts of the mound, at the entrances to the principal trenches. Forty more were placed round my dwelling, and the rest on the bank of the river, where the sculptures were deposited previous to their embarkation on the rafts. The men were all armed. I thus provided for the defence of all my establishment.

Mr. Hormuzd Rassam lived with me; and to him I confided the payment of the wages, and all the accounts. He soon obtained an extraordinary influence amongst the Arabs, and his fame spread through the desert.

I divided my workmen into parties. In each set were generally eight or ten Arabs, who carried away the earth in baskets; and two, or four, Nestorian diggers, according to the nature of the soil and rubbish which had to be excavated. They were overlooked by a superintendent, whose duty it was to keep them to their work, and to give me notice when the diggers approached any slab, or exposed any small object to view, that I might myself assist in the uncovering or removal. I scattered a few Arabs of a hostile tribe amongst the rest, and by that means I was always made acquainted with what was going on, could easily learn if there were plots brewing, and could detect those who might attempt to appropriate any relics discovered during the excavations. The smallness of the sum placed at my disposal, compelled me to follow the same plan in the excavations that I had hitherto adopted, —viz. to dig trenches along the sides of the chambers, and to expose the whole of the slabs, without removing the earth from the centre. Thus, few of the chambers were fully explored; and many small objects of great interest may have been left undiscovered. As I was directed to bury the building with earth after it had been explored, to avoid unnecessary expense I filled up the chambers with the rubbish taken from those subsequently uncovered, having first examined the walls, copied the inscriptions, and drawn the sculptures. The excavations were recommenced, on a large scale, by the 1st of November [1846].

It will be remembered that in chamber B (plan 3), some slabs had fallen with their faces to the ground.[1] I was, in the first place, anxious to raise these bas-reliefs, and to pack them for removal to Busrah. To accomplish this, it was necessary to remove a large accumulation of earth and rubbish—to empty, indeed, nearly the whole chamber, for the fallen slabs extended almost half-way across it. The sculptures from No. 3 to 11 (inclusive) were found to be in admirable preservation, although the slabs were broken by the fall. They were divided into two compartments, separated by an inscription running across the slab. All these inscriptions were precisely similar.

The bas-reliefs, above and below, were of the highest interest. They represented the wars of the king, and the conquest of a foreign nation. The two upper bas-reliefs, on slabs Nos. 3 and 4, formed one subject—the king followed by warriors, in battle with his enemies under the walls of a hostile castle. He stands, gorgeously attired, in a chariot, drawn, as usual, by three horses richly caparisoned. He is discharging an arrow either against the besieged, who are defending the towers and walls; or against a warrior, who, already wounded, is tumbling from his chariot, one of the horses having fallen to the ground. An attendant protects the person of the king with a shield, and a charioteer holds the reins and urges on the horses. A warrior, fallen from the chariot of the enemy, is almost under the horses' feet. Above the king is his presiding Deity, represented—as at Persepolis—by a winged figure within a circle, and wearing a horned cap resembling that of the human-headed lions and bulls. Like the king, he is shooting an arrow, the head of which is in the form of a trident. At the bottom of the first bas-relief are wavy lines, to indicate water or a river, and trees are scattered over both. Groups of men, fighting or slaying the enemy, are introduced in several places; and three headless bodies above the principal figures in the second bas-relief represent the dead in the background.

On the upper part of the two following slabs was the return after victory. In front of the procession are several warriors carrying heads, and throwing them at the feet of the conquerors. Two musicians are playing with a plectrum, on stringed instruments. They are followed by the warriors, who were seen in battle in the previous bas-relief, now unarmed, and holding their standards before them; above them flies an eagle with a human head in his talons. Behind them is the king carrying in one hand his bow, and in the other two arrows.

[1] See above p.132

After the procession, we have the castle and pavilion of the conquering king. The ground plan of the former is represented by a circle, divided into four equal compartments, and surrounded by towers and battlements. In each compartment there are figures apparently engaged in culinary occupations, and preparing the feast; one is holding a sheep, which the other is cutting up: another appears to be baking bread. Various bowls and utensils stand on tables and stools, all remarkable for the elegance of their forms.

The lower series of bas-reliefs contained three subjects—the siege of a castle, the king receiving prisoners, and the king, with his army, crossing a river. The besiegers have brought a battering ram (attached to a moveable tower, apparently constructed of wicker-work) up to the outer wall, from which many stones have already been dislodged and are falling. One of the besieged has succeeded in catching the ram by a chain, and is endeavouring to raise or move it from its place; whilst two warriors of the assailing party are holding it down by hooks, to which they are hanging. Another is throwing fire (traces of the red paint being still retained in the sculpture) from above, upon the engine. The besiegers endeavour to quench the flame, by pouring water upon it from two spouts in the moveable tower. Two figures, in full armour, are undermining the walls with instruments like blunt spears; whilst two others appear to have found a secret passage into the castle. Three of the besieged are falling from the walls; and upon one of the towers are two women, tearing their hair and extending their hands, as if in the act of asking for mercy.

The three following bas-reliefs represented the king receiving captives. The three remaining bas-reliefs[—the passage of the river—] are highly interesting, and curious. [In the first is] a boat containing a chariot, in which is the king, talking with an eunuch, who is pointing with his right hand to some object in the distance, perhaps the stronghold of the enemy. The boat is towed by two naked men, who are walking on dry land; and four men row the vessel with oars. One oar, with a broad flat end, is passed through a rope, hung round a thick wooden pin at the stern, and serves both to guide and impel the boat. It is singular that this is precisely the mode adopted by the inhabitants of Mosul to this day, when they cross the Tigris in barks, perhaps even more rude than those in use, on the same river, three thousand years ago. A charioteer, standing in the vessel, holds by the halters four horses, which are swimming over the stream. A naked figure is supporting himself upon an inflated skin,—a mode of swimming rivers still practised in Mesopotamia. In fact, the three bas-reliefs, with the exception of the king and the chariot, might represent a scene daily witnessed on the banks of the Tigris,—probably the river here represented. The water is shown by undulating lines, covering the face of the slab. On the next slab are two smaller boats; in the first appears to be the couch of the king, and a jar or large vessel; in the other is an empty chariot: they are each impelled by two rowers, seated face to face at their oars. Five men, two leading horses by their halters, are swimming on skins. Two fish are represented in the water. On the third slab is the embarkation—men are placing two chariots in a boat, which is about to leave the shores; two warriors are already swimming over; and two others are filling and tying up their skins on the bank. Behind them, on dry land, are three figures erect, probably officers superintending the proceedings.

Chamber I had only been partly uncovered; the slabs were still half buried. A party of Arabs were employed in removing the remaining earth. As we approached the floor, a large quantity of iron was found amongst the rubbish; and I soon recognised in it the scales of the armour represented on the sculptures. Each scale was separate, and of iron, from two to three inches in length, rounded at one end, and squared at the other, with a raised or embossed line in the centre. The iron was covered with rust, and in so decomposed a state, that I had much difficulty in cleansing it from the soil. Two or three baskets were filled with these relics.

As the earth was removed, other portions of armour were found; some of copper, others of iron, and others of iron inlaid with copper. At length a perfect helmet (resembling in shape, and in the ornaments, the pointed helmet represented in the bas-reliefs) was discovered. When first separated from the earth it was perfect, but immediately fell to pieces. I carefully collected and preserved the fragments, which were sent to England. The lines which are seen round the lower part of the pointed helmets in the sculptures, are thin strips of copper, inlaid in the iron.

Several helmets of other shapes, some with the arched crest, were also uncovered; but they fell to pieces as soon as exposed; and I was only able, with the greatest care, to gather up a few of the fragments which still held together; for the iron was in so complete a state of decomposition that it crumbled away on being touched.

Portions of armour in copper, and embossed, were also found, with small holes for nails round the edges.

Q   227

The slabs numbered 8, 9, 10 and 11 on the plan[1] had fallen from their places, and were broken into several pieces. I raised them, and discovered under them—but of course broken into a thousand fragments—a number of vases of the finest white alabaster, and several vessels of baked clay. I carefully collected these fragments, but it was impossible to put them together. I found, however, that upon some of them cuneiform characters were engraved, and I soon perceived the name and title of the Khorsabad king, accompanied by the figure of a lion.

Whilst I was collecting and examining these curious relics, a workman digging the earth from a corner of the chamber, between slabs 20 and 21, came upon a perfect vase; but unfortunately struck it with his pick, and broke the upper part of it. I took the instrument, and, working cautiously myself, was rewarded by the discovery of two small vases, one in alabaster, the other in glass, (both in the most perfect preservation), of elegant shape, and admirable workmanship. Each bore the name and title of the Khorsabad king, written in two different ways, as in the inscriptions of Khorsabad.[2]

A kind of exfoliation had taken place in the glass vase, and it was incrusted with thin, semi-transparent lamina, which glowed with all the brilliant colours of the opal. This beautiful appearance is a well-known result of age, and is frequently found on glass in Egyptian, Greek, and other early tombs.

It was in the centre of the mound that one of the most remarkable discoveries awaited me. I have already mentioned the pair of gigantic winged bulls, first found there.[3] They appeared to form an entrance, and to be only part of a large building. The inscriptions upon them contained a name, differing from that of the king, who had built the palace in the north-west corner. On digging further I found a brick, on which was a genealogy, the new name occurring first, and as that of the son of the founder of the earlier edifice. This was, to a certain extent, a clue to the comparative date of the newly discovered building.

I dug round these sculptures, expecting to find the remains of walls, but could discover no other traces of building than a few squared stones fallen from their original places. As the backs of the bulls were

[1] Chamber I, plan 3.

[2] The glass and alabaster vases, and many portions of the armour, were among the objects abstracted from the collection sent to England, through the negligence of the authorities at Bombay, where the cases containing them were repacked. The loss of the glass vase is particularly to be regretted.

[3] Above, p. 89.

completely covered with inscriptions, in large and well-formed cuneiform characters, I was led to believe that they might originally have
stood alone. Still there must have been other slabs near them. I
directed a deep trench to be carried, at right angles, behind the northern
bull. After digging about ten feet, the workmen found a slab lying
flat on the brick pavement, and having a gigantic winged figure
sculptured in relief upon it. This figure resembled some already described; and carried the fir-cone, and the square basket or utensil; but
there was no inscription across it. Beyond was a similar figure, still
more gigantic in its proportions, being about fourteen feet in height.
The relief was low, and the execution inferior to that of the sculptures

The Obelisk

discovered in the other palaces. The beard and part of the legs of a winged bull, in yellow limestone, were next found. These remains, imperfect as they were, promised better things. The trench was carried in the same direction for several days; but nothing more appeared. It was now above fifty feet in length, and still without any new discovery. I had business in Mosul, and was giving directions to the workmen to guide them during my absence. Standing on the edge of the hitherto unprofitable trench, I doubted whether I should carry it any further: but made up my mind at last not to abandon it until my return, which would be on the following day. I mounted my horse; but had scarcely left the mound, when a corner of black marble was uncovered, lying on the very edge of the trench. This attracted the notice of the superintendent of the party digging, who ordered the place to be further examined. The corner was part of an obelisk, about six feet six inches in height, lying on its side, ten feet below the surface.

An Arab was sent after me without delay, to announce the discovery; and on my return I found the obelisk completely exposed to view. I descended eagerly into the trench, and was immediately struck by the singular appearance, and evident antiquity, of the remarkable monument before me. We raised it from its recumbent position, and, with the aid of ropes, speedily dragged it out of the ruins. Although its shape was that of an obelisk, yet it was flat at the top, and cut into three gradines. It was sculptured on the four sides; there were in all twenty small bas-reliefs, and above, below, and between them was carved an inscription 210 lines in length. The whole was in the best preservation; scarcely a character of the inscription was wanting; the figures were as sharp and well defined as if they had been carved but

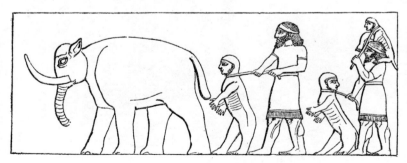

Elephant and monkeys
(Detail of Nimroud obelisk)

a few days before. The king is twice represented, followed by his attendants; a prisoner is at his feet, and his vizir and eunuchs are introducing men leading various animals, and carrying vases and other objects of tribute on their shoulders, or in their hands. The animals are the elephant, the rhinoceros, the Bactrian or two-humped camel, the wild bull, the lion, the stag, and various kinds of monkeys. Amongst the objects carried by the tribute-bearers, may perhaps be distinguished the tusks of the elephant, shawls, vases of the precious metals, fruit, and bars of metal, or bundles of rare wood.[1]

I lost no time in copying the inscriptions, and drawing the bas-reliefs, upon this precious relic. It was then carefully packed, to be transported at once to Baghdad. A party of trustworthy Arabs were chosen to sleep near it at night; and I took every precaution that the superstitions and prejudices of the natives of the country, and the jealousy of rival antiquaries, could suggest.

In the south-west corner of the mound, discoveries of scarcely less interest and importance were made, almost at the same time. The workmen were exploring the walls *a* and *d*[2]; on reaching the end of them, they discovered a pair of winged lions, of which the upper part, including the head, was almost entirely destroyed. They differed in many respects from those forming the entrances of the north-west palace. They had but four legs; the material in which they were sculptured was a coarse limestone, and not alabaster; and behind the body of the lion, and in front above the wings, were several figures, which were unfortunately greatly injured, and could with difficulty be traced. In front were two human figures, one with the head of a lion, raising a sword or stick in one hand as if in the act of striking. Between the two lions, forming this entrance, were a pair of crumbling sphinxes. They differed from all Assyrian sculptures hitherto dis-covered; nor could I form any conjecture as to their original use. They were not in relief, but entire. The human head was beardless; but whether male or female, I could not positively determine. The body was that of a lion. A pair of gracefully formed wings appeared to sup-port a kind of platform, or the base of a column; but no trace of a column could be found. These sphinxes may have been altars for sacrifice, or places to receive offerings to the gods, or tribute to the

---

[1] This monument is now in the British Museum. [One of its bas-reliefs shows the emissary of Jehu, king of Israel, doing homage to the Assyrian king. See plate 35 in H. W. F. Saggs, *The Greatness that was Babylon* (1962).]

[2] See plan 2.

king. There was no inscription upon them, by which they could be connected with any other building.

The whole entrance was buried in charcoal, and the fire which destroyed the building appears to have raged in this part with extraordinary fury. The sphinxes were almost reduced to lime; one had been nearly destroyed; but the other, although broken into a thousand pieces, was still standing when uncovered. I endeavoured to secure it with rods of iron and wooden planks: but the alabaster was too much calcined to resist exposure to the atmosphere. I had scarcely time to make a careful drawing, before the whole fell to pieces. The fragments were too small to admit of their being collected, with a view to future restoration. The sphinxes, when entire, were about five feet in height, and the same in length.

Whilst superintending the removal of the charcoal, which blocked up the entrance formed by the winged lions just described, I found a small head in alabaster, with the high horned cap, precisely similar to that of the large sphinx. A few minutes afterwards, the body of the crouching lion was dug out, and I had then a complete and very beautiful model of the larger sculptures. It had been injured by the fire,

Sphinx from S.W. Palace, Nimroud

but was still sufficiently well preserved to show accurately the form, and details. In the same place I discovered the bodies of two lions, united and forming a platform or pedestal, so much injured by fire, that I was unable to preserve it.

There were no inscriptions between the legs and behind the bodies of the lions just described, as in other buildings at Nimroud and Khorsabad. I had not yet found any sculptures unaccompanied by the name and genealogy of the founders of the edifice in which they had been placed. When no inscription was on the face, it was invariably to be found on the back of the slab. I determined, therefore, to dig at the back of the lions. I was not disappointed in my search; a few lines in the cuneiform character were discovered, and I recognised at once the names of three kings in genealogical series. The name of the first king in the series, or the founder of the edifice, was identical with that of the builder of the N.W. palace; that of his father with the name on the bricks found in the ruins opposite Mosul; that of his grandfather with the name of the builder of Khorsabad. This fortunate discovery served to connect the latest palace at Nimroud, with two other cities or edifices in Assyria; and subsequently with important monuments existing in other parts of Asia.

Whilst excavations were thus successfully carried on in the centre, and amongst the ruins of the two palaces first opened, discoveries of a different nature were made in the S.E. corner, which was much higher than any other part of the mound. I dug to a considerable depth, without meeting with any traces of building. One morning, the superintendent of the workmen informed me that a slab had been uncovered, bearing an inscription. I hastened to the spot, and saw the stone he had described lying at the bottom of the trench. Upon it was a royal name, which I recognised as that on the bull in the centre of the mound. The slab having been partly destroyed, the inscription was imperfect. I ordered it to be raised, with the intention of copying the characters. This was quickly effected with the aid of an iron crow; when, to my surprise, I found that it had been used as the lid of an earthen sarcophagus, which, with its contents, was still entire beneath. The sarcophagus was about five feet in length, and very narrow. The skeleton was well preserved, but fell to pieces almost immediately on exposure to the air: by its side were two jars in baked clay of a red colour, and a small alabaster bottle, all precisely resembling, in shape, similar vessels discovered in Egyptian tombs. There was no other clue to the date, or origin of the sepulchre.

The sarcophagus was too small to contain a man of ordinary size when stretched at full-length; and it was evident, from the position of the skeleton, that the body had been doubled up when forced in. A second earthen case was soon found, differing in form from the first. It resembled a dish-cover in shape, and was scarcely four feet long. In it were also vases of baked clay. Although the skulls were entire when first exposed to view, they crumbled into dust as soon as touched, and I was unable to preserve either of them.

The six weeks following the commencement of excavations upon a large scale, were amongst the most prosperous, and fruitful in events, during my researches in Assyria. Every day produced some new discovery. My Arabs entered with alacrity into the work, and felt almost as much interested in its results, as I did myself. They were now well organised, and I had no difficulty in managing them. Even their private disputes and domestic quarrels were referred to me. They found this a cheaper fashion of settling their differences than litigation; and I have reason to hope that they received an ampler measure of justice than they could have expected at the hands of his reverence, the Cadi. The tents had greatly increased in numbers, as the relatives of those who were engaged in the excavations came to Nimroud and swelled the encampment; for although they received no pay, they managed to live upon the gains of their friends. They were, moreover, preparing to glean,—in the event of there being any crops in the spring,—and to take possession of little strips of land along the banks of the river, upon which they might cultivate millet during the summer. They already began to prepare water-courses, and machines for irrigation. The mode of raising water is very simple. In the first place a high bank, which is never completely deserted by the river, must be chosen. A broad recess, down to the water's edge, is then cut in it. Above, on the edge of this recess, are fixed three or four upright poles, according to the number of oxen to be employed, united at the top by rollers running on a swivel, and supporting a large framework of boughs and grass, which extends to some distance behind, and is intended as a shelter from the sun during the hot days of summer. Over each roller are passed two ropes, the one being fastened to the mouth, and the other to the opposite end, of a sack, formed out of an entire bullock skin. These ropes are attached to oxen, which throw all their weight upon them by descending an inclined plane, cut into the ground behind the apparatus. A trough formed of wood, and lined with bitumen, or a shallow trench, coated with matting, is constructed at the bottom of the poles, and leads to the canal running into the fields. When the sack is drawn up to the roller, the ox turns round at the bottom of the inclined plane. The rope attached to the lower part of the bucket being fastened to the back part of the animal, he raises the bottom of the sack in turning, and the contents are poured into the troughs. As the ox ascends, the bucket is lowered into the stream again. Although this mode of irrigation is very toilsome, and requires the constant labour of several men and animals, it is generally adopted on the banks of the Tigris and Euphrates. In this way all the gardens of Baghdad and Busrah are watered; and by such means the Arabs, who condescend to cultivate,—when, from the failure of the crops, famine is staring them in the face,—raise a little millet to supply their immediate wants.

The principal public quarrels, over which my jurisdiction extended, related to property abstracted, by the Arabs, from one another's tents. These I disposed of in a summary manner, as I had provided myself with handcuffs; and Ibrahim Agha, and the Bairakdar[1] were always ready to act with energy and decision to show how much they were devoted to my service. But the domestic dissensions were of a more serious nature, and their adjustment offered far greater difficulties. They related, of course, always to the women. As soon as the work-men saved a few piastres, their thoughts were turned to the purchase of a new wife, a striped cloak, and a spear. To accomplish this, their ingenuity was taxed to the utmost extent. The old wife naturally enough raised objections, and picked a quarrel with the intended bride, which generally ended in appeal to physical force. Then the fathers and brothers were dragged into the affair; from them it extended to the various branches of the tribe, always anxious to fight for their own honour, and for the honour of their women. At other times, a man repented himself of his bargain, and refused to fulfil it; or a father, finding his future son-in-law increasing in wealth, demanded a higher price for his daughter—a breach of faith which would naturally lead to violent measures on the part of the disappointed lover. Then a workman, who had returned hungry from his work, and found his bread unbaked, or the water-skin still lying empty at the entrance of his tent, or the bundle of faggots for his evening fire yet ungathered, would, in a moment of passion, pronounce three times the awful sentence, and divorce his wife; or, avoiding such extremities, would content himself with inflicting summary punishment with a tent-pole.

[1] [See above, p. 223.]

In the first case he probably repented himself of his act an hour or two afterwards, and wished to be remarried; or endeavoured to prove that, being an ignorant man, he had mispronounced the formula, or omitted some words—both being good grounds to invalidate the divorce, and to obviate the necessity of any fresh ceremonies. But the mullah had to be summoned, witnesses called, and evidence produced. The beating was generally the most expeditious, and really, to the wife, the most satisfactory way of adjusting the quarrel. I had almost nightly to settle such questions as these. Mr. Hormuzd Rassam, who had obtained an immense influence over the Arabs, and was known amongst all the tribes, was directed to ascertain the merits of the story, and to collect the evidence. When this process had been completed, I summoned the elders, and gave judgment in their presence. The culprit was punished summarily, or, in the case of a disputed bargain, was made to pay more, or to refund, as the case required.

It is singular, considering the number of cases thus brought before me, that only on one occasion did either of the parties refuse to abide by my decision. I was sitting one evening in my tent, when a pretty Arab girl rushed into my presence, and throwing herself at my feet, uttered the most dismal lamentations. An old Arab woman, her mother, entered soon after, and a man endeavoured to force his way in, but was restrained by the brawny arms of the Bairakdar. It was some time before I could learn from either the girl or her mother, who were both equally agitated, the cause of their distress. The father, who was dead, had, during his lifetime, agreed to marry his daughter to the man who had followed them to my tent; and the price, fixed at two sheep, a donkey, and a few measures of wheat, had been partly paid. The Arab, who was a stranger, and did not belong to any of the branches of the Jebour from which I had chosen my workmen, had now come to claim his bride; but the girl had conceived a violent hatred for him, and absolutely refused to marry. The mother, who was poor, did not know how to meet the difficulty; for the donkey had already been received, and had died doing its work. She was therefore inclined to give up her daughter, and was about to resign her into the hands of the husband, when the girl fled from her tent, and took refuge with me. Having satisfied myself that the man was of a bad character, and known as a professed thief in a small way (as discreditable a profession as that of a robber on a large scale is honourable), and the girl declaring that she would throw herself into the river rather than marry him, I ordered the mother to give back a donkey, with two sheep by way of interest for the use of the deceased animal, and furnished her privately with the means of doing so. They were tendered to the complainant; but he refused to accept them, although the tribe approved of the decision. As the girl appeared to fear the consequences of the steps she had taken, I yielded to her solicitations, and allowed her to remain under my roof. In the night the man went to the tent of the mother, and stabbed her to the heart. He then fled into the desert. I succeeded after some time in catching him, and he was handed over to the authorities at Mosul; but, during the confusion which ensued on the death of Tahyar Pasha, he escaped from prison, and I heard no more of him. The Arabs, on account of this tragical business, were prejudiced against the girl, and there was little chance of her being again betrothed. I married her, therefore, to an inhabitant of Mosul.

When I first employed the Arabs, the women were sorely ill-treated, and subjected to great hardships. I endeavoured to introduce some reform into their domestic arrangements, and punished severely those who inflicted corporal chastisement on their wives. In a short time the number of domestic quarrels was greatly reduced; and the women, who were at first afraid to complain of their husbands, now boldly appealed to me for protection. They had, however, some misgivings as to the future, which were thus expressed by a deputation sent to return thanks after an entertainment:—'O Bey! we are your sacrifice. May God reward you! Have we not eaten wheaten bread, and even meat and butter, since we have been under your shadow? Is there one of us that has not now a coloured kerchief for her head, bracelets, and ankle-rings, and a striped cloak? But what shall we do when you leave us, which God forbid you ever should do! Our husbands will then have their turn, and there will be nobody to help us.'

These poor creatures, like all Arab women, were exposed to constant hardships. They were obliged to look after the children, to make the bread, to fetch water, and to cut wood, which they brought home from afar on their heads. The bundles of firewood, brought from a considerable distance, were enormous, completely concealing the head and shoulders of those who tottered beneath them. Moreover they were trusted with all the domestic duties, wove their wool and goats' hair into clothes, carpets, and tent-canvass; and were left to strike and raise the tents, and to load and unload the beasts of burden when they changed their encamping ground. If their husbands possessed sheep or cows, they had to drive them to the pastures, and to milk them at night. When moving, they carried their children at their backs during the march, and were even troubled with the burden when employed in their domestic occupations, if the children were too young to be left alone. The men sat indolently by, smoking their pipes, or listening to a trifling story from some stray Arab of the desert. At first the women, whose husbands encamped on the mound, brought water from the river; but I released them from this labour by employing horses and donkeys in the work. And yet the women worked cheerfully, and it was seldom that their husbands had to complain of their idleness. Some were more active than others. There was a young girl named Hadla, who particularly distinguished herself, and was consequently sought in marriage by all the men. Her features were handsome, and her form erect, and exceedingly graceful. She carried the largest burdens, was never unemployed, and was accustomed, when she had finished the work imposed upon her by her mother, to assist her neighbours in completing theirs.

The dinners or breakfasts (for the meal comprised both) of the Arab workmen, were brought to them at the mound about eleven o'clock by the younger children. Few had more than a loaf of millet bread, or millet made into a kind of paste, to satisfy their hunger; wheaten bread was a luxury. Sometimes their wives had found time to gather a few herbs, which were boiled in water with a little salt, and sent in wooden bowls; and in spring, sour milk and curds occasionally accompanied their bread. The little children, who carried their father's or brother's portions, came merrily along, and sat smiling on the edge of the trenches, or stood gazing in wonder at the sculptures, until they were sent back with the empty platters and bowls. The working parties ate together in the trenches in which they had been employed. A little water, drank out of a large jar, was their only beverage. Yet they were happy and joyous. The joke went round; or, during the short time they had to rest, one told a story, which, if not concluded at a sitting, was resumed on the following day. Sometimes a pedlar from Mosul, driving before him his donkey, laden with raisins or dried dates, would appear on the mound. Buying up his store, I would distribute it amongst the men. This largesse created an immense deal of satisfaction and enthusiasm, which any one not acquainted with the character of the Arab, might have thought almost more than equivalent to the consideration.

The Arabs are naturally hospitable and generous. If one of the workmen was wealthy enough to buy a handful of raisins, or a piece of camel's or sheep's flesh, or if he had a cow, which occasionally yielded him butter or sour milk, he would immediately call his friends together to partake of his feast. I was frequently invited to such entertainments; the whole dinner, perhaps, consisting of half a dozen dates or raisins spread out wide, to make the best show, upon a corn-sack; a pat of butter upon a corner of a flat loaf; and a few cakes of dough baked in the ashes. And yet the repast was ushered in with every solemnity;—the host turned his dirty keffiah, or head-kerchief, and his cloak, in order to look clean and smart; appearing both proud of the honour conferred upon him, and of his means to meet it in a proper fashion.

I frequently feasted the workmen, and sometimes their wives and daughters were invited to separate entertainments, as they would not eat in public with the men. Generally of an evening, after the labours of the day were finished, some Kurdish musicians would stroll to the village with their instruments, and a dance would be commenced, which lasted through the greater part of the night. Sheikh Abd-ur-rahman, or some Sheikh of a neighbouring tribe, occasionally joined us; or an Arab from the Khabour, or from the most distant tribes of the desert, would pass through Nimroud, and entertain a large circle of curious and excited listeners with stories of recent fights, plundering expeditions, or the murder of a chief. I endeavoured, as far as it was in my power, to create a good feeling amongst all, and to obtain their willing co-operation in my work. I believe that I was to some extent successful.

The Tiyari, or Nestorian Chaldæan Christians, resided chiefly on the mound, where I had built a large hut for them. A few only returned at night to the village. Many of them had brought their wives from the mountains. The women made bread, and cooked for all. Two of the men walked to the village of Tel Yakoub, or to Mosul, on Saturday evening, to fetch flour for the whole party, and returned before the work of the day began on Monday morning; for they would not journey on the Sabbath. They kept their holidays and festivals with as much rigour as they kept the Sunday. On these days they assembled on the mound or in the trenches; and one of the priests or deacons (for there were several amongst the workmen) repeated prayers, or led a hymn or chant. I often watched these poor creatures, as they reverentially knelt—their heads uncovered—under the great bulls, celebrating the praises of Him, whose temples the worshippers of those frowning idols had destroyed—whose power they had mocked. It was the triumph of truth over paganism.

The women retained their mountain habits, and were always washing themselves on the mound, with that primitive simplicity which characterises their ablutions in the Tiyari districts.[1] This was a cause of shame to other Christians in my employ; but the Chaldæans themselves were quite insensible to the impropriety, and I let them have their way.

As for myself I rose at day-break, and after a hasty breakfast rode to the mound. Until night I was engaged in drawing the sculptures, copying and moulding the inscriptions, and superintending the excavations, and the removal and packing of the bas-reliefs. On my return to the village, I was occupied till past midnight in comparing the inscriptions with the paper impressions, in finishing drawings, and in preparing for the work of the following day. Such was our manner of life during the excavations at Nimroud.

Early in December I had collected a sufficient number of bas-reliefs to load another raft, and I consequently rode into Mosul to make preparations for sending a second cargo to Baghdad. I had soon procured all that was necessary for the purpose; and loading a small raft with spars and skins for the construction of a larger, and with mats and felts for packing the sculptures, I returned to Nimroud.

The raft-men having left Mosul late in the day, and not reaching the Awai until after nightfall, were afraid to cross the dam in the dark; they therefore tied the raft to the shore, and went to sleep. They were attacked during the night, and plundered. I appealed to the authorities, but in vain. The Arabs of the desert, they said, were beyond their reach. If this robbery passed unnoticed, the remainder of my property, and even my person, might run some risk. Besides, I did not relish the reflection, that the mats and felts destined for my sculptures were now furnishing the tents of some Arab Sheikh. Three or four days elapsed before I ascertained who were the robbers. They belonged to a small tribe encamping at some distance from Nimroud—notorious in the country for their thieving propensities, and the dread of my Jebours, whose cattle were continually disappearing in a very mysterious fashion. Having learnt the position of their tents, I started off one morning at dawn, accompanied by Ibrahim Agha, the Bairakdar, and a horseman, who was in my service. We reached the encampment after a long ride, and found the number of the Arabs to be greater

[1] [See above, p. 168.]

than I had expected. The arrival of strangers drew together a crowd, which gathered round the tent of the Sheikh, where I seated myself. A slight bustle was apparent in the women's department. I soon perceived that attempts were being made to hide various ropes and felts, the ends of which, protruding from under the canvas, I had little difficulty in recognising. 'Peace be with you,' said I, addressing the Sheikh, who showed by his countenance that he was not altogether ignorant of the object of my visit. 'Your health and spirits are, please God, good. We have long been friends, although it has never yet been my good fortune to see you. I know the laws of friendship; that which is my property is your property, and the contrary. But there are a few things, such as mats, felts, and ropes, which come from afar, and are very necessary to me, whilst they can be of little use to you; otherwise God forbid that I should ask for them. You will greatly oblige me by giving these things to me.' 'As I am your sacrifice, O Bey,' answered he, 'no such things as mats, felts, or ropes were ever in my tents (I observed a new rope supporting the principal pole). Search, and if such things be found we give them to you willingly.' 'Wallah, the Sheikh has spoken the truth,' exclaimed all the by-standers. 'That is exactly what I want to ascertain; and as this is a matter of doubt, the Pasha must decide between us,' replied I, making a sign to the Bairakdar, who had been duly instructed how to act. In a moment he had handcuffed the Sheikh, and jumping on his horse, dragged the Arab, at an uncomfortable pace, out of the encampment. 'Now, my sons,' said I, mounting leisurely, 'I have found a part of that which I wanted; you must search for the rest.' They looked at one another in amazement. One man, more bold than the rest, was about to seize the bridle of my horse; but the weight of Ibrahim Agha's courbatch across his back, drew his attention to another object. Although the Arabs were well armed, they were too much surprised to make any attempt at resistance; or perhaps they feared too much for their Sheikh, still jolting away at an uneasy pace in the iron grasp of the Bairakdar, who had put his horse to a brisk trot, and held his pistol cocked in one hand. The women, swarming out of the tents, now took part in the matter. Gathering round my horse, they kissed the tails of my coat and my shoes, making the most dolorous supplica-tions. I was not to be moved, however; and extricating myself with difficulty from the crowd, I rejoined the Bairakdar, who was hurrying on his prisoner with evident good will.

The Sheikh had already made himself well known to the authorities by his dealings with the villages, and there was scarcely a man in the country who could not bring forward a specious claim against him— either for a donkey, a horse, a sheep, or a copper kettle. He was consequently most averse to an interview with the Pasha, and looked with evident horror on the prospect of a journey to Mosul. I added considerably to his alarm, by dropping a few friendly hints on the advantage of the dreary subterraneous lock-up house under the governor's palace, and of the pillory and sticks. By the time he reached Nimroud, he was fully alive to his fate, and deemed it prudent to make a full confession. He sent an Arab to his tents; and next morning an ass appeared in the courtyard bearing the missing property, with the addition of a lamb and a kid by way of a conciliatory offering. I dismissed the Sheikh with a lecture, and had afterwards no reason to complain of him or of his tribe; nor indeed of any tribes in the neighbourhood; for the story got abroad, and was invested with several horrible facts in addition, which could only be traced to the imagination of the Arabs, but which served to produce the effect I desired— a proper respect for my property.

During the winter Mr. Longworth,[1] and two other English travellers, visited me at Nimroud. I was riding home from the ruins one evening with Mr. Longworth. The Arabs returning from their day's work, were following a flock of sheep belonging to the people of the village, shouting their war-cry, flourishing their swords, and indulging in the most extravagant gesticulations. My friend, less acquainted with the excitable temperament of the children of the desert than myself, was somewhat amazed at these violent proceedings, and desired to learn their cause. I asked one of the most active of the party. 'O Bey,' they exclaimed almost all together, 'God be praised, we have eaten butter and wheaten bread under your shadow, and are content—but an Arab is an Arab. It is not for a man to carry about dirt in baskets, and to use a spade all his life; he should be with his sword and his mare in the desert. We are sad as we think of the days when we plundered the Aneyza, and we must have excitement, or our hearts would break. Let us then believe that these are the sheep we have taken from the enemy, and that we are driving them to our tents!' And off they ran, raising their wild cry and flourishing their swords, to the no small alarm of the shepherd, who saw his sheep scampering in all directions, and did not seem inclined to enter into the joke.

By the middle of December, a second cargo of sculptures was ready

[1] [Consul-General in Serbia.]

to be sent to Baghdad.[1] I was again obliged to have recourse to the buffalo-carts of the Pasha; and as none of the bas-reliefs and objects to be moved were of great weight, these rotten and unwieldy vehicles could be patched up for the occasion. On Christmas day I had the satisfaction of seeing a raft, bearing twenty-three cases, in one of which was the obelisk, floating down the river. I watched them until they were out of sight, and then galloped into Mosul to celebrate the festivities of the season, with the few Europeans whom duty or business had collected in this remote corner of the globe.

[1] Including the obelisk, nearly all the bas-reliefs forming the south wall of chamber B, plan 3, the slabs from chamber I (same plan), and a human head belonging to one of the gigantic bulls, forming an entrance to the palace in the south-west corner (No. 1, entrance c, plan 2).

XI

AS I WAS drawing one morning at the mound, Ibrahim Agha came to me, with his eyes full of tears, and announced the death of Tahyar Pasha. The Cawass had followed the fortunes of the late Governor of Mosul almost since childhood, and was looked upon as a member of his family. Like other Turks of his class, he had been devoted to the service of his patron, and was treated more like a companion than a servant. In no country in the world are ties of this nature more close than in Turkey: nowhere does there exist a better feeling between the master and the servant, and the master and the slave.

I was much grieved at the sudden death of Tahyar; for he was a man of gentle and kindly manners, just and considerate in his government, and of considerable information and learning for a Turk. I felt a kind of affection for him. The cause of his death showed his integrity. His troops had plundered a friendly tribe, falsely represented to him as rebellious by his principal officers, who were anxious to have an opportunity of enriching themselves with the spoil. When he learnt the particulars of the affair, and that the tribe, so far from being hostile, were peaceably pasturing their flocks on the banks of the Khabour, he exclaimed, 'You have destroyed my house' (*i.e.* its honour), and, without speaking again, died of a broken heart. He was buried in the court-yard of the principal mosque at Mardin. A simple but elegant tomb, surrounded by flowers and evergreens, was raised over his remains; and an Arabic inscription records the virtues and probable reward of one of the most honest and amiable men that it has been my lot to meet. I visited his monument during my journey to Constantinople.

Essad Pasha, who had lately been at Beyrout, was at length appointed to succeed Tahyar, and soon after reached his Pashalic. These changes did not affect my proceedings. Armed with my firman I was able to defy the machinations of the Cadi and the Ulema, who did not cease their endeavours to throw obstacles in my way.

I should weary the reader, were I to describe, step by step, the progress of the work, and the discoveries gradually made in various parts of the great mound. I prefer, therefore, describing at once the results of my labours, during the first three months of the year [1847].

The north-west palace was naturally the most interesting portion of the ruins, and I had satisfied myself beyond a doubt that it was the most ancient building yet explored in Assyria. Not having been exposed to a conflagration like other edifices, the sculptures, bas-reliefs, and inscriptions, which it contained, were still admirably preserved.

When the excavations were resumed after Christmas, eight chambers had been discovered. By the end of the month of April I had explored almost the whole building; and had opened twenty-eight chambers cased with alabaster slabs. The principal part of the edifice seems to have been that to the north. Chambers B and G [see plan 3] contained the most remarkable bas-reliefs; they represented the deeds of the king in war and in the chase, his triumphal return, and the celebration of religious ceremonies. The best artists had evidently been employed upon them; and they excelled all those that had yet been discovered.

The chamber V is remarkable for the discovery of a number of ivory ornaments, of considerable beauty and interest. These ivories, when uncovered, adhered so firmly to the soil, and were in so forward a state of decomposition, that I had the greatest difficulty in extracting them, even in fragments. I spent hours lying on the ground, separating them, with a penknife, from the rubbish by which they were surrounded. The ivory separated itself in flakes. With all the care that I could devote to the collection of the fragments, many were lost, or remained unperceived, in the immense heap of rubbish under which they were buried. Since they have been in England, they have been admirably restored and cleaned, and the ornaments have regained the appearance and consistency of recent ivory, and may be handled without risk of injury.

The most interesting [of these ivories] are the remains of two small tablets, one nearly entire, the other much injured, representing two sitting figures, holding in one hand the Egyptian sceptre or symbol of power. Between the figures is a cartouche, containing a name or words in hieroglyphics, and surmounted by a feather or plume, such as is found in monuments of the eighteenth, and subsequent dynasties, of

Egypt. The chairs on which the figures are seated, the robes of the figures themselves, the hieroglyphics in the cartouche, and the feather above it, were enamelled with a blue substance let into the ivory; and the uncarved portions of the tablet, the cartouche, and part of the figures, were originally gilded—remains of the gold leaf still adhering to them. The forms, and style of art, have a purely Egyptian character, although there are certain peculiarities that would seem to mark the work of a foreign, perhaps an Assyrian, artist.

To the south-east of the great hall Y, I discovered that we had entered chambers formed by walls of sun-dried bricks, covered with a thin coating of plaster, which had been painted with figures and ornaments. The colours had faded so completely, that scarcely any of the subjects or designs could be traced. It required the greatest care to separate the rubbish from the walls, without destroying, at the same time, the paintings, as the plaster fell from the walls in flakes notwithstanding all my efforts to preserve it. I was only able to sketch a few of the ornaments, in which the colours chiefly distinguishable were red, blue, black, and white. The subjects of the paintings, as far as could be judged from the remains, were probably processions, in which the king was represented followed by his eunuchs and attendant warriors, and receiving prisoners and tribute. As the means at my disposal did not warrant any outlay in making mere experiments, without the promise of the discovery of something to carry away, I felt myself compelled, much against my inclination, to abandon the excavations in this part of the mound after uncovering portions of two chambers.

On the western side of the great mound, to the south of the palace in which the discoveries just described were made, there is a considerable elevation. The spot is marked e, on plan 1. To examine the place, a trench was opened on a level with the platform. It was some time before I ascertained that we were cutting into a kind of tower, or nest of upper chambers, constructed entirely of unbaked bricks; the walls being plastered and elaborately painted. I explored three rooms, and part of a fourth, on the southern side of this building. The rooms had been twice painted—two distinct coats of plaster being visible on the walls. The outer coating, when carefully detached, left the under; on which were painted ornaments differing from those above. These painted ornaments were elaborate and graceful in design. The Assyrian bull was frequently portrayed, sometimes with wings, sometimes without. Above the animals were painted battlements, similar to those of castles, as represented in the sculptures. Below them, forming a kind of cornice, were squares and circles, tastefully arranged; and more elaborate combinations were not wanting. The colours employed were blue, red, white, yellow, and black. I doubt whether any green was used in this building; the green on the under coating of plaster, being probably the result of the decomposition of the blue. The pale yellow of the ground, on which the designs were painted, resembles the tint on the walls of Egypt; but it is possible that white had changed to this colour.

In the centre of the mound, to the north of the great winged bulls, I had in vain endeavoured to find traces of building. Excavations to the south disclosed a well-formed tomb built of bricks, and covered with a slab of alabaster. It was about five feet in length, and scarcely more than eighteen inches in breadth in the interior. On removing the lid, parts of a skeleton were exposed to view; the skull and some of the larger bones were still entire, but crumbled into dust when I attempted to remove them. With them were three earthen vessels. A vase of reddish clay, with a long narrow neck, stood in a dish of such delicate fabric, that I had great difficulty in removing it entire. Over the mouth of the vase was placed a bowl or cup, also of red clay. This pottery appears to have stood near the right shoulder of the body. In the dust, which had accumulated round the skeleton, were found beads and small ornaments belonging to a necklace. The beads are of opaque coloured glass, agate, cornelian, and amethyst. With the beads was a cylinder, on which is represented the king in his chariot, hunting the wild bull, as in the bas-relief from the north-west palace. A copper ornament resembling a modern seal, two bracelets of silver, and a pin for the hair, were also discovered. I carefully collected and preserved these interesting remains, which seem to prove that the body had been that of a female.

On digging beyond this tomb, I found a second, similarly constructed, and of the same size. In it were two vases of highly glazed green pottery, elegant in shape, and in perfect preservation. Near them was a copper mirror, and a copper lustral spoon, all Egyptian in form. Many other tombs were opened, containing vases, plates, mirrors, spoons, beads, and ornaments.

Having carefully collected and packed the contents of the tombs, I removed them and dug deeper into the mound. I was surprised to find, about *five feet beneath them*, the remains of a building. Walls of unbaked bricks could still be traced; but the slabs, with which they had been panelled, were no longer in their places, being scattered about without order, and lying mostly with their faces on the flooring of baked bricks. Upon them were both sculptures and inscriptions. Slab succeeded to slab; and when I had cleared away the earth from a space about fifty feet square, the ruins presented a very singular appearance. Above one hundred slabs were exposed to view, packed in rows one against the other, as slabs in a stone-cutter's yard, or as the leaves of a gigantic book. Every slab was sculptured; and as they were placed in a regular series, according to the subjects upon them, it was evident that they had been moved, in the order in which they stood, from their original positions against the walls of sun-dried brick; and had been left as found, preparatory to their removal elsewhere. That they were not thus arranged before being used in the building for which they had been originally sculptured, was evident from the fact that the Assyrians carved their slabs after, and not before, they were placed.

These sculptures resembled, in many respects, some of the bas-reliefs found in the south-west palace, in which the sculptured faces of the slabs were turned towards the walls of unbaked brick. It appeared, therefore, that the centre building had been destroyed, to supply materials for the construction of the more southerly edifice.

The subjects of the sculptures thus found collected together were principally battle-pieces and sieges. Some cities were represented as standing on a river, in the midst of groves of date-trees; others on mountains. Amongst the conquered people were warriors mounted on camels. It may be inferred, therefore, that a part of these bas-reliefs recorded the invasion or conquest of an Arab nation, or perhaps of a part of Babylonia; the inhabitants of the cities being assisted by auxiliaries, or allies from the neighbouring desert.

I have described the singular appearance presented by the ruins in the south-west corner. Several parties of workmen were now engaged in exploring them. As it appeared to me possible that the south-west palace stood above other ruins, by way of experiment I directed long and very deep trenches to be opened in three different directions: nothing, however, was discovered, but a box or square hole, formed by bricks carefully fitted together, containing several small heads in unbaked clay of a dark brown colour. These heads were furnished with beards, and had very high pointed caps (not helmets) or mitres. They were found about twenty feet beneath the surface, and were probably idols placed, for some religious purpose, under the foundations of buildings. Objects somewhat similar, in unbaked clay, were discovered at Khorsabad, buried under the slabs forming the pavement between the gigantic bulls.

Near the entrance *d* of the great hall was found, amidst a mass of charred wood and charcoal, and beneath a fallen slab, part of a beam in good preservation. It appears to be mulberry. This is the only portion of entire wood as yet discovered in the ruins of Assyria.

The south-east corner of the mound, which is considerably higher than any other part, appears to have been the principal burying place of those who occupied the country after the destruction of the oldest of the Assyrian palaces. I have already described two tombs discovered there[1]: many others were subsequently found. Removing these tombs I discovered beneath them the remains of a building, and explored parts of seven chambers. No sculptured slabs or inscriptions were found in them, nor any remains of fragments by which the comparative age of the building could be determined.

Between the palace in the south-west corner and the ruins [on the southern edge of the mound] was a deep ravine; whether an ancient artificial ascent to the platform, gradually deepened and widened by the winter rains, or entirely a natural watercourse, I was unable to determine. Along its sides, to a considerable depth, were exposed masses of brickwork. I directed several trenches to be carried from this ravine into the south-eastern corner, in the expectation of finding buildings beneath the chambers already explored. A few fragments of sculptured alabaster, the remains of a winged bull in yellow limestone, and a piece of black stone bearing small figures, were discovered to the west of the upper building. I could also trace walls of sun-dried brick, still bearing remains of painted ornaments. Finding no sculptured slabs, I did not continue my researches in this part of the ruins.

It only remains for me to mention a singular discovery on the eastern face of the mound, near its northern extremity. I had opened a trench[2] from the outer slope, with a view to ascertain the nature of the wall surrounding the inner buildings. I found no traces of stone, or of alabaster slabs; the wall being built of sun-dried bricks and nearly fifty feet thick. In its centre, about fifteen feet below the surface of the platform, the workmen came upon a small vaulted chamber, built of baked bricks. It was about ten feet high, and the same in width. The arch was constructed upon the well-known principle of vaulted roofs

---

[1] See above, p. 233–4.
[2] *r*, plan 1.

—the bricks being placed sideways, one against the other, and having been probably sustained by a frame-work until the vault was completed. This chamber was nearly blocked up with rubbish, the greater part being a kind of slag. The sides of the bricks forming the arched roof and the walls were almost vitrified, and had evidently been exposed to very intense heat. In fact, the chamber had the appearance of a large furnace for making glass, or for fusing metal. I am unable to account for its use. It is buried in the centre of a thick wall, and I could find no access to it from without. If, therefore, either originally a furnace or serving for any other purpose, it must have been used before the upper part of the wall was built.

The ruins were, of course, very inadequately explored; but with the very small sum at my disposal I was unable to pursue my researches to the extent that I could have wished. If, after carrying a trench to a reasonable depth and distance, no remains of sculpture or inscription appeared, I abandoned it and renewed the experiment elsewhere. By this mode of proceeding I could ascertain, at least, that in no part of the mound was there any very extensive edifice still standing; although it is highly probable that slabs may still be buried under the soil. But there is nothing to point out the spot where such remains may be deposited, and I might have sought after them for months in vain. There were too many tangible objects in view to warrant an outlay in experiments, perhaps leading to no results; and I have left a great part of the mound of Nimroud to be explored by those who may hereafter succeed me in the examination of the ruins of Assyria.

XII

I HAD LONG wished to excavate in the mounds of Kalah Sherghat[1],—ruins rivalling those of Nimroud and Kouyunjik in extent. An Arab, from the Shammar, would occasionally spend a night amongst my workmen, and entertain them with accounts of idols and sculptured figures of giants, which had long been the cause of wonder and awe to the wandering tribes, who occasionally pitch their tents near the place. On my first visit, I had searched in vain for such remains; but the Arabs, who are accustomed to seek for pasture during the spring in the neighbourhood, persisted in their assertions, and offered to show me where these strange statues (carved, it was said, in black stone) were to be found. As there is scarcely a ruin in Mesopotamia without its wondrous tale of apparitions and Frank idols, I concluded that Kalah Sherghat was to be ranked amongst the number, and that all these accounts were to be attributed to the fertile imagination of the Arabs. As the vicinity is notoriously dangerous, being a place of rendezvous for all plundering parties, I had deferred a visit to the ruins, until I could remain amongst them for a short time under the protection of some powerful tribe.

The pastures in the neighbourhood of Mosul having this year been completely destroyed from the want of rain, the three great divisions of the Jebour Arabs sought the jungles on the banks of the Tigris below the town. Abd'rubbou with his tribe descended the river, and subsequently moved towards Kalah Sherghat. I thought this a favourable time for excavating in the great mound; and the Sheikh having promised to supply me with Arabs for the work, and with guards for their defence, I sent Mansour, one of my superintendents, to the spot. I followed some days afterwards, accompanied by Mr. Hormuzd Rassam, the Bairakdar, and several well-armed men, chosen from amongst the Jebours who were employed at Nimroud.

[1] [See above, p. 2.]

We crossed the river on a small raft, our horses having to swim the stream. Striking into the desert by the Wadi Jehennem, we rode through a tract of land, at this time of the year usually covered with vegetation; but then, from the drought, a barren waste. During some hours' ride we scarcely saw any human being, except a solitary shepherd in the distance, driving before him his half-famished flocks. We reached at sunset a small encampment of Jebours. The tents were pitched in the midst of a cluster of high reeds on the banks of the Tigris. They were so well concealed, that it required the experienced eye of a Bedouin to detect them[1] by the thin smoke rising above the thicket. The cattle and sheep found scanty pasture in a marsh formed by the river. The Arabs were as poor and miserable as their beasts; they received us, however, with hospitality, and killed a very lean lamb for our entertainment.

On the following day we passed the bitumen pits, or the 'Kiyara', as they are called by the Arabs. They cover a considerable extent of ground; the bitumen bubbling up in springs from the crevices in the earth. The Jebour, and other tribes encamping near the pits, carry the bitumen for sale to Mosul, and other parts of the Pashalic. It is extensively used for building purposes, for lining the boats on the river, and particularly for smearing camels, when suffering from certain diseases of the skin to which they are liable. Before leaving the pits, the Arabs, as is their habit, set fire to the bitumen, which sent forth a dense smoke, obscuring the sky, and being visible for many miles. We reached the tents of Abd'rubbou early in the afternoon, about ten miles to the north of Kalah Sherghat. The great mound was visible from this spot, rising high above the Zor, or jungle, which clothes the banks of the Tigris.

No Sheikh could have made a more creditable show of friendship than did Abd'rubbou. He rode out to meet me, and without delay ordered sheep enough to be slain to feast half his tribe. I declined, however, to spend the night with him, as he pressed me to do, on the plea that I was anxious to see the result of the excavations at Kalah Sherghat. He volunteered to accompany me to the ruins after we had breakfasted, and declared that if a blade of grass were to be found near the mound, he would move all his tents there immediately for my

---

[1] In the desert, the vicinity of an encampment is generally marked by some sign well known to the members of the tribe. It would otherwise be very difficult to discover the tents, pitched, as they usually are, in some hollow or ravine to conceal them from hostile plundering parties.

protection. In the meanwhile, to do me proper honour, he introduced me to his wives, and to his sister, whose beauty I had often heard extolled by the Jebours, and who was not altogether undeserving of her reputation. She was still unmarried. Abd'rubbou himself was one of the handsomest Arabs in Mesopotamia.

We started for the ruins in the afternoon, and rode along the edge of the jungle. Hares, wolves, foxes, jackals, and wild boars continually crossed our path, and game of all kinds seemed to abound. The Arabs gave chase; but the animals were able to enter the thick brushwood, and conceal themselves before my greyhounds could reach them. Lions are sometimes found near Kalah Sherghat, rarely higher up on the Tigris. As I floated down to Baghdad a year before, I had heard the roar of a lion not far from this spot: they are, however, seldom seen, and we beat the bushes in vain for such noble game.

As for grass, except in scanty tufts at the foot of the trees in the jungle, there appeared to be none at all. In the place of the green meadows of last year, covered with flowers, there was a naked yellow waste, in which even the abstemious flocks of the Bedouin could scarcely escape starvation. As we rode along, Abd'rubbou examined every corner and ravine in the hope of finding an encamping place, and a little pasture for his cattle, but his search was not attended with much success.

The workmen on the mound, seeing horsemen approach, made ready for an encounter, under the impression that we were a foraging party from a hostile tribe. As soon, however, as they recognised us, they threw off the few superfluous garments they possessed. Dropping their shirts from their shoulders, and tying them round the waist by the arms, they set up the war-cry, and rushed in and out of the trenches like madmen.

We heard their shouts from afar, but could see nothing, from the dust they made in throwing out the earth. I found that Mansour, the superintendent, had organised a regular system of warlike defence. We were hailed by scouts as we advanced, and there were well-armed watchmen on all the heights. Near each trench were the matchlocks and spears of the workmen, ready for use. 'What need of all these precautions?' said I to the timid Christian, as he advanced to receive me. 'May God preserve you, O Bey!' replied he. 'Our lives, under your shadow, are, of course, of no value—may yours be prolonged. But all the unbelievers in the world congregate here. If we put a morsel of bread into our mouths—lo! we have to spit it out again, before we can eat it, to meet those accursed Bedouins. If we shut our eyes in sleep, they steal our cauldrons and pots, and we have nothing wherewith to bake our bread; so that if we are not killed, we must be starved. But we have eaten your bread, and shall not go unrewarded after all these sufferings.' The concluding paragraph accounted to some extent for this exaggerated history of their miseries; but I learnt that scarcely a day had elapsed without the appearance of a body of horsemen from some of the tribes of the desert, and that their visits were not always prompted by the most friendly intentions. The general scarcity had unsettled the Arabs, and every one was on the look-out to help himself to his neighbour's property. Moreover, reports had soon been spread abroad that a Frank, acquainted with all the secrets and hidden mysteries of wisdom, had been successfully searching for treasure. Many of those who rode to Kalah Sherghat, expected to return much wealthier men than they went, by seizing the heaps of gold and silver to which, as possessors of the country, they were convinced they had better claims than a stranger.

The principal excavations had been made on the western side of the mound. After I had succeeded in obtaining silence, and calming the sudden fit of enthusiasm which had sprung up on my arrival, I descended into the trenches. A sitting figure in black basalt, of the size of life, had been uncovered. It was, however, much mutilated. The head and hands had been destroyed, and other parts of the statue had been injured. The square stool, or block, upon which the figure sat, was covered on three sides with a cuneiform inscription. The first line, containing the name and titles of the king, was almost defaced; but one or two characters enabled me to restore a name, identical with that on the great bulls in the centre of the mound at Nimroud. On casting my eye down the first column of the inscription, I found the names of his father (the builder of the most ancient palace of Nimroud), and of his grandfather, which at once proved that the reading was correct. An Arab soon afterwards brought me a brick bearing a short legend, which contained the three names entire. I was thus enabled to fix the comparative epoch of the newly-discovered ruins. At no time did I feel the value of the genealogical lists on the different monuments at Nimroud, more than when exploring other remains in Assyria. They enabled me to ascertain the comparative date of every edifice, and rock tablet, with which I became acquainted; and to fix the style of art of each period.

The figure, unlike the sculptures of Nimroud and Khorsabad, was in full, and not in relief; and probably represented the king. The Arabs declared that this statue had been seen some years before; and it is possible that, at some period of heavy rain, it may have been for a short time exposed to view, and subsequently reburied. In other parts of the mound there were ruins of walls, but we found no more sculptures.

Sitting figure in basalt, from Kalah Sherghat

255

Having made a hasty survey of the trenches, I rode to my tent. It had been pitched in the midst of those of my workmen. Abd'rubbou remained with me for the night. Whilst I was examining the ruins, he had been riding to and fro, to find a convenient spot for his tents, and grass for his cattle. Such is the custom with the Arabs. When the grass, within a certain distance of their encampment, has been exhausted, they prepare to seek new pastures. The Sheikhs, and the principle men of the tribe, mount their mares, and ride backwards and forwards over the face of the country, until they find herbage sufficient for the wants of their flocks. Having fixed upon a suitable spot, they return to acquaint their followers with their success, and announce their intention of moving thither on the following morning. The Sheikh's tent is generally the first struck; and the rest of the Arabs, if they feel inclined, follow his movements. If any of the tribe have quarrelled with the chief, and wish to desert him, they seize this occasion, leaving their tents standing until the others are gone, and then moving off in another direction.

Abd'rubbou having, at length, fixed upon a suitable site on the banks of the river, to the south of the mound, he marked out a place for his tents, and sent a horseman to his tribe, with orders for them to move to Kalah Sherghat on the following morning. These preliminaries having been settled, he adjourned to my tent to supper. It was cold and damp, and the Arabs, collecting brushwood and trunks of trees, made a great fire, which lighted up the recesses of the jungle. As night advanced, a violent storm broke over us; the wind rose to a hurricane —the rain descended in torrents—the thunder rolled in one long peal —and the vivid streams of lightning, almost incessant, showed the surrounding landscape. When the storm had abated, I walked to a short distance from the tents to gaze upon the scene. The huge fire we had kindled, threw a lurid glare over the trees around our encampment. The great mound could be distinguished through the gloom, rising like a distant mountain against the dark sky. From all sides came the melancholy wail of the jackals—thousands of these animals having issued from their subterranean dwellings in the ruins, as soon as the last gleam of twilight was fading in the western horizon. The owl, perched on the old masonry, occasionally sent forth its mournful note. The shrill laugh of the Arabs would sometimes rise above the cry of the jackal. Then all earthly noises were buried in the deep roll of the distant thunder. It was desolation such as those alone who have witnessed such scenes can know—desolation greater than the desolation of the sandy wastes of Africa: for there was the wreck of man, as well as that of nature.

Soon after sunrise on the following morning stragglers on horse-back from Abd'rubbou's late encampment began to arrive. They were soon followed by the main body of the tribe. Long lines of camels, sheep, laden donkeys, men, women and children, covered the small plain, near the banks of the river. A scene of activity and bustle ensued. Everyone appeared desirous to outdo his neighbour in vehemence of shouting, and violence of action. A stranger would have fancied that there was one general quarrel; in which, out of several hundred men and women concerned, no two persons took the same side of the question. Everyone seemed to differ from everyone else. All this confusion, however, was but the result of a friendly debate on the site of the respective tents; and when the matter had been settled to the general satisfaction, without recourse to any more violent measures than mere yelling, each family commenced raising their temporary abode. The camels being made to kneel down, and the donkeys to stop in the place fixed upon, the loads were rolled off their backs. The women next spread the coarse, black, goat-hair canvas. The men rushed about with wooden mallets to drive in the stakes and pegs; and in a few minutes the dwellings, which were to afford them shelter until they needed shelter no longer, were com-plete. The women and girls were then sent forth to fetch water, or to collect brushwood and dry twigs for fire. The men, leaving all house-hold matters to their wives and daughters, assembled in the tent of the Sheikh; and crouching in a circle round the entire trunk of an old tree, which was soon enveloped in flames, they prepared to pass the rest of the day in that desultory small-talk, relating to stolen sheep, stray donkeys, or successful robberies, which fills up the leisure of an Arab, unless he be better employed in plundering, or in war.

There is a charm in this wandering existence, whether of the Kurd or the Arab, which cannot be described. I have had some experience in it, and look back with pleasure to the days I have spent in the desert, notwithstanding the occasional inconveniences of such a life, not the least of them being a strong tendency on the part of all nomads to profess a kind of communist philosophy, supposed in Europe to be the result of modern wisdom; but which appears to have been known, from the earliest times, in the East. Friends and strangers are not always exempted from the rules of this philosophy, and their property is made no less free with than that of Job was by Arabs and Chaldees, some four thousand years ago. Still this mode of life has not always a bad effect on human nature; on the contrary, it frequently acts favourably. One cannot but admire the poor half-naked Arab, who, intrusted with a letter or a message from his Sheikh to the haughty Pasha of Baghdad, walks proudly up to the great man's sofa, and seats himself, unbidden, upon it as an equal. He fulfils his errand as if he were half ashamed of it. If it be too late to return to his tent that night, or if business still keep him from the desert, he stretches himself under a tree outside the city gate, that he may not be degraded by sleeping under a roof or within walls.

Leaving Abd'rubbou and his Arabs to pitch their tents, and settle their domestic matters, I walked to the mound. The trenches dug by the workmen around the sitting figure, were almost sufficiently extensive to prove, that no other remains of building existed in its immediate vicinity. Removing the workmen, therefore, from this part of the mound, I divided them into small parties, and employed them in making experiments in different directions. Wherever trenches were opened, remains of the Assyrian period were found, but only in fragments; such as bits of basalt with small figures in relief, portions of slabs bearing cuneiform inscriptions, and bricks similarly inscribed. Many tombs were also discovered. Like those of Nimroud, they had been made long after the destruction of the Assyrian building, and in the rubbish and earth which had accumulated above it.

Although I remained two days at Kalah Sherghat I was not able to find the platform of sun-dried bricks upon which the edifice, now in ruins and covered with earth, must originally have been built. Remains of walls were found in abundance; but they were evidently of a more recent period than the Assyrian building, to which the inscribed bricks and the fragments of sculptured stone belonged. The trenches opened by the workmen were deep; but still they did not, I think, reach the platform of the older building. The ruins were consequently not thoroughly explored. I saw no remains of the alabaster or Mosul marble, so generally employed in the palaces to the north of Kalah Sherghat. As quarries of that stone do not exist in the neighbourhood, unbaked bricks alone may have been used; and if so, the walls built with them could no longer, without very careful examination, be distinguished from the soil in which they are buried.

The principal ruin at Kalah Sherghat, like those of Nimroud, Khorsabad, and other ancient Assyrian sites, is a large square mound, surmounted by a cone or pyramid, rising nearly in the centre of the north side of the great platform. Immediately below this cone, and forming a facing to the great mound, is a wall of well-hewn stones or slabs, carefully fitted together, and bevelled at the edges. The battlements still existing on the top of this wall, are cut into gradines, resembling in this respect the battlements of castles and towers represented in the Nimroud sculptures. It is probably an Assyrian work, and the four sides of the mound may originally have been similarly cased.

The position of Kalah Sherghat is well adapted to a permanent settlement. The lands around are rich, and could be irrigated without much labour. If the population of Mesopotamia were more settled than it now is, the high road between Mosul and Baghdad would be carried along the western banks of the Tigris; and Kalah Sherghat might soon become a place of importance, both as a station and as a post of defence. At present, caravans, carrying on the trade between those two cities, are compelled to make a considerable detour to the left of the river. The road through the desert to the right of the Tigris would be direct and short. Water could, of course, be easily obtained during the whole journey, and there are no streams to interrupt the progress of a caravan. There can be little doubt that, in the days of the Arab supremacy, a flourishing commerce was carried on through this wilderness, and that there was a line of settlements, and stations on both sides of the river; but its banks are now the encamping places of wild tribes; and no merchant dares to brave the dangers of the desert, or to compound, if he escapes them, by the payment of an enormous blackmail to the Arab Sheikhs, through whose pasture-grounds his camels must pass.

The principal mound of Kalah Sherghat is one of the largest ruins with which I am acquainted in Assyria, having a circumference of 4685 yards.[1] A part of it, however, is not artificial. Irregularities in the face of the country, and natural eminences, have been united into one great platform by layers of sun-dried bricks. It is, nevertheless, a stupendous structure, yielding in magnitude and extent to no other artificial mound in Assyria. In height it is unequal; to the south it slopes off nearly to the level of the plain, whilst to the north, where it is most lofty, its sides are perpendicular, in some places rising nearly one hundred feet above the plain.

I will not attempt to connect, without better materials than we now possess, the ruins of Kalah Sherghat with any ancient city whose name

[1] *Journal of the Royal Geographical Society*, vol. xi, p. 5.

occurs in the sacred books, or has been preserved by ancient geo-graphers.[1] Of the geography of ancient Assyria, we know scarcely anything. When even the site of Nineveh could not recently be determined with any degree of certainty, we can scarcely expect to be able to identify the ruins of less important places. An extended know-ledge of the monuments of Assyria, and an acquaintance with the contents of the inscriptions, may, hereafter, enable us not only to fix the position of these cities, but to ascertain the names of many moie, which must have existed in so well-peopled a country, and may have perished on the fall of the Empire.

Having directed Mansour to continue the excavations, I prepared to return to Mosul. Abd'rubbou offered to accompany me, and as the desert between Kalah Sherghat and Hammum Ali was infested by roving parties of the Shammar and Aneyza Arabs, I deemed it prudent to accept his escort. He chose eight horsemen from his tribe, and we started together for the desert.

We slept the first night at the tents of a Seyyid, or descendant of the Prophet, of some repute for sanctity, and for the miraculous cure of diseases, which he effected by merely touching the patient. The Arabs are fully persuaded of the existence of his healing power; but I never saw anyone who even pretended to have been cured, although there was certainly no lack of subjects for the Seyyid to practise upon. The old gentleman's daughter, a dark, handsome girl, was claimed by a Sheikh of the Jebours, to whom, according to some accounts, she had been betrothed. The greater part of the night was spent in quarrelling and wrangling upon the subject. Although my tent was pitched at some distance from the assembly, the discordant voices, all joining at the same time in the most violent discussion, kept me awake until past midnight.

On the morrow I started early with Abd'rubbou and his horsemen. We struck directly across the desert, leaving my servants and baggage to follow leisurely along the banks of the river, by a more circuitous but safer road. When we were within four or five miles of that part of the Tigris at which the raft was waiting for me, I requested Abd'rubbou to return, as there appeared to be no further need of an escort. Mr. Hormuzd Rassam and myself galloped over the plain. We disturbed, as we rode along, a few herds of gazelles, and a solitary wolf, or a jackal; but we saw no human beings. Abd'rubbou and his Arabs were less fortunate; they had scarcely left us when they observed a party of

[1] [It is the site of the city Ashur.]

horsemen in the distance, whom they mistook for men of their own tribe returning from Mosul. It was not until they drew nigh that they discovered their mistake. The horsemen were plunderers from the Aneyza. The numbers were pretty equal. A fight ensured, in which two men on the side of the enemy, and one of the Jebour, were killed; but the Aneyza were defeated, and Abd'rubbou carried off, in triumph, a couple of mares.

A few days after my return to Nimroud, the Jebour were compelled, from want of pasturage, to leave the neighbourhood of Kalah Sherghat. The whole desert, as well as the jungle on the banks of the river, which generally supplied, even in the driest seasons, a little grass to the flocks, was dried up. Abd'rubbou, with his tribe, moved to the north, and migrated to the sources of the Khabour. The desert to the south of the town was now only frequented by wandering parties of plunderers, and, the position of my workmen at Kalah Sherghat becoming daily more insecure, I found it necessary to withdraw them —had I not, they would probably have run away of themselves. I renounced the further examination of these ruins with regret, as they had not been properly explored; and I have little doubt, from the fragments discovered, that many objects of interest, if not sculptured slabs, exist in the mound.

Although I was unable, at this time, to remove the sitting figure, I have, since my return to England, at the desire of the Trustees of the British Museum, sent orders for its transport to Baghdad. This has been accomplished under the directions of Mr. Ross. It will, I trust, be ere long added to the Assyrian remains now in the national collection.[1]

[1] [This sitting figure, of Shalmaneser III (858–824 B.C.), is now in the Nimrud Central Saloon of the British Museum.]

XIII

ASSYRIA PROPER, LIKE Babylonia, owed its ancient fertility as much to artificial irrigation as to the rains which fell during the winter and early spring. The Tigris and Euphrates, unlike the Nile, did not over-flow their banks and deposit a rich manure on the face of the land. They rose sufficiently, at the time of the melting of the snows in the Armenian hills, to fill the numerous canals led from them into the adjacent country; but their beds were generally so deep, or their banks so high, that, when the stream returned to its usual level, water could only be raised by artificial means.

The great canals dug in the most prosperous period of the Assyrian Empire, and used for many centuries by the inhabitants of the country —probably even after the Arab invasion—have long since been choked up, and are now useless. When the waters of the rivers are high, it is still only by the labour of man that they can be led into the fields. I have already described the rude wheels constructed for the purpose along the banks of the Tigris. Even these are scarce. The government, or rather the local authorities, levy a considerable tax upon machines for irrigation, and the simple buckets of the Arabs become in many cases the source of exaction or oppression. Few are, consequently, bold enough to make use of them. The land, therefore, even near the rivers, is entirely dependent upon the rains for its fertility.

Such is the richness of the soil of Assyria, that even a few heavy showers in the course of the year, at the time of sowing the seed, and when the corn is about a foot above the ground, are sufficient to ensure a good harvest. It frequently, however, happens that the season passes without rain. Such was the case this year. During the winter and spring no water fell. The inhabitants of the villages, who had been induced to return by the improved administration and conciliatory measures of the late Pasha, had put their whole stock of wheat and

barley into the ground. They now looked in despair upon the cloudless sky. I watched the young grass as it struggled to break through
the parched earth; but it was burnt up almost at its birth. Sometimes a
distant cloud hanging over the solitary hill of Arbela, or rising from
the desert in the far west, led to hopes, and a few drops of rain gave
rise to general rejoicings. The Arabs would then form a dance, and
raise songs and shouts, the women joining with the shrill tahlehl. But
disappointment always ensued. The clouds passed over, and the same
pure blue sky was above us. To me the total absence of verdure in
spring was particularly painful. For months my eye had not rested
upon a green thing; and that unchanging yellow, barren waste, has a
depressing effect upon the spirits. The Jaif, which the year before had
been a flower garden and had teemed with life, was now as naked and
bare as a desert in the midst of summer. I had been looking forward to
the return of the grass to encamp outside the village, and had meditated
many excursions to ancient ruins in the desert and the mountains; but
I was doomed to disappointment like the rest.

The Pasha issued orders that Christians, as well as Mussulmans,
should join in a general fast and in prayers. Supplications were offered
up in the churches and mosques. The Mohammedans held a kind of
three days' Ramazan, starving themselves during the day, and feasting
during the night. The Christians abstained from meat for the same
length of time. If a cloud were seen on the horizon, the inhabitants of
the villages, headed by their mullahs, would immediately walk into
the open country to chant prayers and verses from the Koran. Sheikhs
—crazy ascetics who wandered over the country, either half clothed
in the skins of lions or gazelles, or stark naked—burnt themselves with
hot irons, and ran shouting about the streets of Mosul. Even a kind
of necromancy was not neglected, and the Cadi and the Turkish
authorities had recourse to all manner of mysterious incantations,
which were pronounced to have been successful in other parts of the
Sultan's dominions on similar occasions. A dervish, returning from
Mecca, had fortunately brought with him a bottle of the holy water of
Zemzem. He offered it, for a consideration, to the Pasha, declaring that
when the sacred fluid was poured out in the great mosque, rain must
necessarily follow. The experiment had never been known to fail.
The Pasha paid the money—some twenty purses—and emptied the
bottle; but the results were not such as had been anticipated; and the
dervish, when sought after to explain, was not to be found.

There was no rain, not even the prospect of a shower. A famine appeared to be inevitable. It was known, however, that there were abundant supplies of corn in the granaries of the principal families of Mosul; and the fact having been brought to the notice of the Pasha, he at once ordered the stores to be opened, and their contents to be offered for sale in the market at moderate prices. As usual, the orders were given to the very persons who were speculating upon the miseries of the poor and needy—to the Cadi, the Mufti, and the head people of the town. They proceeded to obey, with great zeal and punctuality, the orders of his Excellency; but somehow or another overlooked their own stores and those of their friends, and ransacked the houses of the rest of the inhabitants. In a few days, consequently, those who had saved up a little grain for their own immediate wants were added to the number of the starving; and the necessities and misery of the town were increased.

The Bedouins, who are dependent upon the villages for supplies, now also began to feel the effects of the failure of the crops. As is generally the case in such times, they were preparing to make up for their sufferings by plundering the caravans of merchants, and the peaceable inhabitants of the districts within reach of the desert. The Shammar and other formidable tribes had not yet encamped in the vicinity of Mosul; still casual plundering parties had made their appearance among the villages, and it was predicted that as soon as their tents were pitched nearer the town, the country without the walls would be not only very unsafe, but almost uninhabitable.

These circumstances induced me to undertake the removal of the larger sculptures as early as possible. The dry season had enabled me to carry on the excavations without interruption. I determined to send the sculptures to Busrah in the month of March or April, foreseeing that as soon as the Bedouins had moved northwards from Babylonia, and had commenced their plundering expeditions in the vicinity of Mosul, I should be compelled to leave Nimroud.

The Trustees of the British Museum had not contemplated the removal of either a winged bull or lion, and I had at first believed that, with the means at my disposal, it would have been useless to attempt it. They wisely determined that these sculptures should not be sawn into pieces, to be put together again in Europe, as the pair of bulls from Khorsabad. They were to remain, where discovered, until some favourable opportunity of moving them entire might occur; and I was directed to heap earth over them, after the excavations had been brought to an end. Being loath, however, to leave all these fine specimens of Assyrian sculpture behind me, I resolved upon attempting the removal and embarkation of two of the smallest and best preserved. I had wished to secure the pair of lions forming the great entrance into the principal chamber of the north-west palace[1]; the finest specimens of Assyrian sculpture discovered in the ruins. But after some deliberation I determined to leave them for the present; as, from their size, the expense attending their conveyance to the river would have been very considerable.

I formed various plans for lowering the smaller lion and bull, for dragging them to the river, and for placing them upon rafts. Each step had its difficulties, and a variety of original suggestions and ideas were supplied by my workmen, and by the good people of Mosul. At last I resolved upon constructing a cart sufficiently strong to bear any of the masses to be moved. As no wood but poplar could be procured in the town, a carpenter was sent to the mountains with directions to fell the largest mulberry tree, or any tree of equally compact grain, he could find; and to bring beams of it, and thick slices from the trunk, to Mosul.

By the month of March this wood was ready. I purchased from the dragoman of the French Consulate a pair of strong iron axles, formerly used by M. Botta in bringing sculptures from Khorsabad. Each wheel was formed of three solid pieces, nearly a foot thick, from the trunk of a mulberry tree, bound together by iron hoops. Across the axles were laid three beams, and above them several cross-beams, all of the same wood. A pole was fixed to one axle, to which were also attached iron rings for ropes, to enable men, as well as buffaloes, to draw the cart. The wheels were provided with moveable hooks for the same purpose.

Simple as this cart was, it became an object of wonder in the town. Crowds came to look at it, as it stood in the yard of the vice-consul's khan; as long as the cart was in Mosul, it was examined by every stranger who visited the town. But when the news spread that it was about tol eave the gates, and to be drawn over the bridge, the business of the place was completely suspended. The secretaries and scribes from the palace left their divans; the guards their posts; the bazaars were deserted; and half the population assembled on the banks of the river to witness the manœuvres of the cart. A pair of buffaloes, with the assistance of a crowd of Chaldæans and shouting Arabs,

---

[1] Entrance a, chamber B, plan 3.

forced the ponderous wheels over the rotten bridge of boats.[1] The cart was the topic of general conversation in Mosul until the arrival, from Europe, of some children's toys—barking dogs and moving puppets—which gave rise to fresh excitement, and filled even the gravest of the clergy with wonder at the learning and wisdom of the Infidels.

To lessen the weight of the lion and bull, without in any way interfering with the sculpture, I reduced the thickness of the slabs, by cutting away as much as possible from the back. Their bulk was thus considerably diminished; and as the back of the slab was never meant to be seen, being placed against the wall of sun-dried bricks, no part of the sculpture was sacrificed. As, in order to move these figures at all, I had to choose between this plan and that of sawing them into several pieces, I did not hesitate to adopt it.

To enable me to move the bull from the ruins, and to place it on the cart in the plain below, a trench was cut nearly two hundred feet long, about fifteen feet wide, and, in some places, twenty feet deep. A road was thus constructed from the entrance, in which stood the bull, to the edge of the mound. About fifty Arabs and Nestorians were employed in the work.

On opening this trench it was found that a chamber had once existed to the west of hall Y (plan 3). The only bas-relief discovered was lying flat on the pavement, where it had evidently been left when the adjoining slabs were removed. It has been sent to England, and represents a lion hunt. This small bas-relief is remarkable for its finish, the elegance of the ornaments, and the great spirit of the design. The work of different artists may be plainly traced in the Assyrian edifices. Frequently where the outline is spirited and correct, and the ornaments designed with considerable taste, the execution is defective or coarse; evidently showing, that whilst the subject was drawn by a master, the carving of the stone had been intrusted to an inferior workman. In many sculptures some parts are more highly finished than others, as if they had been retouched by an experienced sculptor. The figures of the enemy are generally rudely drawn and left unfinished, to show probably that, being those of the conquered or

[1] The bridge of Mosul consists of a number of rude boats bound together by iron chains. Planks are laid from boat to boat, and the whole is covered with earth. During the time of the floods this frail bridge would be unable to resist the force of the stream; the chains holding it on one side of the river are then loosened, and it swings round. All communication between the two banks of the river is thus cut off, and a ferry is established until the waters subside, and the bridge can be replaced.

Warrior hunting the lion

captive race, they were unworthy the care of the artist. It is rare to find an entire bas-relief equally well executed in all its parts.

Whilst making this trench, I also discovered, about three feet beneath the pavement, a drain, which appeared to communicate with others previously opened in different parts of the building. It was probably the main sewer, through which all the minor water-courses were discharged. It was square, built of baked bricks, and covered in with large slabs and tiles.

As the bull was to be lowered on its back, the unsculptured side of the slab having to be placed on rollers, I removed the walls behind it. An open space was thus formed, large enough to admit of the sculpture when prostrate, and leaving room for the workmen to pass on all sides of it. The principal difficulty was of course to lower the mass: when once on the ground, or on rollers, it could be dragged forwards by the united force of a number of men; but, during its descent, it could only be sustained by ropes. If they chanced to break, the sculpture would be precipitated to the ground, and would, probably, be broken in the fall. The few ropes I possessed had been expressly sent to me, across the desert, from Aleppo; but they were small. From Baghdad I had obtained a thick hawser, made of the fibres of the palm. In addition I had been furnished with two pairs of blocks, and a pair of jack-screws belonging to the steamers of the Euphrates expedition. These were all the means at my command for moving the bull and lion. The sculptures were wrapped in mats and felts, to preserve them, as far as possible, from injury in case of a fall; and to prevent the ropes chipping or rubbing the alabaster.

The bull was ready to be moved by the 18th of March. The earth had been taken from under it, and it was now only supported by beams resting against the opposite wall. Amongst the wood obtained from the mountains were several thick rollers. These were placed upon sleepers or half beams, formed out of the trunks of poplar trees, well greased and laid on the ground parallel to the sculpture. The bull was to be lowered upon these rollers. A deep trench had been cut behind the second bull, completely across the wall. A bundle of ropes coiled round this isolated mass of earth served to hold two blocks, two others being attached to ropes wound round the bull to be moved. The ropes, by which the sculpture was to be lowered, were passed through these blocks; the ends, or falls of the tackle, as they are technically called, being led from the blocks above the second bull, and held by the Arabs. The cable having been first passed through the trench, and then round the sculpture, the ends were given to two bodies of men. Several of the strongest Chaldæans placed thick beams against the back of the bull, and were directed to withdraw them gradually, supporting the weight of the slab and checking it in its descent, in case the ropes should give way.

My own people were reinforced by a large number of the Abou Salman. I had invited Sheikh Abd-ur-rahman to be present, and he came attended by a body of horsemen. The men being ready, and all my preparations complete, I stationed myself on the top of the high bank of earth over the second bull, and ordered the wedges to be struck out from under the sculpture to be moved. Still, however, it remained firmly in its place. A rope having been passed round it, six or seven men easily tilted it over. The thick, ill-made cable stretched with the strain, and almost buried itself in the earth round which it was coiled. The ropes held well. The mass descended gradually, the Chaldæans propping it up with the beams. It was a moment of great anxiety. The drums and shrill pipes of the Kurdish musicians increased the din and confusion caused by the war-cry of the Arabs, who were half frantic with excitement. They had thrown off nearly all their garments; their long hair floated in the wind; and they indulged in the wildest postures and gesticulations as they clung to the ropes. The women had congregated on the sides of the trenches, and by their incessant screams, and by the ear-piercing tahlehl, added to the enthusiasm of the men. The bull once in motion, it was no longer possible to obtain a hearing. The loudest cries I could produce were lost in the crash of discordant sounds. Neither the hippopotamus-hide whips of the Cawasses, nor the bricks and clods of earth with which I endeavoured to draw attention from some of the most noisy of the group, were of any avail. Away went the bull, steady enough as long as supported by the props behind; but as it came nearer to the rollers, the beams could no longer be used. The cable and ropes stretched more and more. Dry from the climate, as they felt the strain, they creaked and threw out dust. Water was thrown over them, but in vain, for they all broke together when the sculpture was within four or five feet of the rollers. The bull was precipitated to the ground. Those who held the ropes, thus suddenly released, followed its example, and were rolling, one over the other, in the dust. A sudden silence succeeded to the clamour. I rushed into the trenches, prepared to find the bull in many pieces. It would be difficult to describe my satisfaction, when I saw it lying precisely where I had wished to place it, and uninjured! The Arabs no sooner got on their legs again, than, seeing the result of the accident, they darted out of the trenches, and, seizing by the hands the women who were looking on, formed a large circle, and, yelling their war-cry with redoubled energy, commenced a most mad dance. Even Abd-ur-rahman shared in the excitement, and, throwing his cloak to one of his attendants, insisted upon leading off the debkhé. It would have been useless to endeavour to put any check upon these proceedings. I preferred allowing the men to wear themselves out,—a result which, considering the amount of exertion and energy displayed both by limbs and throat, was not long in taking place.

I now prepared to move the bull into the long trench which led to the edge of the mound. The rollers were in good order; and, as soon as the excitement of the Arabs had sufficiently abated to enable them to resume work, the sculpture was dragged out of its place by ropes.

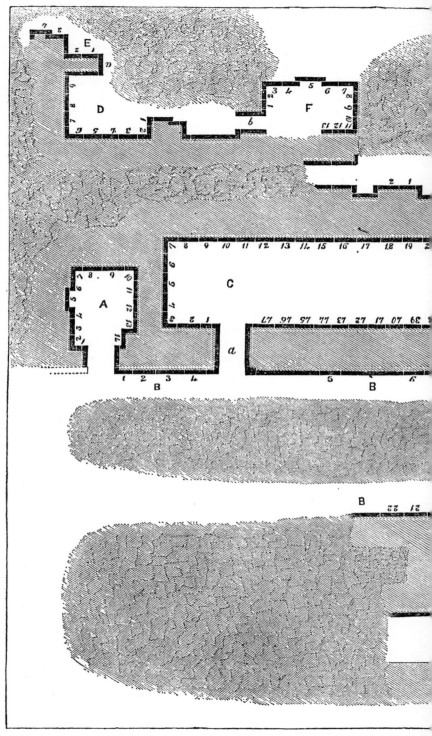

PLAN 4. Excava

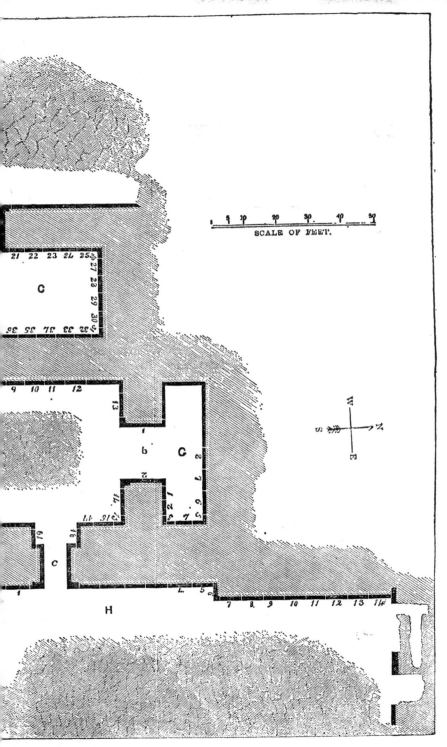

SCALE OF FEET.

ruins at Kouyunjik

Sleepers were laid to the end of the trench, and fresh rollers were placed under the bull as it was pulled forwards by cables. The sun was going down as these preparations were completed. I deferred any further labour to the morrow. The Arabs dressed themselves; and, placing the musicians at their head, marched towards the village, singing their war songs, and occasionally raising a wild yell, throwing their lances into the air, and flourishing their swords and shields over their heads.

I rode back with Abd-ur-rahman. The Arab Sheikh, his enthusiasm once cooled down, gave way to moral reflections. 'Wonderful! Wonderful! There is surely no God but God, and Mohammed is his Prophet,' exclaimed he, after a long pause. 'In the name of the Most High, tell me, O Bey, what you are going to do with those stones. So many thousands of purses spent upon such things! Can it be, as you say, that your people learn wisdom from them; or is it, as his reverence the Cadi declares, that they are to go to the palace of your Queen, who, with the rest of the unbelievers, worships these idols? As for wisdom, these figures will not teach you to make any better knives, or scissors, or chintzes; and it is in the making of those things that the English show their wisdom. But God is great! God is great! Here are stones which have been buried ever since the time of the holy Noah—peace be with him! Perhaps they were under ground before the deluge. I have lived on these lands for years. My father, and the father of my father, pitched their tents here before me; but they never heard of these figures. For twelve hundred years have the true believers (and, praise be to God! all true wisdom is with them alone) been settled in this country, and none of them ever heard of a palace under ground. Neither did they who went before them. But lo! here comes a Frank from many days' journey off, and he walks up to the very place, and he takes a stick (illustrating the description at the same time with the point of his spear), and makes a line here, and makes a line there. Here, says he, is the palace; there, says he, is the gate; and he shows us what has been all our lives beneath our feet, without our having known anything about it. Wonderful! Wonderful! Is it by books, is it by magic, is it by your prophets, that you have learnt these things? Speak, O Bey; tell me the secret of wisdom.'

The wonder of Abd-ur-rahman was certainly not without cause, and his reflections were natural enough. Whilst riding by his side I had been indulging in a reverie, not unlike his own, which he suddenly interrupted by these exclamations. A stranger laying open monuments buried for more than twenty centuries, and thus proving to those who dwelt around them, that much of the civilisation and knowledge of which we now boast, existed amongst their forefathers when our 'ancestors were yet unborn', was, in a manner, an acknowledgement of the debt which the West owes to the East.

This night was, of course, looked upon as one of rejoicing. Sheep were as usual killed, and boiled or roasted whole; they formed the essence of all entertainments and public festivities. They had scarcely been devoured before dancing was commenced. There were fortunately relays of musicians; for no human lungs could have furnished the requisite amount of breath. When some were nearly falling from exhaustion, the ranks were recruited by others. And so the Arabs went on until dawn. It was useless to preach moderation, or to entreat for quiet. Advice and remonstrances were received with deafening shouts of the war-cry, and outrageous antics as proofs of gratitude for the entertainment, and of ability to resist fatigue.

After passing the night in this fashion, these extraordinary beings, still singing and capering, started for the mound. Everything had been prepared on the previous day for moving the bull, and the men had now only to haul on the ropes. As the sculpture advanced, the rollers left behind were removed to the front, and thus in a short time it reached the end of the trench. There was little difficulty in dragging it down the precipitous side of the mound. When it arrived within three or four feet of the bottom, sufficient earth was removed from beneath it to admit the cart, upon which the bull itself was then lowered by still further digging away the soil. It was soon ready to be dragged to the river. Buffaloes were first harnessed to the yoke; but, although the men pulled with ropes fastened to the cart, the animals, feeling the weight behind them, refused to move. We were compelled, therefore, to take them out; and the Tiyari, in parties of eight, lifted by turns the pole, whilst the Arabs, assisted by the people of Naifa and Nimroud, dragged the cart. I rode first, with the Bairakdar, to point out the road. Then came the musicians, with their drums and fifes, drumming and fifing with might and main. The cart followed, dragged by about three hundred men, all screeching at the top of their voices. The procession was closed by the women, who kept up the enthusiasm of the Arabs by their shrill cries. Abd-ur-rahman's horsemen performed divers feats round the group, dashing backwards and forwards, and charging with their spears.

We advanced well enough, although the ground was very heavy

until we reached the ruins of the former village of Nimroud.[1] It is the custom, in this part of Turkey, for the villagers to dig deep pits to store their corn, barley, and straw for the autumn and winter. These pits generally surround the villages. Being only covered by a light framework of boughs and stakes, plastered over with mud, they become, particularly when half empty, a snare and a trap to the horseman, who, unless guided by some one acquainted with the localities, is pretty certain to find the hind legs of his horse on a level with its ears, and himself suddenly sprawling in front. The corn-pits around Nimroud had long since been emptied of their supplies, and had been concealed by the light sand and dust, which, blown over the plain during summer, soon fill up every hole and crevice. Although I had carefully examined the ground before starting, one of these holes had escaped my notice, and into it two wheels of the cart completely sank. The Arabs pulled and yelled in vain. The ropes broke, but the wheels refused to move. We tried every means to release them, but unsuccessfully. After working until dusk, we were obliged to give up the attempt. I left a party of Arabs to guard the cart and its contents, suspecting that some adventurous Bedouins, attracted by the ropes, mats, and felts, with which the sculpture was enveloped, might turn their steps towards the spot during the night. My suspicions did not prove unfounded; for I had scarcely got into bed before the whole village was thrown into commotion by the reports of fire-arms and the war-cry of the Jebour. Hastening to the scene of action, I found that a party of Arabs had fallen upon my workmen. They were beaten off, leaving behind them, however, their mark; for a ball, passing through the matting and felt, struck and indented the side of the bull.

Next morning we succeeded in clearing away the earth, and in placing thick planks beneath the buried wheels. After a few efforts the cart moved forwards amidst the shouts of the Arabs. The procession was formed as on the previous day, and we dragged the bull triumphantly down to within a few hundred yards of the river. Here the wheels buried themselves in the sand, and it was night before we contrived to place the sculpture on the platform prepared to receive it, and from which it was to slide down on the raft. The night was passed in renewed rejoicings, to celebrate the successful termination of our

---

[1] The village was moved to its present site after the river had gradually receded to the westward. The inhabitants had been then left at a very inconvenient distance from water.

labours. On the following morning I rode to Mosul, to enjoy a few days' rest after my exertions.

The bull having thus been successfully transported to the banks of the river, preparations were made, on my return to Nimroud, for the removal of the second sculpture. My preparations were completed by the middle of April. I determined to lower the lion at once on the cart and not to drag it out of the mound over the rollers. This sculpture, during its descent, was supported in the same manner as the bull had been; but, to avoid a second accident, I doubled the number of ropes and the coils of the cable. Enough earth was removed to bring the top of the cart to a level with the bottom of the lion. As the lion was cracked in more than one place, considerable care was required in lowering and moving it. Both, however, were effected without accident. The lion and bull were at length placed side by side on the banks of the Tigris, ready to proceed to Busrah, as soon as I could make the necessary arrangements for embarking them on rafts.

The sculptures, which I had hitherto sent to Busrah, had been floated down the river on rafts, as far only as Baghdad. There they had been placed in boats built by the natives for the navigation of the lower part of the Tigris and Euphrates. These vessels were much too small and weak to carry either the lion or the bull; and, indeed, had they been large enough, it would have been difficult, if not impossible, in the absence of proper machinery, to lift such heavy masses into them. I resolved, therefore, to attempt the navigation of the lower as well as of the upper part of the river with rafts; and to embark the lion and bull, at once, for Busrah. The raftmen of Mosul, who are accustomed to navigate the Tigris to Baghdad, but never venture further, pronounced the scheme to be impracticable, and refused to attempt it, [although in the river below] Baghdad there is depth of water and nothing to impede the passage of large boats. It was impossible by the most convincing arguments, even though supported by the exhibition of a heap of coins, to prevail upon the raftmen of Mosul to construct such rafts as I required, or to undertake the voyage. I applied therefore to Mr. Hector,[1] and through him found a man at Baghdad, who declared himself willing to make the great sacrifice generally believed to be involved in the attempt. He was indebted in a considerable sum of money, and being the owner of a large number of skins, now lying useless, he preferred a desperate undertaking to the prospect of a debtor's prison.

[1] [Mr. Alexander Hector gives details of the arrangements in 38977, 195.]

Mullah Ali—for such was the name of my raft-contractor—at length made his appearance. He was followed by a dirty half-naked Arab, his assistant in the construction of rafts; and, like those who carried on his trade some two thousand years before, by a couple of donkeys laden with skins ready for use. Like a genuine native of Baghdad, he had exhausted his ingenuity in the choice of materials for the composition of his garments. There could not have been a more dexterous mixture of colours than that displayed by his antari, cloak, and voluminous turban. He began, of course, by a long speech, protesting, by the Prophet, that he would undertake for no one else in the world what he was going to do for me; that he was my slave and my sacrifice, and that the man who was not was worse than an infidel. I cut him short in this complimentary discourse. He then, as is usual in such transactions, began to make excuses, to increase his demands, and to throw difficulties in the way. On these points I declined all discussion, directing Ibrahim Agha to give him an insight into my way of doing business, to recommend him to resign himself to his fate, as the contract had been signed, and to hint that he was now in the power of an authority from which there was no appeal.

Mullah Ali made many vain efforts to amend his condition, and to induce, on my part, a fuller appreciation of his merits. He expected that these endeavours might, at least, lead to an additional amount of bakshish. At last he resigned himself to his fate, and slowly worked, with his assistant, at the binding together of beams and logs of wood with willow twigs to form a framework for a raft. There were still some difficulties and obstacles to be surmounted. The man of Baghdad had his own opinions on the building of rafts in general, founded upon immemorial customs and the traditions of the country. I had my theories, which could not be supported by equally substantial arguments. Consequently he, who had all the proof on his side, may not have been wrong in declaring against any method, in favour of which I could produce no better evidence than my own will. But, like many other injured men, he fell a victim to the 'droit du plus fort', and had to sacrifice, at once, prejudice and habit.

I did not doubt that the skins, once blown up, would support the sculptures without difficulty as far as Baghdad. The journey would take eight or ten days, under favourable circumstances. But there they would require to be opened and refilled, or the rafts would scarcely sustain so heavy a weight all the way to Busrah. However carefully the skins are filled, the air gradually escapes. Rafts, bearing merchandise, are generally detained several times during their descent, to enable the raftmen to examine and refill the skins. If the sculptures rested upon only one framework, the beams being almost on a level with the water, the raftmen would be unable to get beneath them to reach the mouths of the skins when they required replenishing, without moving the cargo. This would have been both inconvenient and difficult to accomplish. I was therefore desirous of raising the lion and bull as much as possible above the water, so as to leave room for the men to creep under them.

It may interest the reader to know how these rafts, which have probably formed for ages the only means of traffic on the upper parts of the rivers of Mesopotamia, are constructed. The skins of full-grown sheep and goats are used. They are taken off with as few incisions as possible, and then dried and prepared. The air is forced in by the lungs through an aperture which is afterwards tied up with string. A square framework, formed of poplar beams, branches of trees, and reeds, having been constructed of the size of the intended raft, the inflated skins are tied to it by osier and other twigs, the whole being firmly bound together. The raft is then moved to the water and launched. Care is taken to place the skins with their mouths upwards, that, in case any should burst or require filling, they can be easily opened by the raftmen. Upon the framework of wood are piled bales of goods, and property belonging to merchants and travellers. When any person of rank, or wealth, descends the river in this fashion, small huts are constructed on the raft by covering a common wooden *takht*, or bedstead of the country, with a hood formed of reeds and lined with felt. In these huts the travellers live and sleep during the journey. The poorer passengers seek shade or warmth, by burying themselves amongst bales of goods and other merchandise, and sit patiently, almost in one position, until they reach their destination. They carry with them a small earthen *mangal* or chafing-dish, containing a charcoal fire, which serves to light their pipes, and to cook their coffee and food. The only real danger to be apprehended on the river is from the Arabs; who, when the country is in a disturbed state, invariably attack and pillage the rafts.

The raftmen guide their rude vessels by long oars—straight poles, at the end of which a few split canes are fastened by a piece of twine. They skilfully avoid the rapids; and, seated on the bales of goods, work continually, even in the hottest sun. They will seldom travel after dark before reaching Tekrit, on account of the rocks and shoals, which abound in the upper part of the river; but when they have passed that place, they resign themselves, night and day, to the sluggish stream. During the floods in the spring, or after violent rains, small rafts may float from Mosul to Baghdad in about eighty-four hours; but the large rafts are generally six or seven days in performing the voyage. In summer, and when the river is low, they are frequently nearly a month in reaching their destination. When the rafts have been unloaded, they are broken up, and the beams, wood, and twigs are sold at a considerable profit, forming one of the principal branches of trade between Mosul and Baghdad. The skins are washed and afterwards rubbed with a preparation of pounded pomegranate skins, to keep them from cracking and rotting. They are then brought back, either upon the shoulders of the raftmen or upon donkeys, to Mosul or Tekrit, where the men engaged in the navigation of the Tigris usually reside.

On the 20th of April, there being fortunately a slight rise in the river, and the rafts being ready, I determined to attempt the embarkation of the lion and bull. The two sculptures had been so placed on beams that, by withdrawing wedges from under them, they would slide nearly into the centre of the raft. The high bank of the river had been cut away into a rapid slope to the water's edge.

In the morning Mr. Hormuzd Rassam informed me that signs of discontent had shown themselves amongst the workmen, and that there was a general strike for higher wages. They had chosen the time fixed upon for embarking the sculptures, under the impression that I should be compelled, from the difficulty of obtaining any other assistance, to accede to their terms. Several circumstances had contributed to this manœuvre. As I have already mentioned, the want of rain had led to a complete failure of the crops, and the country around Nimroud was one yellow barren waste. The villagers were consequently leaving the plain and migrating to the Kurdish hills, or to the lands under Mardin watered by the Khabour; where, by dint of irrigation, they could hope to raise millet, and other grain, sufficient to meet their wants until the winter rains might promise better times. The country around Nimroud was deserted; not a human being was to be seen within some miles of the place. Abd-ur-rahman, whose crops had failed like the rest, and who could no longer find pasture for his flocks in the Jaif, had followed the example of the villagers, and was moving northwards. I consequently remained alone with my workmen, and the few Arabs who were cultivating millet along the banks of the Tigris. The time chosen by the Jebour to demand higher wages, and to threaten to leave me, was not, therefore, ill-chosen. They were persuaded that I should be compelled to agree to their demands, or to leave the lion and bull where they were. It was not, however, my intention to do either.

I found, on issuing from the house, that the Arabs had already commenced their preparations for departure. A few of the Sheikhs were hanging about the doors of my court-yard with gloomy expectant looks, anxious to learn my decision, and little doubting that, on seeing the signs of packing, I would at once yield. However reasonable their demands might have been, the unceremonious fashion in which they were urged was somewhat repugnant to my feelings. I was aware that one or two of the chiefs, who did not work, but managed to raise money from those who did, were the originators of the scheme. I ordered my Cawass and the Bairakdar to seize them at once, and then took leave of those who were preparing to depart. Their plans were somewhat disconcerted, and they went on sullenly with their arrangements. When at length their preparations for the march were completed, they moved off at a very slow pace, looking back continually, not believing it possible that I would obstinately persist in my determination to refuse a compromise. As a last attempt a deputation of one or two Sheikhs came to express a disinterested anxiety for my safety should the Jebour leave the country. I did my best to quiet their alarms by employing the Tiyari to put my premises into a state of defence, and to reopen all the loop-holes, which Ibrahim Agha had industriously made in the walls surrounding my dwelling, when they had been first built. Defeated in all their endeavours to make me sensible of the danger of my position, they walked sulkily off to join their companions, who took care to encamp for the night within sight of the village.

Many families, however, refusing to desert me, pitched their tents under the walls of my house. The wives, too, of those who were going, had been to me, sobbing and weeping, protesting that the men, although anxious to remain, were afraid to disobey their Sheikhs.

The tents of the Abou Salman were still within reach, and I despatched a horseman, without delay, to Sheikh Abd-ur-rahman with a note, acquainting him with what had occurred, and requesting him to send me some of his Arabs to assist in embarking the bull. There was a rival tribe of the Jebour encamping at some distance from Nimroud, and I also offered them work.

In the evening, Abd-ur-rahman, followed by a party of horsemen, came to Nimroud. He undertook at once to furnish me with as many men as I might require to place the sculptures on the rafts, and sent orders to his people to delay their projected march.

Next morning, when the Jebour perceived a large body of the Abou Salman advancing towards Nimroud, they repented themselves of their manœuvre, and returned in a body to offer their services on any terms that I might think fit to propose. But I was well able to do without them. I refused, therefore, to listen to any overtures, and commenced my preparations for embarking the lion and bull with the aid of the Chaldæans, the Abou Salman, and such of my Arab workmen as had remained with me.

The beams of poplar wood, forming an inclined plane from beneath the sculptures to the rafts, were first well greased. A raft, supported by six hundred skins, having been brought to the river bank, opposite the bull, the wedges were removed from under the sculpture, which immediately slided down into its place. The only difficulty was to prevent its descending too rapidly, and bursting the skins by the sudden pressure. The Arabs checked it by ropes, and it was placed without any accident. The lion was then embarked in the same way, and with equal success, upon a second raft of the same size as the first; in a few hours the two sculptures were properly secured, and before night they were ready to float down the river to Busrah. Many slabs, and about thirty cases containing small objects discovered in the ruins, were placed on the rafts with the lion and bull.

After the labours of the day were over, sheep were slaughtered for the entertainment of Abd-ur-rahman's Arabs, and for those who had helped in the embarkation of the sculptures. The Abou Salman returned to their tents after dark. Abd-ur-rahman took leave of me, and we did not meet again; the next day he continued his march towards the district of Jezirah. I heard of him on my journey to Constantinople; the Kurds by the road complaining that his tribe were making up the number of their flocks, by appropriating the stray sheep of their neighbours. I had seen much of the Sheikh during my residence at Nimroud; and although, like all Arabs, he was not averse to ask for what he thought there might be a remote chance of getting by a little importunity, he was, on the whole, a very friendly and useful ally.

On the morning of the 22nd, all the sculptures having been embarked, I gave two sheep to the raftmen to be slain on the bank of the river, as a sacrifice to ensure the success of the undertaking. The carcases were distributed, as is proper on such occasions, amongst the poor. A third sheep was reserved for a propitiatory offering, to be immolated at the tomb of Sultan Abd-Allah. This saint still appears to interfere considerably with the navigation of the Tigris, and had closed the further ascent of the river against the infidel crew of the Frank steamer the 'Euphrates',[1] because they had neglected to make the customary sacrifice. All ceremonies having been duly performed, Mullah Ali kissed my hand, placed himself on one of the rafts, and slowly floated, with the cargo under his charge, down the stream.

I watched the rafts until they disappeared behind a projecting bank of the river. I could not forbear musing upon the strange destiny of their burdens; which, after adorning the palaces of the Assyrian kings, had been buried unknown for centuries beneath a soil trodden by Persians under Cyrus, by Greeks under Alexander, and by Arabs under the first successors of their prophet. They were now to visit India, to cross the most distant seas of the southern hemisphere, and to be finally placed in a British Museum. Who can venture to foretell how their strange career will end?

I had scarcely returned to the village, when a party of the refractory Jebour presented themselves. They were now lavish in professions of regret for what had occurred. They laid the blame upon their Sheikhs, and offered to return at once to their work, for any amount of wages I might think proper to give them. The excavations at Nimroud were almost brought to a close, and I had no longer any need of a large body of workmen. Choosing, therefore, the most active and well-disposed amongst those who had been in my service, I ordered a little summary punishment to be inflicted upon the captive Sheikhs, who had been the cause of the mischief, and then sent them away with the rest of the tribe.

After the departure of the Abou Salman, the plain of Nimroud was a complete desert. The visits of armed parties of Arabs became daily more frequent, and we often watched them from the mound, as they rode towards the hills in search of pillage, or returned from their expeditions driving the plundered flocks and cattle before them. We were still too strong to fear the Bedouins; but I was compelled to put my house into a complete state of defence, and to keep patrols round

---

[1] [For a good summary of the Euphrates Expedition, in which the two vessels *Euphrates* and *Tigris* were utilized, see Seton Lloyd, *Foundations in the Dust* (Penguin Books, 1955), pp. 101 ff.]

my premises during the night to avoid surprise. The Jebour were exposed to constant losses, in the way of donkeys or tent furniture, as the country was infested by petty thieves, who issued from their hiding-places, and wandered to and fro, like jackals, after dark. Nothing was too small or worthless to escape their notice. I was roused almost nightly by shoutings and the discharge of firearms, when the whole encampment was thrown into commotion at the disappearance of a copper pot or an old grain sack. I was fortunate enough to escape their depredations.

The fears of my Jebour increased with the number of the plundering parties, and at last, when a small Arab settlement, within sight of Nimroud, was attacked by a band of Aneyza horsemen, who murdered several of the inhabitants, and carried away all the sheep and cattle, the workmen protested in a body against any further residence in so dangerous a vicinity. I determined, therefore, to bring the excavations to an end.

I now commenced burying with earth those parts of the ruins which still remained exposed, according to the instructions I had received from the Trustees of the British Museum. Had the numerous sculptures been left, without any precaution being taken to preserve them, they would have suffered, not only from the effects of the atmosphere, but from the spears and clubs of the Arabs, who are always ready to knock out the eyes, and to otherwise disfigure, the idols of the unbelievers. The rubbish and earth removed on opening the building, was accordingly heaped over the slabs until the whole was again covered over.

But before leaving Nimroud and reburying its palaces, I would wish to lead the reader once more through the ruins of the principal edifice, as they appeared when fully explored. Let us imagine ourselves issuing from my tent near the village in the plain. We ascend the mound, but see no ruins, not a stone protruding from the soil. There is only a broad level platform before us, perhaps covered with a luxuriant crop of barley, or may be yellow and parched, without a blade of vegetation, except here and there a scanty tuft of camel-thorn. Low black heaps, surrounded by brushwood and dried grass, a thin column of smoke issuing from the midst of them, are scattered here and there. These are the tents of the Arabs; and a few miserable old women are groping about them, picking up camel's-dung or dry twigs. One or two girls, with firm step and erect carriage, are just reaching the top of the mound, with the water-jar on their shoulders, or a bundle of brushwood on their heads. On all sides of us, apparently issuing from underground, are long lines of wild-looking beings, with dishevelled hair, their limbs only half concealed by a short loose shirt, some jumping and capering, and all hurrying to and fro shouting like madmen. Each one carries a basket, and as he reaches the edge of the mound, or some convenient spot near, empties its contents, raising at the same time a cloud of dust. He then returns at the top of his speed, dancing and yelling as before, and flourishing his basket over his head; again he suddenly disappears in the bowels of the earth, from whence he emerged. These are the workmen employed in removing the rubbish from the ruins.

We will descend into the principal trench, by a flight of steps rudely cut into the earth, near the western face of the mound. As we approach it, we find a party of Arabs bending on their knees, and intently gazing at something beneath them. Each holds his long spear, tufted with ostrich feathers, in one hand; and in the other the halter of his mare, which stands patiently behind him. The party consists of a Bedouin Sheikh from the desert, and his followers; who, having heard strange reports of the wonders of Nimroud, have made several days' journey to remove their doubts and satisfy their curiosity. He rises as he hears us approach, and if we wish to escape the embrace of a very dirty stranger, we had better at once hurry into the trenches.

We descend about twenty feet, and suddenly find ourselves between a pair of colossal lions, winged and human-headed, forming a portal. In the subterraneous labyrinth which we have reached, all is bustle and confusion. Arabs are running about in different directions; some bearing baskets filled with earth, others carrying the water-jars to their companions. The Chaldæans or Tiyari, in their striped dresses and curious conical caps, are digging with picks into the tenacious earth, raising a dense cloud of fine dust at every stroke. The wild strains of Kurdish music may be heard occasionally issuing from some distant part of the ruins.

We issue from between the winged lions, and enter the remains of the principal hall. On both sides of us are sculptured gigantic winged figures; some with the heads of eagles, others entirely human, and carrying mysterious symbols in their hands. To the left is another portal, also formed by winged lions. One of them has, however, fallen across the entrance, and there is just room to creep beneath it. Beyond this portal is a winged figure, and two slabs with bas-reliefs; but they have been so much injured that we can scarcely trace the subject upon them. Further on there are no traces of wall, although a deep trench has been opened. The opposite side of the hall has also disappeared, and we only see a high wall of earth. On examining it attentively, we can detect the marks of masonry; and we soon find that it is a solid structure built of bricks of unbaked clay, now of the same colour as the surrounding soil, and scarcely to be distinguished from it.

The slabs of alabaster, fallen from their original position, have, however, been raised; and we tread in the midst of a maze of small bas-reliefs, representing chariots, horsemen, battles, and sieges. Perhaps the workmen are about to raise a slab for the first time; and we watch, with eager curiosity, what new event of Assyrian history, or what unknown custom or religious ceremony, may be illustrated by the sculpture beneath.

Having walked about one hundred feet amongst these scattered monuments of ancient history and art, we reach another door-way, formed by gigantic winged bulls in yellow limestone. One is still entire; but its companion has fallen, and is broken into several pieces —the great human head is at our feet.

We pass on without turning into the part of the building to which this portal leads. Beyond it we see another winged figure, holding a graceful flower in its hand, and apparently presenting it as an offering to the winged bull. Adjoining this sculpture we find eight fine bas-reliefs. There is the king, hunting, and triumphing over, the lion and wild bull; and the siege of the castle, with the battering-ram. We have now reached the end of the hall, and find before us an elaborate and beautiful sculpture, representing two kings, standing beneath the emblem of the supreme deity, and attended by winged figures. Between them is the sacred tree. In front of this bas-relief is the great stone platform, upon which, in days of old, may have been placed the throne of the Assyrian monarch, when he received his captive enemies, or his courtiers.

To the left of us is a fourth outlet from the hall, formed by another pair of lions. We issue from between them, and find ourselves on the edge of a deep ravine, to the north of which rises, high above us, the lofty pyramid. Figures of captives bearing objects of tribute—ear-rings, bracelets, and monkeys—may be seen on walls near this ravine; and two enormous bulls, and two winged figures above fourteen feet high, are lying on its very edge.

As the ravine bounds the ruins on this side, we must return to the yellow bulls. Passing through the entrance formed by them, we enter a large chamber surrounded by eagle-headed figures: at one end of it is a doorway guarded by two priests or divinities, and in the centre another portal with winged bulls. Whichever way we turn, we find ourselves in the midst of a nest of rooms; and without an acquaintance with the intricacies of the place, we should soon lose ourselves in this labyrinth. The accumulated rubbish being generally left in the centre of the chambers, the whole excavation consists of a number of narrow passages, panelled on one side with slabs of alabaster; and shut in on the other by a high wall of earth, half buried, in which may here and there be seen a broken vase, or a brick painted with brilliant colours. We may wander through these galleries for an hour or two, examining the marvellous sculptures, or the numerous inscriptions that surround us. Here we meet long rows of kings, attended by their eunuchs and priests—there lines of winged figures, carrying fir-cones and religious emblems, and seemingly in adoration before the mystic tree. Other entrances, formed by winged lions and bulls, lead us into new chambers. In every one of them are fresh objects of curiosity and surprise. At length, wearied, we issue from the buried edifice by a trench on the opposite side to that by which we entered, and find ourselves again upon the naked platform. We look around in vain for any traces of the wonderful remains we have just seen, and are half inclined to believe that we have dreamed a dream, or have been listening to some tale of Eastern romance.

Some, who may hereafter tread on the spot when the grass again grows over the ruins of the Assyrian palaces, may indeed suspect that I have been relating a vision.

XIV

THE CHAMBERS AT Nimroud had been filled up with earth, and the sculptures thus preserved from injury. The surrounding country became daily more dangerous from the incursions of the Arabs of the desert. It was time, therefore, to leave the village. As a small sum of money still remained at my disposal, I proposed to devote it to an examination of the ruins opposite Mosul; particularly of the great mound of Kouyunjik. Although excavations on a small scale had already been made there, I had not hitherto had time to superintend them myself, and in such researches the natives of the country cannot be trusted. There was good reason to doubt whether any edifice, even in an imperfect state, still existed in Kouyunjik. Almost since the fall of the Assyrian empire, a city of some extent has stood on the banks of the Tigris in this part of its course. The alabaster slabs, which had once lined the walls of the old palaces, had been frequently exposed by accident or by design, and as the ruins offered an inexhaustible mine of building materials, the removal of slabs, and the destruction of sculptures, may have been going on for centuries.

By the middle of May, I had finished my work at Nimroud. My house was dismantled. The windows and doors were taken out; and, with the little furniture that had been collected together, were placed on the backs of donkeys and camels to be carried to the town. The Arabs struck their tents and commenced their march. I remained behind until every one had left, and then turned my back upon the deserted village.

Halfway between Mosul and Nimroud the road crosses a low hill. From its crest, both the town and the ruins are visible. On one side, in the distance, rises the pyramid, in the midst of the broad plain of the Jaif; and on the other may be faintly distinguished the great artificial mound of Kouyunjik, and the surrounding remains. The whole space over which the eye ranges from this spot was probably once covered

286

with the buildings and gardens of the Assyrian capital—that great city of three days' journey. To me, of course, the long dark line of mounds in the distance were objects of deep interest. I reined up my horse to look upon them for the last time—for from no other part of the road are they visible—and then galloped on towards Mosul.

In excavating at Kouyunjik, I pursued the plan I had adopted at Nimroud. I resided in the town. The Arabs pitched their tents on the summit of the mound, at the entrances to the trenches. The Tiyari encamped at its foot, on the banks of the Khausser, the small stream which flows through the ruins. Here the men and women found a convenient place for their constant ablutions. They were still obliged, however, to fetch water, when required for other purposes, from the Tigris; that from the Khausser being considered heavy and unwholesome. It is rarely drunk by those who live near the stream, if other water can be obtained from wells, or even from natural pools formed by the rain. The nearness of the ruins to Mosul enabled the inhabitants of the town to gratify their curiosity by a constant inspection of my proceedings; and a great crowd of gaping Mussulmans and Christians was continually gathered round the trenches. I rode to the mound early every morning, and remained there during the day.

The French Consul had carried on his excavations for some time at Kouyunjik, without finding any traces of building. He was satisfied with digging pits or wells, a few feet deep, and then renouncing the attempt, if no sculptures or inscriptions were uncovered. By excavating in this desultory manner, if any remains of building existed under ground, their discovery would be a mere chance. An acquaintance with the nature and position of the ancient edifices of Assyria, will at once suggest the proper method of examining the mounds which enclose them. The Assyrians, when about to build a palace or public edifice, appear to have first constructed a platform, or solid compact mass of sun-dried bricks, about thirty or forty feet above the level of the plain. Upon it they raised the monument. When the building was destroyed, its ruins, already half buried by the falling in of the upper walls and roof, remained of course on the platform; and were in process of time completely covered up by the dust and sand, carried about by the hot winds of summer. Consequently, in digging for remains, the first step is to search for the platform of sun-dried bricks. When this is discovered, the trenches must be opened to the level of it, and not deeper; they should then be continued in opposite directions, care being always taken to keep along the platform. By these means, if there be any ruins they must necessarily be discovered, supposing the trenches to be long enough; for the chambers of the Assyrian edifices are generally narrow, and their walls, or the slabs which cased them if fallen, must sooner or later be reached.

At Kouyunjik, the accumulation of rubbish and earth was very considerable, and trenches were dug to the depth of twenty feet, before the platform of unbaked bricks was discovered. Before beginning the excavations, I carefully examined all parts of the mound, to ascertain where remains of buildings might most probably exist; and at length decided upon continuing my researches where I had commenced them last summer, near the south-west corner.

The workmen had been digging for several days without finding any other remains than fragments of calcined alabaster, sufficient, however, to encourage me to persevere in the examination of this part of the ruins. One morning as I was in Mosul, two Arab women came to me, and announced that sculptures had been discovered. They had hurried from the mounds as soon as the first slab had been exposed to view; and blowing up the skins, which they always carry about with them, had swum upon them across the river. They had scarcely received the present claimed in the East by the bearers of good tidings, than one of my overseers, who was generally known from his corpulence as Toma Shishman, or fat Toma, made his appearance, breathless from his exertions. He had hurried as fast as his legs could carry him over the bridge, to obtain the reward carried off, in this instance, by the women.

I rode immediately to the ruins; and, on entering the trenches, found that the workmen had reached a wall, and the remains of an entrance. The only slab as yet uncovered had been almost completely destroyed by fire. It stood on the edge of a deep ravine which ran far into the southern side of the mound.

As the excavations of Kouyunjik were carried on in precisely the same manner as those of Nimroud, I need not trouble the reader with any detailed account of my proceedings. The wall first discovered proved to be the side of a chamber. In a month nine chambers had been explored.

The palace had been destroyed by fire. The alabaster slabs were almost reduced to lime, and many of them fell to pieces as soon as uncovered. The places, which others had occupied, could only be traced by a thin white deposit, left by the burnt alabaster upon the wall of sun-dried bricks, and having the appearance of a coating of plaster.

In its architecture, the newly discovered edifice resembled the palaces of Nimroud, and Khorsabad. The bas-reliefs were, however, much larger in their dimensions than those generally found at Nimroud, being about ten feet high, and from eight to nine feet wide. The winged, human-headed bulls, forming the entrances, were from fourteen to sixteen feet square. The slabs, unlike those I had hitherto discovered, were not divided in the centre by bands of inscription, but were completely covered with figures. The bas-reliefs were greatly inferior in general design, and in the beauty of the details, to those of the earliest palace of Nimroud; but in many parts they were very carefully and minutely finished: in this respect Kouyunjik yields to no other known monument in Assyria.

Inscriptions were not numerous. They were all much defaced, and I had great difficulty in copying even a few characters from some of them. The name of the king, occurring both on the backs of slabs and on bricks, resembles that occupying the second place in the genealogical list in the short inscriptions on the bulls and lions of the southern, or most recent, palace of Nimroud. He was the son of the builder of Khorsabad. There are certain peculiarities in the bas-reliefs, in the ornaments, and in some of the characters used in the inscriptions, which distinguish the sculptures, and connect them, at the same time, with those of Khorsabad.

In the earth, above the edifice of Kouyunjik, a few earthen vases and fragments of pottery were discovered. One or two small glass bottles entire, and many fragments of glass, were taken out of the rubbish; and on the floors of the chambers were several small oblong tablets of dark unbaked clay, having a cuneiform inscription over the sides. Detached slabs of limestone, covered with inscriptions, were also found in the ruins.

The first chamber seen on entering the trenches from the ravine, was that marked A, on plan 4. All the slabs within the chamber had been much injured.

The southern extremity of hall B had been completely destroyed by the water-duct which had formed the ravine. Its width was about forty-five feet, and the length of the western wall, from the entrance of chamber A (to the south of which it could not be traced) was nearly one hundred and sixty feet. The first and second slabs[1] on the west

[1] Nos. 1 and 2, plan 4.

side of the hall appear to have been occupied by one subject, the burning and sacking of a city. The two slabs were greatly injured, and in many places had been entirely destroyed.

Head of a winged bull (style of Khorsabad and Kouyunjik)

[After two further slabs, one of them completely destroyed], the wall was interrupted by an entrance formed by two winged bulls, nearly 16½ feet square, and sculptured out of one slab. The human heads of these gigantic animals had disappeared. This entrance was narrow, scarcely exceeding six feet, differing in this respect from the entrances at Nimroud. The pavement was formed by one slab, elaborately carved with figures of flowers resembling the lotus, and with other ornaments. Behind the bull was a short inscription containing the name and titles of the king.

Of the slabs forming the rest of the wall, to the end of the chamber, only two were sufficiently well preserved to be drawn, even in part— those numbered 9 and 13 in the plan. On No. 9, the king, seated within a castle, was receiving his vizir, who was accompanied by his attendants. Behind the king stood two eunuchs, raising fans or fly-flappers over his head. Without the walls were prisoners, their hands confined by manacles: and within were represented the interiors of several houses and tents. To the tent-poles were suspended some utensils, perhaps vases hung up, as is still the custom in the East, to cool water. The castle, built on a mountain, had probably been captured by the Assyrians, and the bas-relief represented the king celebrating his victory.

On slab No. 13 was recorded the conquest of a mountainous country. The enemy occupied the summit of a wooded hill, which they defended against numerous Assyrian warriors who were seen scaling the rocks. Others, returning from the combat, were descending the mountains driving captives before them, or carrying away the heads of the slain.

A spacious entrance at the upper end of the hall opened into a small chamber [with further slabs]. A third entrance, narrower than that on the opposite side of the hall, led into a chamber to the east. Beyond this entrance the slabs had almost all been completely destroyed. As the trench now approached the ravine, and there appeared to be no chance of finding any sculptures, sufficiently well preserved to be drawn, I removed the workmen to another part of the ruins.

The doorway on the west side of the hall led into a second hall,[1] the four sides of which were almost entire. The bas-reliefs had unfortunately suffered greatly from the fire, and in many places the slabs had disappeared altogether. No. 30 was better preserved than [most of the] slabs. The king stood in a chariot, holding a bow in his left hand, and raising his right in a token of triumph. He was accompanied by a charioteer, and by an attendant bearing an umbrella, to which was hung a long curtain falling behind the back of the king, and screening him entirely from the sun. The remaining bas-reliefs in this chamber appear to have recorded similar events—the conquests of the Assyrians, and the triumphs of their king.

Upon the walls of chamber D, were the siege and capture of a city, standing on the banks of a river in the midst of forests and mountains. On the bottom of slab No. 7 was a fisherman fishing with a hook and

[1] Hall C, plan 4.

line in a pond. Upon his back was a wicker basket, containing the fish he had caught. This was almost the only fragment of sculpture that I was able to move and send to England, as a specimen of the bas-reliefs of Kouyunjik.

After my departure from Mosul, Mr. Ross continued the excavations, and discovered several other slabs and the openings into three new chambers. The subjects of the bas-reliefs appear to have been nearly the same as those preceding them.

This was the extent of my discoveries at Kouyunjik. The ruins were evidently those of a palace of great extent and magnificence. From the size of the slabs and the number of the figures, the walls, when entire and painted, as they no doubt originally were, must have been of considerable beauty, and the dimensions of the chambers must have added greatly to the general effect. At that time the palace rose above the river, which swept round the foot of the mound. Then also the edifice, now covered by the village of Nebbi Yunus, stood entire above the stream, and the whole quadrangle was surrounded by lofty walls cased with stone, their towers adorned with sculptured alabaster, and their gateways formed by colossal bulls. The position of the ruins proves, that at one time this was one of the most important parts of Nineveh; and the magnificence of the remains, that the edifices must have been founded by one of the greatest of the Assyrian monarchs.

Mr. Ross having been requested, by the Trustees of the British Museum, to carry on the excavations, on a small scale, in Kouyunjik, he judiciously made experiments in various parts of the mound. His discoveries are of great interest, and tend to prove that there were more buildings than one on the platform; but whether they were all of the same epoch I have no means of judging; Mr. Ross not having yet sent me the copies of any inscriptions from the palace last explored by him.

In a mound, so vast as that of Kouyunjik, it is probable that many remains of the highest interest still exist. Hitherto only two corners of the mound have been partially explored; and in both have ruins, with sculptures and inscriptions, been discovered. They have been exposed to the same great conflagration which apparently destroyed all the edifices built upon the platform. It is possible, however, that other parts of these palaces may be found, which, if they had not escaped altogether the general destruction, may at least be sufficiently well preserved to admit of the removal of many important relics. Further researches at Kouyunjik could scarcely fail to be productive of many interesting and important results.

My labours in Assyria had now drawn to a close. The funds assigned to the Trustees of the British Museum for the excavations had been expended, and from the instructions sent to me, further researches were not, for the present at least, contemplated. It now, therefore, only remained for me to wind up my affairs in Mosul, to bid adieu to my friends there, and to turn my steps homewards, after an absence of some years. The ruins of Nimroud had been again covered up, and its palaces were once more hidden from the eye. The sculptures taken from them had been safely removed to Busrah, and were now awaiting their final transport to England. The inscriptions, which promise to instruct us in the history and civilisation of one of the most ancient and illustrious nations of the earth, had been carefully copied. On looking back upon the few months that I had passed in Assyria, I could not but feel some satisfaction at the result of my labours. Scarcely a year before, with the exception of the ruins of Khorsabad, not one Assyrian monument was known. Almost sufficient materials had now been obtained to enable us to restore much of the lost history of the country, and to confirm the vague traditions of the learning and civilisation of its people, hitherto treated as fabulous. It had often occurred to me during my labours, that the time of the discovery of these remains was so opportune, that a person inclined to be superstitious might look upon it as something more than accidental. Had these palaces been by chance exposed to view some years before, no one would have been ready to take advantage of the circumstance, and they would have been completely destroyed by the inhabitants of the country. Had they been discovered a little later, it is highly probable that there would have been insurmountable objections to their removal. It was consequently just at the right moment that they were disinterred; and we have been fortunate enough to acquire the most convincing and lasting evidence of that magnificence, and power, which made Nineveh the wonder of the ancient world, and her fall the theme of the prophets, as the most signal instance of divine vengeance.

Before my departure I was desirous of giving a last entertainment to my workmen, and to those who had kindly aided me in my labours. A small village on the western side of Kouyunjik was chosen for the festivities, and tents for the accommodation of all the guests were pitched around it. Large platters filled with boiled rice, and divers inexplicable messes, only appreciated by Arabs, and those who have

lived with them,—the chief components being garlic and sour milk—
were placed before the various groups of men and women, who
squatted in circles on the ground. Dances were then commenced, and
were carried on through the greater part of the night, the Tiyari and
the Arabs joining in them, or relieving each other by turns. The
dancers were happy and enthusiastic, and kept up a constant shouting.
The quiet Christian ladies of Mosul, who had scarcely before this
occasion ventured beyond the walls of the town, gazed with wonder
and delight on the scene; lamenting, no doubt, that the domestic
arrangements of their husbands did not permit more frequent indul-
gence in such gaieties.

At the conclusion of the entertainment I spoke a few words to the
workmen, inviting any who had been wronged, or ill-used, to come
forward and receive such redress as it was in my power to afford, and
expressing my satisfaction at the successful termination of our labours
without a single accident. One Sheikh Khalaf, a very worthy man,
who was usually the spokesman on such occasions, answered for his
companions. They had lived, he said, under my shadow, and, God be
praised, no one had cause to complain. Now that I was leaving, they
should leave also, and seek the distant banks of the Khabour, where
at least they would be far from the authorities, and be able to enjoy
the little they had saved. All they wanted was each man a teskerè, or
note, to certify that they had been in my service. This would not only
be some protection to them, but they would show my writing to their
children, and would tell them of the days they had passed at Nimroud.
Please God, I should return to the Jebour, and live in tents with them
on their old pasture grounds, where there were as many ruins as at
Nimroud, plenty of plunder within reach, and gazelles, wild boars,
and lions for the chase. After Sheikh Khalaf had concluded, the women
advanced in a body and made a similar address. I gave a few presents
to the principal workmen and their wives, and all were highly satisfied
with their treatment.

A few days afterwards, the preparations for my departure were
complete. I paid my last visit to Essad Pasha, called upon the principal
people of the town, and on the 24th of June was ready to leave Mosul.

I was accompanied on my journey to Constantinople by Mr.
Hormuzd Rassam, Ibrahim Agha, and the Bairakdar, and by several
members of the household of the late Pasha; who were ready, in
return for their own food and that of their horses, to serve me on the
road. We were joined by many other travellers, who had been waiting

for an opportunity to travel to the north in company with a sufficiently strong party. The country was at this time very insecure. The Turkish troops had marched against Beder Khan Bey, who had openly declared his independence, and defied the authority of the Sultan. The failure of the crops had brought parties of Arabs abroad, and scarcely a day passed without the plunder of a caravan and the murder of travellers. The Pasha sent a body of irregular horse to accompany me as far as the Turkish camp, which I wished to visit on my way. With this escort, and with my own party, all well armed and prepared to defend themselves, I had no cause to apprehend any accident.

Mr. and Mrs. Rassam, all the European residents, and many of the principal Christian gentlemen of Mosul, rode out with me to some distance from the town. On the opposite side of the river, at the foot of the bridge, were the ladies who had assembled to bid me farewell. Beyond them were the wives and daughters of my workmen, who clung to my horse, many of them shedding tears as they kissed my hand. The greater part of the Arabs insisted upon walking as far as Tel Kef with me. In this village supper had been prepared for the party. Old Gouriel, the Kiayah, still rejoicing in his drunken leer, was there to receive us. We sat on the house-top till midnight. The horses were then loaded and saddled. I bid a last farewell to my Arabs, and started on the first stage of our long journey to Constantinople.

Glossary of Oriental Terms

(Page references are to explanations in the text, usually provided by Layard, but not always at first occurence. Terms which occur once only, with an explanation at that point, are not included.)

Anderun	family quarters amongst the Bakhtiyaris.
Antari	a bodice.
Bairakdar	approximately 'Sergeant'.
Bouyourouldi	11.
Cawass	an armed personal servant acting principally as courier and bodyguard.
Debkhè	a type of native dance.
Firman	an imperial edict issued by the Sultan of Turkey.
Hyta	85 n.
Iwan	183.
Jerid	a mounted tournament.
Kelek	18.
Kiayah	84 n.
Melek	167 n.
Mutesellim	173.
Rais	155.
Raki	174 n.
Sardaub	a room below ground level, usually ventilated by a north-facing air-vent on the roof, to provide cooler quarters during the hot weather. It is often more comfortable than Layard's translation 'cellar' (138) might imply.
Serai	147.
Su-bashi	182.
Suiter	217 n.
Tahlehl	127.
Tatar	36.
Ulema	82 n.

Index

Abraham and Nimrod, story of 76
Ainsworth, W.F. 17
Al Hather=Hatra, q.v.
Alison, Charles 48, 51, 54, 55, 56, 128 n.
Arabs, domestic disputes among 235–7
  encampment of 257
  mode of life of 238–9
  womenfolk and domestic establishment of 75, 117–8, 237–8
Armour, excavation of 227
Asses, wild 219–20
Austen, Benjamin 5–6
Austen, Marianne 3
Awai dam 68, 75, 240

Baasheikha 82, 91
Badger, Rev. G. P. 42 n., 74 n.
Bas-reliefs, Assyrian 86–7, 95–6, 130–4, 225–8, 248, 266, 284, 289–92 et passim
Bathing by Nestorian women 168, 179, 240
Birch, Samuel 60, 61
Bisitun 20, 41
Botta, P. E. 3 n., 36, 39, 41, 46, 68, 69–72, 74, 140–1, 265
British Museum 1, 18, 53–6, 58–62, 72, 221, 261, 264, 292, 293
Budge, Sir E. A. W. 45 n.
Bulls, Assyrian colossal 1, 44, 47, 92, 132, 228, 247, 249, 264, 265, 284, 290
Burgess, Edward 33 n., 37, 38

Canning, Sir Stratford 35–7, 39, 40, 42 n., 43, 44, 46–51, 53, 55, 58, 59, 71–2, 89–90, 134, 221

Chaldaean Christians 189–91 et passim; see also: Nestorians
Churches, Nestorian 159, 161
Copper ore 181
Cuneiform, decipherment of 52, 56–8

Disraeli, Benjamin 6
Drought 262–3

Egyptian symbols 81

Festivities 125–8, 239, 273, 293–4
Foundation deposits 248–9
Furnace 250

Hatra 18, 108, 120–2
Hector, Alexander 35, 38, 41–2, 54, 90
Hector, George 54
Helmets, excavation of 227
Hincks, Dr. E. 57
Hunting: in desert 253
  in Tiyari mountains 162

Irrigation 234–5, 262
Ivories 81, 245–6

Kala Tul 26, 29, 31
Kalah Sherghat 18, 66, 67, 251–60
Karamles 83, 91
Keritli Oglu 47, 73, 75, 82, 87–8, 90 n., 91, 192
Khorsabad 36, 39, 43, 69–71, 77, 140–1, 228, 233, 264, 265
Kouyunjik (Kuyunjik) 17–8 et passim
  excavation of 69, 134, 286–92
Kurdish chief, unwelcome visit of 103–5

297